PYTHON
PROGRAMMING
PATTERNS

ISBN 0-13-040956-1

90000

9 780130 409560

PYTHON PROGRAMMING PATTERNS

Thomas W. Christopher

Prentice Hall PTR
Upper Saddle River, NJ 07458
www.phptr.com

Library of Congress Cataloging-in-Publication Data Available

Acquisition Editor: *Mary Franz*
Editorial Assistant: *Noreen Regina*
Editorial/Production supervision: *Rose Kernan*
Composition: *Argosy, Inc.*
Marketing Manager: *Dan DePasquale*
Manufacturing Manager: *Alexis Heydt-Long*
Manufacturing Buyer: *Maura Zaldivar*
Cover Design: *Anthony Gemmellaro*
Cover Design Director: *Jerry Votta*
Series Design: *Gail Cocker-Bogus*

 © 2002 Prentice Hall PTR
Prentice-Hall, Inc.
Upper Saddle River, NJ 07458

The publisher offers discounts on this book when ordered in bulk quantities.
For more information, contact Corporate Sales Department, Prentice Hall PTR, One Lake Street, Upper Saddle River, NJ 07458. Phone: 800-382-3419; FAX: 201-236-7141; E-mail (Internet): corpsales@prenhall.com

Printed in the United States of America

10 9 8 7 6 5 4 3 2 1

ISBN 0-13-040956-1

Pearson Education Ltd., *London*
Pearson Education Australia Pty., Limited, *Sydney*
Pearson Education Singapore, Pte. Ltd
Pearson Education North Asia Ltd., *Hong Kong*
Pearson Education Canada, Ltd., *Toronto*
Pearson Education de Mexico, S.A. de C.V.
Pearson Education Japan, *Tokyo*
Pearson Education Malaysia, Pte. Ltd.
Pearson Education, *Upper Saddle River, New Jersey*

Contents

Introduction

The major purpose of this book is to teach the Python programming language and, in doing so, to concentrate on facilities that make it easier to write moderately large programs, say 5,000 lines or so. Programming in the large is more difficult than writing short scripts. Writing a 5,000-line program is not just 100 times as much work as writing a 50-line program. The way you write a 50-line script does not work for 5,000-line programs.

The secret for successfully writing larger programs is modularization, breaking them into understandable, manageable components. Your goal will not only be to make the software comprehensible, writable, debuggable, and maintainable, but to make it reusable. The best way to write a 5,000-line program is not to have to write all 5,000 lines right then. If somebody else has written code you need and it is available, use it. The library of modules available with Python is large and full of useful code.

When you do write code, it is best to make it reusable. There is no reason to implement the same kind of thing over again. This means you typically will need to over-design the code, to make it more general than you need the first time. The object-oriented design patterns, that we will look at in Chapter 5, are useful ways to think about the design. They are stylized ways of using things which make the design clean and help you remember how to use the objects.

When you are implementing your designs, of course, there are numerous patterns available to reuse: data structures, algorithms, mathematics, concurrent and object-oriented patterns. Where there are well known ways of doing things, it is not cost effective to be creative.

Design and Programming Techniques

We will be looking at several kinds of software designs, components, and techniques. The fundamental way to organize software is the *module*. At a higher level, modules can be grouped into *packages*. Python's handling of modules and packages are the subject of Chapter 3.

Defining classes of objects is fundamental to many techniques. *Objects* and *classes* are the subject of Chapter 4 and *object-oriented design techniques* are the subject of Chapter 5.

Python has some built-in functions that are useful for *functional programming*. We discuss these in "Functional Programming" in Chapter 6.

Data types are not just sets of values. They include the operators, functions, and methods of manipulating those values. *Abstract Data Types*, ADTs, are data types implemented in software as opposed to the "concrete" data types built in to the language. Python has excellent facilities for implementing ADTs. You can define with "special methods" how your data type will respond to operators such as addition, $x + y$, or subscripting, $x[i]$. We devote Chapter 14 to looking at most the special methods. Chapter 15 is devoted to the subscripting and "slicing" special methods used to implement abstract container data types. Chapter 16 and Chapter 17 give examples of abstract container data types: priority queues and sets.

Concurrency involves allowing several threads of control (mini-programs) to run interleaved over the same period of time interacting with each other. They improve performance by allowing one part of the program to execute while another is waiting information to arrive. They also aid in program design, since it is often easier to design and understand the smaller programs than it is to design and understand a program that tries to do all their functions together. We discuss concurrency in Chapter 18, including the facilities available in Python's `threading` module, the monitor pattern (used to protect data from getting scrambled by concurrent access), and the dangers of deadlock and how to avoid it. Chapter 19 is devoted to an example monitor, `Shareddb`, that protects a shared data base from being mangled by concurrent updates and protects the transactions using it from deadlock. Chapter 20 presents another monitor, `RunQueue`, that allows thread objects to be reused. `TransactionQueue` is a variant of `RunQueue` to be used with `SharedDB` which automatically reschedules transactions that need to be tried again when they were unable to commit their changes to a data base.

Chapter 21 is devoted to *regular expressions* and Python's `re` module. Regular expressions are widely used to extract significant parts of text strings. The chapter includes an example scanner used by the parser presented in the next chapter. Chapter 22 shows how to use the TCLLk *parser* to recognize and execute simple statements. The behavior of the parser is specified by a context-free grammar augmented with "action symbols." Parsers are the next level up from regular expressions, facilitating the processing of text with nested subexpressions. The parser is an example of a *framework*: the parser is in control and you must write code that plugs into it.

Software

This book comes with software available through the author's web site, *toolsofcomputing.com*. Some of the software is described in this book; some is not because it would not demonstrate any new principles. There are three varieties of software:

Abstract Data Types

This book contains and describes the abstract container data types:

- `DEQueue`: a doubly ended queue,
- `prioque` and `prioqueunique`: priority queues,
- `DisjointUnion`: implementing the union-find algorithm,
- `Set` and `PureSet`: a set.

Also included is a prototype ADT implementation of rational numbers. Not discussed in the book, but available through the web site are multi-maps, directed graphs, undirected graphs, and bit sets.

Concurrent Programming

This book contains implementations of objects to aid in writing concurrent programs:

- `Future`: an assign-once variable,
- `Latch`: a single element buffer,
- `SharedDB`: a transaction-oriented monitor to share Python's dictionary-like data bases.

- `RunQueue`: a queue to allow reuse of threads,
- `TransactionQueue`: a version or `RunQueue` for transactions accessing a `SharedDB` object.

Included with the software, but not described in the book, are the translation of classes from the Tools of Computing thread package in Java, described in our book *High-Performance Java Platform Computing*.[1] This includes the `SharedTableOfQueues` data structure that resembles JavaSpaces and the Linda system.

Parsing Framework

Chapter 22 shows the use of a parser generator and parser, the TCLLk system. TCLLk is available at the web site. The parser generator takes context-free grammars and generates parsing tables for them, if possible. The tables can be translated for use in a number of programming languages including Python, Java, and Icon. All the ports are available, not just the Python.

Included with TCLLk is a class StringScanner that provides an alternative to regular expressions for extracting usable parts of strings.

What the Book is Not

Because of the space that must be devoted to presenting the Python language, this book cannot be a hard-core object-oriented design patterns book. Chapter 5 describes most of the usual design patterns and they are demonstrated throughout the book in the implementations of software, but they are not the exclusive interest.

---

1. Thomas W. Christopher and George K. Thiruvathukal, *High-Performance Java Platform Computing*, Prentice Hall PTR, 2000, ISBN 0-13-016164-0.

Acknowledgments

I would like to thank my wife Patricia Guilbeault and my son Nick Guilbeault for providing my life with a sense of meaning and belonging that has allowed me to devote my attention to writing this book.

My appreciation goes to the Department of Computer Science at Illinois Institute of Technology in Chicago where I was a professor for about 20 years.

Thanks are due also to my editor at Prentice Hall, Mary Franz, and the group of reviewers she found for this book: Guido van Rossum, the inventor of Python; Gordon McMillan; Konstantin Läufer; Geoffrey Furnish, Python/C++ SIG chair; and Alan Jeffrey. Their suggestions certainly improved the quality of the book. I must admit that I was deeply anxious about submitting my unpolished work to such a knowledgeable group of reviewers.

Finally, I would like to thank Mr. Nack Po Paik and his wife Sun Ja Paik (nee Kim), the proprietors of Cafe Express South at Main and Hinman in Evanston, where I spend hours working each week. They have made their cafe a special place for the neighborhood knowledge workers. Thanks go to Joann Lomax who has served me coffee there during the time I was working on this book and whose cheerfulness has helped keep my spirits up.

Thomas Christopher
Evanston, Illinois

1

Getting Started

The two major thrusts of this book are to teach the Python programming language and to concentrate on the facilities and techniques that are useful for writing medium-size programs–of about 5,000 lines.

In this chapter, after considering the question, "Why would we write larger programs in Python?" we begin our look at the expression evaluation in the Python programming language. Since you can run Python interactively, the material in this chapter will let you start using Python immediately as a calculator.

1.1 Why Write Larger Programs in Python?

How do you write programs of several thousand lines in Python?

The first response may be, "Will I want to?" Python is gaining popularity as a scripting language. Scripting languages are typically used for writing short programs, particularly small utility programs for system administration. So, are you going to use Python for writing larger programs? Yes, for several reasons.

First, if Python is your first language, you will be tempted to use it for writing all programs, to avoid the learning curve involved with mastering another programming language. After all, you want the program done soon.

Second, perhaps you are like the author. The author has implemented several parallel programming systems in C, has been an expert assembly language programmer for more than one computer, and knows what a pain it is to write and debug code in lower-level lan-

1

guages. Sure, other programs are more efficient for the machine to execute, but writing and debugging in Python is a more efficient way to spend one's time. Maybe the program is not going to be used very often, so it may be a net financial loss to waste your time rather than the computer's.

Third, maybe you have decided to program a prototype. Often, you do not know all of what you want a program to do until you have a version to try out. Or maybe you're not sure how to implement parts of the program. Python is a much easier language in which to try out ideas than either C or C++.

So our bet is that you will be writing larger programs by yourself in Python. This brings us back to the question, How can you do that best?

It is a problem. A 5,000-line program is not just a 50-line program 100 times as long. The way you write a 50-line script does not work for writing 5,000-line programs.

The fundamental problem is the seven-plus-or-minus-two problem from cognitive psychology: You are able to keep only seven plus or minus two things in mind at one time: a range of from five to nine things. You can probably keep a lot of what you need in mind when you are writing a 50-line script. Even if you cannot, you can glance around the screen as necessary to remind yourself. Suppose you try writing a 5,000-line program the way you do a script: You just start typing. At some point the question will hit you, "Now, what was I going to do?" You will have about 200 screens of text to look through. By the time you find the information you need in one part of the program, you will have forgotten some of why you were looking it up—and this is while you are writing it and it is fresh in your mind. Just try to fix it or extend it a couple of months after you wrote it.

Remember that a program may have 5,000 lines, but that does not mean you have written 5,000 lines of code. You may have written considerably more than 5,000 lines: You may have written debugging code for parts of your program or you may have had to rip out parts of your program and rewrite them when they could not be made to work correctly or did not work with other parts of the program. On the other hand, you may have written fewer than 5,000 lines: If you reused code that already existed, you did not have to write that much of the program again.

So, the best way to write a 5,000-line program is to write far fewer than 5,000 lines; and the way to do that is to reuse code. If you do have to write new code, the best code to write is code you can use again in other programs.

If you do write code, you'll write faster if you do not invent too much. Creativity is fun, but it is slow and error-prone. If the techniques are already known, it is not cost-effective to reinvent them. That's why schools teach algorithms and data structures. It is best to use methods you know will work.

To reuse code, you must understand it—at least you must understand how to use it and how to fit it into other programs. Remember the 7 ± 2 principle: The less you have to know to use the code, the better able you are to fit it into other code. If it's too complicated, you will not be able to use it at all.

"Programming-in-the-large," as writing larger programs is sometimes called, is a lot different from writing code. You don't think so much of program statements and flow of control; you think of components and of plugging them together. Object-oriented programming, which much of this book deals with, is a technology devoted to software components.

At a deeper level of programming, *patterns* play a role. Kinds of objects and styles of plugging them together have been identified as object-oriented design patterns. But many programming patterns were discovered before object-oriented programming led to a focus on identifying "patterns." Those patterns were studied under the names "data structures," "algorithms," "process synchronization," and such. We will look at a number of these throughout the book.

1.2   Running Python

Unlike pure compilers, Python does not distinguish strongly between compile-time and run-time. If you tell Python to execute a program that has not been compiled yet, Python compiles it and executes it. If the program imports another file of Python source code, Python pauses to translate that.

You do not have to prepare a Python program beforehand. You can type the commands to the Python interpreter directly from the command line. Just type `python` in a command window, and the Python interpreter will start reading and executing the commands you type into the window.

Of course, you are not going to type thousand-line programs each time you run them. You will edit the Python commands into a file and have Python execute it. There are several ways to tell Python which file to execute. You can run the Python interpreter from a command line by giving it the file name:

```
python filename
```

Or you can use the `.py` extension on Python files under Windows and associate the Python interpreter with them. Then clicking on the Python file will run the interpreter. Under Linux and Unix, you can set the access rights of the Python code file to executable and begin the file with the comment `#!/usr/bin/python`, which tells Linux to pass the rest of the file to the Python interpreter at `/usr/bin/python`. You will have to change the path if you have stashed Python in some other directory. If you do not wish to keep track of where the Python interpreter is stored, you can use `#!/usr/bin/env python`, which asks Unix or Linux to find the Python interpreter on the system path and run it.

Python also has a GUI development environment, called IDLE. We do not discuss it here, but you may find it more comfortable to use than the shell command line interface.

Python expressions are very much like expressions in most other programming languages, such as C++ and Java. If you know them, you are well on your way to knowing Python; but there are some differences, and we will mention them as we go along.

An advantage of an interactive system like Python is that you can fire up the interpreter, try things out, and see how they work. For example[*]:

```
C:\WINNT\system32>python
Python 2.1 (#15, Apr 16 2001, 18:25:49) [MSC 32 bit (Intel)] on win32
Type "copyright", "credits" or "license" for more information.
>>> 1+2*3
7
>>>
```

Here we typed the `python` command in a command window on a PC running Windows NT. Python came up, identified itself, and displayed a command prompt, `>>>`. We typed in an expression, `1+2*3`. Python evaluated it and wrote out the answer, `7`, on a separate line and

---

[*]   Most of the examples in this book were run using an earlier version of Python, but some have been run under version 2.1. You may find a few differerences in the format of program outputs, depending on which version you use.

then issued another command prompt. Since the time of FORTRAN, the symbol "*" has been used to indicate multiply, and multiplication is performed before addition. Section 1.9 discusses all the operators in Python and their precedence. The operators with higher precedence numbers are performed before neighboring operators with lower precedences.

1.3   Numbers

Examples and explanations of identifiers and numeric and string literals are shown in Table 1–1 on page 23. Python allows mixed-mode arithmetic. Integer constants are written without a decimal point. Floating-point constants are written with a point or exponent.

```
>>> 1+1
2
>>> 1+1.0
2.0
>>> 1+1e0
2.0
```

A number may be an integer, a long integer, a floating-point number, or a complex number. Whereas the range of integers is limited by the computer's word length (at least 32 bits), long integers (with a trailing "L") are limited only by memory size:

```
>>> 999999999999999
OverflowError: integer literal too large
>>> 999999999999999L
999999999999999L
```

An integer, regular or long, may be written in decimal, octal (leading "0"), or hexadecimal (leading "0x") format:

```
>>> 17
17
>>> 021
17
>>> 0x11
17
```

There are no literals for full complex numbers, only for real numbers and imaginary numbers (trailing "j"). You get complex numbers by adding a real number and an imaginary number:

```
>>> 1j
1j
>>> 1+1j
(1+1j)
>>> 1j*1j
(-1+0j)
```

You can assign a value to an identifier (variable).

```
>>> x=1+1
>>> x
2
>>> x=1+1.0
>>> x
2.0
```

There are a couple of things to notice here. One is that we did not have to declare the variable x before we assigned a value to it; the assignment itself created it. Moreover, there were no restrictions on the type of value that variable x could hold. We assigned it an integer; then we assigned it a float; no problem.

It is an error to try to access a variable that has not been assigned a value yet:

```
>>> y
Traceback (most recent call last):
  File "<stdin>", line 1, in ?
NameError: name 'y' is not defined
```

There is a value, None, that can be used to represent that a value is not present. It is used particularly as a null or NIL value to indicate the end of a linked list or the absence of a subtree. It is also the value returned by functions that "do not return a value." When you assign None to a variable, it is defined, so you can access it without getting an error. However, when you type a command in the command line that evaluates to None, Python does not write anything out:

```
>>> y=None
>>> y
>>>
```

Observe that y has the value None, so the expression y did not cause an error; but since y has the value None, neither did Python write out a value. We can ask if y is equal to None, and be told yes, it is.

```
>>> y==None
1
```

(Python reports 1 for true.)

You can delete a variable with the del statement:

```
>>> del y
>>> y
Traceback (most recent call last):
  File "<stdin>", line 1, in ?
NameError: name 'y' is not defined
```

The del statement deletes a variable or, as we will see, an element from a data structure.

You can find out the type of a value at run-time using the built-in type() function. For example, you can ask whether the variable x contains an integer with an expression:

$$type(x) \; is \; type(2)$$

That is, we asked if the type of x and the type of the literal 2 are the same. Why did we use the is operator rather than ==? The is operator tests whether two objects are really the same object, and is in some cases faster than ==, which tests whether the two have equal values. It probably does not make any difference in this case.

The ability to assign a value of any type to any variable makes Python a *dynamically typed* language. We can distinguish three ways that programming languages handle data types:

- *Statically typed* languages, like C and FORTRAN: The programmer has to declare the data types of variables. Since the compiler knows what the types of all variables and constants are, it can deduce the types of all expressions and generate the actual machine instructions to perform the operations.
- *Dynamically typed* languages, like Python, LISP, and Icon: These languages associate the data type with values. Any value can be assigned to any variable. Only at run-time can the system figure out the actual machine instructions to execute.
- *Type-ignorant* languages, like assembly language, BCPL, and BLISS: These languages associate types with instructions, not

with variables. It is up to the programmer to remember what type value is stored in what location and to use the correct instruction to process it. These languages would not use the same + operator to perform both integer and floating-point arithmetic.

As a practical matter, dynamically typed languages are a lot easier to use interactively, but they have some major problems for developing software systems. They typically are not compiled into machine language, although it is possible in some cases for a compiler to deduce at compile time what the run-time data types will be. This is especially true of some "functional" programming languages, like Haskell. But dynamically typed languages are typically implemented with interpreters that check the types of operands each time an operation is executed. For systems that are going to be used intensively, this can produce a slowdown in performance.

Worse yet for developing software systems, a lot of debugging is moved from compile time to execution time in dynamically typed languages. One of the most common programming errors is using illegal operand types for an operator or function call. A compiler for a statically typed language can detect illegal operand types at compile time, and the programmer can fix the problem before the program runs. The interpreter for a dynamically typed language will detect this problem only when the program runs, so the problem must be detected during program testing, when the operation is executed—indeed when control takes the path through the code that will result in the operation being executed with the wrong types of operands.

You can argue that statically typed programs also need thorough testing, that all instructions need to be executed anyway, and all paths through the code. Though that may be true in the abstract, as a practical matter, type mismatches reveal logic errors, and a compiler's guarantee of finding them is a great aid in eliminating those errors early.

So Python's dynamic typing is a convenience in writing small programs and in hacking around interactively, but it is an inconvenience in writing larger programs. We will just have to live with that.

1.4 Lists, Strings, and Tuples

Python has a number of powerful, built-in data types. Three of these are sequences: lists, strings, and tuples. Sequences contain elements numbered from zero up to the length of the sequence minus one.

Python's array-like object is a *list*. You can create a list by writing its contents in brackets.

```
>>> [1,2,3]
[1, 2, 3]
```

You subscript a list the same way you would subscript an array in C.

```
>>> z=[4,5,6]
>>> z[1]
5
```

You can assign to a position in a list using a subscript on the left side of an assignment operator.

```
>>> z[1]=7
>>> z
[4, 7, 6]
```

The way to find the current length of a list is to use the `len()` function:

```
>>> len(z)
3
```

You can use negative subscripts to index elements from the right end of the sequence:

```
>>> z[-1]
6
>>> z[-3]
4
```

In Python you can quote a *string* with either double or single quotes. As in C and C++, the elements of a list are numbered from zero up to the length of the string minus one. You can subscript strings the way you can lists:

```
>>> x='abc'
>>> x[0]
'a'
>>> len(x)
3
```

When you subscript a string, you cannot get the character at that position, since there is no character data type. You get a string of length one that contains the character at that position. Unlike many other languages, strings in Python are *not* arrays of characters.

Strings are immutable values; you cannot assign to parts of strings:

```
>>> x[0]='d'
Traceback (most recent call last):
  File "<stdin>", line 1, in ?
TypeError: object doesn't support item assignment
```

Suppose you want to allocate an array x of size 10 in Python. You could call the built-in range() function to create a list:

```
>>> x=range(10)
>>> x
[0, 1, 2, 3, 4, 5, 6, 7, 8, 9]
```

but that initializes it to contain the integers 0, 1,..., 9. What if you want all the elements to be initialized to zero? You can do that as follows:

```
>>> x=[0]*10
>>> x
[0, 0, 0, 0, 0, 0, 0, 0, 0, 0]
```

Here the [0] creates a list of length one containing zero. The "*" operator replicates the list, creating a new list containing as many copies as the integer operand specifies.

The range() function can specify the start and step sizes for the sequence:

```
>>> range(10)
[0, 1, 2, 3, 4, 5, 6, 7, 8, 9]
>>> range(1,5)
[1, 2, 3, 4]
>>> range(1,10,2)
[1, 3, 5, 7, 9]
>>> range(5,0,-1)
[5, 4, 3, 2, 1]
```

If you call range(n), it gives you a list of integers starting at zero and increasing by one up to but not including n. If you call range(m,n), it will give you the integers from m up to but not including n. You can provide a step size as a third parameter, range(m,n,k). If k is negative, you can have a descending sequence. But range gives only a sequence of *integers*, even if you pass in floating point numbers.

```
>>> range(10.0)
[0, 1, 2, 3, 4, 5, 6, 7, 8, 9]
```

Tuples are like lists, but you cannot change their contents. They are written with parentheses around them rather than brackets.

```
>>> x=(1,2,3)
>>> x
(1, 2, 3)
```

You subscript a tuple to get an element, just as you would a list:

```
>>> x=(1,2,3)
>>> x[1]
2
```

As with strings, since tuples are immutable, you *cannot* assign to a position in a tuple:

```
>>> x[1]=4
Traceback (innermost last):
  File "<stdin>", line 1, in ?
TypeError: object doesn't support item assignment
```

If you are creating a tuple on the right side of an assignment, you do not have to put parentheses around the elements:

```
>>> x=1,2,3
>>> x
(1, 2, 3)
```

The same also applies to return statements in functions. If you want to return multiple values, just list the expressions whose values you want to return, separated by commas in the return statement.

```
>>> def sumdif(a,b):
...     return a+b,a-b
...
>>> sumdif(5,7)
(12, -2)
```

(The function definition should be reasonably clear. The def statement declares a function, sumdif, of two parameters, a and b. The body is a return statement, indented beneath the header.)

A sequence of expressions separated by commas can also be used as a statement, just as a single expression, typically a function call, is a statement.

If you want a tuple of zero elements, use open and close parentheses:

```
>>> ()
()
```

If you want a tuple of one element, you must put a comma before the close parenthesis. If you do not, it will be interpreted as a parenthesized expression.

```
>>> (1,)
(1,)
>>> (1)
1
```

A comma is always permitted to follow the last expression in a tuple or a list:

```
>>> [1,2,3,]
[1, 2, 3]
>>> (1,2,)
(1, 2)
```

There is a *slicing* operation that looks like subscripting. The bounds of the slice are separated by a colon. Slice x[m:n] indicates the elements in x from position m up to but not including position n. If you slice a list, tuple, or string, you get a copy of the elements in the indicated positions:

```
>>> x=1,2,3
>>> x[1:3]
(2, 3)
>>> z=[5,6,7]
>>> z[1:3]
[6, 7]
>>> y = 'abc'
>>> y[1:3]
'bc'
```

Just as you can assign a new value to an element of a list, you can assign a new list of elements to a slice of a list, but not to a slice of a string or a tuple, of course.

```
>>> z[1:3]=[10,11,12]
>>> z
[5, 10, 11, 12]
>>> z[1:3]=[]
>>> z
[5, 12]
```

Similarly, you can delete a slice of a list with a del statement.

```
>>> del z[0:1]
>>> z
[12]
```

You can also use negative subscripts with slices.

```
>>> z=[4,5,6]
>>> z[1:-1]
[5]
```

You can leave out the starting or ending position in a slice; they will default to the start or end of the entire sequence.

```
>>> z[:2]
[4, 5]
>>> z[1:]
[5, 6]
>>> z[:]
[4, 5, 6]
```

Lists have additional operations, "methods" written like a function call following the list connected by a dot; for example, L.append(x) adds an element x to the end of list L; L.pop() removes and returns the element from the end; L.insert(k,x) inserts x at position k in list L:

```
>>> z=[4,5,6]
>>> z
[4, 5, 6]
>>> z.append(7)
>>> z
[4, 5, 6, 7]
>>> z.pop()
```

```
7
>>> z
[4, 5, 6]
>>> z.insert(1,4.5)
>>> z
[4, 4.5, 5, 6]
```

The "+" operator is used for concatenation; the "*" operator is used for replication.

```
>>> [1,2]+[3,4]
[1, 2, 3, 4]
>>> [1,2]*3
[1, 2, 1, 2, 1, 2]
>>> (5,6)+(7,8)
(5, 6, 7, 8)
>>> (5,6)*3
(5, 6, 5, 6, 5, 6)
>>> "ab"+"cd"
'abcd'
>>> "ab"*3
'ababab'
```

1.5   Logical Values

Python does not have a Boolean or logical data type. Instead, like C, it uses zero for false and anything else for true. Comparison operations return one for true and zero for false. The relational operators are much as you would find in other languages.

```
>>> 1<2
1
>>> 1>2
0
```

You can use the comparison operators on two lists, tuples, or strings. The comparison is lexicographic; in other words, it proceeds left to right until the results of the comparison are known.

```
>>> [1,2]<[3,4]
1
>>> [1,2]>[3,4]
0
>>> [1,2]==[1,2]
1
>>> "ab"=="a"+"b"
```

```
1
>>> (1,2)==[1,2]
0
>>> (1,[2,3])==(1,[1+1,1+2])
1
```

The logical operators are `and`, `or`, and `not`. The `and` and `or` operators are short-circuited: They do not evaluate their right operands if the left operand determines the value of the expression:

```
>>> 0 and 5/0
0
>>> 1 or 5/0
1
```

The zero determines the value of the `and` operation just as the one determines the value of the `or`, so the divide by zero was not executed; however, it is executed if the left-hand side does not determine the value:

```
>>> 1 and 5/0
Traceback (most recent call last):
  File "<stdin>", line 1, in ?
ZeroDivisionError: integer division or modulo by zero
```

Empty sequences also count as false, and nonempty sequences as true:

```
>>> not []
1
>>> not [1,2,3]
0
>>> not ''
1
>>> not 'ab'
0
```

1.6 Dictionaries

One of the most flexible and useful data types is the *dictionary*, also known as a table or map, which dates back to tables in SNOBOL4, at least. A dictionary is like a list in that you can subscript it to assign and look up elements; but unlike a list, you can subscript with almost any object, not just with an integer. The subscript is called the key, and you can associate any value with it. You can also put as many keys and values into the dictionary as you wish, up to the limits of memory. The dictionary will grow automatically to accommodate them.

You create a dictionary by using braces:

```
>>> d={}
>>> d
{}
```

You can put an association into the dictionary using a subscripted assignment. The following statements associate the integer 2 with the integer 1 and the integer 3 with the string abc:

```
>>> d[1]=2
>>> d["abc"]=3
>>> d
{'abc': 3, 1: 2}
```

In this dictionary, the keys are 1 and 'abc' and their values are 2 and 3 respectively. If you subscript a dictionary with a key that it contains, you get the associated value. If you subscript with a key that it does not contain, you get an error:

```
>>> d["abc"]
3
>>> d[3]
Traceback (innermost last):
  File "<stdin>", line 1, in ?
KeyError: 3
```

If you are unsure whether a dictionary contains a key, there are several ways to find out. You can use the dictionary's get() method, supplying a special value to return if the key is not present. The following asks for the value of key 3, but the value 4 if key 3 is not present:

```
>>> d.get(3,4)
4
```

If the key is present, get() returns its value:

```
>>> d.get(1,4)
2
```

If you do not specify a value to return if the key is not present, `get()` uses the value `None`.

```
>>> d.get(3)==None
1
```

Or you can just ask the dictionary if it has the key:

```
>>> d.has_key(3)
0
>>> d.has_key("abc")
1
```

You can use the `del` statement to delete associations from the dictionary.

```
>>> del d[1]
>>> d[1]
Traceback (innermost last):
  File "<stdin>", line 1, in ?
KeyError: 1
```

Python does restrict you to using a string or tuple rather than a list as the key. The reason is that it uses *hashing* to look up keys in the dictionary. When you use a sequence as the key, Python calculates an integer hash code from its contents, and that is why Python rejects lists. If the key can change, then its hash value can change. In that case, Python will start looking in the wrong place and will not be able to find the key in the dictionary again. Generally, Python will use any object as a key that it can hash and compare for equality.

1.7   Assignments

There are other forms of assignment in Python. We have already seen the single equal sign assigning the value on the right-hand side to the variable on the left. You can assign the same value to several targets at the same time by using multiple instances of the assignment operator:

```
>>> x=y=1
>>> x
1
>>> y
1
```

You can unpack a sequence inside an assignment statement by listing variables on the left side of the assignment operator:

```
>>> a,b=1,2
>>> a
1
>>> b
2
>>> a,b="gh"
>>> a
'g'
>>> b
'h'
>>> (a,(b,c))=[1,"gh"]
>>> a,b,c
(1, 'g', 'h')
```

You can use an augmented assignment operator, combining the operator with an equals sign, to update the value of the target. The variable on the left-hand side of the assignment is used both as the left operand for the operator and as the target for the assignment; thus:

```
>>> x=3
>>> x+=10
>>> x
13
```

1.8 Garbage Collection

Lists in Python are allocated when you need them, like the storage you allocate with `malloc()` in C or `new` in C++. Unlike those other languages, you do not have to explicitly free the storage when you no longer need it; Python has automatic storage reclamation. It figures out when you no longer need objects you have allocated and frees their storage automatically. This is a great convenience. In languages without automatic storage reclamation, you can seriously contort your algorithms trying to keep track of when some storage should be freed, and you can often get it wrong. It is not so serious if you fail to free some storage you are no longer using, although if your program runs long enough, it can run out of free storage and crash. It's worse when you free storage before all parts of your program are done with it. It can be reallocated, leaving two different parts of your program thinking they are manipulating different objects, when really they are overwriting parts of the same memory. Your program crashes, with very strange bugs.

Earlier versions of Python used reference counts to reclaim storage. With each list or other object, it keeps a count of the number of variables, list elements, and so on that point to it. When you assign a variable a pointer to an object, the object's reference count goes up. When you overwrite the pointer, the reference count goes down. When the count goes to zero, the object certainly is available for collection. If there are no pointers to the object, there is no way to access it anymore; there's no way for your program to find it. The problem is that if you have cycles of references, objects may become inaccessible without their reference counts going to zero. Consider the following:

```
>>> x=[0]
>>> x[0]=x
>>> x=1
```

We create a list of length one and assign it to x. It has a reference count of one because x points to it. Then we put a reference to the list itself in its one element. Its reference count is now 2, because x and x[0] both point to the list. Finally, we assign a new value to x. The reference count of the list goes to one, because x no longer points to it, but it still contains a pointer to itself. Its storage will never be collected. Its reference count says it still has pointers to it, but we have no way to reach it anymore to clear out the self-reference. If you put the statements in a loop, for example:

```
>>> while 1:
...        x=[0]
...        x[0]=x
...        x=1
...
```

your program would eventually crash for lack of memory. We need to emphasize that this applies to all Python objects that contain references to other objects; it doesn't apply only to lists.

More recent versions of Python include a garbage collector that can reclaim even circularly linked, inaccessible structures. They will keep on running the loop for as long as you have patience.

1.9   Operators

Now let us take a tour through Python's operators. Python has 14 levels of operator precedence in expressions, enough that it may be difficult to keep track of which operators bind more tightly than others. When in doubt, use parentheses. Table 1–2 on page 25 lists the groups of operators by precedence level, with the higher level binding more tightly than the lower. Here we examine the operators in order, from those operators that bind most tightly to those that bind least.

Identifiers, literals, and expressions in parentheses, brackets, or braces can be used as elements in all other expressions.

```
(expression)
(expressions)
 [expressions]
{expr:expr, expr:expr,..}
`expression`
```

We discuss the back-quote string construction operators in Chapter 9.

Next come the function call, attribute access, subscription, and slicing operators.

```
f(args)
x.attr
x[i]
x[i:j]
```

Exponentiation, x^y, associates to the right, so that `x**y**z = x**(y**z) = ` x^{y^z}.

Negation, bit-wise complement, and unary plus (no operation for numbers)

```
-x
~x
+x
```

bind less tightly than exponentiation, so `-x**y` is `-(x**y)`. As we will soon see, the logical "`not`" operator is of much lower precedence than these.

Multiplication, division, and modulus (or remainder) come next:

```
x * y
x / y
x % y
```

Operator % will also work with floating-point numbers and has a special function for strings. Operator * replicates sequence types.

    Addition and subtraction are as usual in programming languages:

```
x + y
x - y
```

 Operator + also performs concatenation on sequences; see Chapters 8
and 9.

    The shift operators apply to integers or long integers.

```
x << y
x >> y
```

The bits in x are shifted left (<<) or right (>>) the number of positions
indicated by y. The right shifts are *arithmetic*; the sign bit will be shifted
in at the top, preserving the sign of the x operand. Since >> truncates
toward minus infinity, it is not a good substitute for division when the
left operand is negative.

    The bit-wise and operation, x & y ands the corresponding bits in
two integers or long integers. It is of lower precedence than shifts, so
you do not have to use parentheses to shift a bit and mask with it. However, the length of << and >> compared to & may trick you into thinking
they are lower in precedence, so be careful.

    The bitwise exclusive-or (xor) operation, x ^ y xors the corre-
sponding bits in two integers or long integers. It has its own precedence
level, lower than & but higher than |, the bitwise OR operation.

    The bitwise or operation, x|y ors the corresponding bits in two
integers or long integers.

    The relational operators are much like they are in other languages:

```
x < y
x <= y
x > y
x >= y
x == y
x != y
x <> y
x is y
x is not y
x in y
x not in y
```

Operators != and <> both mean *not equal*. The comparison operators <,
<=, >, >=, == and != can be applied to structured objects. They compare
the structured objects' components.

The comparison operators can be chained, so that `x<y<=z` is equivalent to `x<y and y<=z`.

Operators `x is y` and `x is not y` test whether two names reference the same object, so they will be much faster than `==` and `!=` for structured objects, but they do not compare the contents.

Operations `x in y` and `x not in y` search a sequence to see if an element is present or not. They are discussed with sequence types in Chapter 8.

The logical `not` operator, `not x` returns 1 (true) if `x` is false; it returns 0 (false) if `x` is true. Notice that it has a much lower precedence than the other unary operators. Its precedence level is much more convenient, since if it had the precedence of other unary operators, it would almost always require parentheses around the expression following it.

The logical `and` operation `x and y` will return true if both `x` and `y` are true, or nonzero. Like the `&&` operator in C, it is *short-circuited*: It will not evaluate `y` if `x` determines the value of the expression. It first evaluates `x` and returns `x` if `x` is false. If `x` is true, it evaluates and returns the value of `y`.

Similarly, the logical `or` operation `x or y` will return true if either `x` or `y` is true, or nonzero. In Python, like C, nonzero is considered to be true and zero false. Like the `||` operator in C, the `or` operator is also *short-circuited*: It will not evaluate `y` if `x` determines the value of the expression. It first evaluates `x` and returns the value of `x` if `x` is true. If `x` is false, it evaluates and returns the value of `y`. By "x is true or false" we mean that `x` would be considered true or false in an `if` or `while` statement. Empty lists and strings, for example, also count as false. The logical `or` operation has the lowest precedence of all Python operators.

1.10 Wrap-Up

In this chapter we took a quick look at how to run the Python interpreter and at Python built-in data types and expressions. In addition to the usual integer and floating point, Python provides long integers to do unbounded precision arithmetic and complex numbers for engineering computations. There is no "logical" data type: Python uses zero for false and nonzero for true. Python provides 14 precedence levels of operators.

There are three types of sequences in Python: lists, tuples, and strings. You can change the contents of lists, but strings and tuples are immutable. Python has dictionaries that allow you to associate values with keys using a syntax that resembles subscripting.

Python is dynamically typed, so values of different data types can be assigned to the same variable. In fact, the same code can be executed with operands of different data types.

Table 1–1
Python lexical formats.

Examples	Remarks
_x_ x10 frog	An identifier is a letter or an underscore followed by zero or more letters, digits, and underscores.
1 10	A decimal is written as a string of decimal digits, the leftmost of which may not be a zero, because that's used to signal an octal number.
0 0377	An octal number is written as a zero followed by zero or more octal digits. (By this rule, zero is written in octal.)
0xffffffff 0XC63	A hexadecimal number is composed of hexadecimal digits preceded by a zero and an "X" in either upper or lower case. The hexadecimal digits are the decimal digits and the first six letters of the alphabet, in either upper or lower case, representing ten through fifteen.
0xffffffffL 037777777777L 4294967295L	A long integer literal is written as any form of integer literal followed by an "L" in either upper or lower case. Using a lowercase "l" will cause confusion.
0.1 1.1 .1 0. 1. 0.1E1 1.1e10 .1e+1 0.E0 1.e-10 10e-2	A floating-point literal must contain either a decimal point or an exponent or both. Generally, it should not begin with a zero (so as not to confuse the integer part with an octal number), but as a special case, a zero may precede a decimal point. The fraction part begins with a decimal point and contains one or more decimal digits. The grammar makes special cases of a zero or a decimal integer followed by a decimal point with no digits following it. An exponent begins with an "E" in either upper or lower case, followed optionally by a sign, and then followed by one or more decimal digits.

Table 1–1
Python lexical formats. (Continued)

Examples	Remarks

`2j`
`2.0J`
`0j`
	An imaginary number is a decimal integer or a floating-point number or a zero followed by a "J" in either upper or lower case. It gives you a complex number with a zero real part. You get other complex numbers by adding a real number and an imaginary number, but that is an expression rather than a literal.

`' '`
 	
`"abc"`
 	
`U'xyz'`
 	
`r"\s"`
 	
`"""a`
`bc"""`
	A string can be surrounded by single or double quotes or by a triple single quote or a triple double quote. The triple quotes allow the string to extend across multiple lines. Otherwise, it must be completed on the same line it begins on. The newlines in the multiline string are considered part of the string.
	The backslash is an incorporation character. The backslash and certain following characters are replaced by a single special character.
	An uppercase or lowercase "U" in front of the string means the string is in Unicode. An uppercase or lowercase "R" in front of the string indicates a "raw string," which means that backslash-plus-character sequences lose their special meanings and the two characters are included as is. (Still, the backslash is always assumed to be followed by another character, so you cannot end any string with an odd number of backslashes.)
	If you write several strings in a row, separated only by white space, Python will concatenate them for you before the program runs.

Table 1–2
Operators and precedence levels.

Precedence	Operators		
1	x or y		
2	x and y		
3	not y		
4	x < y x > y x == y x is y x in y	x <= y x >= y x != y x is not y x not in y	x <> y
5	x | y		
6	x ^ y		
7	x & y		
8	x << y	x >> y	
9	x + y	x - y	
10	x * y	x / y	x % y
11	– y	~ y	+ y
12	x ** y		
13	f(args) x[i]	x.attr x[i:j]	
14	(expression) (expressions) [expressions] {expr:expr, expr:expr,..} `expression`		

2

Statements

In this chapter, we look at many of Python's statement types, although some are reserved for later, more appropriate chapters. The `def` statement is used for creating functions and the `return` statement for returning values from functions. The `for` and `while` statements are used for looping. The `break` statement is used to jump out of loops and the `continue` statement to go on to the next iteration. The `if-elif-else` statement is used for executing statements conditionally. The `print` statement is used to write the values of expressions to the output. The `assert` and `raise` statements report problems detected during program execution. The `import` statement is used to let a program use functions and other things declared in other files. Expression, assignment, and delete statements were covered in Chapter 1.

This chapter includes a number of example functions and programs: functions to detect whether a string is balanced with respect to parentheses, to compute Fibonacci numbers, and to compute a square root. We present, as an example of top-down programming, a program to perform the core behavior of the Unix `wc` utility: counting the number of characters, words, and lines in a file.

2.1 Python Statements

Python is a purely structured programming language: It has sequential, conditional, and looping statements, and it omits the labels and goto's. Table A–1 lists the types of Python statements.

27

2.1.1   Defining Functions

In Python, you define functions with a `def` statement. Consider the following definition of a function that calculates the cube of a number:

```
>>> def cube(x):
...     return x*x*x
...
>>> cube(5)
125
```

The `def` line is the function header. It has the name of the function, `cube`, followed by the list of parameters in parentheses and a final colon. A colon ends all header lines that introduce nested statements.

The Python interpreter gives a "..." prompt for the lines of the body of the function. You have to indent all the statements in the body of any compound statement by the same amount, preferably by the same sequence of white space characters. Python documentation refers to the body of a compound statement as a *suite,* and we usually do so as well. Statements are written on separate logical lines. If the statement is too long to fit on one line, you can continue it to the next line in either of two ways:

1. End the physical line with a backslash.
2. End the physical line while there are still open parenthesized or bracketed subexpressions.

The `return` statement computes the value of the function and returns it to the caller. We tested the function by passing it 5 and it responded 125.

As a special case, if there is only one line in the suite, you can place it on the same line after the header:

```
>>> def cube(x): return x*x*x
...
>>> cube(5)
125
```

In Python, the `def` statement is executable. When Python executes it, it compiles the function into a function object, which it assigns to the function name. If we ask about the value of `cube`, we get:

```
>>> cube
<function cube at 7f64c0>
```

You can assign a new value to `cube` and lose the function:

```
>>> cube=8
>>> cube
8
```

2.1.2 `for` and `print`

The `for` statement in Python is used to iterate through a list. It assigns each element of the list to a variable. The `print` statement writes out the values of expressions. Here is a simple example:

```
>>> x=['a','b','c']
>>> for y in x:
...        print y,y
...
a a
b b
c c
```

Variable `y` is assigned each of the elements of list `x` from left to right (or from position zero up to the highest position, if you prefer). The body of the `for` loop is executed once for each value assigned to `y`. As with the `def` statement, the body is introduced by the colon and must be indented beneath the `for`.

The `print` statement prints out the values that follow it. Since `y` appears twice, it is printed twice. The comma not only separates the values to be written, it also causes a blank to be inserted between them in the output.

Why is there a `print` statement? We saw the Python interpreter write out the values of expressions typed in to it. Well, at the top level, the command interpreter executes expressions as you type them in, and if they produce a value, it writes out that value; but it doesn't write out values of expressions executed within compound statements like functions and `for` statements, so we need the `print` statement to do the writing.

The forms of the print statement are:

```
print
print e1, ..., en
print e1, ..., en ,
print >>file
print >>file, e1, ..., en
print >>file, e1, ..., en ,
```

If the list of expressions does not end with a comma, Python terminates a line after writing out their values. If there is a comma, Python does not end the line, so the next `print` will continue writing on the same line. If there is a `>>file`, Python will write out the expressions to the indicated file object.

The `for` statement has either the form:

```
for targetlist in expressionlist do:
    suite
```

or the form:

```
for targetlist in expressionlist do:
    suite
else:
    suite
```

Typically the `targetlist` is a single variable and the `expression-list` is a single expression yielding a sequence, but you can use more variables or expressions:

```
>>> for x,y in (1,2),[3,4],'ab': print x,y
...
1 2
3 4
a b
```

The variables in the `targetlist` are assigned the values in the sequence given by the `expressionlist`. If there is a single expression in the `expressionlist`, its value is the sequence. If there are multiple expressions in the `expressionlist`, they form a tuple that is the sequence. For each assignment, the suite following the `for` header is executed.

When the sequence is exhausted, the suite in the `else` clause is executed and control leaves the `for` statement. If control leaves before the sequence is exhausted, for example by a `break` statement, the `else` clause is skipped.

Naturally, you use `range()` in `for` statements to iterate over a sequence of numbers:

```
>>> x=['a','b','c']
>>> for y in range(len(x)):
...     print x[y],x[len(x)-y-1]
...
a c
```

```
b  b
c  a
```

Since a string is a sequence, a `for` statement can iterate over the characters in it. Consider:

```
>>> for y in "abc": print y,
...
a b c
```

2.1.3 Example: `bal()`

Now consider the function `bal()`, shown in Figure 2–1. It is to return true if the string it is passed is balanced with respect to parentheses. That means two things: 1) that the number of open parentheses is equal to the number of close parentheses; and 2) that if you match close parentheses to open parentheses, the matching close parenthesis is to the right of its open parenthesis.

There are several things to notice about the function `bal()`:

- It is supposed to return true or false, but you don't see the identifiers `true` or `false` in it. Python uses zero for `false` and nonzero for `true` and does not have defined identifiers for them.
- An `if` statement begins with a line of the form:
  ```
  if expression:
  ```
  with a suite indented beneath it that will be executed if the expression is true (nonzero).
- The `elif` line is a combination of `else` and `if` lines. It prevents your having to indent further and further with each `else-if` statement.

```
def bal(s):
    d=0
    for c in s:
        if c=="(":
            d=d+1
    elif c==")":
            d=d-1
            if d<0:
                return 0
    return d==0
```

Figure 2–1
Function `bal()`: test to see if a string has balanced parentheses.

The function `bal()` works by letting variable `c` be assigned each character of the parameter string `s`, from left to right. Variable `d` keeps a count of the number of open parentheses minus the number of close parentheses that the algorithm has seen. It will return `true` at the end if `d` equals zero, indicating that the number of open and close parentheses are equal. It also checks as it goes left to right through the string that at no point does the number of close parentheses exceed the number of open parentheses. If at any point `d` goes negative, there can be no way the close parenthesis just seen can match an open parenthesis to its left.

Here is a test of `bal()`:

```
>>> bal("")
1
>>> bal("(")
0
>>> bal(")")
0
>>> bal("(a(bc)d(e(f)g)h(i)j)k")
1
```

2.1.4   Example: `fib()`

As another example, consider the Fibonacci function, `fib()`, in Figure 2–2. Fibonacci numbers are defined as follows: The first two Fibonacci numbers, f_0 and f_1, are arbitrary values, here 0 and 1. The ith Fibonacci number is, f_i, where $i>1$, is defined as $f_{i-1}+f_{i-2}$. Here we generalize the definition, extending it to numbers less than zero, by $f_{i-2}=f_i-f_{i-1}$.

There are three things to notice in the definition of function `fib()`:

- Functions can be recursive. Function `fib()` calls itself except in the cases of the two values, f_0 and f_1.
- Here you see the `else` statement.
- Here you also see the relational expression, `0<=n<=1`. This form of relational expression is quite uncommon in programming languages. It is equivalent to, and is translated into, `0<=n and n<=1`.

```
def fib(n):
    if 0<=n<=1: return n
    elif n>1: return fib(n-1)+fib(n-2)
    else: return fib(n+2)-fib(n+1)
```

Figure 2–2
Function `fib()`: Fibonacci numbers both ways from zero.

Here is a test of `fib()`:

```
>>> for i in range(-10,11):
...     print fib(i),
...
-55 34 -21 13 -8 5 -3 2 -1 1 0 1 1 2 3 5 8 13 21 34 55
```

2.1.5 `if` Statement

The full form of an `if` statement is as follows:

```
if expression:
    suite
elif expression:
    suite
elif expression:
    suite
else:
    suite
```

The `if` clause is required. Any number of `elif` clauses can be used, including zero. The `else` clause is optional. The `if` and `elif` clauses are tried one at a time. The suite of statements is executed for the first `if` or `elif` clause whose expression evaluates true (nonzero), and then control leaves the `if` statement. If none of the expressions evaluate true, the `else` clause, if any, is executed.

2.1.6 `break`

You can escape from a loop by executing the `break` statement. Its form is simply `break` and it causes control to jump to the next statement following the innermost enclosing loop. We will see an example in the example of the `sqrt()` function.

2.1.7 `while` Statement

Python also has `while` statements that execute a loop as long as an expression evaluates true. The full form is:

```
while expression :
    suite
else:
    suite
```

The `else` clause is optional. When the expression evaluates false, the suite of the `else` clause, if any, is executed and control leaves the while statement. If control jumps out of the suite of the while clause (e.g., by a break statement), the else clause is not executed. Here is a while loop that might be used for Fibonacci number calculation:

```
while a<n:
        a,b=b,a+b
```

2.1.8 else in Loops

Both the for and while loops in Python have optional else clauses. The suite of statements following the else is executed if the loop terminates normally, but not if control jumps out of it in some way. This is quite useful in searches. Consider the following code:

```
for i in range(len(L)):
        if f(L[i]):
                print "found",i
                break
else:
    print "not found"
```

Here the loop is looking for the index i of the first element in list L for which function f returns true. If the loop finds the item, it writes out a message and breaks out of the loop. If it doesn't find any item for which f() returns true, it prints out a message reporting failure.

Using the keyword "else" to indicate normal termination seems a bit strange, but that's how Python was designed.

2.1.9 Example: sqrt()

Consider Figure 2–3, which shows a function, sqrt(), to calculate square roots. It has several points of interest.

```
def sqrt(x,e=None):
        x=float(x)
        if not e: e=x/10000.0
        y=x/2.0
        while y*y < x-e or x+e < y*y:
                y = (y + x/y)/2.0
        return y
```

Figure 2–3
Square root routine.

- The `sqrt()` function takes an optional second parameter, `e`, which is to indicate the absolute precision required. If the user calls the function with just one parameter, `x`, parameter `e` defaults to the value `None`. `None` is a built-in value in Python that is often used to mean that a value is not present. It is also used to represent a `NIL` or `null` pointer in list processing.
- The value `None` counts as false, hence the statement `if not e: e=x/10000.0` to assign `e` to a fraction of `x` if it isn't provided explicitly. If `e` is passed the value zero, it will also be considered to be false and be assigned `x/10000.0`. That is just as well; the function might loop endlessly trying to get a floating-point number to converge exactly.
- To avoid repeated conversions, `x` is converted to a floating-point number at the beginning if it is not already a float.
- The algorithm calculates an approximation `y` of the square root of `x` by starting with a guess, `x/2`, and repeatedly assigning `y` the average of `y` and `x/y`. Variable `y` is considered to be close enough when $x-e < y^2 < x+e$.
- We use the logical `or` operator in the `while` loop's test. It will continue looping while y^2 is less than `x-e` or greater than `x+e`.

(By the way, Python already has a better square root function. See `sqrt()` in the `math` module.)

Python's logical operators are `and`, `or`, and `not`. If you are a C, C++, or Java programmer, you will have to remember not to use `&&`, `||`, and `!`. As with C, C++, and Java, the `and` and `or` operators are *short-circuited*; that is, they evaluate the left-hand subexpression first, and if it determines the value of the overall expression, they do not evaluate the right-hand subexpression. This is important in tests such as `0<=i<len(x)` and `x[i]==y`, when you want to do the right part of the test only if subscripts are in bounds. As with most other languages, the `and` operator has a higher precedence than the `or` operator, so `x or y and z` associates as `x or (y and z)`.

A difference to be aware of is that the `not` unary operator has a much lower precedence than in many other languages. It has a higher precedence than `and`, but lower than the relational operators. In Figure 2–3, we could have written the `while` line as:

```
while not x-e <= y*y <= x+e:
```

2.1.10 `continue`

You can use the `continue` statement to force control to return to the loop header of the innermost and attempt to begin the next iteration. Its form is `continue`.

If the loop is a `while` loop, it will evaluate the expression again to decide whether to execute another iteration or leave the loop. If it is a `for` statement, it will reenter the loop if the controlling sequence has more elements to assign to the target.

2.1.11 `pass`

The pass statement, `pass`, performs no operation, but is used when the syntax of Python requires a statement. You might use it in an `if-elif-elif` statement when the first, special case is to do nothing. We will see other examples in later chapters.

2.1.12 `assert`

Python has a statement type that allows you to put in an assertion that can be checked at run-time. The common forms of the `assert` statement are:

```
assert expression
assert expression , data
```

In both forms, the expression is evaluated. If the expression is `true`, control goes on to the next statement. If the expression is `false`, the `assert` statement "raises an exception." That typically means that your program will terminate with a traceback telling you the location of the assertion that failed (file and line) and the value of the data you supplied, if any. For example:

```
>>> x=1
>>> y=2
>>> assert x==y
Traceback (innermost last):
  File "<stdin>", line 1, in ?
AssertionError
```

The reason for the data option in the `assert` statement is that you may wish to know the data values that failed the test.

```
>>> assert x==y, [x,y]
Traceback (innermost last):
```

```
File "<stdin>", line 1, in ?
AssertionError: [1, 2]
```

You can turn off assertion checking by running Python with the `-o` option; for example, `python -o progname.py`. See Chapter 13 for a discussion of the various ways to run Python.

2.1.13   `raise` and `try-except` Statements

The `assert` statements are for debugging. It is also possible to call conditions to the program's attention with a `raise` statement. The simplest form of the `raise` statement is

raise ExceptionClass

where *ExceptionClass* names the kind of thing that went wrong; for example, `raise ValueError`. It is also possible to pass data back from the `raise` to further describe the exception:

raise ExceptionClass,data

A program can catch and handle an exception with a `try` statement. A simple version is:

```
try:
    code that raises the exception
except ExceptionClass:
    code to handle the problem
```

There can be more than one `except` clause. If the code between the `try` and the `except` raises an exception, Python tries to find an `except` clause that matches. If it finds one, it executes its suite and leaves the `try` statement. If it does not find one, it goes back to the next active surrounding `try` statement. The `raise` statement does not need to be located between the `try` and `except` headers. It can be in a function called from there. If there is no matching `except` clause, Python stops executing and writes out an error message, as it does when the `assert` statement detects a problem.

You can include a variable in the `except` clause to receive any data being passed back by the `raise`:

```
except ExceptionClass, variable:
    code to handle the problem
```

You can include more than one `except` clauses to handle different kinds of exceptions:

```
try:
        readdata()
except BadDataError:
        print "try again"
except ValueError:
        print "try again"
```

You can also include an `else` clause to be executed only if the suite following the `try` is executed without an exception.

```
try:
    search()
except Found,x:
        report(x)
else:
        report( "not found")
```

There are many more options than the few discussed here. In Chapter 11 we will study exception handling in Python.

2.2 Example: Word Count

2.2.1 Top-Down Programming

Structured programming was an early invention that was going to revolutionize programming, making it easy and reliable. Loosely, it consisted of restricting control constructs to sequential, conditional, and repetitive statements and function calls. Structured programming led to a realization about programs: Structured programs had a hierarchical structure. Compound statements contained statements within them, which could contain other statements within them. Similarly, functions could call other functions that could call other functions. Except for a few cases of recursion, functions could be placed in a hierarchy according to the depth of their call nesting. You could visualize a tree of functions, with the main program at the root—at the top of the diagram, given the inverted way we draw trees. Arrayed beneath it are the functions it calls, the functions they call, and so forth.

Given this tree, several questions arose: In what order should you design and implement the program? Should you design from the top down, deciding what your main program should do, then what the functions it calls should do, and then what the functions they call should do, going down the tree? Or should you first design the functions at the leaves of the tree, then the functions that call them, and work your way up? Or should you sort of jump around the tree? This last option didn't arouse much support; it seemed too undisciplined.

The argument for designing from the bottom up seemed pretty good. You would want to implement from the bottom up. After all, how would you call a function if you didn't have it implemented yet?

But there was an argument against bottom-up design. Typically, all you start off knowing about the program is what you want it to do, a high-level consideration. You don't really know what you want the functions way down the tree to do until you know how they fit into achieving the overall goal. So though you might need to implement the program from the bottom up, you need to design from the top down.

This line of thinking led to the top-down programming method. It works as follows.

2.2.2   Program wc

Suppose we want to write a Python word count program like the wc program in Unix. The wc program reads a file, or reads its input; counts the number of characters, words, and lines; and writes out the counts.

Top-down programming says we should start with the goal we want to achieve:

```
write the counts of the number of characters,
    words, and lines in a file
```

Now we break this down into other goals or actions using structured programming constructs: sequences of actions or goals, if's, loops, and functions. Our next step might be:

```
open the file
count the characters, words, and lines
write out the counts
```

Next, we might want to work on getting the counts, so we might expand the middle action into:

```
count the characters, words, and lines
-------------------------------------
initialize the counts
while there are lines remaining
```

```
add one to the number of lines
add the number of characters in the line to the number of characters
add the count of the number of words in the line to the number of words
```

And so it goes, down to lower and lower levels. At any point, we get to call a function rather than writing the code in line.

Using this method, there are three reasons for putting a part of the code into a function:

1. You want to make your program easier to understand. A block of code is easier to read and understand if it isn't too long. You should make functions with clear names for parts of the program to make the parts that use them easier to understand. You should have a lot of functions that are called from only one place.
2. You are going to use the same code in more than one place, differing only by some variables and constants. You can put the code into a function and pass the parts that vary as parameters.
3. You are processing a recursive data structure.

Following the top-down design method, we arrive at a `wc` program like the one given in Figure 2–4. We will call this `wc1.py`, since we anticipate creating other versions.

The `import` statements provide the way to get at functions and variables declared in other files. A lot of the Python system is provided in *modules;* that is, Python code in files. We know that we can use the facilities provided in two of them. The `sys` module has a variable `argv` that means the same thing as the `argv` parameter to the `main()` function in a C program. It is a list of strings with one string per command line parameter. Suppose we want to apply our `wc1` program to the file `fib.py`. We would type in the command:

```
python wc1.py fib.py
```

The first element of the `argv` list will be the name of the file (`'wc1.py'` in this case) that was passed to the Python interpreter. The subsequent elements are the command line parameters being passed to the Python program. So `argv` will contain `['wc1.py','fib.py']`.

The way we reference a variable in a module we have imported is by `modulename.variblename`. So we refer to `argv` as `sys.argv`. Module `sys` also contains a variable `stdin` that contains the standard input file. We refer to it as `sys.stdin`. If a module contains a function we want, we

```
#!/usr/bin/python
import sys
import string
#
#let f be the input file
#
if len(sys.argv)>=2:
    f=open(sys.argv[1],"r")
else:
    f=sys.stdin
#
#set counts of characters, words, and lines:
#
c = w = L = 0
#
#read and count
#
line = f.readline()
while line:
    L = L+1
    c = c+len(line)
    w = w + len(string.split(line))
    line=f.readline()
#
#report results
#
print c,w,L
```

Figure 2–4
A word count (wc1.py) program.

use the same syntax to get at it–a def statement, after all, assigns the function value to a variable.

The wc1 program assigns the input file to variable f. If there is no file name given on the command line, it assigns sys.stdin to f. If there is a file name given, it must open the file using the built-in function open(). It takes the file name as its first argument and the mode as the second. The modes include r for reading, w for writing, and a for appending. Mode w empties an existing file before writing, whereas a does not. (If you are accessing a binary file, which wc1 is not, you would use rb, wb, or ab.)

There is another use of this dotted notation later in the program, f.readline(). This says that a file object has a readline() method. It's equivalent to a member function, if you know C++. Method readline() will read the next line from a text file and return it as a string.

The line will contain the termination character, so even a blank line will have characters in it. On end of file, `readline()` will return an empty string.

Now consider the `while` loop beginning `while line:`. A string is considered `true` if it has any characters in it and is considered `false` if it is empty. So this loop will continue to execute until we come to the end of file. The same rule applies to other sequences, like lists: An empty list is considered to be false; a non-empty list, true.

Finally, the `string` module has functions that are useful for processing strings. The function `string.split(line)` will return a list of all the substrings of `line` that are separated by white space. "White space" means blanks, tabs, line termination characters, and such. The program counts all chunks of non-white-space characters as words.

Whereas we had to use module `sys` to get at the command line arguments and the standard input file, the use of the string module was completely optional. It was used in Python 1 and proved so popular that its operations were made into strings methods in Python 2. (In Python 2 style, we would count the words with: `w += len(line.split())`.)

2.3 Wrap-Up

We have now seen most of Python's statement types: expressions, assignments and `del` statements in Chapter 1; function definition and `return`, `print`, looping, loop escape, conditional, `assert`, `raise`, and `try-except` statements here. We are still missing the `class`, `exec`, `try-finally`, and `global` statements and details on `import`, `raise`, and `try-except` statements. We will come to these in later chapters.

2.4 Exercises

2.1. Write a function `factorial(n)` that will compute n!, i.e. `1*2*3*...*n`.

2.2. Write a version of `bal(s,open,close)` that checks whether a string is balanced with respect to arbitrary pairs of opening and closing characters that are passed in as parameters. Parameters `open` and `close` are strings of the same length. Character `open[i]` is an opening character and `close[i]` is the corresponding closing character.

2.3. Write a version of `fib(n)` that uses loops to calculate the value and will give the correct answer even if it cannot be contained in an integer.

⬗ Some Problems with Top-Down Programming

- It does not help with choosing data structures. Data structures are at least as important as code. When and how should the data structures be chosen during top-down programming?
- Top-down programming was not designed for reuse, since code is written for a particular context, but we want to be able to reuse a lot of the code we write.
- Designing top-down invites us to write the program as we design, but it is hard to test code when the functions it calls haven't been written yet.
- When we invent a goal or activity name for a section of code, we are assuming we can program it. We may write other code assuming that we can implement that part, but when we come to it, we may discover that we are not able to program it.
- It does not help with designing interfaces, the coordinated collections of functions in modules (Chapter 3) or methods in classes (Chapter 4).

2.4. Write a function, `pal(s)`, that checks whether string `s` is a palindrome—the same sequence of characters forward and backward. It is to return `1` if `s` is a palindrome and `0` if it is not.

2.5. Write an insertion sort function, `sort(x)`. It is to sort the list `x`, in place. Insertion sort works by keeping the initial part of the list sorted, say `x[0:i]`. (Remember, this means all the items from `0` up to but not including `i`.) At the beginning, the single item in `x[0:1]` is sorted. The item `x[i]` is moved down to its proper place by repeatedly exchanging it with its predecessors until it is in place, at which point `x[0:i+1]` is sorted. The process continues until all items have been moved to their proper places.

2.6. Write a function `reverse(x)` that reverses the list `x` in place.

3

Modules and Packages

Writing large programs can be a problem. One aspect of the problem is just the quantity of code that must be written. Being able to reuse code is a great help, but a problem with top-down design is that it is not directed at reusability. Each section of code you write, you write in a particular context, with particular inputs and outputs. It is natural that each piece of code is specialized, and that makes it harder to reuse elsewhere later.

However, the quantity of code to be written is not the largest problem. The problem is writing correct, maintainable code. In fact, part of the problem is even getting the code completed. Programs can exceed the capacity of one person to implement, even the capacity of one person to understand.

One important way to manage the complexity of software systems is *modularity*–breaking the system down into smallish, meaningful, coherent chunks. These chunks have an interface, preferably small, through which the rest of the system interacts with them. They hide the details of their implementation from the rest of the system.

In this chapter, we study Python's modules, one way of grouping code to hide details from the outside. We look at how to import modules, how to access the names they declare, and how to organize them into packages.

▌ **Principles of modular programming**

- A system should be composed of modules. A module is a self-contained collection of related code.
- A module should be devoted to one kind of thing; it should have a single theme, you might say. That means, among other things, that if you need to look something up, you know where to look.
- A module should provide *encapsulation*. A module has an interface to the outside world. It makes certain functions, variables, and data definitions visible. Users of the module should need to know only the interface, not the details of how the module is implemented. Conversely, a module should hide the details of its implementation from the outside. There may be some functions and variables and data structures that only the code in the module uses. These should be hidden from the users of the module.
- Modules should be used for *information hiding*. Although some people use it as a synonym for encapsulation, information hiding originally meant hiding major design decisions inside modules. Information hiding allows the design decisions to be reconsidered without having to change the rest of the program. You might want to change a data structure or an algorithm. You might want to do a first implementation that is simple to debug, but change it later if it's too inefficient. If you hide a major design decision in the implementation in a module, you should be able to change the decision without having to change any other part of your program.
- Modules in a system should form *layers*. Each layer of a system provides facilities that can be used by the layers above it. This concept has become important in operating systems, where it is sometimes said that each layer of the system provides a "virtual machine" for the layer above to run on. The code for each layer is written using the facilities provided by the lower layers.

3.1 Importing Modules

The syntax of module imports is shown in Table 3–1 on page 49. When you tell Python to import a module, M,

```
import M
```

you will get a reference to a module object in variable M. M is also the name of the module that Python tries to find. Python first tries to look up module M in memory, in case it has already been loaded. If Python finds the module in memory, Python assigns the module object to the identifier M in the current scope. If the module is not already in memory, Python tries to find it in the search path, as we will describe shortly. The module name M corresponds to a file with a name M.pyc (for already compiled modules) and M.py (for source code). If there are files with both names M.pyc and M.py, Python will use whichever has the more recent modification time. If M.py is more recent, Python will recompile it and store the compiled version in M.pyc to use the next time. There could also be a file M.pyo for an optimized, compiled version, the result of using the -o option on the Python command line.

When a module is loaded, its code is executed with its own global name space. The code assigns values to names in this name space. At the end of initialization, the name space becomes the attributes of the module object, a dictionary available through the module object's special __dict__ attribute.

You can import any number of modules in one import statement, listing the module names separated with commas. For example:

```
import sys, os, math
```

3.2   Importing Names from Modules

Once you have imported module M, you can refer to variables, classes, and functions in it with qualified names, such as M.x. If you wish to refer to them without qualification, you could make assignments to local variables, for example, x=M.x or you can import the names directly, using the from-import statement:

```
from M import x
```

In this case, the identifier M is not assigned a value, but module M is loaded if it has not been already and x is assigned the value of x within M. You can import more than one name at a time:

```
from M import x, y, z
```

If you wish to import all the names defined in a module, you can use '*' for the import list:

```
from M import *
```

Actually, this only imports all those names defined in the module except for those beginning with an underscore. Those names are considered private. Importation of all names is fine for some modules, but other modules have a larger number of names, and a great many of them are for specialized purposes only. Importing them all would fill up the local namespace with a large number of names, and it would increase the risk that some of these names might collide with names being used for other purposes. You could be using some of the names yourself, or perhaps worse, the same name could be used in different modules.

Filling up a namespace with a large number of unused names is called "namespace pollution." Namespace pollution is made even worse by the fact that if you import a module that itself imports * from a third module, you get all the names from the third module.

3.3 Avoiding Namespace Pollution

There are a number of techniques for avoiding namespace pollution, or cluttering up your namespace with a large number of names with the attendant risks of mistaken and inconsistent uses.

One way is to avoid using the `from modname import *` statement except in special cases. You may also need to refer to modules by different names than their own. The name of one module may be a name of a function or class you need to use frequently in another module, or it may be a very intuitive name for a variable or function in your module. You need to import the module, but assign it to a variable with a different name. You can do this with the `as` clause:

```
import modname as varname
```

This imports the module with the name `modname`, but assigns the module object to `varname`. You can also use the as phrase in the `from-import` statement; for example:

```
from M import x as y, y as z
```

to rename the objects being imported from a module.

In version 2.1 of Python, a feature was added to modules that allows you to restrict the names that another module can import from them with `from ... import *`. Assign a list of names to attribute `__all__` and only those names can be imported with a *; for example:

```
__all__=["PureSet","emptySet"]
```

3.4   Reloading Modules

When you are debugging a module, M, interactively, you repeatedly need to make changes in the module and try it again. The problem is that you cannot just change the module's source file and import it again with the `import` statement, `import M`.

The import statement will first look for module M in memory; finding it there, it will assign the module object to the variable M. You need to force Python to reload the module from disk by calling the `reload()` function. Calling `reload(M)` has Python reload the module corresponding to the module object. The reload is done in place, overwriting attributes of the same module object. Since all the places in your program where you have imported the module will have references to the same module object, the reload will work retroactively for all of them. You do not have to reload other modules that import the module you have changed; their references to the module are fine.

However, there are some problems with reloading modules. Although the module object is the same, the objects contained in the module are not. When you execute:

```
import M
from M import f
```

you get a reference to the `f` contained in the module at the instant the `from-import` statement is executed. Suppose `f` is a function, and you change its code in the module source and reload the module:

```
reload(M)
```

If you call

```
M.f()
```

you will get the new function definition, but if you call

```
f()
```

you get the old one. The `from M import f` assignment to `f` is not re-executed. One way around this is to reload not only the module you've changed, but all the modules that import names from it. If you've changed module M and module N that imports a name from M, you need to reload them in order:

```
reload(M)
```

```
reload(N)
```

Another alternative, of course, especially during program debugging, would be to import the module only as a whole, not import names from it.

Another problem with reloading is that it does not clear out the dictionary of attributes in the module object it is reloading. If you remove a function or class definition from the module source code, it will still be present in the module object after reloading. This is likely to be confusing: "I thought I got rid of that."

3.5   Search Paths

When Python searches for modules, it looks in each directory in a search path in order. You can find the search path in a list in the `sys` module, `sys.path`. The elements of the list are strings that are paths to directories in the computer's file system. This list is initialized either in an installation-dependent manner or from the environment variable `$PYTHONPATH`. The first element of the list, `sys.path[0]`, is the directory containing the script that invoked the Python interpreter. If there was no script, for example, because Python is being executed interactively, `sys.path[0]` is the empty string, and it tells Python to search the current directory first. Since Python searches the directories in the path in order, it will look for a module in the directory containing the script or in the current directory first. However, certain built-in modules are not on the search path; for example, there is no module `sys` in any of the directories listed in `sys.path`.

Python does a case-sensitive import. It looks for a module whose name exactly matches the identifier being imported. Some operating systems have case-insensitive file systems, so hedgehog.py, Hedgehog.py, HedgeHog.py and HEDGEHOG.py are indistinguishable. If you wish to use a case-insensitive import, set the `PYTHONCASEOK` environment variable before starting the Python interpreter.

No matter what order you use to search for modules, there is a potential problem with name collisions. If you have a module with the same name as a system module, you will hide the system module. This may not seem to be a problem, but it is when another standard Python module tries to access the module you have hidden; it will get yours instead. It is another example of namespace pollution–not of the names

Table 3–1
Import statement syntax.

```import mod1, mod2 ,...```	The import statement allows you to load and initialize a module (if it hasn't already been loaded).
```import mod1 as name1,``` ```mod2 as name2,...```	```import m``` imports module m and assigns the variable m a reference to the module object. You can then get at a variable or other member x in m as m.x.
```from mod import ident1,``` ```ident2, ...```	```import m as n``` imports m but assigns it to variable n.
```from mod import ident1 as name1,``` ```ident2 as name2, ...```	```from m import x``` imports module m, but doesn't assign the module to a variable. Instead, it assigns the module's attribute x to variable x. With ```as y```, it assigns the value of the attribute to variable y.
```from mod import *```	```from m import *``` imports m and assigns all its attributes to variables with their same names. The module names can be qualified:

```from __future__ import facility```	```ident1.ident2....,```
	indicating importing from a package. The ```from __future__ import``` does not import a module. It allows access to a new feature of Python that is available but not standard yet. It must come before any statements that can generate executable code, since it may influence code generation. Examples:
	```import math```
	
	```import math as mathfns```
	
	```from math import sin```
	
	```from math import sin as sine```
	
	```from math import *```
	
	```from __future__ import```
	```nested_scopes```

being used within your program, but of names in the space of modules. Packages provide a way to get around this module namespace pollution.

3.6   Packages

Packages try to get around the problem of module namespace pollution by creating hierarchical names for modules, of the form:

```
packagename.subpackage1.subpackage2.....modulename
```

When you import a hierarchical name that your program has not seen before, Python searches for the module roughly the same way as it searches for a simple module. Python searches the `sys.path` list, looking for a subdirectory with the name `packagename`. Within that directory, it looks for a subdirectory with name `subpackage1`, and so on, until it finds the file `modulename`. There are, however, a number of complications.

A first consideration is what the naming conventions should be for packages. One suggestion is to use Internet domain names of the companies and organizations that are the sources of the packages. For example, the company Tools of Computing LLC (of which the author is a principal) has a domain `toolsofcomputing.org` to distribute its open source, publicly licensed software. The software available in this book might be in several packages:

- `toolsofcomputing_org.adt`, for the abstract data types;
- `toolsofcomputing_org.threads`, for the threading modules;
- `toolsofcomputing_org.tcllk`, for the parsing modules; and
- `toolsofcomputing_org.PPPexamples`, for Python programming pattern examples.

After you import a module from a package, using, for example,

```
import toolsofcomputing_org.adt.Set
```

you can refer to class `Set` in module `Set` as `toolsofcomputing_org.adt.Set.Set`. What do you get if you just refer to `toolsofcomputing_org`? You get a module object. Internally, a package becomes a module: Following a path through packages and subpackages simply involves fetching attributes from module objects.

If `toolsofcomputing_org` is not already loaded, the subdirectory `toolsofcomputing_org` must be found on the search path, a module object created for it, subdirectory `adt` found in it, and a module created for that. A Python file (`Set.py`, `Set.pyc` or `Set.pyo`) must be found in `adt`, a module must be created for the Python file, and that module must be initialized. Indeed, as module objects `toolsofcomputing_org`, and `toolsofcomputing_org.adt` are created, they are initialized as well. Their attributes can be more submodules: whatever attributes their initialization code creates. Their initialization code is found in files `__init__.py` within their directories. Indeed, a directory without an `__init__.py` file will not be recognized as a package.

The command `import toolsofcomputing_org.adt` does not automatically import all the modules in directory `toolsofcomputing_org/adt` and in its subpackages; however, you can have the `__init__.py` files import modules and subpackages themselves. For example, the file `toolsofcomputing_org/adt/__init__.py` could contain

```
import Set
import PureSet
import prioque
import prioqueunique
import rational
import DEQueue
```

which would make those modules available as `toolsofcomputing_org.adt.Set`, and so on. The downside is that they would all always be loaded, whether they are needed or not.

When we are importing another module in the same package directory, we can simply use its name. We do not have to write an entire path to it.

Consider trying to import all the modules in a package with the '*' option:

```
from toolsofcomputing_org.adt import *
```

The '*' option with package imports is problematic. Because Python is case-sensitive, but not all operating systems are, Python cannot be certain of knowing what internal names to use for the Python code files in a package directory. You can get around this by making the package initialization code define a variable `__all__`. Upon encountering a '*' option on an import list, Python will import all the modules whose names are in the `__all__` list of the source package's module object. Since the package's module object is created and initialized before Python tries to import these contained names, its `__all__` attribute will have already been assigned a value. For example, the file `toolsofcomputing_org/adt/__init__.py` could contain:

```
__all__=["Set","PureSet","prioque","prioqueunique",
         "rational","DEQueue"]
```

which would make the `from-import` statement equivalent to

```
from toolsofcomputing_org.adt import Set,PureSet,prioque,
        prioqueunique,rational,DEQueue
```

3.7   Example Stack Module

Suppose we need a stack, or a LIFO data structure. We can push things on the top of the stack. We can pop them off the top. We can look at the top element. In a language with static or dynamic arrays, we might allocate an array to hold the elements and keep an integer index of the top element. In Python, however, we keep the stack in a list and change the size of the list as we push and pop. This module has functions to treat a list as a stack. Function `new()` will create a new, empty stack. It is not needed if we know that a stack is really just a list. Function `push(stk, v)` pushes value `v` on the top of the stack `stk`. Function `pop(stk)` pops the top value off the stack `stk` and returns it. Function `top(stk)` returns the top value on stack `stk` without removing it. Function `isempty(stk)` returns `true` if stack `stk` is empty, and returns `false` otherwise.

Here is a test of the module:

```
>>> import stack1
>>> s=stack1.new()
>>> s
[]
>>> stack1.push(s,1)
>>> stack1.push(s,2)
>>> stack1.push(s,3)
>>> s
[1, 2, 3]
>>> len(s)
3
>>> stack1.pop(s)
3
>>> stack1.top(s)
2
>>> stack1.isempty(s)
0
>>> stack1.pop(s)
2
>>> stack1.pop(s)
1
>>> stack1.isempty(s)
1
```

Now look at the code in Figure 3–1. Function `push(skt,s)` calls list's `append()` method, `stk.append(v)`, which increases the length of `stk` by one and puts the value `v` at the end (i.e., the rightmost, or highest, position).

```
def new():
    return []
def push(stk,v):
    stk.append(v)
def pop(stk):
    tmp=stk[-1]
    del stk[-1]
    return tmp
def top(stk):
    return stk[-1]
def isempty(stk):
    return len(stk)==0
```

Figure 3–1
Stack operations (stack1.py).

Function `pop(stk)` saves a copy of the last element in `stk`, removes that element, and returns it. It shows two things of interest:

1. Negative subscripts—You can use negative subscripts to access elements relative to the right end of the list. For indices, `i`, in the range 1 to `len(x)`, `x[-i]` is the same as `x[len(x)-i]`.
2. The `del` statement—You use the `del` statement to delete things. In this case, the statement `del stk[-1]` deletes the last element of `stk`.

The implementation of `pop()` was designed to show negative subscripts and the `del` statement. Actually, lists have their own `pop()` method that does just what we want.

Although this shows how a module can be used, we would not implement stacks this way in Python. In Chapter 4 we will look at creating our own classes of objects. We would create a stack class that has the appropriate methods, and create stack objects as instances of this class. In fact, we present a doubly-ended queue class in "DEQueue," Chapter 15, Section 15.2, that includes two `stack1` commands, `push()` and `pop()`, among its methods.

3.8   Critique of Modules

Let us consider how well Python's modules suit our needs when writing modular programs. We want a module to provide a separate scope for declarations. We should be able to declare variables and functions in the module without the names colliding with those declared elsewhere. Python handles this well: Each module is in a separate file. When

Python imports it, Python creates a separate scope and executes the code for the module within that scope. This satisfies another desire: We want a module to execute some initialization code to set up its data structures.

We want the ability to import the names from another module to access the variables and function there. This is handled in Python by the `import` and `from-import` statements.

We want the ability to restrict the visibility of some names declared in the module so that they can be seen only by code inside the module. That is, we want encapsulation. Python doesn't provide this completely. All names in a module are visible, although those beginning with an underscore are not as visible; they will not be imported from a module with a `from name import *` statement.

3.9   Wrap-Up

With modules, we particularly have to worry about namespace pollution, the appearance of a multitude of confusing and potentially conflicting names. Some namespace pollution is internal to a Python program. Some is external to the program, within the search path that Python uses when hunting for modules being imported. Some forms of the import statement help to combat internal namespace pollution. To help combat external pollution, we can use Python packages. Packages are kept in directory hierarchies on the module search path and are translated into trees of modules when loaded. They allow us to partition the names into subspaces where they will not conflict.

3.10   Exercises

3.1. Try to write two modules that import names from each other; for example, module A contains a `from B import X` statement and module B contains a `from A import Y` statement. What happens? Use function `dir(M)` to get a list of the names defined in module `M`.

3.2. Critique the design of packages in Python.

3.3. Critique the `from name import *` statement in Python.

4

Objects and Classes

This chapter presents details on Python's classes and inheritance, the facilities essential for object-oriented programming. The classes contain methods, functions that apply to class instances. These methods access and assign attributes of the instance. Python provides multiple inheritance, so you can use methods of more than one superclass to manipulate an instance. Multiple inheritance can be confusing if there is more than one way to inherit from the same superclass, so-called diamond inheritance.

Unlike statically-typed object-oriented languages, you do not have to use inheritance in Python. All that is required is that an object have a method with the proper name and parameters available when you call it. There are no visibility restrictions on attribute names in instances that are used by methods in different classes.

4.1 Instances and Classes

You create a class object by executing a `class` statement, e.g.:

```
class point: pass
```

You create an instance of a class by calling the class name as a function:

```
p=point()
```

Both classes and instance objects have *attributes*. You get an attribute with the syntax:

```
object . attribute_name
```

The instance has a reference to its class in a special attribute __class__, so that p.__class__ is point.

Both classes and class instances have dictionaries, named __dict__. You reference the class point's dictionary as point.__dict__ and the instance p's dictionary as p.__dict__. The relationships between p and point and their dictionaries are shown in Figure 4–1.

4.2   Class Declarations

The basic form of a class statement is:

```
class name:
    suite
```

where name is the name of the class being declared and suite is a suite of statements to execute. All the statements in the suite of a class declaration are typically def statements, although they do not have to be.

The class declaration is an executable statement. Like a def statement, it creates an object and assigns it to the name in the current scope. The def statement creates a function object. The class statement creates a class object. But here is an important difference: The suite in a function is not executed until the function is called. The statements in a

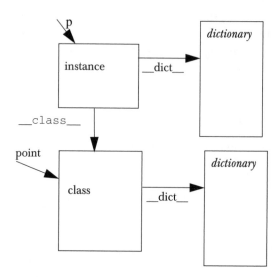

Figure 4–1
Instances and classes.

class declaration are executed while the class statement is being executed.

When a function is called, it is executed with its own local environment where local variables are stored. When the function returns, the local environment is discarded. Like a function, the statements in a class declaration are executed with the declaration's own local environment. Unlike a function, however, when the class statement finishes executing, the local environment is not thrown away. It is saved in the `__dict__` dictionary of the class object. The suite of statements in a class declaration is executed to create a dictionary of class *attributes*, the names known in the class. In other object-oriented languages, these are known as class variables.

The most common statement to include in a class declaration is the `def` statement, which is used to create the "methods" that operate on instances of the class (which we discuss in the next section); but it is possible to execute other assignments as well.

When you want to get the value of one of these names, you can use the dot operator. The form `ClassName.attribute` gives you the value of the attribute defined in the *class*. For example:

```
>>> class W:
...       y=1
...
>>> W.y
1
```

creates a class named `W` and assigns the value `1` to an attribute `y`. Note that `y` is an attribute of the *class object itself*, not of instances of the class. More confusing still, we can get at class attributes through instances of the class as well as through the class object. The way to get an instance of a class is by calling the class as we would call a function. So:

```
>>> z=W()
>>> z.y
1
```

shows that we can also get the value of `y` through the instance, `z`, of the class `W`.

4.3 Instances

The purpose of a `class` is to create instances of it. We can use this for something as simple as implementing what are called `structs` or records in other languages. For example, `class point: pass` declares a class object called point. The `pass` statement executes no operation. We need it because the syntax requires a class statement to have a suite of one or more statements as a body.

We can create an *instance* of the class point by calling `point()` as a function:

```
>>> p=point()
```

We can then assign values to attributes of the point using the dotted notation and access them the same way:

```
>>> p.x=1
>>> p.y=2
>>> p.x
1
>>> p.y
2
```

But when we create a point, it doesn't start with any attributes.

```
>>> q=point()
>>> q.x
Traceback (innermost last):
  File "<stdin>", line 1, in ?
AttributeError: x
```

This is a major difference between instances of classes in Python and `structs` or records in most other languages. In most languages, you have to declare the attributes (fields, members) of the `structs` or records. In Python, the first assignment to an attribute creates it. The attributes are kept in the __dict__ dictionary of the instance:

```
>>> p.__dict__
{'x': 1, 'y': 2}
```

Assignment to an attribute is equivalent to an assignment to the attribute name in the __dict__ dictionary.

A problem with Python then is, "What if we want the instance of the class to start off with a set of attributes?" To do this, we can provide

an initialization procedure in our declaration of the class that will be
called when an instance is created:

```
>>> class point:
...     def __init__(self):
...             self.x=0
...             self.y=0
...
>>> q=point()
>>> q.x
0
```

Here we have redeclared point, replacing pass with a function definition. The function name is __init__. When Python creates an instance
of the point, it calls the __init__(self) function and passes it a reference to the point it has just created. Function __init__(self) then
assigns zero to both attributes x and y via the parameter self. Just as
with the assignments from outside, these assignments create the
attributes.
      The __init__() function is an initializer. Although it is called by
Python just after the instance is created to initialize it, you can call it
again at any later time to reinitialize the object.
      If you want to know what attributes are defined in an instance of a
class, you can use the dir(), as in "directory," function:

```
>>> dir(p)
['x', 'y']
```

4.4 Methods

A def statement within a class declaration declares a *method*, a function
that operates on instances of the class. Consider the following:

```
>>> class X:
...     def f(self,y): return y
...
```

We declared a class X containing a method f. The rule is that methods
can be called only for instances of the class or a subclass. When they are
called, their first argument will be given a reference to the instance and
their other arguments will be taken from the argument list. So method f
takes two parameters: The first one, self, will be given a reference to an

instance of class x. The second one will be given a value by the argument of the call.

The __init__() method shown in the preceding section is an example of a *special method*. There are many other special methods, and they are discussed in Chapters 14 and 15. The special methods are called when an instance is used in a special context; for example, as an operand for a binary operator.

The normal way to call a method is to use the dot operator. For example:

```
>>> z=X()
>>> z.f(5)
5
```

The call `instance.name(args)` will call the method `name` declared in the class of `instance` and pass it the `instance` as its first parameter and the other `args` as the subsequent parameters. You use this first parameter to access the *attributes* of the *instance*.

If you are familiar with other object-oriented languages, you will notice that there are no "class methods" or "static methods" in a class definition; in other words, there are no methods that do not require a reference to a class instance. Instead, you would call functions in the module that contains the class and have them assign values to variables in the module.

Let's look at the data type of a method. If we look up a method in the class object, we get an *unbound method* object:

```
>>> X.f
<unbound method X.f>
```

This means that it is a method, but it isn't attached to any instance of the class yet. If, however, we look it up in an instance, we get a bound method. Thus:

```
>>> z=X()
>>> z.f
<method X.f of X instance at 007DCEFC>
```

gives us a method object that is bound to an instance of the class x. We can call the bound instance as a function of one parameter:

```
>>> g=z.f
>>> g(7)
7
```

But we cannot call the unbound method, f, as a function of one parameter. It needs two parameters, the first being an instance:

```
>>> g=X.f
>>> g(7)
Traceback (most recent call last):
  File "<stdin>", line 1, in ?
TypeError: unbound method must be called with class
instance 1st argument
>>> g(z,7)
7
```

By the way, methods are not stored in the class object as unbound methods, but rather as functions. A class object contains a special attribute, __dict__, that is a dictionary containing the namespace of the class. If you look up a method in that dictionary, you find a function. Thus:

```
>>> X.__dict__["f"]
<function f at 007B2464>
```

When it looks up a function in a class object, the dot operator creates a method object. Figure 12-4 shows a picture of the relationships between method objects, classes, and modules.

Now, to show a use of the instance reference, consider the counter class shown in Figure 4-2. Instances of the counter class have an attribute, count, that starts at zero by default, or at another value specified when the object is created. The method call c.bump() will add one to c.count. The call c.bump(k) will add k to c.count. The __init__() method is called automatically when an instance of the class is created and assigns its parameter val to the count attribute of the instance. This creates the count attribute, since, like variables, attributes are created when they are first assigned a value. The val=0 parameter specifies that the default value is zero. Method bump() adds its parameter by to count and returns the new value. The default increment is specified by the parameter specification, by=1.

Notice, by the way, that there is no requirement that you call the first parameter of a method self. It is a custom in Python. Java and C++

```
""" counter objects:
x=counter()
x=counter(initVal)
x.count
x.bump()
x.bump(increment) """
class counter:
    "creates counter objects"
    def bump(this,by=1):
       this.count+=by
       return this.count
    def __init__(self,val=0):
       self.count=val
```

Figure 4–2
Counter class, file `counterObj.py`.

programmers may prefer the name `this`, but many Python programmers
strongly object to using anything other than `self`, or perhaps `s` for short.
Here is a test of the `counter` class:

```
>>> from counterObj import counter
>>> c=counter()
>>> c.count
0
>>> c.bump()
1
>>> c.count
1
>>> counter.__doc__
'creates counter objects'
>>> d=counter(3)
>>> d.count
3
>>> d.bump(2)
5
```

Also notice that both the `counterObj` module and the counter class
begin with string literals. These are documentation strings. You can look
up these strings as the __doc__ attributes of the objects containing them:

```
>>> print counterObj.__doc__
 counter objects:
x=counter()
x=counter(initVal)
x.count
x.bump()
```

```
x.bump(increment)
>>> counter.__doc__
'creates counter objects'
```

You also need to distinguish between methods that are contained in classes and attributes of objects that contain functions. Here we create a function, `hi()`, that writes out the string "hi". Then we assign it as the `bump` attribute of `counter` object c.

```
>>> def hi():print "hi"
...
>>> c.bump=hi
>>> c.bump()
hi
```

When we call `c.bump()`, we get the `hi()` function, not the `bump` method of the class. From this and the earlier discussion of bound method objects, we can see what Python does with a reference like `c.bump`. First it tries to find attribute `bump` of object c. If it finds it, it uses that. If it doesn't find an attribute with that name, Python looks in the class of object c to find a function `bump`. If it finds one, it creates a bound method object containing that function and the object c.

Finally, let us remark again on the scope of names in methods. In most object-oriented languages, code in a method can refer to the attributes of an object that contains it by just using the name of the attribute. In Python, it must use an explicit reference to the object, such as `self`, and reference the attributes with the dot operator.

So what do the variable names in the method refer to? The same as in any function, they are either local variables, global variables defined in the surrounding module, or built-in names of the Python system.[1]

4.5   Single Inheritance

Classes without inheritance are enough for what is called object-based programming. You can create new data types (called abstract data types) that have their own operations. But for object-oriented programming, you need inheritance. Python allows a class to inherit from one or more classes—multiple inheritance. We discuss single inheritance first, and then expand the discussion to multiple inheritance.

---

1. Prior to version 2.1, all functions in Python had three levels of scope, even those defined in class statements. In version 2.1, it is optional to have one level of scope for each nested function. In version 2.2, that feature will become standard. See "Nested Scopes" in Chapter 6.

A class declaration with single inheritance has the form:

```
class name(superclass):
    suite
```

where `superclass` is an expression that yields a class object. In other languages, like Java, the class declarations are handled by the compiler, so the superclass would be a name of a class. In Python, class declarations are executable, so the `superclass` is an expression that yields a class at run-time. You could have an array of classes and a loop creating a subclass of each, something like:

```
for i in range(len(X)):
    class C(Y[i]): ...
    X[i]=C
```

although it is hard, offhand, to think of any use for doing so. Executing the same class declaration more than once is more likely to be a bug.

When we say the subclass *inherits* from its superclass, we mean that the subclass starts with all the superclass's methods. The subclass can add new methods and attributes beyond those possessed by the superclass. The subclass can *override* methods that it would inherit from its superclass; that is, it can provide its own declarations of some of the methods declared in the superclass. Then, when someone calls the method, they get the version provided by the subclass.

Because objects in the subclass get all the attributes and methods of the superclass, they can be used in any place an object of the superclass can be. They will respond to the same operations. This gives an "is-a" relationship between instances of the subclass and its superclass. If class y inherits from class x, an instance of y is an x. The is-a relationship provides what is called "polymorphism." At a particular place in the program, you may not be sure precisely what class of object is being operated on, only that it has a certain *interface*, that is, that it will respond to certain method calls. (Actually, polymorphism is the wrong name. It means "multiple forms," but the interface is more analogous to a form and the implementation to a substance. The interface is the same. It is the implementations that can be different.)

So what do you use inheritance for? It has a great many different uses. We discuss some of them here and some in later chapters. Many of the uses have been given names and have been classified as object-oriented design patterns, which we discuss in Chapter 5.

```
import counterObj
class settableCounter(counterObj.counter):
    "creates settable counter objects"
    def set(self,to):
      self.count=to
```

Figure 4–3
Class `settableCounter`.

One use for inheritance is to add functionality. Consider the class `settableCounter` in Figure 4–3. It is a subclass of class `counter` shown in Figure 4–2. As we've already seen, `counter` provides three things to its user: an attribute `count` that contains the current count; an `__init__()` method that allows the counter to be initialized to a particular value or to default to zero; and a `bump()` method that allows you to increase the count either by one by default or by an explicit amount, positive or negative.

The class `settableCounter` adds a method `set()` that allows you to assign an explicit value to the current count. You may be wondering why we would need a `set()` method. Why not just assign a value to `count`? Well, with the current implementation, that would work; but does `counter` actually promise that you will be able to assign to `count`? It is possible to implement `counter` so that you can only read count, but not assign to it. The actual count can be hidden. We'll see how to do this in Chapter 14.

Here is an example of a `settableCounter` in action:

```
>>> from settableCounter import settableCounter
>>> x=settableCounter(1)
>>> x.count
1
>>> x.bump()
2
>>> x.set(10)
>>> x.count
10
```

Clearly, when we create a `settableCounter`, we get an object that has the methods declared in its class and in its superclass, `counter`. When we created it, the `__init__()` method in the superclass was executed, setting `count` initially to 1. We got at the attribute `count` as easily as in a `counter` object. When we called `bump()`, we called the `bump()` method declared in the superclass, `counter`. When we called `set()`, we got the method declared in `settableCounter`.

Here's how it works: As discussed earlier, when we access an object using the dot operator—for example, `x.y`—Python first looks for a `y` attribute of object `x`. If it finds one, that's what it returns. Otherwise, it looks through a series of classes for a definition. It first looks in `x`'s class. Then, if it doesn't find it there, it looks in `x`'s superclass. It will keep on looking in superclasses until it finds the class attribute `y` or it comes to a class that has no superclasses.

In the `settableCounter` example, when we referred to `x.count`, Python found it in `x`'s dictionary of attributes. When we referred to `set()`, Python found it in `x`'s class object. When we referred to `bump()`, Python found it in `x`'s class's superclass. Similarly, when we created a `settableCounter`, Python found the `__init__()` method in the superclass, `counter`, and executed that. These namespaces are shown in the contour diagram in Figure 4–4. The boxes represent nested namespaces. You start searching for a name in the innermost name space and move to each enclosing namespace in turn.

4.6 Visibility

If you know other object-oriented languages such as Java, you will find some differences between them and Python regarding visibility. Classes in other object-oriented languages declare the visibility of their attributes. If an attribute is declared *private*, only that class can see it. If it

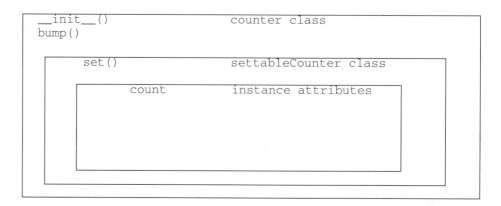

Figure 4–4
Contour model of scopes (namespaces) in a `settableCounter` instance.

is *public*, anyone using an object of that class can see it. And there is usually a *protected* visibility that says that code in that class and any subclass can see the attribute, but code outside those classes cannot. Of course, the same visibility restrictions can also be used on methods.

Python objects have a single pool of attributes. In other languages, each class has its own separate pool of attributes in the instance object. Suppose you want to use some private attribute exclusively in one class. In the other languages, each class can use the same private name as any other class, and all will be kept separate. Thus you can program a class without worrying too much about what private attribute names its superclasses are using. In Python, if two of the classes use the same name for different purposes, they will clobber each other's data and the program will probably crash.

These visibility restrictions are considered important to object-oriented programming. One goal is to have objects provide *encapsulation*: An object is supposed to provide an interface to the outside users of the object and hide details from them internally. Thus, programmers are required to program to the interface. The implementation of the object can change, but its users will not have to change their code.

Python has no such visibility restrictions. All attributes and methods are visible to everyone. Anyone who wishes to use knowledge about the implementation of an object can do so. That can result in more efficient code. It can also result in a crash if the implementation changes. The language does nothing to prohibit programmers from "breaking encapsulation."

However, Python does provide "name mangling" to help hide names in classes. If you begin the name of an attribute of a class with two underscores, and you don't end it with any underscores, it is automatically rewritten to include the class name. Here's an example:

```
>>> class XX:
...     def __init__(self):
...             self.__x=0
...
>>> z=XX()
>>> dir(z)
['_XX__x']
```

As you can see, attribute __x in class XX was renamed to _XX__x. It doesn't prevent anyone from accessing it, but it does make it more unpleasant, which should serve to discourage casual use. Just as important, this keeps the attributes used privately by one class separate from those used by another.

As in other object-oriented languages, a method declared in a subclass will *hide* a method in a superclass with the same name. Python stops looking for a method as soon as it finds one with the right name. Unlike some other object-oriented languages, there is *no method overloading* in Python. Method overloading allows you to declare several methods with the same name but different signatures; that is, different numbers or types of parameters. All those methods will be visible at the same time. The compiler will look at a method call and choose the correct method to execute for the argument list given in the call. Python has no such facility. There are no type declarations, so the types of parameters cannot be specified to help in choosing which method is being called, and the parameter-passing conventions are so loose, even the number of parameters would not be a good way to choose a method.

4.7 Explicit Initializer Chaining

In many object-oriented languages, the initialization code for class instances (i.e., the class's constructor) will automatically call the initialization code for its superclasses when it begins executing. But there is nothing special about the __init__() method. Python will only call one __init__() method, the first it finds. In Python, you will have to call __init__() methods of superclasses yourself.

How? The problem is, suppose settableCounter had an __init__() method:

```
def  __init__(self,x): ...
```

that needed to call the __init__() method of its superclass, counter. It couldn't just call

```
self.__init__  #won't work
```

That would call settableCounter's __init__() method again, since Python will start searching at the class of object self and stop at the first __init__() method it finds.

Other object-oriented languages have a keyword like super to give a method access to names known in the superclass. Python uses the class name of the superclass. Remember that you can get an unbound method object by writing *classname.methodname*. You use that to get a method in a superclass whose name is hidden:

```
counter.__init__(self,x) #would work
```

Now let's criticize the design of `counter` and `settableCounter`. It is part of the design to have an attribute `count` visible from outside. With the obvious implementation, users are invited to assign values to it, rather than use the `set()` method. It is considered poor object-oriented design to ever allow the users of a class to assign values to its attributes directly. Instead, they are supposed to call methods to ask the object to do things for them.

Also, `settableCounter` knows the implementation of `counter` and assigns a value directly to `count` in the `set()` method. This is not as bad as allowing unrelated code to assign to `count`. Classes generally provide a more lenient interface to their subclasses than to the rest of the world, so it is probably okay for `settableCounter` to access the `count` attribute. But this still binds the classes together, so that a change to `counter` may force a change in `settableCounter`. It would be better to program defensively and prevent changes in one class from propagating into another.

This discussion becomes more complicated still if we use the special methods `__getattr__()` and `__setattr__()` discussed in Chapter 14. They allow what looks like an attribute access to actually call a method. However, we did not use these in `counter` and `settableCounter`, and their discussion will have to wait until Chapter 14.

4.8 Example: Set Implementation

Now let's consider a more elaborate example: A class `AbstractSet` (Figure 4–5) is a superclass of two other classes, `ListSet` (Figure 4–6) and `DictSet` (Figure 4–7). A *set*, in the mathematical sense, is a collection of elements (objects) without duplications. These classes may be considered a kind of sketch of how sets could be implemented. These three classes provide two implementations of sets as follows:

- `AbstractSet` declares all the set operations, but it doesn't implement them all. It provides some common code, but leaves many operations up to the subclasses.
- `ListSet` implements a set using a list to hold the elements.
- `DictSet` implements a set using a dictionary to hold the elements.

```
"""Abstract Set:
common set operations"""
class AbstractSet:
  def contains(self,x): raise NotImplementedError,"set.contains()"
  def insert(self,x): raise NotImplementedError,"set.insert()"
  def delete(self,x): raise NotImplementedError,"set.delete()"
  def members(self): raise NotImplementedError,"set.members()"
  def new(self): raise NotImplementedError,"set.new()"
  def copy(self): raise NotImplementedError,"set.copy()"
  def size(self): raise NotImplementedError,"set.size()"

  def __init__(self): pass # i.e. do nothing

  def insertAll(self,elems):
    for x in elems: self.insert(x)
    return self

  def removeAny(self):
    e=self.members()
    if len(e)>0:
      x=e[0]
      self.delete(x)
      return x
    return None

  def union(self,s):
    r=self.copy()
    for x in s.members():
      r.insert(x)
    return r

  def intersection(self,s):
    r=self.new()
    for x in self.members():
      if s.contains(x):
                  r.insert(x)
    return r

  def __str__(self):
    r=self.members()
    return "{"+str(r)[1:-1]+"}"
  __repr__ = __str__
```

Figure 4–5
AbstractSet.

```
"""ListSet
List implementation of an abstract set"""
import AbstractSet
class ListSet(AbstractSet.AbstractSet):
    def __init__(self,elems=()):
        AbstractSet.AbstractSet.__init__(self)
        self.rep=[]
        self.insertAll(elems)

    def contains(self,x):
      return x in self.rep

    def insert(self,x):
      if x not in self.rep:
        self.rep.append(x)
      return self

    def delete(self,x):
      if x in self.rep:
        self.rep.remove(x)
      return self

    def members(self):
      return self.rep[:]

    def new(self):
      return ListSet()

    def copy(self):
      c=ListSet()
      c.rep=self.rep[:]
      return c

    def size(self):
      return len(self.rep)
```

Figure 4–6
ListSet.

Why have two implementations? Lists and dictionaries may each be more efficient than the other for some set sizes and some uses, although in Chapter 17, we will settle on the dictionary implementation of sets and provide one that has a more complete collection of methods than these.

```
"""DictSet
Dictionary implementation of an abstract set"""
import AbstractSet
class DictSet(AbstractSet.AbstractSet):
    def __init__(self,elems=()):
      AbstractSet.AbstractSet.__init__(self)
      self.rep={}
      self.insertAll(elems)

    def contains(self,x):
      return self.rep.has_key(x)

    def insert(self,x):
      self.rep[x]=x
      return self

    def delete(self,x):
      if self.rep.has_key(x):
        del self.rep[x]
      return self

    def members(self):
      return self.rep.keys()

    def new(self):
      return DictSet()

    def copy(self):
      c=DictSet()
      c.rep=self.rep.copy()
      return c

    def size(self):
      return len(self.rep)
```

Figure 4–7
DictSet.

The operations provided by these sets are as follows:

- s=ListSet(elems) or s=DictSet(elems)—Creates a set initially containing the elements of the (optional) sequence elems.
- s.insert(x)—Adds element x to set s if it is not already present. Returns s.
- s.contains(x)—Returns true (1) if s contains x, false (0) otherwise.

- `s.delete(x)`—Removes element x from set s. Performs no operations if s does not contain x. Returns s.
- `s.members()`—Returns a list of all the elements of set s.
- `s.new()`—Returns a new empty set of the same type as s, e.g., a `ListSet` for a `ListSet`.
- `s.copy()`—Returns a copy of set s.
- `s.size()`—Returns the number of elements in set s.
- `s.insertAll(q)`—Inserts all the elements in sequence q into the set s. Returns s.
- `s.removeAny()`—Removes and returns an arbitrary element of set s. If s is empty, it returns `None`.
- `s.union(t)`—Returns a new set of the same type as s that contains all the elements contained in either s or t.
- `s.intersection(t)`—Returns a new set of the same type as s that contains all the elements contained in both s and t.
- `str(s)`—Returns a string representation of s, listing all the elements. This is the __str__() method; it tells `str()` how to do its job.
- `repr(s)`—This is the __repr__() method. For these sets, it is the same as `str(s)`.

You can find all the methods in `AbstractSet`, but not all of them are implemented there. Those methods that contain `raise NotImplemented-Error` are actually implemented in the subclasses. In a language like Java, we would have to declare them "abstract," which would tell the compiler that they must be implemented in a subclass and that instances of `AbstractSet` cannot be created, because only instances of subclasses that have the code for the methods can be created.

Python doesn't have any special way to declare "abstract" methods, but this is the custom. You raise a `NotImplementedError` for the abstract method; if the method hasn't been overridden at run-time, you will find out about it.

What about removing a method from a class by implementing a subclass that overrides it with a method that raises `NotImplementedError`? You can do that, but it is considered an extremely bad programming practice. An instance of the subclass is supposed to have an is-a relationship to its superclass. That means that it can be used anywhere an instance of the superclass can be used, but if it lacks one of the methods of the superclass, then it cannot be used anywhere that method is needed.

The __init__() method for AbstractSet does nothing when it is called—the pass statement performs no operation. Why is it present? It is there to honor the programming practice that a class instance ought to be given a chance to initialize itself. If at some future time we were to change AbstractSet so that it did need to perform some initialization, it is easier already to have the __init__() method and the subclasses already calling it.

Why have an AbstractSet? It is not essential in Python, although it would be in statically-typed object-oriented languages. It documents the operations that all sets must have. If you specify that an algorithm requires an AbstractSet, then that algorithm should use only the operations that AbstractSet provides. Since ListSet and DictSet are subclasses of AbstractSet, either of them can be provided to the algorithm and it will still work.

In object-oriented languages that use static typing, the AbstractSet class would be required to allow ListSet and DictSet objects to be used interchangeably. Variables and attributes would have to be declared with the AbstractSet class, and then objects of either subclass could be assigned to them. Python does not require this. Any object that has the required methods can be used. We could eliminate AbstractSet here if we were willing to duplicate the code for the insertAll(), removeAny(), union(), intersection(), and __str__() methods.

The reason that AbstractSet would be required in statically-typed languages, but not in Python, is that the compiler of a statically-typed language must know the value of every expression. You have to declare the types of variables and functions. The compiler would need these to check that you are performing only permissible operations and to figure out the data types of their results. So you would need the class AbstractSet in order to declare all the methods you could call for a set. This would allow you to declare a variable AbstractSet and assign either a ListSet or a DictSet to it and use them without knowing which one is there.

Python, however, doesn't know in general what kind of value a variable contains or whether an operation will work or not. All that's required is for Python to find the methods it's calling at run-time. So we didn't really need AbstractSet. If both ListSet and DictSet implement all the set operations, they can be used interchangeably.

However, ListSet and DictSet do not implement all the set operations. Some set operations, such as union and intersection, are implemented in `AbstractSet`. This demonstrates one of the most trivial uses for inheritance: code sharing.

The basis for the division of methods between those implemented in `ListSet` and `DictSet` on one hand and those implemented in `AbstractSet` on the other is this: `ListSet` and `DictSet` contain those methods that depend on the implementation of the set, on the kind of data structure it uses. `AbstractSet` implements those methods that are the same for all implementations.

A method can call other methods for the same object. If those methods are defined in different classes, two cases occur: *up calls* and *down calls*. If a method in a subclass calls a method in a superclass, it is called an up call (super to sub is interpreted as above to below). If a method in a superclass calls a method in a subclass, it is called a down call.

If you come from a non-object-oriented background, you may be saying, "I can see how an up call works. The subclass imports the super-class, so it knows the methods defined there. But how does the super-class know the names of methods defined in a subclass?" The question, however, assumes that the compiler must know what method is being called before the program runs. If you are calling a method on an object from outside the object's classes, you usually don't know what the actual class of the object will be. You just know it is supposed to have a method with a certain name, say M, that will do a certain kind of thing for you. At run-time, Python searches for method M in the class and superclasses of the object. It's exactly the same with the call `self.M()` within a method. Again, Python will take the actual class of the current object, `self`, and search that class and its superclasses for method M. Where will Python find M? Maybe in the same class the call is in, maybe in a superclass, maybe in a subclass. You don't know. You shouldn't have to care.

In each of `ListSet` and `DictSet`, there is an example of an up call. In the `__init__()` method there is a call of `insertAll()`, defined in `AbstractSet`, to initialize the set to the sequence of elements. It is in `AbstractSet` because it does not depend on the implementation of the set.

Method `insertAll()` contains a down call to `insert()`. Method `insert()` does depend on the representation of the set. At run-time this down call will either call the `insert()` in `ListSet` or the `insert()` in `DictSet`, depending on which type of set is present.

There are two other things to notice about the __init__() methods in ListSet and DictSet:

1. They call the __init__() method of AbstractSet, which is somewhat pointless, since it does nothing. This is considered a good programming practice. A class should be given the chance to initialize itself. Knowing that a class's initialization method does nothing is the sort of knowledge you shouldn't use. It shouldn't be part of the public definition of the class. It could be changed in some later release.

2. They initialize an attribute, rep, to the representation of a set. ListSet initializes it to an empty list. DictSet initializes it to an empty dictionary.

ListSet keeps the elements of the set in a list. It checks for the presence of an element with the in operator. It uses list's append() method to insert an element into the set and remove() to delete it. The members() method just returns a copy of the list. The new() method returns a new ListSet, while copy() returns a new ListSet with a copy of the current object's rep attribute.

DictSet keeps the elements as keys in a dictionary. To insert an element, the element is put into the dictionary with itself as its value. The value isn't actually important, only the key. It checks for the presence of an element by the dictionary's has_key() method. It deletes an element with a del statement. It gets a list of the members of the set using the dictionary's keys() method.

In both ListSet and DictSet, there are if statements to test for the presence of an element before removing it. These are necessary to avoid having Python raise an error if the element isn't present.[2]

AbstractSet has the code that can be common to all sets. The method insertAll() iterates over a sequence, inserting all the elements into the set. The call t.union(s) copies set t and then inserts all the elements of set s into it. The call t.intersection(s) uses new() to create a new set of the same class as t, and then inserts all the elements of t into it that are also in s.

Later in the book, we will look at object-oriented design patterns. There are two present here:

• Factories–The new() method is a factory method. It manufactures a new set object. When it is called in AbstractSet, we

---

2. Although raising an error can aid in program debugging, I am personally annoyed by it: When I want to make sure something isn't in the list or dictionary, I hardly ever care if it was there before.

don't know what kind of set it will create. Why do we have it? Because when we create an actual set, we must specify the actual class, but `AbstractSet` shouldn't have to know anything about the actual sets, only what is common to them. It is the subsets that know about, well, about themselves.

- Template methods—The methods `union()` and `intersection()` are being used as template methods. They have the basic algorithm, but they are missing the details. These details are filled in by methods like `contains()` and `insert()`, which are defined in subclasses. The idea of a template method is that the superclass contains the general algorithm, but omits some details that are filled in by methods in a subclass. Thus the same algorithm can be implemented in several versions, sharing much of the code between them.

4.9 Critique

Now let's criticize the design of these set classes. On the positive side, they do make good use of object-oriented programming techniques, and they do allow more than one implementation of sets to be used interchangeably in the same program.

On the negative side, there are two points:

First, they are not complete. There ought to be a relative complement method to give a new set containing all the elements of one set that are not in another. Although it could be programmed, it's used a lot and it's logically one of the standard set operations.

Second, they do not have identical interfaces. You can put lists into other lists and search for them, but you cannot make list keys for hash tables, so there are operations that will succeed for `ListSet`s that will fail for `DictSet`s. In the following code, we create a `ListSet` and a `DictSet` and try to insert a list, [7,8], into each and look it up. We succeed only for the `ListSet`.

```
>>> import DictSet
>>> import ListSet
>>> y=ListSet.ListSet([4,5,6])
>>> x=DictSet.DictSet([1,2,3])
>>> x
{3, 2, 1}
>>> y
{4, 5, 6}
>>> y.insert([7,8])
{4, 5, 6, [7, 8]}
>>> y.contains([7,8])
```

```
1
>>> x.insert([7,8])
Traceback (most recent call last):
  File "<stdin>", line 1, in ?
  File "DictSet.py", line 14, in insert
    self.rep[x]=x
TypeError: unhashable type
```

4.10   Example: `BaseTimer`

Here is another example of a template method. Figure 4–8 gives the
code for a class named `BaseTimer`. This class will help us time the execution of algorithms. To use it, we create a subclass containing the algorithm:

```
class alg(BaseTimer):...
    def __init__(self,...):...
    def xeq(self): ...#do algorithm
```

This subclass must contain a method named `xeq()`, which will actually
execute the algorithm. The `__init__()` method, if any, can be used to
save parameters for the trial, for example, the size of the data set to use.
    To run the timing trial, create an instance of the subclass contain-
ing the algorithm, call its `run()` method, and then call its `duration()`
method to get the time:

```
t=alg(N,....)
t.run()
print "run time for size",N,"is",t.duration()
```

```
import time
class BaseTimer:
    #Template method:
    # xeq(self)--perform algorithm
    def run(self):
      start=time.clock()
      self.xeq()
      self.__duration=time.clock()-start
    def duration(self): return self.__duration
```

Figure 4–8
BaseTimer.

Figure 4–9 shows a script, TimeListSet.py, to find the execution time of ListSet. There is another script to time DictSet, which is almost the same. The built-in function xrange() is like range(), but it does not construct an entire list. When used in a for statement, xrange() generates the elements that would be in the list created by range() with the same parameters. This script is executed with the command line python TimeListSet *start* *end* *step*, where *start* is the initial data set size, *end* is the terminating size, and *step* is the increment in size. Because these are converted to integers and passed to xrange(), data set size *end* is not included.

Here are the first two times given by TimeListSet:

```
TimeSet, size= 10000 , time= 18.6961543995
TimeSet, size= 20000 , time= 85.1229013743
```

And here are the first two given by TimeDictSet:

```
TimeSet, size= 10000 , time= 0.188048481022
TimeSet, size= 20000 , time= 0.356522127812
```

Clearly, for large set sizes, DictSets are a lot faster.

```
import BaseTimer
import ListSet
class TimeSet(BaseTimer.BaseTimer):
    def __init__(self,N):
      self.s=ListSet.ListSet()
      self.N=N
      self.r=xrange(N)
    def xeq(self):
      for i in self.r:
        self.s.insert(i)
      for i in self.r:
        self.s.insert(i)
      for i in self.r:
        self.s.delete(i)
from sys import argv
for i in range(int(argv[1]),int(argv[2]),int(argv[3])):
    t=TimeSet(i)
    t.run()
    print "TimeSet, size=",i,", time=",t.duration()
```

Figure 4–9
Script to time ListSet.

4.11   Inheritance As Classification

A common use for inheritance is the hierarchical classification of objects. Suppose there is one superclass that has many subclasses. Since all the subclasses have the same operations as their superclass, they can be used wherever the superclass is expected. The superclass, then, specifies what is common to all the subclasses, and the subclasses can indicate how they differ from the common characteristics. The superclass specifies the general kind of thing, and the subclasses specify variations. This fits in with how we define things. Actually, there are two common ways that we define things: using an abstract, Aristotelian definition or using a definition by reference to an example.

In an Aristotelian definition, we define a thing by the category of thing that it is and then by how it differs from the other things in that category. Using an Aristotelean definition, the superclass is the category of thing, and the methods and attributes in the subclass specify the differences from the category.

When you are using inheritance in this Aristotelian sense, the superclass is often an *abstract class.* An abstract class is something like a "bird," whereas the subclasses will be things like robins, penguins, and ostriches. An abstract class is not intended to be used itself to create objects, only to group together its subclasses, just as there is no instance of "bird" that is not some particular kind of bird.

When you implement an abstract class in Python, you often do not provide implementations for all the methods shared by members of the subclasses. Some methods have no behavior that is common to all instances.

`AbstractSet`, Figure 4–5, is an example of an abstract class. The superclass provides an interface that can have several implementations. The algorithms that use the objects don't need to know the implementation; they only need to know the interface. There are seven methods that are not defined in `AbstractSet`, but only in subclasses.

In other object-oriented languages like Java, `AbstractSet` would have to provide *method signatures* for the methods that are to be provided by the subclasses. Method signatures give the name of the method, the number and types of parameters, and the result type. The compiler needs this information to be able to compile calls to the methods.

In Python, there are no parameter types or result types to put in signatures, and methods are looked up at run-time. We did not have to put `defs` in `AbstractSet` for the seven methods. We did, however, put them in and made them all raise a `NotImplementedError` exception. If an instance of `AbstractSet` itself is created, a `NotImplementedError` will be raised when it is first used. If a subclass is coded without all the required methods, it will be raised as soon as a missing method is called. `NotImplementedError` was invented for precisely this purpose. It allows you to put `def`s for the required methods in the superclass, which is good for documentation, and it gives a more precise error message than that the attribute was not found. For an example of the error messages, here we create an instance of `AbstractSet` and try to call the `copy()` method and then to call a nonexistent `remove()` method.

```
>>> import AbstractSet
>>> x=AbstractSet.AbstractSet()
>>> x.copy()
Traceback (most recent call last):
  File "<stdin>", line 1, in ?
  File "AbstractSet.py", line 9, in copy
    def copy(self): raise NotImplementedError,"set.copy()"
NotImplementedError: set.copy()
>>> x.remove(1)
Traceback (most recent call last):
  File "<stdin>", line 1, in ?
AttributeError: 'AbstractSet' instance has no attribute
'remove'
```

So, if you are defining classes the way Aristotle suggested, you have an abstract superclass and you create concrete subclasses of it–"concrete" meaning that all the details are filled in, all the methods are defined. But that's not the way we usually understand things. Mentally, we usually use a paradigm, an example instance, and relate other things to it. For example, most people in the U.S. seem to use the robin as a paradigmatic bird. Other birds are considered birds because they resemble robins: feathers, beaks, wings, nests, eggs, flying, and soon. What about penguins and ostriches? Well, they are a lot like robins–feathers, wings, beaks–but penguins swim instead of flying and they aren't big on nests. Ostriches run.

When you program using a paradigmatic definition, you use a concrete superclass that represents the example object, and concrete subclasses that represent the related things.

Would that have worked with `ListSet` and `DictSet`?

If we made `ListSet` the paradigm, it would try to have its own list, and then the `DictSet` would override that with its own dictionary. If we used different attribute names for the data structures, then each instance of a `DictSet` would have both a list and a dictionary. But we programmed both of them to use the attribute name `rep` for their data structures. That would save space in `DictSet`, since it could override `ListSet`'s list with its own dictionary.

But is that safe? `ListSet` contains code that assumes it's manipulating a list. If any of that code is executed, the program will crash. So `DictSet` would have to override all of `ListSet`'s list manipulation code. We wrote `ListSet` and `DictSet` in such a way that that could happen. All the data structure specific code is in separate methods that can be overridden. If we had been writing `ListSet` in isolation, would we have done that? Would we have been so careful? Probably not. And if we weren't careful, we would have to override all the methods, rather than being able to share code for `union` and `intersection` and the others. And even if there were a few methods in `ListSet` that didn't need to be overridden, would it be safe to use them? If someone changed the implementation of `ListSet`, it could break our code. In this case, at least, where we are providing different implementations, an `AbstractSet` class, designed to be overridden, is much better choice.

In Python, we can get around all this discussion of whether to inherit from an abstract superclass or a concrete one. We do not have to inherit at all. All we have to do is provide classes with the proper interface, the proper collection of methods. To adapt an old saying, if it looks like a duck and walks like a duck and quacks like a duck, I don't care whether it "really" is a duck: I'll treat it like a duck.

4.12 Multiple Inheritance

In Python, a class may inherit from more than one superclass. This is called *multiple inheritance*. It is not absolutely essential, but it does have a few uses.

For example, lists, being mutable, cannot be used as keys in dictionaries. But suppose we need to use lists as keys. Suppose we aren't interested in looking up lists by their contents, but by their identities; that is, when we look up the same list object, we want to find it, but when we look up a different list object with the same contents, we do not. Here's what we can do.

First, we create a class `Hashable` that provides the functions that a dictionary needs to use an object as a key.[3] See Figure 4–10. The two methods are `__hash__()`, which a dictionary calls to decide where in the

---

3. This code was developed before version 2.1 of Python came out. In version 2.1 and beyond, you will also have to override the special method `__eq__()` in `Hashable`.

```
class Hashable:
    def __hash__(self):
      return id(self)
    def __cmp__(self,other):
      return id(self)-id(other)
```

Figure 4–10
Class Hashable in Hashable.py, pre-version 2.1.

hash table to start looking for the key, and __cmp__(), which it calls to compare two keys to see if they are equal. Both our methods will use the id() built-in function, which returns a different integer for each object. Any object inheriting these methods from Hashable will be placed in a hash table by its identity, rather than by its contents.

Now all we have to do is create a kind of list that inherits from Hashable. It would be nice to have a class that inherits from both Hashable and list, but Python's list data type is not a class. However, there is a trivial way around that. The Python library contains a module with a class UserList, which behaves exactly like a list. (It contains a list and passes all list operations on to it.) Since UserList is a class, we can inherit from it. So we create a class ListKey, Figure 4–11, that is both a list and a Hashable. All the methods are provided by its superclasses. It doesn't need any contents of its own.

To understand what is happening with multiple inheritance, we need to understand the order in which Python searches the superclasses to find a method. It is no longer as simple as searching from a class to its one superclass along a chain until you find the method. Suppose a class has two superclasses and they both define the method. Which one gets used? Or does Python raise an exception if there are more than one?

```
import UserList,Hashable
class ListKey(Hashable.Hashable,UserList.UserList):
    pass
```

Figure 4–11
Class ListKey in ListKey.py.

```
class A: pass
class B(A):
    def f(self): print "f() in B"
class C(B): pass
class D(B) :
    def f(self): print "f() in D"
class E(C,D) : pass
```

Figure 4–12
Diamond inheritance example.

To examine this, we are using a contrived example. Consider the collection of five classes given in Figure 4–12. A picture of the inheritance hierarchy is shown in Figure 4–13.

Class E inherits from both C and D; C and D both inherit from B; and B inherits from A. Notice that both B and D define a method f(). Suppose we have an instance of an E and call method f(). Which one do we get? Let's try it:

```
>>> import abcde
>>> x=abcde.E()
>>> x.f()
f() in B
```

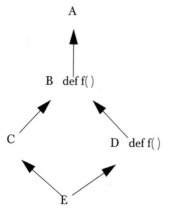

Figure 4–13
Class hierarchy, diamond inheritance example.

Okay, we get the f() method in B, even though the one in D is closer to E. In fact, the one in D lies between E and B. You might think that the definition of f() in D ought to hide the one in B from E.

The way it actually works, Python does a depth-first search for the method. When it comes to a class with more than one superclass, Python searches them and their superclasses one at a time, from left to right. So the search path from E would be E, C, B, A; then, after backing down to E, up again to D, B, and A. So, looking for f(), Python will examine E and C and then find it in B. Python won't look any further to see it in D. This leads some people to argue that the search order should be "depth first up to joins." Since the paths join at B, B wouldn't be searched until both C and D have been, but that's not how Python does it.

The contour diagram we used in Figure 4–4 won't work as easily here, since the box for one class is not enclosed in a single box. But we can use the contour model if we are willing to have classes included more than once. The boxes for the search path C-B-A would be included in the boxes for the search path D-B-A, as shown in Figure 4–14.

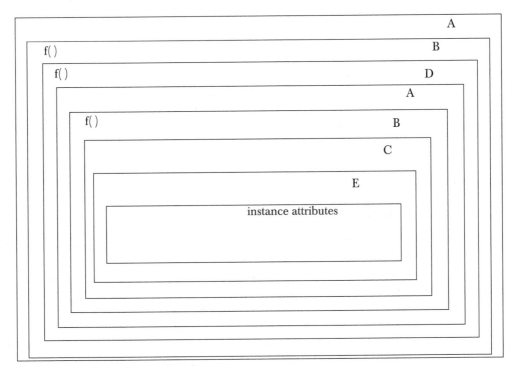

Figure 4–14
Contours for abcde.

4.13   Recapitulation of the Scope of Names

It is important to understand the scopes of names used in methods. There are unqualified names–in other words, variable names–and qualified names of the form `object.attribute`.

Unqualified names in methods are the same as unqualified names in other functions. They name parameters and local variables of the method, variables in the surrounding module, or built-in variables of the Python system. They *never* refer to attributes of the instance of the class or of the class itself. This is unlike many other object-oriented languages, so if you know them, you have to be careful using Python.

Your methods *must* get at attributes of the instance or the class using qualified names. Your method's first parameter will point to the instance your method is being called for. The custom is to call this parameter `self`, to remind you of its meaning. You get at all attributes of the instance using this parameter; that is, by `self.name`. When `name` isn't found in the attributes of the instance, Python searches the class of the instance and its superclasses using a depth-first, left-to-right search. If it finds a function in a class with the `name` you are searching for, Python gives you a bound method object that allows you to call the method for the current object. You can use this to make up calls or down calls, wherever the method is found in the class hierarchy. It's the same as calling the method from outside the object.

You can also look up functions directly in classes, which gives you an unbound method object. To call it, you have to provide it an instance as its first parameter. You use this to make explicit up calls to superclass implementations of overridden methods. A method uses this to call the method it is overriding.

4.14   Testing Objects and Classes

If you have a reference to something and you want to know if it is an instance of some class, you can use the `isinstance(obj,c)` built-in function. This will return true if the object `obj` is an instance of the class `c`, or any subclass of `c`, so `if isinstance(x,AbstractSet):`*stuff* will execute the *stuff* if `x` is an instance of a `ListSet` or a `DictSet`.

The function `isinstance()` works for types as well as for classes. If `c` is a type object, it will return true if `obj` is an object of that type. One way to get a type object is to use the `type(x)` built-in function, which will give you the type object for `x`'s type: For example, `if isinstance(x,type(1)):`*stuff* will execute the stuff if `x` is an integer.

Similarly, you can find type objects in the `types` module. If you have imported `types`, then `if isinstance(x,types.IntType )`:*stuff* will do the same thing.

Unlike many other object-oriented languages, classes in Python are not types. The `type(x)` call for instance `x` of class `C` will not give you `C`. (Jpython, an implementation of Python in Java, may be an exception to this.) All class instances are objects of type `types.InstanceType`. The way you can find `x`'s class is by using its special attribute `__class__`. So `if x.__class__ is AbstractSet` :*stuff* will execute the stuff if `x` is an instance of a `AbstractSet`, but neither `ListSet` nor `DictSet`. A "special attribute" is an attribute that's built in to an instance object and is always present.

Classes themselves are objects of type `types.ClassType`. The types are of type `types.TypeType`. Figure 4–15 diagrams the relationships among instances, classes, and types.

You can test classes' relationships in an inheritance hierarchy with the `issubclass(c1,c2)` built-in function, which returns true if class `c1` is the same as `c2` or if `c1` inherits from `c2`.

```
>>> class X:pass
...
>>> y=X()
```

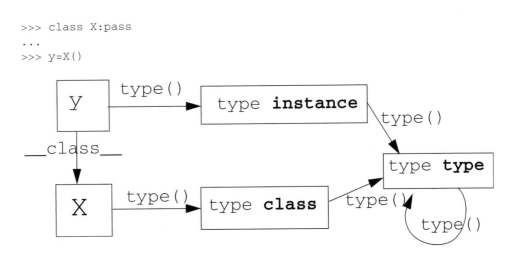

Figure 4–15
Relationships among instances, classes, and types.

4.15 Wrap-Up

In this chapter, we've seen the object-oriented features of Python. Python provides the essentials: classes, methods, and inheritance—indeed, multiple inheritance.

Python diverges from many other object-oriented languages in several ways:

- *No visibility restrictions*: Python does not provide private, or other limited scopes, of attributes and methods. This means that encapsulation cannot be enforced, but must be programmed on the honor system. Name mangling can be used to indicate which methods and attributes are intended to be private, but it doesn't make them invisible or prevent access to them.
- *Absence of overloading*: Python does not permit one of several methods with the same name to be called, depending on the numbers and types of parameters.
- *The diamond inheritance anomaly*: Because of its strictly depth-first search for methods, Python allows a method in a superclass to override one in a subclass, rather than only allowing methods in subclasses to override methods from superclasses.
- *A single pool of instance attributes*: All attributes used by all the classes in an inheritance hierarchy are put in a single dictionary. Attribute name collisions are a likely source of bugs. Name mangling can make it a bit easier to keep separate the attributes intended to be private.

4.16 Exercises

4.1. Try out `TimeListSet` and `TimeDictSet` to see at what point dictionaries become more efficient than lists.

4.2. Why must the superclasses of `ListKey` be listed in the order they are—`Hashable` first, then `UserList`?

4.3. Fix `Hashable` to work with version 2.1 of Python, if any changes are needed. (For example, see if `__eq__()` causes problems.)

4.4. Show how to reimplement the `set new()` method in `AbstractSet` itself, using `self.__class__`.

4.5. Implement a relative complement operation for the sets. `X.relativeComplement(Y)` is a new set containing all the elements of `X` that are not in `Y`.

4.6. Prevent an `AbstractSet` from being created rather than a subclass, by having it raise a `NotImplementedError` in its `__init__()` method.

4.7. Critique multiple inheritance.

4.8. Should classes be types? That is, should the type of an instance be its class?

5

Object-Oriented Patterns

Computer science is full of design patterns. Structured programming breaks actions down into sequences, loops, and conditionals. Modular programming builds layers. Data structures and algorithms are patterns. Concurrent programming has its critical sections, monitors, bounded buffers, producers and consumers, and clients and servers.

Object-oriented programming involves a number of patterns that deal with how objects can be plugged together as components. Here we present a basic collection of object-oriented design patterns. Many of the patterns appear in examples in subsequent chapters.

5.1 Concept of Design Patterns

The great innovation of object-oriented programming was that objects were not viewed simply as replacement data structures to be manipulated by algorithms, but rather as software components that can be plugged together. Polymorphism provided a way to create plug-compatible components. All one object needed to know about an object that it had a reference to was that the other object would perform certain operations when asked to.

The idea of object-oriented design patterns was presented by Erich Gamma, Richard Helm, Ralph Johnson, and John Vlissides (often referred to as GoF, a reference to the "Gang of Four") in their book, *Design Patterns: Elements of Reusable Object-Oriented Software* (Addison Wesley, 1995). They pointed to Christopher Alexander, who discussed design patterns in architecture as solutions to recurring problems. Each solution is used repeatedly, with variations, so that no two uses are identical, but they are recognizably on the same pattern.

It should be clear that computer science is full of design patterns. Data structures are named *linked lists, trees, hash tables, heaps,* and so on. Algorithms have such names as *heap sort, union/find,* and *merge.* Patterns in concurrent programming have such names as *mutual exclusion, monitors, barriers,* and *producer/consumer.*

Object-oriented design patterns use objects linked together and use the inheritance hierarchies. Gamma, Helm, Johnson, and Vlissides distinguish among categories of problems to further divide OODPs. They distinguish among:

- creational patterns, involved in the creation of objects and structures;
- structural patterns, involving linked structures of objects; and
- behavioral patterns, involving dynamic flow-of-control issues.

We use this division in our discussion, and we present many of the patterns that Gamma et al. present. Most of them are used elsewhere in this book. The presentation here is less formal than theirs. For precise definitions, you may want to refer to their book.

Before we begin, we need to consider some aspects of object-oriented programming. First, objects provide interfaces. An interface is a set of methods the object can execute. The methods have signatures: the name and the required parameters.

One object may have links to other objects and use them to perform its functions. Some linked clusters of objects may be thought of as a single, extended object, since there is a single entry object and the other objects hold parts of its information and perform parts of its functions.

When one object uses another object, it will call methods in that other object. The other object must provide the methods the first object needs. This makes interfaces very important. Objects supply interfaces to the objects that use them. Objects require objects they use to have particular interfaces. We sometimes need to think of interfaces as sets of signatures. One interface is a superset of another if its set of method signatures is a superset of the other's. Generally, you can plug in and use another object if its interface includes the interface you need.

Of course, it is not only the interface you need; you need the object to perform the right kinds of actions. You might wish to think of this as a contract. The object you are using has a contract to perform certain actions when requested. Similarly, the classes you write provide contracts about how their objects will behave. If the objects in a system fulfill their contracts when the objects they use fulfill theirs, you should have confidence that the system will work.

Statically-typed object-oriented languages require you to declare the types of all variables, parameters, and attributes. For those languages, the compiler can at least check that objects are supplying the required interfaces. Python uses dynamic typing, so in general it is not possible to figure out before the program runs whether it will crash due to an interface incompatibility.

Object-oriented programming uses inheritance. There are several uses for inheritance. Inheritance allows us to organize classes into hierarchies. Objects of subclasses of the same superclass are conceptually related, and they have similarities reflected by their method signatures. They are supposed to obey the same commands their superclass provides. Subclasses provide varieties of that same conceptual class of object. This is the other side of inheritance providing classification. But there are two quite concrete uses for inheritance:

- extending the interface of the superclass, and
- refining the implementation of the superclass. (If more than one subclass exists, they can provide alternate implementations for the superclass.)

These two uses for inheritance form the basis for a number of design patterns. This brings us to an additional problem with Python: Python is dynamically typed. We are not required to specify precisely the interface that an object will have. Indeed, we are not able to. Many of the patterns can be distinguished by their inheritance of interfaces. With Python, the distinctions among a number of patterns are less clear.

5.2   Creational Patterns

Creational patterns provide ways of creating objects. The simple way to create an object is to call the object's class as a constructor as many times as we wish, creating the entire object each time. The creational patterns eliminate different aspects of this way of creating objects.

Factory functions create and return objects. If you call a factory to create an object, you do not know precisely what the class of the object will be. You only know that the factory promises that the object has a particular interface.

If you use a *prototype* object, you can create a copy of it. Again, you do not have to know its precise class. You only need to know that the object provides the interface you want and that you can create copies of it. A prototype allows you to construct the object beforehand, perhaps interactively, perhaps with a large amount of computation or a large number of remote accesses. It may be much more efficient to copy an object rather than having to recreate it.

If you use a *singleton*, you are restricting a class to have a single instance. You would use this if there is no purpose in having more than one of some object in your program, or if the object represents an external object provided by your computer system and there is only one of them.

If you use a *builder*, you can specify how a compound object is to be put together. An example we will see in Chapter 22 is the semantics phase of a language processor. The semantics phase is to build a tree representation of a program. You may consider the entire tree to be an object that is built as expressions and statements of the program are recognized. The semantics phase is a builder that constructs the tree from subtrees under command of the parser.

5.2.1   Factories

When we write code to use objects, we usually do not require a specific class. We usually require an object that provides the particular methods we are using. We do not know precisely what class of object we are using. However, if we create an object by calling its class, we do know at that point precisely what the class is.

▶ **Examples of Factories**

Factory methods can be found in Figures 4–5, 4–6, and 4–7. The method new() is a factory to create an instance of either a ListSet or a DictSet.

Figure 15–2 shows a skeleton of a factory class–a class with a factory method for the creation of multidimensional array objects.

Chapter 20 includes the factory function TransactionQueue that creates an instance of a RunQueue with special initialization.

Figure 21–3 includes three factory functions–mkToken(), mkErrorToken(), and mkActionToken()–that recycle or create token objects.

A great use of many creational patterns is to avoid having to know precisely what class of object we are creating. There are advantages to not knowing precisely what class object we are using, merely knowing that it has the interface we need; those advantages are also present when we create an object. As an example, when we open a database (see Chapter 10), we do not want to know precisely what kind of database it is. We want it to open; we want certain methods–in the case of Python's library, subscripting by the key to fetch and assign records; and we want the ability to close it when we are finished. It would be complicated if we had to write our own code to figure out the precise kind of database and open it with the precise class we need to access it. The Python library module `anydb` provides an `open()` function that will try to import the appropriate database module for a database file and open the file with that module.

These considerations led to the use of *factories*. A factory is a function that is called to give us an object with a certain interface. It is up to the factory to choose the precise class of the object and to initialize it. There are several varieties of factories. You can have a *factory function*, like the `open()` function in the `anydb` module.

You can have a *factory method*. That is, you have one object that has a factory method. When you call the method, it returns another object. Reasons you might wish to use a factory method include:

- You can create instances of factory classes with different attributes that they can use to instantiate objects. This allows you to easily create objects for different needs.
- You can substitute factory objects of different classes. The different implementations of the factory methods can create objects of different classes or be initialized in different ways.
- You can store and pass around objects with factory methods. The user of the factory does not need to know what class of object is being created or how it is being created or initialized. Certainly it does not need to know how to initialize the object itself.

Often the implementation of a factory method is overridden in a subclass. The `new()` method in our implementation of sets in Chapter 4 is such a factory method. Having a reference to an `AbstractSet`, `s`, you can call `s.new()` to get a new set. The subclasses `ListSet` and `DictSet` provide definitions of `new()` that create a new set of their own kind, so the call will return a new set of the same class as the actual class of `s`.

You can also have an *abstract factory*. An abstract factory is an interface that provides, a collection of factory methods that can create objects of related classes; for example, graphical components for the same GUI system. You have an object that implements the interface and call factory methods in it to create objects guaranteed to work together. You do not need to know the precise system of the objects you are using; you do not need to know the particular factory object.

Factory methods and abstract factories can be used even if you are only creating one kind of object. In Python, you can write special methods that are called by syntactic constructs. Instead of having to use something that looks like a function call, you could use something that looks like subscripting to call the method. We use this in Chapter 15 when we consider how to implement multidimensional arrays in Python. It allows us to create an array by specifying its bounds in brackets, the way most programming languages allow us to create arrays.

5.2.2   Prototypes

A *prototype* is simply an object that is copied to create other objects like itself. This is particularly useful if a large expense is incurred in creating the objects, or if the objects are created interactively.

Interactive creation of objects is becoming quite common (for example, with Java beans). A system with a graphical interface allows programmers to create instances of graphical or business application objects, link them together, and set parameters in them. Then, when the system containing them runs, they are created and plugged together as the programmer specified.

This could be implemented either by the graphical system generating a module that would construct and initialize the objects, or simply by saving the collection of objects in compressed form in a file, perhaps using the `cPickle` or `shelve` modules. When the program runs, it loads the collection of objects from the prototype on disk.

5.2.3   Singletons

A module is an example of a *singleton*. No matter how many times it is imported, there is only one copy. The singleton object-oriented design pattern extends this to classes. A singleton class can have at most a single instance created. All users have to use that one instance.

How do you enforce this in Python? You could have the class in a separate module that creates the instance when the module is loaded. All users of the class could be asked to get a reference to it from an attribute in the module. Or you could have a factory function in the

▶ Singletons

The `ArrayFactory` discussed in Chapter 15 is an example of a singleton. We do not need more than one copy.

Similarly, `EmptySet` in, Figure 17–2 is a singleton. It is a set with no elements, and it cannot be modified. All such sets are equivalent.

The states of a `Splitter` object, Figure 9–4, are singletons. They are featherweights, containing no attributes. There is no need for more than one of each.

module that creates the single instance upon first call and returns that instance for all subsequent calls.

Why would you use a singleton class when you need only one of something, rather than just using a module? There are a couple of reasons:

Modules do not have inheritance. You may need only a single copy of something, but there are several kinds of that thing. For example, you might have a singleton to give you access to the underlying computer hardware. It would be different for different kinds of computers or for different hardware configurations. You could have different modules and put the proper one into the search path when building the Python system; or you could use the singleton pattern, have all of them available, and choose which one to instantiate when the program runs.

You might also want to use a singleton class if you wish to access its object with a wider variety of syntax than only calling attribute functions.

5.2.4   Builders

A builder object has methods that allow you to construct compound objects or subsystems. The methods allow you to construct components and plug them together. For example, suppose you need to build a tree. The builder object can have methods to create each node type you might need in the tree, and can contain a stack of subtrees. You can build the tree in postfix order by calling node constructors. The constructors for leaf nodes create a node and push it on the stack. The constructors for internal nodes 1) create the internal node, 2) take references to subtrees off the stack and put them in the internal node, and 3) push a reference to the internal node on the stack. When you have finished creating all the nodes, you pop the reference to the root from the stack.

In a trivial way, you could consider an output file to be a builder. It constructs a file out of the strings you write.

▶ Builder

> Figure 22–12 contains a builder pattern in the class `CalcSemantics`. Its superclass, `ActionSemantics`, will invoke methods in it to build the nodes of an abstract syntax tree.

5.3 Structural Patterns

Structural patterns deal with organizing multiple objects into components. Many of the patterns are surprisingly alike in structure, but they differ in the problems they are designed to solve.

5.3.1 Decorator, Protection Proxy, Adapter, and Bridge

The patterns for *Decorator, Protection Proxy, Adapter,* and *Bridge* have the same picture, shown in Figure 5–1. Basically, one object sits in front of another, as A sits in front of B in the figure. One big difference among the patterns is the relationship between the interface provided by object A and the interface provided by object B. In the decorator pattern, A's interface is a superset of B's. In the Protection Proxy pattern, A's interface is no larger than B's, and may be a subset. In the Adapter pattern, A's interface is different from B's. The Bridge pattern may be considered a variety of Decorator, and so A's interface will be a superset of B's.

The biggest difference among these patterns is the intent of the pattern. Let us consider them individually.

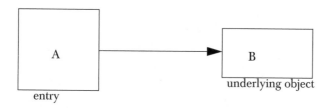

Figure 5–1
Decorator, Protection Proxy, Adapter, or Bridge.

Decorator

Suppose you want an object that is a lot like another object, but has a few additional features. You could use inheritance, creating a subclass with the extra operations. You can also use the decorator pattern: Create a new class that has all the operations you want. Objects of the new class will contain a reference to an object of the old class and pass on many of the operations to it.

▶ **Decorator**

Figure 14–7 gives a base class to make writing decorators easy (if not computationally efficient). It uses Python's attribute access special methods.

The purpose of a decorator is to add facilities to an object. Object A (in Figure 5–1) provides more methods than object B, or at least implements some of them in a different way. In this way, the decorator is like a subclass, since one of the functions of a subclass is to add methods to those provided by the superclass.

Why would you use a decorator rather than a subclass? There are a couple of circumstances in which it might be preferable:

- You want to keep the methods separate. You do not want methods in object B to make down calls to methods in object A, but rather to other methods in B. If you make A's class a subclass of B's, you may have problems.
- You have several decorators that you wish to use in different combinations. If you made them all subclasses of B, then you would only be able to use one at a time, or you would have to create subclasses for all useful combinations of them. If you wish to have them perform their operations in different orders, you would have to create subclasses for all useful permutations. When you chain the decorators in this fashion, you approach another pattern, the *chain of responsibility.*

Some difficulties may arise when using decorators. One is that the underlying object is different from the decorator object. It has a different identity and a different address. The `is` and `is not` operators will not recognize the decorator and the underlying object as the same. The object may not be able to place itself–the string of decorators and the

base object–into a data structure unless it has a pointer to the first decorator in the list. That would give a circular linked data structure that will
not be collected by reference counting (although with a garbage collector in Python 2, this is not a problem). An alternative is to have an entry
object that passes a reference to itself to the next decorator, and have all
the decorators other than the first expect a reference to the entry object
as one of their parameters. This makes the entry object into a kind of
adapter, because it changes the interface.

Similarly, the decorators may be too separate. You might need
them to modify attributes in the same underlying object, rather than just
in themselves. This would require them to follow the chain of pointers,
or to contain a pointer to the ultimate object.

Protection Proxy

A proxy is an object that controls access to another object. A protection
proxy protects its underlying object from certain kinds of accesses. In
Chapter 17, we present PureSet, a class that prevents the user of an
object from changing the contents of the object. Because the protection
proxy prohibits some accesses, it provides a subset of the interface of
the underlying object–the opposite of a decorator. You would use a protection proxy when you need to prevent some objects or threads from
performing certain operations on an object.

▌ **Protection Proxy**

> Figure 17–2 shows a protection proxy, `PureSet`, that removes the methods
> from a set that can change the set's contents.
>
> Chapter 19 is devoted to a kind of protection proxy, distributed
> through the classes `Transaction` and `SharedDB`, that protect a database
> from inconsistent concurrent updates.

▌ **Adapter**

> Chapter 21 presents an adapter called Scanner that converts an input file
> into an input stream of tokens.

Adapter

Suppose you want to use a component, B, but it doesn't have the right interface. You can use an adapter object to sit in front of the object B and change the calls to the ones the object needs. For example, you might want to read the contents of a list as if they were lines in a file. You could write an adapter that would obey all the file operations, but would get the elements of the list and convert them into strings.

An adapter changes an interface. It provides a different interface than the underlying object does. The adapter is particularly useful for plugging together two objects that were developed separately. One object assumes that the object it is using has one interface, but the object you need it to use has a different interface. You can write an adapter to convert from the expected interface to the one that is actually available.

There is an alternative way to provide an adapter. In Figure 5–1, instead of A having a separate class, you could combine A and B by making A's class a subclass of B's. A would add methods to B's interface. The downside to this approach is that it would make A into a kind of decorator, adding to an interface rather than translating, and it would allow the user to mix calls from the two interfaces, which might not be meaningful.

Bridge

A bridge pattern in effect breaks one class into two that can be subclassed separately. The idea is that there are two major uses for inheritance: adding to the interface and providing alternative implementations. Suppose you need to do both: Suppose you need three interfaces, P, Q, and R, and three implementations, X, Y, and Z. Using subclasses to combine any interface with any implementation, you would have to provide nine subclasses: PX, PY, PZ, QX, QY, QZ, RX, RY, and RZ. If there are M interfaces and N implementations, you would have to provide $M \times N$ subclasses.

The bridge pattern breaks the object into two parts. In Figure 5–1, part A handles the interface and part B handles the implementation. So part A is an interface subclass, including P, Q, or R; and part B is an implementation subclass, including X, Y, or Z. This converts the number of subclasses needed for M interfaces and N implementations to $M + N$.

5.3.2   Façade

A façade pattern provides a single entry point to a subsystem, as pictured in Figure 5–2. The subsystem may have several objects that must work together. The façade allows you to control them all through one object.

▸ **Façade**

> The `LLkParser` presented in Chapter 22 is a kind of a façade. It hides the interactions of the scanner, semantics, error recovery, and parsing from the user behind a single method, `parse()`.

Just as you write a function to perform a sequence of operations with a single call, so you would use a façade to access a collection of objects in a coordinated way. You would not wish to have references to all of them and to have to call their methods in a special order, any more than you would wish to write out algorithms inline.

In Chapter 22, we show a façade: a parser for a calculator language. It coordinates calling a scanner to read tokens (numbers, identifiers, and operators) from an input, finding the phrases, evaluating the expressions or building a tree, and recovering from and reporting

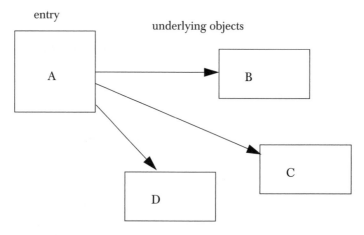

Figure 5–2
Façade.

errors. The user, after creating the parser, has only to call the `parse()` method to have it perform all its operations and return the semantic value (e.g., a tree) for the file it processed.

5.3.3 Proxy

A proxy pattern allows one object to represent and control access to another object. There are several kinds of proxies:

- A protection proxy limits accesses to an underlying object, as we discussed earlier.
- A virtual proxy creates an object when it is first accessed. You would use this when the creation of the object is expensive. For example, you could use a proxy to avoid loading image files from the Internet unless they need to be displayed.
- A remote proxy allows you to access objects on other machines as if they were on the local machine. Figure 5–3 shows the function of a remote proxy. A call to a method in the proxy packs the parameters in a message and sends it to another machine, where a remote object server unpacks the message and calls the same method in the actual object. Whatever the call returns is packed into a response message that is sent back to the remote proxy, which unpacks it and returns it.

There are other uses, such as loading persistent objects when they are accessed and storing them when they are no longer needed. You might call that a variety of a virtual proxy. If you are using a multi-threading system, you could use a proxy to lock an object while it is

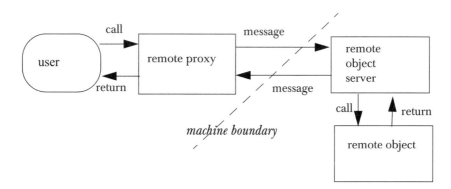

Figure 5–3
Remote proxy.

being accessed. This might be considered a variety of protection proxy.

5.3.4   Composite

A composite pattern is a general way of constructing rooted trees. The situation is this: You want a tree composed of several types of nodes. Some of the nodes are internal nodes; some are leaves. You want a general way of attaching children (subtrees) to an internal node, removing them, and getting a reference to the ith child.

The solution is to use a composite class that all the nodes can inherit from. The composite keeps a list of children and provides methods to add and remove children and to look up the ith child. Figure 5–4 shows a simple `Composite` class. With the `Composite` class, there is a uniform way to manipulate the children of any node in the tree.

Figure 5–5 shows a test program for the composite class. The `Node` class allows you to create a node with a name and a list of zero or more children. Its `__str__()` method is called by Python to convert it into a string (e.g., for printing out a node and all its subtrees). These special methods are discussed in Chapter 14. When the test is run, it writes out:

```
x(v(u,w),z(y))
x(z(y),v(u,w))
```

```
class Composite:
    def __init__(self):
      self.__children=[]
    def addChild(self,x):
      self.__children.append(x)
    def removeChild(self,x):
      self.__children.remove(x)
    def getChild(self,i):
      return self.__children[i]
    def numChildren(self):
      return len(self.__children)
```

Figure 5–4
Composite class.

```
class Node(Composite.Composite):
    def __init__(self,name,*kids):
      Composite.Composite.__init__(self)
      self.name=name
      for x in kids:
        self.addChild(x)
    def __str__(self):
      n=self.numChildren()
      if n>0:
        x=self.name+"("
        for i in xrange(self.numChildren()):
          x+=str(self.getChild(i))+','
        return x[:-1]+")"
      else:
        return self.name
t=Node("x",
    Node("v",Node("u"),Node("w")),
    Node("z",Node("y")))
print t
s=t.getChild(0)
t.removeChild(s)
t.addChild(s)
print t
```

Figure 5–5
Test program for the composite class.

5.4 Behavioral Patterns

The behavioral patterns deal in one way or another with the execution of the program. A number of them are used in the examples in this book.

5.4.1 Template Method and Strategy

The template method and the strategy patterns both have similar functions: They separate the specific details of an algorithm from its general form. They are the object-oriented equivalent of passing parameters that are functions.

In both, methods in one class call methods in another class to do parts of an algorithm. For example:

- A sorting method might call a comparison function to determine the order of two items.
- A general container data type might have different representations. Its algorithms would call methods to handle the elementary

insertion, lookup, and deletion operations for the particular representation of the container.

The difference between the template method and strategy patterns is in where the methods are located. In the template method pattern, the general algorithm is in a superclass and the specific methods are overridden in subclasses. We saw examples of the template method while we were discussing sets in Chapter 4. The `AbstractSet` class provided a number of representation-independent methods, but the actual implementations of sets were provided in the `ListSet` and `DictSet` subclasses. The methods that had to know the actual implementation were implemented in the subclasses; for example: `insert()`, `delete()`, `members()`, and `copy()`. The fact that these methods are defined in subclasses does not in itself make them template methods. The fact that they are called by methods in `AbstractSet` does.

▸ Template Methods

> Template methods are used extensively in the implementation of `AbstractSet`, `ListSet`, `DictSet`, and `BaseTimer` in Chapter 4.

A template method requires a method defined in a concrete subclass called by a method in superclass, by a so-called down call. Template methods allow you to create specialized versions of classes, varying their behavior by using different implementations of the methods in subclasses.

Another example from Chapter 4 is the implementation of `BaseTimer`, a class that is to time algorithms. A subclass would provide an `xeq()` method that contains the algorithm to be timed. The `BaseTimer` class provides the code to read the clock, call `xeq()` to run the algorithm, and compute the duration.

The strategy pattern (see Figure 5–6) differs by putting the methods that specialize the algorithm in one or more separate objects. Instead of the *context* object x doing a down call to a template method through `self.method(...)`, the algorithm calls the method through `self.strategyObjRef.method(self,...)`. Here we show `self` being passed to the strategy method so it will be able to access attributes in the object x. This is not always necessary.

Figure 5–6
Strategy.

In Chapter 16, we use strategies to specialize priority queues, choosing how the priorities are ordered and how a priority is modified when an item is inserted again. These methods do not get a reference to the queue itself, since they need only two priorities to compare, or two priorities to compute a new priority from.

▶ Strategy

The priority queues in Chapter 16 use strategies to compare the priorities of the elements they contain and to choose the replacement priorities of objects being reinserted into the queues.

The minimal error recovery used in the parsers discussed in Chapter 22 is a strategy using the `PanicMode` object. We actually convert this to a chain of responsibility by plugging another strategy in front of it.

Of these two patterns, the strategy pattern is more flexible. You do not have to declare new subclasses of the context or create a factory to choose the correct one. You can simply plug in the desired strategy object when you create the object that needs it.

5.4.2   Chain of Responsibility

The chain of responsibility pattern links together a chain of objects to handle a method call (see Figure 5–7). The call goes to the first object in the chain and is passed along from object to object until one of them handles it successfully. For example:

- In a compiler, the symbol table might be implemented as a chain of responsibility ordered from innermost scope to outermost. To look up an identifier, the innermost scope is asked first.

Figure 5–7
Chain of responsibility.

If it finds the identifier, it can return its information; otherwise it asks the next outer scope about the identifier, and so on until one of the scopes has the identifier or until it comes to the end of the chain. A special last scope will report failure to find any identifier—it is "where identifiers are not if they are not anywhere else."

- Keyboard macros in the old DOS system used a chain of responsibility. Each TSR (terminate and stay resident program) that took keyboard commands linked itself on a chain. A keystroke was passed to each in turn to see if it would handle it. If none of them did, the character was buffered for the application program to read. These TSR programs often were written to relink themselves at the beginning of the chain to get first chance at the keystrokes.

- In a graphical user interface, a mouse click might be processed by the innermost object that encloses the location of the click and is prepared to handle it. The objects can be asked one at a time from innermost to outermost to handle the click, until one of them reports complete success.

Notice that there are similarities between the chain of responsibility pattern and other patterns. First, the chain of responsibility searching for the first object to handle a method call resembles searching for a method using inheritance. A class and its superclasses are searched in a particular order, looking for the first to define a method.

▶ Chain of Responsibility

The parsers discussed in Chapter 22 use a chain of responsibility to handle syntax errors.

The resemblance to inheritance also implies a resemblance to the decorator pattern. Decorators can be chained together and calls can be passed along the chain. The intention, however, is different. Decorators are used to add functionality to an object and may be considered components of the same conceptual object, as the instance of a subclass is the same object as its superclass.

The objects in a chain of command are not considered part of a single conceptual object, nor are they thought of as operating as a unit. They are separate objects that can handle a call and are given their chances one at a time.

Similarly, a chain of responsibility can be used like a strategy. In Chapter 22, we show a parser object that has a default strategy for recovering from syntax errors (`PanicMode`), but we actually create a parser that has another strategy plugged in front of the default error recovery object. What is normally a strategy has become a chain of responsibility.

5.4.3   Iterator

Container data types are objects that hold other objects. Python itself offers lists, tuples, and dictionaries as concrete container data types. This book presents several container abstract data types (ADTs), including doubly-ended queues, priority queues, and sets. Container abstract data types call for *iterators*. Many of the algorithms that use containers require iterating over the items in the container. Encapsulation requires that we not know how the ADT is implemented, so we must not look in the representation of the data and iterate over it directly. Therefore, container ADTs must supply higher-level facilities for iteration.

In Python, containers are invited to provide their own iterators. The __getitem__() special method allows you to implement your own subscripting: X.__getitem__(i) implements X[i]. If the X.__getitem__(i) special method returns the ith item of container x from *i=0* to *len(X)-1*, then x can be used to control a for loop. The DEQueue shown in Chapter 15 provides __getitem__() for this purpose.

The reason we might not use __getitem__() for iteration is that for some containers, it is a lot slower to look up items one at a time by position than it is to process them in internal order. Iterators try to provide the efficiency of processing the items in internal order.

▶ **Iterator**

> Chapter 22 shows an internal iterator method, `walk()`, in the node classes
> of abstract syntax trees. See Figure 22–12.
>
> Chapter 17 presents a class, `SetEnumeration`, that exemplifies an
> external iterator. The special method `__getitem__()` makes an object into
> its own external iterator. The method is discussed in Chapter 15.
> Examples are DEQueue (doubly-ended queue) in Figure 15–1, Set in
> Figure 17–1, `prioque` (priority queue) in Figure 16–2, and `prioqueunique`
> (a priority queue whereby adding an element will replace an instance that
> is already present) in Figure 16–3.
>
> The example of Splitter in Chapter 9 shows a kind of external
> iterator implemented using the state pattern. It does not iterate over the
> contents of a container, but rather returns one at a time the substrings and
> separators contained in a string.

In Chapter 17, we describe a class, `SetEnumeration`, that delivers the
elements of a set one at a time. If `x` is a `Set` (as defined in Chapter 17, not
in Chapter 4), the call `x.elements()` yields a `SetEnumeration` object that
can control either `while` or `for` loops, delivering the elements of the set,
one at a time, in an arbitrary order, either by:

```
e=s.elements()
while e:
    x=e.nextElement()
    ...
```

or by:

```
for x in s.elements():
    ...
```

An iterator object you use to control loops is called an *external iterator*. It
is somewhat difficult to program an external iterator to deliver the
nodes in a tree or other graph. The easiest way to examine the elements
of a tree or graph is in a recursive function, but translating the recursive
calls into explicit manipulations of a stack is a pain. A way around this is
to use an *internal iterator*. An internal iterator for a recursive data structure is a recursive method that applies a function parameter to each
item.

```
class X:
    ...
    def iterate(self,f):
      self.sub1.iterate(f)
      self.sub2.iterate(f)
      f(self)
```

Figure 5–8
Internal iterator over tree nodes, class X.

Consider the internal iterator method `iterate()` for node class `X` in Figure 5–8. Here `X` is assumed to be a tree node and to have two subtrees pointed to by `sub1` and `sub2`. The iterator does a postorder walk by calling itself recursively for `sub1` and `sub2` and then calling function `f()` for this node. In this case, the items being delivered to the function are the tree nodes themselves.

If the tree is just a container, we would want to iterate over the objects it contains, not over the nodes themselves, so we would pass the contents to the function, as shown in Figure 5–9. Here we have changed the order to "inorder" (sorted order for binary search trees) and assumed that attribute `data` contains the element to be processed.

It takes some effort to translate a loop for use with an internal iterator. For example, if we want to write a loop like this:

```
for x in T:
    body #using variables a, b, c
```

```
class BSTNode:
    ...
    def iterate(self,f):
      self.sub1.iterate(f)
      f(self.data)
      self.sub2.iterate(f)
```

Figure 5–9
Internal iterator over tree contents.

we would translate it into something like this:

```
class LoopBody:
    def __init__(self, a,b,c):
      initialize attributes a, b, ... used by
        the body from a,b,c
    def __call__(self,x):
      body where x is the loop index and other
        vars are in self.a, self.b, self.c
lb=LoopBody(a,b,c)
T.iterate(lb)
a,b,c=lb.a, lb.b, lb.c
```

That is, the body of the loop is converted into a `__call__()` method in a new class. When a class instance is called as a function, its `__call__()` method is executed. An instance of the class is created with all the variables needed other than the loop index; is passed to the container `T`'s `iterate()` method; and is called for each item in the container. The item is passed to the body as parameter `x`. When the `iterate()` method returns, the results of the loop can be retrieved from attributes of the instance.

We include an example of an internal iterator in Chapter 22 for trees constructed for a calculator language. Although internal iterators are easier to write for many containers, external iterators are easier to use and allow you to simultaneously iterate over more than one container.

5.4.4   Visitor

The *visitor* pattern is an alternative way of providing new recursive methods for the data structures. Suppose you want to have a new recursive function F that you can call for a tree t. You could write a method F for each class of node in t and have each of them call F for subtrees recursively, something like the routine shown in Figure 5–10. A node of class x has subtree pointers sub1 and sub2, and z in this case is an additional data structure used to communicate data among the calls.

The problem with this approach is that you have to go into the classes for the tree nodes and modify them each time you need to add another recursive method. If the set of classes is relatively stable otherwise, it would be better to package it away and not modify it. It would be better not to have to load all the methods written for all applications using the tree for each of them. In short, it would be better not to have to modify the node classes.

```
class X:
    ...
    def F(self,z):
        ...
        self.sub1.F(z)
        ...
        self.sub2.F(z)
        ...
```

Figure 5–10
Recursive method F in node class X.

The visitor pattern can be used with internal iterators to walk over the tree, and put all the methods in a separate object. The idea is this: An internal iterator applies a method of an object to each node in a tree (or other graph structure—here we will assume it is a tree). The object has one implementation of the method for each class of node in the tree. The appropriate one of the implementations is called for each node.

▶ Visitor

Figure 22–12 includes an example of a visitor pattern: class `WriteOut` combined with method `walk()`.

The visitor pattern avoids having to modify the node classes. For each new method you need, you create a new class. Suppose you have node classes X, Y, and Z, and you need a new recursive method F. Suppose further that the nodes have an internal iterator, `iterate()`, that visits the nodes in the proper order for method F.

Instead of modifying the code for classes X, Y, and Z, you could write a class F as shown in Figure 5–11. Now instead of a method F in each node class, X, Y, Z, there is a method in F named after each node type. We are assuming that an instance of the visitor class, F, is passed to an internal iterator that calls it for each node in the tree. That is, instead of calling method F of node t,

```
t.F(data_z)
```

with the `data_z` object being passed in to communicate among the method calls, you call

```
f=F(data_init)
t.iterate(f)
```

where the `data_init` object is being used to initialize the attributes of `f`. The `iterate()` method of `t` is the kind shown in Figure 5–8.

The iterator calls the object `f` for each node in the tree, `t`, as `f(self)`, invoking `f`'s `__call__(self,node)` method. The `__call__()` method is a dispatcher. It looks up the name of the class of the node it is passed and finds its method with that name. The built-in `getattr()` function looks up an attribute for an object: `obj.name` is the same as `getattr(obj,'name')`.

The `__call__()` method calls the method it has looked up, passing it the node. That method then operates on the node as easily as when it was method `F` in the node class.

Here the methods do not need to take an extra parameter, `z`, to communicate among themselves. They share the object `self`. We do show a parameter `z` on the initialization, to relate the object initialization to the parameter `z` in the method `F` in Figure 5–10.

We have been discussing the visitor pattern in conjunction with an internal iterator, but an internal iterator is not required. The visitor object can handle the recursion itself. In this version of the visitor pattern, each node has some method such as `accept()`, shown in Figure 5–12. The `accept()` method receives a visitor object and calls it, passing it the node.

Now the node-class-specific method in the visitor has to call the `accept()` methods of the subnodes, usually passing itself as the visitor as sketched in Figure 5–13.

```
class F:
    def __init__(self,z):
      self.z=z
    def __call__(self,node):
      getattr(self,node.__class__.__name__)(node)
    def X(self,node): #process node of class X
      ...
    def Y(self,node): #process node of class Y
      ...
    def Z(self,node): #process node of class Z
      ...
```

Figure 5–11
Visitor class F, an alternative to Figure 5–10.

```
class X:
    ...
    def accept(self,visitor):
      visitor(self)
```

Figure 5–12
Accept a visitor in node class X.

```
class F:
    def __init__(self,z):
      self.z=z
    def __call__(self,node):
      getattr(self,node.__class__.__name__)(node)
    def X(self,node): #process node of class X
      ...
      node.sub1.accept(self)
      ...
      node.sub2.accept(self)
      ...
    def Y(self,node): #process node of class Y
      ...
    def Z(self,node): #process node of class Z
      ...
```

Figure 5–13
Visitor class F controlling recursion itself.

We include an example of a visitor, class `WriteOut` in Chapter 22, Figure 22–12. In Exercise 22.1, you are asked to redo a recursive function as a visitor pattern. The visitor pattern is often used along with the composite pattern, since visitors are typically applied to trees and composites are used to construct trees.

In some other object-oriented languages, you would not need to write your own dispatch function for F. You could use method overloading to select the version of the method that corresponds to the type of the node.

5.4.5   Observer

The observer pattern is important for event-driven programming. The observer pattern addresses the problem, "What if one object needs to know when an event occurs in another object, or when another object changes its state?" An example of this is in graphical user interfaces, where objects responsible for handling user requests need to observe mouse clicks and keystrokes.

▶ **Observer**

> The `Set` and `SetEnumeration` classes presented in Chapter 17 exemplify the observer pattern. `SetEnumeration` objects are iterators that deliver the elements of a set one at a time. They observe changes in the contents of the set, allowing them to deliver elements that were added after the iterators were created, or to omit delivering elements that have been removed.

The obvious solution, shown in Figure 5–14, is to have the object that changes its state inform the other object that needs to know. The observer pattern formalizes this solution. There is an observed object and zero or more observers. The observed object keeps a list of current observers. When the observed object changes its state, it runs through the list of observers and calls a method in each one of them to inform them of the change. The observed object has two additional methods: one to register an observer and the other to remove an observer.

The `SetEnumeration` objects discussed in Chapter 17 are observers of sets. They are external iterators that deliver the elements of a set one at a time to a loop. They start off with a list of the elements of a set. When an element is added to the set, the `SetEnumeration` object is informed so it can return the new element. If an element is removed from a set, the `SetEnumeration` object is informed so it can avoid returning the element.

5.4.6 Command

The command pattern creates an object that can be used to perform a command later. For example, instead of calling a method directly, using `p.f(q)`, you could create an object that will call the method later:

```
class CMD:
    def __init__(self,x,y):
      self.x=x
      self.y=y
    def doItNow(self):
      self.x.f(self.y)
c=CMD(p,q)
```

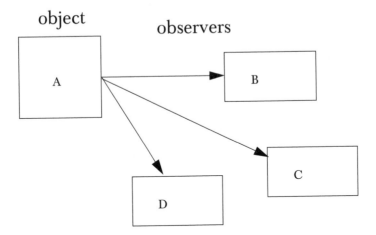

Figure 5–14
Observer.

Later, you can call the method by executing `c.doItNow()`.

Why would you ever wish to do this? One big use is in graphical user interfaces. You wish to display buttons. When the user clicks the button, some method needs to be called. You could have a separate class for each button that knows what to do when the button is pushed; but it is more flexible to have a single class for a button that takes a caption to be displayed and a command object, `c`. When the button is clicked, it executes the command, `c.doItNow()`.

We use versions of the command pattern in Chapter 20. The commands are objects with `run()` methods that are to be run concurrently in threads. The commands are enqueued in `RunQueues` to be removed by threads and run.

▶ Command

Chapter 20 is devoted to the command pattern. Command objects are created and submitted to RunQueue objects to be executed concurrently.

5.4.7   Memento

The *memento* pattern allows you to save the state of an object and restore it later. This has a couple of uses:

- You can save the state of a computation to be able to restart it if the program crashes or has to be cancelled.
- You can restart part of a computation if it could not run to completion the first time.

The memento pattern makes the implementation of an object responsible for saving and restoring its state. To implement the memento pattern, an object, x, needs such methods as:

- `memento=x.getMemento()`—assigns `memento` an object that contains x's state and can be used to reinitialize it; and
- `x.setMemento(memento)`—restores x's state from the memento.

Our implementation of transaction queues in Chapter 20 assumes that the command objects are given support mementos. Alas, our example of Transaction Queue, "Dining Philosophers," uses only a degenerate form of memento, since the commands do not change their state while being executed.

▸ **Memento**

`TransactionQueue` in Chapter 20 uses a memento pattern to save a command, allowing it to be restarted if a transaction's attempt to commit changes to a database fails.

5.4.8   Interpreter

The interpreter pattern involves creating a representation of executable expressions that contain methods that will interpret them. Expressions are usually represented as a tree with nodes for operators, numbers, and variables, and subtrees representing subexpressions. The usual components of the interpreter pattern are:

- a *syntax tree*, a collection of node classes;
- a recursive `eval()` or `interpret()` method in each node of the syntax tree; and

- an additional object to hold additional data needed by the inter-pretation: symbols and maybe an evaluation stack.

Figure 5–15 shows a few example node classes for expression trees. The `eval()` method will evaluate the subtree rooted in the expression rooted in its node. The evaluation involves recursive evaluation of the subtrees. For example, the `Add` node corresponds to a '+' operator. Its `eval()` method calls itself recursively for the left and right subtrees, adds their values, and returns the result. The `Number` nodes just contain a number that is returned when the node is evaluated.

Interpreter

"Building a Tree" in Section 22.3, in Chapter 22, discusses a tree representation of a calculator program that implements the interpreter pattern.

The additional object in this case is a dictionary that stores the values of variable identifiers. It is passed around the tree during the recursive calls, since it must be shared by all nodes in the tree. The `Var` node contains an identifier that it looks up in the dictionary to find the value to return. The `Asgn` node corresponds to an assignment. It has an identifier and a subexpression. It recursively evaluates the subexpression and assigns its value to the identifier in the dictionary.

The interpreter pattern is often implemented as a combination of the composite and visitor patterns. The composite is used to build expression trees and the visitor is used to walk over them in a certain order. Conditional (`if-else`) expressions do cause problems for using a visitor pattern: The evaluation order of a conditional expression depends on the truth of subexpressions, but a simple visitor pattern using an Iterator would visit all the nodes in a fixed order. The form of visitor pattern using an `accept()` method, sketched in Figure 5–13, works better.

A more complete interpreter pattern is presented in Chapter 22. The syntax tree is built, using the builder pattern for a sequence of statements on text lines, and is then evaluated with an interpreter pattern.

```
class Add:
    def __init__(self,x,y):
        self.left=x
        self.right=y
    def eval(self,d):
        L=self.left.eval(d)
        R=self.right.eval(d)
        return L+R
class Var:
    def __init__(self,id):
        self.id=id
    def eval(self,d):
        return d[self.id]
class Asgn:
    def __init__(self,id,e):
        self.id=id
        self.e=e
    def eval(self,d):
        x=self.e.eval(d)
        d[self.id]=x
        return x
class Number:
    def __init__(self,n):
        self.n=n
    def eval(self,d):
        return self.n
```

Figure 5–15
Interpreter fragment: classes.

5.4.9   State

The *state* pattern allows objects, in effect, to change their types. Conceptually, an object can be in one of several states. The object will respond to method calls differently depending on the state it is in.

The concept is that the object is like a finite state machine. A finite state machine is in one of a finite number of states. It reads input symbols and changes its state based on the symbol read and the state it is in.

In this model, method calls are analogous to input symbols, and the object receiving method calls is analogous to the machine reading the input symbols. The problem is how to represent the states. You could represent a state with an attribute. Each method would look at the contents of the attribute and decide what to do based on the contents. Changing the state simply requires assigning a new value to the attribute.

The state pattern also uses an attribute, but the attribute contains an object that is delegated handling the method calls. Figure 5–16 gives a picture of the state pattern. The "context object" is the object that the rest of the system sees. It points to only one of the state objects at a time. When it receives a method call, the context object passes it on to the current state object, which performs the operation. If the state is supposed to change, the state object changes the state attribute in the context to point to the new state object. The code might look like this:

```
class context:
    def __init__(self,...):
       self.state=stateA #initial state
       ...
    def methodX(self, arg1, arg2, ...):
       return self.state.methodX(self, arg1, arg2, ...)
    ...
...
class StateB:
    def methodX(self, context, arg1, arg2,...):
       ... context ... #do operation on context object
       context.state=stateC #successor state
       ...
...
stateA=StateA()
stateB=StateB()
stateC=StateC()
```

The idea is that the module defines the context class and the state classes. Each state class is a singleton "flyweight" class; there is only one copy of each state class and it contains no data of its own. When an instance of the context is created, it will assign the state object for its initial state to its state attribute.

▶ State

The example splitter in Chapter 9 shows an iterator implemented using the state pattern.

A method call to a context object will delegate the call to the same method in the current state. The method in the state object gets one additional parameter, a reference to the context object. The method in the state object performs all the operations required on the attributes of the context object, not the attributes of itself. If the state is to be changed, the new state object is assigned to the state attribute in the context object. The next method call will be handled by a method of the new state.

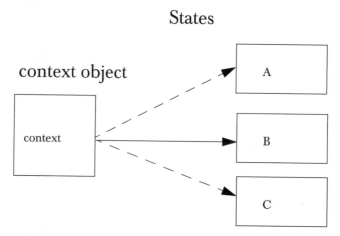

Figure 5–16
State.

5.5   Wrap-Up

In this chapter we have looked at the object-oriented design patterns that we make use of elsewhere in the book. The design patterns involve ways of creating objects, ways of plugging objects together, and ways of using objects to control execution of a program.

The general principle behind these design techniques is to maintain flexibility. We program to an interface, allowing any object that obeys the interface to be plugged in and used. This flexibility has major payoffs in allowing us to reuse code.

5.6   Exercises

5.1. Add two internal iterators to the `Composite` class (Figure 5–4). One, `preorder()`, will visit the nodes in pre-order; in other words, it will apply a function to a node before visiting all the subtrees left to right. The other, `postorder()`, will visit the nodes in post-order; in other words, it will apply a function to a node after visiting all the subtrees left to right.

5.2. Add an external iterator to the `Composite` class (Figure 5–4). The external iterator is to deliver the nodes of the tree in post-order; in other words, it will deliver a node after delivering all the nodes in all the subtrees, left to right. You may find it useful to add a `__parent` attribute to `Composite` when the node is added beneath another. You may also find it convenient to add a `x.findChild(y)` method to return the index of child `y` of node `x`.

5.3. The `Composite` class (Figure 5–4) makes no distinction between internal nodes and leaves. Create a different class, `LeafComposite`, that has the same methods as `Composite`, but raises a `LeafError` when you attempt to add, remove, or access a child. Add a method, `isLeaf()`, to both `Composite` and `LeafComposite` to indicate whether a node is a leaf.

6

Functions

In all approaches to program design, functions are essential for constructing larger programs. Python provides more flexibility in defining and calling functions than many other languages. You can call a function in the conventional way, assigning arguments to parameters by their position in an argument list. You can also pass arguments specifying the name of the parameter that gets the value, so-called keyword parameters. When you define a function, you can specify that some parameters must be passed but that others are optional. For the optional parameters, you specify the default value to be assigned to the parameter if no argument is passed for it. You can allow the function to receive a variable-length parameter list and a variable number of keyword parameters with arbitrary names.

Python has several built-in functions that can be used for functional programming. Functional programming views a program as a composition of functions instead of statements. The functions take their data from their parameters and return all their results directly. There are no mutable objects. There are no global assignments or side effects. Since all the communication among parts of the program is restricted to parameters and results, a program should be easier to debug; there's no question about "Who clobbered this variable?"

Here we take a look at Python's functions: function definitions, function calls, and built-in functions.

6.1   Parameter and Argument Lists

Arguments are passed by pointer. Every Python variable may be considered a pointer to the actual object that holds the value. When Python calls a function, the function's parameters are given copies of the pointers to the argument. This is equivalent to an assignment statement assigning the arguments to the parameters.

If the argument is immutable, for example a number, a string, or a tuple, this behaves like call-by-value. It is as if the function is given a copy of the argument. If the argument is mutable, for example, a list, the function can change the contents of the argument. In Python, you can return values by modifying a mutable argument, but having the function return a tuple of values that you assign to a sequence of variables is probably easier to understand: e.g., x,y=f(x,y).

6.1.1   Positional and Keyword Arguments

Consider the distl function shown in Figure 6–1. It has two parameters, Item and List. It is supposed to distribute the item across the list (or any other sequence), returning a list of the same length as parameter List, each element of which is a tuple composed of the Item and the corresponding element of List.

You can call distl the usual way, by passing the Item argument first in the argument list and the List argument second, thus:

```
>>> distl(10,range(5))
[(10, 0), (10, 1), (10, 2), (10, 3), (10, 4)]
```

The arguments passed by position are called, naturally, positional arguments.

```
def distl(Item,List):
    L=[]
    for x in List:
      L.append((Item,x))
    return L
```

Figure 6–1
Function distl from dist.py.

But Python also allows you to pass the argument by giving the name of the parameter that is to receive the argument, for example:

```
>>> distl(Item='x',List='abcde')
[('x', 'a'), ('x', 'b'), ('x', 'c'), ('x', 'd'), ('x', 'e')]
>>> distl(List=(1,2,3),Item=0)
[(0, 1), (0, 2), (0, 3)]
```

These arguments are called keyword arguments and have the form `parametername=value`. You can mix positional and keyword arguments. The only restriction is that all the positional arguments must come before the keyword arguments, so the general form of a call is:

$$fn(positional\_args, keyword\_args)$$

where, of course, either the positional arguments or the keyword arguments or both may be omitted.

Why would you use keyword arguments? Often the arguments have no natural, intuitive order. If the parameter names are well chosen, it may be easier to remember the parameters by name than by position.

Also, some arguments may be needed only for certain values of other arguments. Without keyword arguments, you would have to pass all of them, even though some are irrelevant. With keyword arguments, you can omit those you don't need. To make arguments optional, however, you will need defaulted parameters or an extra keyword parameter, as described in the next subsection.

6.1.2   Function Parameters

The most general form of a function definition is:

```
def fn(positionals, defaulteds, *extra_positionals,
       **extra_keywords):
    body
```

where each part of the parameter list is optional.

The *positionals* are a sequence of identifiers. They *must* be assigned values in the call by their positions in the argument list or by keyword arguments.

6.1.2.1 Parameter Sublists

One strange facility in Python is the ability to specify a sublist in a parameter list. The sublist is a list of parameter names in parentheses; for example, here's how we might define head and tail functions:

```
def hd((x,y)):return x
def tl((x,y)):return y
```

The argument passed to that parameter must be a sequence of the same length as the sublist. The parameters are assigned the elements of the sequence. This works the same way as multiple targets in an assignment statement.

There are not many uses for sublists of parameter lists.

6.1.2.2 Defaulted Parameters

The *defaulteds* are a sequence of parameters of the form *name=expression*. These parameters have default values that will be used if no value is assigned to the parameter in the call. When the def statement is executed, creating the function object, the expression is evaluated and its value is saved to assign to the parameter. Figure 6–2 gives an example using defaulted parameters.

```
"""upto(subject,set=' \t\n',start=0,end=end of string)
search subject sequence for element in set
from start to (but not including) end.
return position, or end"""

def upto(subject,set=' \t\n',start=0,end=None):
    N=len(subject)
    if end is None: end=N
    if start<0: start += N
    if end<0: end+=N
    if not 0 <= start <= end <= N: raise IndexError
    for i in range(start,end):
      if subject[i] in set: return i
    return end
```

Figure 6–2
upto.py.

The `upto()` function is supposed to search a `subject` string (or list or tuple) for the first occurrence of a character that is included in its string parameter `set`. It will search the positions from parameter `start` up to, but not including, `end`. It is to return the first (lowest) position of a character included in `set`. If it doesn't find such a character, it will return the position `end`.

The function uses defaulted parameters. If `end` is not supplied in the call, it defaults to the end of the `subject` string. If `start` is not supplied, it defaults to the beginning of the subject. If `set` is not supplied, it defaults to whitespace—specifically, a blank, tab, or newline.

Notice here that `subject` does not have a default value. It must be supplied in any call. Both `set` and `start` have obvious constant initial values. Parameter `end`, however, is given the default value `None`. It is supposed to default to the end of the subject string. Why didn't we specify `end=len(subject)`? We couldn't. The default value for `end` is computed when the `def` statement is executed, when the function is defined. The `subject` parameter only becomes available later, when the function is called. What we had to do was assign a distinctive constant value to `end` that we could examine when the function is run. If we find that value, we assign `end` the default value we really wanted.

Notice further that we try to follow Python's conventions about negative indices. If a position, either `start` or `end`, is negative, we take it from the end of the subject string. Also, if either `start` or `end` refers to a position outside the string or if `end` is less than `start`, we raise an `Index-Error`, a built-in error type. Here is an example execution:

```
>>> upto('abcdefghijklm nopqrstuvwxyz')
13
>>> upto('abcdefghijklm nopqrstuvwxyz','dt')
3
>>> upto('abcdefghijklm nopqrstuvwxyz','dt',4)
20
>>> upto('abcdefghijklm nopqrstuvwxyz','dt',4,10)
10
>>> upto('abcdefghijklm nopqrstuvwxyz','dt',4,-10)
17
>>> upto('abcdefghijklm nopqrstuvwxyz','dt',-26,-10)
3
>>> upto('abcdefghijklm nopqrstuvwxyz','dt',-36,-10)
Traceback (most recent call last):
  File "<stdin>", line 1, in ?
  File "upto.py", line 11, in upto
    if not 0 <= start <= end <= N: raise IndexError
```

```
IndexError
>>> upto('abcdefghijklm nopqrstuvwxyz','dt',-26,30)
Traceback (most recent call last):
  File "<stdin>", line 1, in ?
  File "upto.py", line 11, in upto
    if not 0 <= start <= end <= N: raise IndexError
IndexError
```

6.1.2.3   Extra Positional Parameters

To be able to receive extra positional parameters, put an asterisk followed by an identifier at the end of your parameter list. (It may only be followed by an extra-keywords parameter.) It will be given a tuple containing all the positional arguments in the call beyond those that are assigned to the preceding arguments. The tuple will be empty if there are no additional parameters, for example:

```
>>> def t(*a): return type(a)
...
>>> t(1,2)
<type 'tuple'>
```

You can use the extra positionals parameter to write functions like the built-in `max` and `min` functions that can take a list of any number of values. Consider the function `avg()` in Figure 6–3 that computes the mean of any number of values.

```
"""avg(L) avg(x, ...)
calculate the average"""

import types

def avg(*L):
    if len(L)==1 and (type(L[0]) is types.ListType or\
        type(L[0]) is types.TupleType):
      L=L[0]
    x=0.0
    if len(L)==0: return x
    for y in L: x+=y
    return x/len(L)
```

Figure 6–3
avg.py.

Function `avg()` may be called with any number of numeric values in its argument list and it will compute their average. The first `if` statement checks to see if there is only a single argument and it is either a list or a tuple. If so, the average is taken of the contents of that sequence, since like `max()` and `min()`, it can also take a list or tuple of values as a single argument and compute their average. Here is an example of its execution:

```
>>> avg(1,2,3,4,5,6)
3.5
>>> avg([1,2,3,4,5,6])
3.5
>>> avg((1,2,3,4,5,6))
3.5
>>> avg()
0.0
>>> avg([])
0.0
```

6.1.2.4   Extra-Keyword Parameters

A function can also receive a dictionary of extra-keyword arguments. These are the keyword arguments that do not name any positional or defaulted parameters. To get them, put two asterisks followed by an identifier at the very end of the parameter list.

Here's an example:

```
>>> def makedict(**D): return D
...
>>> makedict(a=1,b=2)
{'b': 2, 'a': 1}
```

You might want to use an extra-keyword parameter when there are many possible parameters but very few are always required.

6.1.2.5   No Overloading

Some languages allow you to declare several functions with the same name but with different parameter lists. The compiler or the run-time system chooses which one to actually call, given the numbers and types of the arguments. Python does not provide overloading; it really can't. Being a dynamically-typed language, Python does not declare the types of parameters, so type information cannot be used. Moreover, the extra-positional and extra-keyword parameters prevent using the length of the parameter list to choose among function definitions.

On the other hand, the very flexibility provided by positional, defaulted, extra-positional, and extra-keyword parameters give you all the flexibility in calling functions that overloading would provide; it simply requires you to do the pattern matching yourself to see what code to execute.

6.1.3   Return Values

If a function returns by falling off the end of its code, it returns `None`. A return statement can return zero, one, or multiple values. When it returns no value:

```
return
```

it is actually returning `None`. If it returns multiple values, for example:

```
return x,y+1
```

it is returning a tuple of values, exactly as if it were written:

```
return (x,y+1)
```

The unpacking assignment statement works nicely with this. It allows a function to return multiple results directly without having to change the contents of mutable objects. For example:

```
p,q,x=f(x,y,z)
```

can be interpreted to mean function `f` is taking two "in" parameters, `y` and `z`, one "in/out" parameter `x`, and "out" parameters, `p` and `q`.

6.2   Three-Level Scopes

There are three scopes for variable names used in a function: the *local* scope of parameters and local variables; the *global* scope of variables defined in the surrounding module; and the *built-in* scope containing the names built into the Python system and always available. As of Python version 2.1, it is possible to access several nested scopes of surrounding functions as well. We consider nested scopes in the next section. Except for that section, we consider only the traditional three levels of scopes.

When you refer to a variable in a function, Python first looks to see if it is a local variable. It uses that variable if it exists. If it isn't local, Python looks to see if it is global and uses that variable if it finds one. If the variable isn't either local or global, Python looks for a built-in variable with that name.

When a function starts running, it has local variables for all its parameters. Whenever you first assign a value to a variable in a function, it creates a local variable with that name, with one exception: You cannot assign a new value to a global variable in a function if the assignment always creates a new local variable; so Python allows you to specify that certain names are to be taken as global variables. For this you use the `global` statement. When you include the statement:

```
global id1, id2, ...
```

in a function, Python will interpret the identifiers `id1`, `id2`, and so on as global variables. There will be no local variables with those names. An assignment to any of them will assign to the variable of that name in the module, in fact creating it if it isn't already there.

6.3   Functional Programming

Functional programming views a program as a function that transforms input into output. The function may be a composition of other functions, which are compositions of other functions and so on. There are no statements. There are no assignments to global variables, and, in fact, no side effects of function execution.

One effect of that is that instead of a `for` statement assigning a variable the elements of a list and executing other statements for each assignment, in functional programming there are functions that apply other functions to each element of a list.

Python has a number of facilities for functional programming.

6.3.1   Lambda Functions

Python has three built-in functions, `filter(f,L)`, `map(f,L)`, and `reduce(f,L)`, that apply functions to the items in a list. They, and similar functions you write yourself, need functions to apply, and it can be a nuisance to have to write a `def` statement for each of those functions, especially those that are just expressions. Python eases the burden by allowing you to write some simple functions inside expressions by using lambda expressions:

```
lambda parameterList : expression
```

A lambda expression is introduced by the keyword `lambda`. There is no function name for a lambda function. The parameter list is like a parameter list of a `def`'d function, but it is not written in parentheses. The body of the function is an expression–no statements are allowed.

Why "lambda"? It is not an acronym. It comes from early work on the theory of functions. The notation was $\lambda x.e$, meaning a function of one parameter, *x*, whose definition is the expression *e*. The word *lambda* has been used in Lisp and various functional languages. The designer of Python clearly was aware of this history.

A lambda expression has the same scopes as if it were a function created in a `def` statement:

1. local, here consisting solely of the parameters;
2. global, those variables defined in the surrounding module; and
3. built-in.

This means, in particular, that if you use a lambda expression in a function, it will not be able to see the local variables of the function. We'll see a work-around for this in Figure 6–4 when we examine the `map()` function.

6.3.2   Map

You can use the `map()` built-in function to apply a function to every element of a list or other sequence, creating a list of the results. Its call has the form:

```
map(function, sequence)
```

For example:

```
>>> map(lambda x:-x,range(5))
[0, -1, -2, -3, -4]
```

Here the lambda function `lambda x:-x` is applied to every element of the list returned by `range(5)`, and a new list is constructed from their values. Notice that the lambda function takes one parameter, `x`, which will be given each element of the list it is being mapped over.

An example of its use is shown in Figure 6–4. The `distr()` function is like the `dist1` function shown in Figure 6–1, but when it pairs an item with each element of a list, it places the item on the right rather than the left. For example:

```
>>> import dist
>>> dist.distr(range(5),10)
[(0, 10), (1, 10), (2, 10), (3, 10), (4, 10)]
```

```
def distr(List,Item):
    return map(lambda x,Item=Item: (x,Item), List)
```

Figure 6–4
Function distr: mapping a lambda expression.

Here `map()` applies a lambda function to `List`. The body of the lambda expression is simply the tuple constructor, `(x,Item)`, which is to pair the list element `x` with `Item`.

Strangely, though, the lambda function has two parameters rather than one. Its first parameter, `x`, as in Figure 6–4, gets an element of the list the lambda function is being mapped over. So what is this `Item=Item` parameter? Recall that a function knows variables in only three scopes: local, global, and built-in. The parameter `Item` passed in to `distr()` is local to the `distr` function, but it is neither local to the lambda function nor is it defined in the module. Therefore, the body of the lambda function can't see it.

So, here's the trick: We create a parameter `Item` in the lambda function. The lambda function can see its parameters. We give this parameter a default value, the value of `Item` in the surrounding `distr` function at the time the lambda function is created. If we don't pass an argument to the lambda function's `Item` parameter, it will have its default value; and since the `map()` function will be passing the lambda function a single parameter, we are safe: the `Item` parameter of the lambda function will have the same value as the `Item` parameter of `distr()`.

With the introduction of nested function scopes, this trick will become unnecessary. We will redo `distr` using nested scopes in Section 6.3.5.

The `map()` function can also apply a function of n arguments to n sequences and produce a list of the values returned. The form of the call is:

```
map(function, sequence0, sequence1, ...)
```

The result will be:

```
[function(sequence0[0], sequence1[0],...),
 function(sequence0[1], sequence1[1],...),...]
```

For example:

```
>>> map(lambda x,y:y-x,[0,1,2],[2,1,0])
[2, 0, -2]
```

If you only want to apply a standard unary or binary operator to the elements of one or two sequences, you don't have to write a lambda function. The `operator` module has functions for most of Python's operators (and a few others as well). For example, `operator.sub(x,y)` is the same as `x-y`.

You may use `None` as the function in `map()`. It will be interpreted as the identity function: It will return its arguments. In the case of a single argument list, `L`, `map(None,L)` returns a copy of the list `L`:

```
>>> map(None,range(5))
[0, 1, 2, 3, 4]
```

But in the case of more than one argument sequence, `map(None,L0,L1,...)` returns tuples of the corresponding elements of the argument sequences; for example:

```
>>> map(None, (1,2),(3,4))
[(1, 3), (2, 4)]
>>> map(None,'abc','def')
[('a', 'd'), ('b', 'e'), ('c', 'f')]
```

`None` makes `map()` behave like the built-in function `zip()`:

```
>>> zip((1,2,3),[4,5,6])
[(1, 4), (2, 5), (3, 6)]
```

6.3.3   Reduce

The `reduce()` built-in function can be used to *accumulate* a value over the elements of a sequence. For example, `reduce(operator.add,range(1,5))` adds the elements of the list `range(1,5)` together:

```
>>> import operator
>>> reduce(operator.add,range(1,5))
10
```

The call `reduce(operator.mul,range(1,5))` multiplies them:

```
>>> reduce(operator.mul,range(1,5))
24
```

The call `reduce(f,s)` returns `f(...f(s[0],s[1]),...s[n-1])`, where `len(s)==n`. You can also provide an initial value. The call `reduce(f,s,init)` returns `f(...f(f(init,s[0]),s[1]),...s[n-1])`.

Notice that the reduction works left to right through the sequence, so `reduce(operator.sub,range(1,5))` yields -8–i.e., 1–2–3–4. It would be a little more useful if it ran right to left, as in APL, since that would give an alternating sum−1−2+3−4 = −2. (It's useful in calculating approximations to mathematical functions.) We can get this in Python with a little more work by reversing the list and reversing the subtraction:

```
>>> reduce(lambda x,y:y-x,range(4,0,-1))
-2
```

6.3.4   Filter

The built-in function `filter(f,s)` creates a new list out of the elements of sequence `s` for which function `f` returns true. For example, to get a list of integers in the range zero through 25 that are multiples of 3, we could do something like this:

```
>>> filter(lambda x:x%3==0,range(26))
[0, 3, 6, 9, 12, 15, 18, 21, 24]
```

If you specify `None` as the function, you get a list of those elements of the sequence that can be considered true, or nonzero; for example:

```
>>> filter(None,map(lambda x:x%3,range(26)))
[1, 2, 1, 2, 1, 2, 1, 2, 1, 2, 1, 2, 1, 2, 1, 2, 1]
```

6.3.5   Nested Scopes

As of Python version 2.1, you can nest function scopes so that an inner function can see local variables in the surrounding functions. Since this change may break some existing code, it is not the default behavior, but it will become the default behavior in later versions of Python. Figure 6–5 shows how the `distr` function (seen in Figure 6–4) can be rewritten with nested scopes.

```
""" distr(List,Item)
distribute item onto list from right"""

from __future__ import nested_scopes

def distr(List,Item):
    return map(lambda x: (x,Item), List)
```

Figure 6–5
Nested distr: distr using nested scopes.

Note two important points about this module:

1. The line `from __future__ import nested_scopes` makes nested scopes available for this code. It looks like a module import statement, but it is not. The reserved module name `__future__` is used for features being introduced into the language. They are already implemented, but they are not the default yet. We are saying that we want to use the new `nested_scopes` facility.

    The `from __future__ import` ... statement must precede all statements that can generate code, since it may change the functioning of the compiler. However, it has to follow the initial module documentation string.

2. Unlike the `distr()` in Figure 6–4, the lambda function did not have to include a second parameter `Item=Item`. It can see the `Item` parameter of the surrounding `distr()` function.

6.3.6   Example: Functional Programming Lists of Files

Python's functional programming facilities are useful for processing lists as in-memory databases. Here's an example of processing lists of files.

The module `os` has a large number of functions for processing files. The `listdir(d)` function will give a list of files in directory *d*. Here we filter the files in the current directory (indicated by `'.'`) to select only the Python source files:

```
filter(lambda x:x[-3:]=='.py',os.listdir('.'))
```

The `os.path` module contains a function `getsize(f)` that gives the size of the file `f`. Passing the result of the previous function, we can add up the sizes of all the Python source files in the current directory with this:

```
reduce(operator.add,
    map(os.path.getsize,
        filter(lambda x:x[-3:]=='.py',
            os.listdir('.')))))
```

6.3.7 Apply

Sometimes you need to apply a function to an argument list that really
is a list. For example, suppose we have a list `args`:

```
>>> args=[1,2]
```

and we need to apply function `f` to it. For the purpose of our example,
let's let `f=operator.add`. Sure, it's trivial; in this case, we could just
write:

```
>>> f(args[0],args[1])
3
```

But it won't always be this trivial. The function may take variable numbers of parameters, and it would be a pain to have to write a bunch of
`if` statements, one for each possible length of argument list, choosing an
appropriate call, such as:

```
if len(args)==1: f(args[0])
elif len(args)==2: f(args[0],args[1])
elif len(args)==3: f(args[0],args[1],args[2])
...
```

There is an easy way around this. The `apply(f,args)` call applies
the function `f` to the arguments in the sequence `args`. Continuing the
example from above:

```
>>> apply(f,args)
3
```

More generally, you can apply a function to both a sequence of
positional arguments and a dictionary of keyword arguments. The form
for this is:

$$apply(\mathit{fn},\ \mathit{posargs},\ \mathit{kwargs})$$

where `posargs` is a sequence of positional arguments and `kwargs` is a
dictionary of keyword arguments. The keys in `kwargs` must be strings.
Using the `distr` function of Figure 6–4:

```
>>> apply(dist.distr,[range(5)],{"Item":10})
[(0, 10), (1, 10), (2, 10), (3, 10), (4, 10)]
```

In fact, `apply()` turned out to be so useful that it was added to Python's syntax. The call `fn(*posargs,  **kwargs)` is equivalent to `apply(fn,posargs,kwargs)`

Either of the `*posargs` or the `**kwargs` may be omitted; for example:

```
>>> dist.distr(**{"Item":10,"List":range(5)})
[(0, 10), (1, 10), (2, 10), (3, 10), (4, 10)]
```

But that's not the case with `apply()`. The third argument of `apply()` may be omitted, but the second argument must be a sequence:

```
>>> apply(dist.distr,{"Item":10,"List":range(5)})
Traceback (most recent call last):
  File "<stdin>", line 1, in ?
TypeError: apply() 2nd argument must be a sequence
>>> apply(dist.distr,(),{"Item":10,"List":range(5)})
[(0, 10), (1, 10), (2, 10), (3, 10), (4, 10)]
```

6.3.8   Eval

The built-in function `eval(s)` evaluates the string `s` as a Python expression.

```
>>> eval("[1,2]")
[1, 2]
```

You can also give `eval()` dictionaries to look up variables in: `eval(s,globals)` will look up all names in the `globals` dictionary first and then in the built-in scope. The call `eval(s, globals, locals)` will look for identifiers first in the `locals` dictionary, then the `globals`, and then in the built-in scope. You can use the built-in functions `locals()` and `globals()` to access the current directories explicitly.

```
>>> eval("x+y",{"x":1,"y":2},{"x":3})
5
```

6.4   Function Objects

6.4.1   Kinds of Functions

In essence, a function is any object that can be followed with an argument list in parentheses. Python has many types of function objects.

Of course, there are the functions you define yourself, with `def` statements and `lambda` expressions, which are of the type `types.FunctionType`. (The `types` module has names for the built-in types.)

```
>>> type(lambda x:x)
<type 'function'>
>>> def id(x):return x
...
>>> type(id)
<type 'function'>
```

There are the built-in functions, which are of the type `types.BuiltinFunctionType`:

```
>>> type(abs)
<type 'builtin_function_or_method'>
```

A method is a function that you apply to an object with a dot notation. For example, lists have the built-in method `append()`. The call `L.append(x)` will insert `x` at the end of the list `L`. Methods of the built-in types, like lists, are of `types.BuiltinFunctionType` or `types.BuiltinMethodType` (those are two names for the same type):

```
>>> type([].append)
<type 'builtin_function_or_method'>
```

Class statements can give you several different kinds of functions. The class itself is a function, since it can be called to produce an instance of the class:

```
>>> class C:
...     def id(self,x):return x
...     def __call__(self): return 1
...
>>> type(C)
<type 'class'>
```

A method is declared in a `def` statement within a `class` statement. When you use the form `class_name.method_name`, you get a type `types.MethodType` (also known as `types.UnboundMethodType`, but written out as `<type 'instance method'>`). We examine these in detail in Chapter 12.

```
>>> type(C.id)
<type 'instance method'>
>>> c=C()
>>> type(c.id)
<type 'instance method'>
```

When a class has a `__call__()` method in it, you call that method by calling a class instance itself as a function. The class instance has the type `types.InstanceType`:

```
>>> c()
1
>>> type(c)
<type 'instance'>
```

The built-in function `callable()` will return false for any object that can never be used as a function and true for any object that can at least sometimes be used that way. If `callable(f)` is false, `f(...)` will always result in an error. If `callable(f)` is true, `f(...)` may still fail, of course, for the wrong number of arguments.

In these examples, `callable()` will return true for id, abs, C, C.id, c.id, and c.

6.4.2   Assigning Attributes to User Functions

As of Python version 2.1, you can assign attributes to user-defined (`def` and `lambda`) function objects just as you can assign to class instances. Functions have a special attribute, `__dict__`, that contains a dictionary of such attributes:

```
>>> g=lambda x:x
>>> g
<function <lambda> at 007E2FAC>
>>> g.y=2
>>> g.y
2
>>> g.__dict__
{'y': 2}
```

```
>>> del g.y
>>> g.y
Traceback (most recent call last):
  File "<stdin>", line 1, in ?
AttributeError: y
```

6.5 Built-In Functions

To try to make Python's built-in functions a bit more comprehensible, we can divide them into several groups, although some might be considered to belong in more than one group.

6.5.1 Arithmetic Functions

Python's built-in arithmetic functions are mostly unremarkable. See Table 6–1. A more comprehensive set of mathematical functions is available in the `math` module, and for complex operands in the `cmath` module. Several arithmetic built-in functions are type conversions.

Table 6–1
Arithmetic built-in functions.

Function	Explanation
`abs (x)`	Absolute value of x. If x is complex (x,y), it gives you $\sqrt{x^2 + y^2}$.

`coerce (x, y)`	Returns a tuple of x and y converted to a common type, e.g.:
	 `>>> coerce(1L,2)`
	 `(1L, 2L)`
	 `>>> coerce(1L,2.0)`
	 `(1.0, 2.0)`

`complex (real)` `complex (real, imag)`	Constructs a complex number.
`divmod (a, b)`	Returns the tuple `(a/b,a%b)`.
`float (x)`	Converts x to a floating-point number.

Table 6–1
Arithmetic built-in functions. (Continued)

Function	Explanation
`int (x)` `int (x, radix)`	Converts x to an integer. If x is a string, it allows you to specify a radix, e.g., 2, 8, 10, or 16 for binary, octal, decimal, or hexadecimal conversion. (It will also convert long integers and floating-point numbers to integers.)
`long (x)`	Converts x to a long integer.
`max (s)` `max (a0,a1,...)`	Returns the maximum value in sequence s, or of the arguments a0, a1, ...
`min (s)` `min (a0,a1,...)`	Returns the minimum value in sequence s, or of the arguments a0, a1, ...
`pow (x, y)` `pow (x, y, z)`	x^y or (x^y) modulus z.

`round (x)`
`round (x, n)`
	Returns the floating-point number x rounded to n decimal digits after the decimal point. Parameter n defaults to zero.
	`>>> round((1/3.0),2)`
	`0.33000000000000002`

Maximum and minimum functions can be given any number of numeric operands or a single sequence of values. The `pow()` function can compute one number to a power modulus a third number. It is used in encryption and decryption in public key systems. Combining the exponentiation and modulus can be a lot faster than performing them separately.

6.5.2   Sequence Operations

Sequence operations include the functional programming-related functions `map()`, `zip()`, `reduce()`, `filter()`, and `apply()` that were discussed in an earlier section.

The `list()` function converts a sequence to a list; it generates a new list with the contents of the operand sequence. The `tuple()` function converts a sequence to a tuple. If the operand is already a tuple, Python just returns it, since tuples are pure values.

Table 6–2
Sequence-related built-in functions.

Function	Explanation

`apply (function, args)`
`apply (function, args,`
`        keywords)`
	See `apply`, Section 6.3.7.

`filter (function, list)`	See `filter`, Section 6.3.4.
`len (s)`	Returns the length of the sequence `s`.
`list (sequence)`	Converts the sequence to a list, i.e., returns a list each of whose elements is the corresponding element of the sequence.
`map (function, list,` `    ...)`	See `map`, Section 6.3.2.

`range ( stop)`
`range (start, stop)`
`range (start, stop,`
`        step)`
	Returns a list of integers, `[start, start+step, start+2*step,...]` up or down to but not including `stop`. Parameter `start` defaults to `0` and `step` defaults to `1`.

`reduce (function,`
`        sequence)`
`reduce (function,`
`        sequence,`
`        initializer)`
	See `reduce`, Section 6.3.3.

Table 6–2
Sequence-related built-in functions. (Continued)

Function	Explanation

`slice ( stop)`
`slice (start, stop)`
`slice (start, stop,`
`    step)`
	Creates a slice object with attributes `start`, `stop`, and `step`. Such objects are created by some forms of slicing syntax and can be used when implementing abstract data types. See Chapter 15.

`tuple (sequence)`	Converts the sequence to a tuple, i.e., returns a tuple the length of the sequence with each element being an element of the sequence.

`xrange (stop)`
`xrange (start, stop)`
`xrange (start, stop,`
`    step)`
	Like `range()`, but doesn't actually build a list. It can be used following the `in` in a `for` statement to save space.

`zip (seq1, ...)`	Equivalent to map`(None,seq1, ...)`.

The `range()` function actually generates a list containing the integers in the specified sequence. The `xrange()` function has the same interface as `range()`. It creates an object that can deliver the numbers in the sequence when used in a `for` statement following the `in`. Since `xrange()` doesn't actually construct the list, it uses less memory.

Function `slice()` just produces a slice object with `start`, `stop`, and `step` attributes. These objects are generated by Python in some array slicing contexts. It is of most relevance for programming abstract data types. See Chapter 15.

6.5.3   String Functions

Most of Python's string operations are methods built in to string objects, but Python does provide a number of built-in functions for converting characters and strings. Functions `hex()` and `oct()` convert their integer arguments to their hexadecimal and octal string representations.

Function `chr(i)` converts its integer argument to a character, more precisely, a one-character string whose character has number `i` in the ASCII encoding. Function `ord(c)` works the other way: It gives the numeric value of the character c. Function `unichr(i)` is like `chr()`, but produces a string with the Unicode character with number i.

There are two general ways to convert objects to string representations. Function `str(x)` converts x to a form for a human to read. Function `repr(x)` is supposed to convert object x to a string that, if evaluated as a Python expression, will recreate the object.

Function `intern(s)` returns string s or a copy of the string s. Each call to `intern()` with an equal string will return the identical string. You use this to speed up string compares and to save storage. Equal strings may be different objects; in other words, both have the same characters, but they were created at different times. It is faster to compare strings for identity, `(x is y)`, than for equality, `(x == y)`, since Python only has to compare the memory addresses for identity, but must compare the characters in the strings for equality. Therefore, if you are frequently going to compare a set of strings for equality, you can speed up your program by interning them and just comparing their interned values, as shown here:

```
>>> "ab"=="a"+"b"
1
>>> "ab" is "a"+"b"
0
>>> intern("ab") is intern("a"+"b")
1
```

By interning strings that are used throughout your data structures, all occurrences of the string will occupy the same block of storage, rather than many blocks. This can save a lot of storage. The downside, however, is that the storage for the interned strings will never be garbage collected.

6.5.4 Object Identity, Comparison, and Types

There are a number of functions that deal with object identity, comparisons, and types. Function `id(x)` returns an integer unique to the object x. Different objects have different `id()` values. If `id(x)==id(y)`, x is y.

The function `cmp(x,y)` is called for relational operators such as `<`. It is to return a negative value if x is less than y, zero if they are equal, and a positive value if x is greater than y. The comparisons compare the contents of the built-in sequences left to right, so even different lists may compare equal. However, different kinds of sequences will not compare equal. When dictionaries are compared, their contents are sorted by

Table 6–3
String-related built-in functions.

Function	Explanation
chr (i)	Returns the character (in a one-character string) whose ASCII code is integer i. This is equivalent to (″%c″ % i); see Chapter 9.
hex (x)	Returns a string representation of integer i converted to hexadecimal representation: >>> hex(65) '0x41' It is *not* equivalent to (″%x″ % i), which does not put 0x on the front.
intern (s)	Returns string s or a copy of the string s. Each call to intern() with an equal string will return the identical string. You use this to speed up compares and to save storage. See the discussion in the text.

oct (x)	Converts integer x to a string representation of it as an unsigned octal integer.
	>>> oct(65)
	'0101'
	>>> oct(-1)
	'037777777777'
	It is *not* equivalent to ('%o' % x), which does not put ″0″ on the front.

ord (c)	Returns the integer number of the single character in string c. Works for both Latin (8-bit character) and Unicode.
repr (x)	Returns a string representation of object x. It is the same as 'x'. If possible, it is to produce a string that can be evaluated (with function eval()) to create a copy of the object.

Table 6–3
String-related built-in functions. (Continued)

Function	Explanation
`str (x)`	Returns a string representation of object x. Unlike `repr()`, `str()` does not attempt to be the inverse of `eval()`. It attempts to make the translated string legible.
`unichr (i)`	Returns the character (in a one-character Unicode string) whose Unicode code is integer i.
`unicode (string[, encoding[, errors]])`	For Unicode string conversion. It is not discussed here.

Table 6–4
Object identity, types, classes, and comparison built-in functions.

Function	Explanation
`callable (object)`	True if the object can be called as a function, false if it cannot be. True for functions, class names, methods, or instance objects with a `__call__()` method, etc.
`cmp(x, y)`	Compares x and y and returns negative if $x<y$, 0 if $x==y$, and positive if $x>y$.

`coerce(x, y)`	Returns tuple (x, y) of x and y converted to a common type, e.g.:
	`>>> coerce(1L,2)`
	`(1L, 2L)`
	`>>> coerce(1L,2.0)`
	`(1.0, 2.0)`

Table 6–4

Object identity, types, classes, and comparison built-in functions. (Continued)

Function	Explanation
hash(object)	Computes a hash value for an object, an integer that tells a dictionary where in its table to start looking when the object is used as a key. Objects that cannot be used as keys in dictionaries do not have a hash value.
id(object)	Returns an integer representing the identity of the object. Different objects have different id() values, even if they compare equal.
isinstance(object, C)	True if object is an instance of class c (or a subclass) or if object's type is c. See Section 4.3.
issubclass(class1, class2)	True if class1 is class2 or a subclass of class2. See Section 4.3.
type(obj)	Returns a type object that represents the type of object obj.

key and compared. There are ways to allow cmp() to compare instances of classes; they are discussed in Chapter 14.

Function callable(x) returns true if x can be called as a function, false if it cannot be. Of course, even if x can be called as a function, a particular call may fail if the parameter list isn't right. Functions, of course, are callable. So are methods, the function attributes of classes, which we looked at in Chapter 4. Classes are callable; they are called as functions to create instances. And instances of classes are callable if the class defines a __call__() special method. This was discussed in Section 6.4. The various forms of callable objects are discussed in Chapter 12 and used in the function actionRoutineInfo in Figure 22–11.

The type(x) function will give you a type object that represents the type of object x. There is a single type object for each data type. You can look them up in the module types. For example, type(10) is the same type object as types.IntType. Function isinstance(x,t) can be used to see if the type of object x is type t; isinstance(10,types.IntType) returns true.

Function isinstance() is also used to test the class of instance objects. Function issubclass() tests whether one class object is or inherits from another. We discussed this in Chapter 4.

The function hash(x) is supposed to compute a hash code for object x. It is only supposed to produce a hash code if x can be used as a key in a dictionary. The hash code tells the dictionary where to start looking for the key in its table. The dictionary will then use cmp() to test whether a key it has found is the one desired. Therefore, if two objects, x and y, are to be treated as equal keys, cmp(x,y) must return zero and hash(x) must equal hash(y). If they are to be treated as different keys, their hash values may still be equal.

Function coerce(x,y) is supposed to return a tuple of x and y converted to a common type. It is commonly used with numbers before performing arithmetic. It can also be used with abstract data types; that is discussed in Chapter 14.

6.5.5   Run-Time Compilation and Evaluation

Python does not distinguish between compile-time and run-time. It can translate programs into its internal, interpretive code while the program is running; indeed, it does that when you import modules (although Python leaves the translated code in files to avoid recompiling if the code hasn't changed).

Table 6–5
Run-time evaluation-related built-in functions.

Function	Explanation

__import__(name)
__import__(name,
   globals)
__import__(name,
   globals, locals)
__import__(name,
   globals, locals,
      fromlist)
	Called by the import statement. It exists to be replaced for some special uses. It is not discussed further here.

compile(string, filename, kind)	Compiles a string at run-time. See Chapter 13.

Table 6–5
Run-time evaluation-related built-in functions. (Continued)

Function	Explanation

`eval (expression)`
`eval (expression,`
`    globals)`
`eval (expression,`
`    globals, locals)`
	Evaluates the string `expression` as if it is a Python expression:
	`>>> eval("[1,2]")`
	`[1, 2]`
	You can also give `eval()` dictionaries to look up variables in: `eval(s,globals)` or `eval(s, globals, locals)`:
	`>>> eval("x+y",{"x":1,"y":2},{"x":3})`
	`5`

`execfile (file)`
`execfile (file,`
`    globals)`
`execfile (file,`
`    globals,`
`    locals)`
	Executes the file as Python code. See Chapter 13.

`reload (M)`	Reloads the module `M`. You use this while debugging code. After changing the code in `M.py`, you need to reload it. Note that you pass `reload` the module object, not the name. You will also have to re-execute all the statements `from M import names` to get the new versions.

Table 6–5 lists the built-in functions that are used for translating or executing source code at run-time or with loading modules. Function `eval()` was discussed in Section 6.3.8. The descriptions of most of these functions are given in Chapter 13.

As was discussed in Chapter 3, you will need the `reload(M)` function when you are debugging modules interactively. If you fix a bug in a module, you need to import the new version into the Python session. You can't just say `import M`. After the module has been imported for the first time, the `import` statement just returns the module object that was constructed when it was first loaded. To force it to load the new one, you need to pass the module object to `reload()`. The reloaded module overwrites the module object, so you do not have to import it again, but if you wrote `from M import x`, you will have to execute that statement again to get the new `x`. Similarly, if the module contains a class declaration, you will have to create new instances of the class to see any changes in it. A final warning: If you eliminated a variable, function, or class in the module, reloading will not eliminate the old value. Reloading overwrites. It does not clear.

6.5.6 Environment-Related

Several functions let you examine the variables currently available or the attributes of objects. Function `globals()` gives you a dictionary containing the global variables and their values. Function `locals()` gives you the local variable dictionary; for example:

```
>>> def locs(x,y):return locals()
...
>>> locs(1,2)
{'x': 1, 'y': 2}
```

Function `locals()` returns the same thing as `globals()` if it is executed outside a function.

Table 6–6
Environment-related built-in functions.

Function	Explanation
`dir()` `dir(object)`	Without a parameter, gives a list of the names of the variables that would be returned by `locals()`—the keys of the dictionary returned by `locals()`. With a parameter, gives a list of the names of the attributes of the object.
`globals()`	Gives a dictionary whose keys are the global variables and whose values are their values.

Table 6–6
Environment-related built-in functions. (Continued)

Function	Explanation
`locals()`	Inside a function, gives a dictionary whose keys are the local variables and whose values are their values. Outside a function, gives the dictionary of global variables.
`vars()` `vars(object)`	Without a parameter, `vars()` behaves like `locals()`. With a parameter, it returns the `__dict__` attribute of the object, or raises an exception if the object does not have a `__dict__` attribute.

The call `vars()`, without a parameter, will behave like `locals()`. When called with a parameter, `vars(x)`, it will give you the `__dict__` attribute of x, if it has one. As an example:

```
>>> class P:pass
...
>>> vars(P)
{'__module__': '__main__', '__doc__': None}
>>> p=P()
>>> vars(p)
{}
>>> p.x=1
>>> p.y=2
>>> vars(p)
{'x': 1, 'y': 2}
```

Function `dir()` returns a list of variable names, rather than a dictionary. Continuing the example:

```
>>> dir(P)
['__doc__', '__module__']
>>> dir(p)
['x', 'y']
```

When called without a parameter, `dir()` returns a list of the names of the variables that `locals()` would return in a dictionary, for example:

```
>>> def showdir(x,y):return dir()
...
>>> showdir(1,2)
['x', 'y']
```

These are useful for writing out the state of a computation during debugging.

6.5.7   Attribute Access

An object with attributes is much like a dictionary. It has attributes with names and values, although, of course, you access an attribute with `x.name` rather than `x['name']`. Python has some built-in functions that make objects closer to dictionaries, allowing you to assign, look up, and delete attributes by their string names.

Table 6–7
Attribute-related built-in functions.

Function	Explanation
`delattr(object, name)`	Deletes the `value` of the attribute of `object` with the string `name`. Raises an exception if the object doesn't have an attribute with that name.
`dir(object)`	Gives a list of the names of the attributes of object.
`getattr(object, name)` `getattr(object, name, default)`	Returns the value of the attribute of object with the name `name`, a string. It returns `default` if there is no such attribute. If there is no default parameter, it raises an exception if there is no such attribute.
`hasattr(object, name)`	Returns true if the object has an attribute with the given name.
`setattr(object, name, value)`	Assigns the `value` to the attribute of `object` with the (string) `name`.
`vars(object)`	Returns the `__dict__` attribute of the object, i.e., returns a dictionary of attributes and their values. It raises an exception if the object does not have a `__dict__` attribute.

```
>>> class P:pass
...
>>> p=P()
>>> dir(p)
[]
>>> getattr(p,'x','none')
'none'
>>> getattr(p,'x')
Traceback (most recent call last):
  File "<stdin>", line 1, in ?
AttributeError: 'P' instance has no attribute 'x'
>>> hasattr(p,'x')
0
>>> setattr(p,'x',1)
>>> hasattr(p,'x')
1
>>> getattr(p,'x')
1
>>> vars(p)
{'x': 1}
```

Figure 6–6
Attribute functions in action.

Figure 6–6 is an example of using the attribute functions.

6.5.8   I/O Functions

Python provides one function to open files and two functions to read from the standard input. These are listed in Table 6–8. They are discussed in Chapter 7.

Table 6–8
I/O-related built-in functions.

Function	Explanation
input() input(prompt)	Writes prompt, if any, and reads a Python expression from the standard input and evaluates it. Very unsafe.

Table 6–8
I/O-related built-in functions. (Continued)

Function	Explanation

`open(filename)`
`open(filename, mode)`
`open(filename, mode,`
   `bufsize)`
	Opens a file. Discussed in Chapter 7.

`raw_input()` `raw_input(prompt)`	Writes prompt, if any, and reads input from standard input.

6.6 Wrap-Up

In this chapter we examined Python's rich collection of parameter list options for receiving positional, defaulted, extra-positional, and extra-keyword parameters. We also looked at the calls that can include positional and keyword arguments.

We looked at Python's built-in functions, with extra emphasis on the functions used in a functional programming style. We also looked at the wide variety of data types in Python that can, in certain circumstances, be used as functions.

6.7 Exercises

6.1. Create a class `Intern` with a single method, `intern(s)`, that will perform the operations of the `intern()` built-in function; for instance `x` of `Intern` and strings `s` and `t`, `x.intern(s)==s`, `x.intern(t)==t`, and if `s==t`, `x.intern(s)` is `x.intern(t)`.

6.2. Write a function `mkArray(d,val=None)` where `d` is a sequence of `n` integers that will create an `n`-dimensional array defined as follows:

- If `n==0`, it returns `val`.
- If `n>0`, it returns a list of length `d[0]`, all of whose elements are the result of calling `mkArray(d[1:],val)` for each element, for example:

```
>>> mkArray([],5)
5
>>> mkArray([2],5)
```

```
[5, 5]
>>> mkArray([2,3],5)
[[5, 5, 5], [5, 5, 5]]
```

6.3. Write a function `trans(z)` that transposes the multidimensional array `z`. Parameter `z` must be a list of lists. Let `len(z)` be `m`. Each of the lists in `z` is of the same length, `n`. The result will be a new list of length `n` of lists of length `m`, for example:

```
>>> trans([range(1,5),range(11,15)])
[[1, 11], [2, 12], [3, 13], [4, 14]]
```

Generally,

```
trans([[a0,a1,...],[b0,b1,...],...])
```

will be

```
[[a0,b0,...],[a1,b1,...],...]
```

Do not use loops in this code. Use only built-in functions and a functional programming style.

7

Input/Output

A major use for Python is writing system scripts, programs to deal with files and directories. Python is also becoming popular for Web server programming. For these uses, you need to know not only Python's built-in file operations, but also the file- and directory-related functions found in several Python modules, particularly os and os.path, which we look into in this chapter. For some of these uses, you will also need access to databases. Python has a number of modules to make databases look like dictionaries. We look into some of those modules in Chapter 10.

7.1 File Objects

File objects are used to read and write disk files. File-like objects have a wide variety of uses, including construction or decomposition of strings and communication over the Internet.

The open() built-in function opens a file and returns a file object. You can call it with one, two, or three parameters:

```
f=open(path)
f=open(path, mode)
f=open(path, mode, bufsize)
```

The path gives the path to the file: zero or more directories followed by the file name. The modes are:

- 'r'—Open for reading. This is the default.

- 'w'—Open for writing. This will replace a current file with the same name.
- 'a'—Open for appending. Data will be added to the end of a currently existing file.
- 'r+'—Open for both reading and writing.
- 'w+'—Open for both reading and writing. The file is truncated to empty.
- 'rb', 'wb', 'ab', 'r+b', 'w+b'—Open as a binary file.

The bufsize integer tells the system how large a buffer to allocate.

Every disk file has a *length*. Every open disk file has a *current file position*, from which a read will take bytes or at which a write will place bytes. The current file position will be moved past the characters read or written. When a file is open for reading, 'r', or reading and writing, 'r+', the current file position is initialized to the beginning of the file. When a file is opened for writing, 'w', or writing and reading, 'w+', the length and the current file position are both set to zero. When the file is opened for appending, 'a', the current file position is set to the end of the file.

You can perform a number of operations on a file object. These are given in Table 7–1.

Table 7–1
File operations.

Operation	Meaning
f=open(path) f=open(path, mode) f=open(path, mode, bufsize)	Open a file for input, assign f the open file object. The mode is one of 'r', 'w', 'a', 'r+', 'w+', 'rb', 'wb', 'ab', 'r+b', 'w+b'.
f.read()	Reads in the entire file and returns its contents as a string.
f.read(n)	Reads in at most n bytes of the file and returns them as a string. It returns fewer, of course, if the file has fewer than n bytes left.

Table 7–1
File operations. (Continued)

Operation	Meaning
f.readline()	Reads the next line of the file and returns it as a string. The line terminating character, "\n", is at the end of the string. It returns an empty string, "", on end of file. An empty string counts as false to while and if statements.
f.readlines()	Reads all the remaining lines and returns them in a list.
f.write(s)	Writes the characters in string s to the file.
f.writelines(L)	Writes all the strings in list L into the file. L must be a list, not a tuple. The strings in L must contain their own line termination characters to be lines in the file: The characters are written as is, without any other characters being added.
print >> f, s_1, ... s_n, print >> f, s_1, ... s_n	Writes the strings s_1 through s_n to the file f. A blank is placed between each string. A line termination character is written following the strings, unless there is a trailing comma. A trailing comma suppresses line termination.
f.close()	Closes the file. Further I/O operations on the file are not permitted.
f.flush()	Forces the buffered bytes to be written out.
f.truncate()	Resets the file length to zero.
f.truncate(n)	Sets the file size to be no more than n bytes. If n is shorter than the current length of the file, the bytes beyond position n are chopped off. The value of n should not be larger than the length of the file.

Table 7–1
File operations. (Continued)

Operation	Meaning
`f.seek(offset, from)`	Sets the current file position. This is the position from which bytes will be read or to which bytes will be written. If `from` is 0, the current position is set to `offset`. If `from` is 1, this current position is set to the current position plus `offset`. If `from` is 2, the position is set to the length of the file plus the `offset`; a negative offset leaves the file position somewhere within the file, whereas a positive position extends the file with zeros to the position requested. To extend the file, it needs to be opened with `'r+'` or `'w+'` mode (or `'r+b'` or `'w+b'`).
`f.tell()`	Returns the current file position.
`f.isatty()`	Returns true if the file is an interactive terminal.
`f.fileno()`	Returns the file descriptor number, an integer, for an open file.

When reading a text file, you will usually use the `readline()` method. It returns the next line of the file as a string. More precisely, it will read from the current file position up to the next line termination character, or to the end of the file if there is no such character. The string will include the trailing line termination character, typically '\n'. Upon end of file, it returns an empty string. Thus the usual way to read a text file is:

```
L=f.readline()
while L:
    ... #process the line
    L=f.readline()
```

The `while` loop will terminate when the string `L` is empty, which will occur upon coming to the end of file `f`. It will not terminate before, even for an empty line, since `L` will include the termination character.

For a binary file, you can use the `read(n)` method, which will return up to `n` characters of the file as a string, starting from the current file position. It will return fewer, of course, if the file has fewer than `n` characters remaining. Again, on end of file, `read()` will return an empty string. You will typically use `f.read(1)` to process the file a character at a time.

Since files can be arbitrarily large, you typically read and process a little bit at a time. Strangely, Python makes it easy to read the entire file all at once. When called for a freshly opened file object, `f.read()` will read in the entire file as a string, and `f.readlines()` will read it in as a list of lines. If you have already been reading the file, these calls will return the remaining portion, beginning at the current file position.

You can write characters into the file with the `f.write(s)` method, which will write the characters in string `s` into file `f`. This does not write a line termination character into the file. You will have to include it yourself.

Similarly, `f.writelines(L)` will write all the strings in list `L` to the file `f`. Again, no line termination is added. You will have to terminate the strings by adding termination characters yourself.

The `os` module contains many attributes and methods for manipulating files and file names. The attribute `os.linesep` contains the line termination character or characters for the system you are running on: `'\015\012'` for Windows and `'\012'` for Unix and Linux systems. You should use this to add line termination characters to lines you are writing; it will make your code more portable.

The call `f.tell()` will return the current file position of `f`. You can set the position with `f.seek(off, from)`. The parameter `from` tells whether the offset `off` is from the front of the file (`from==0`), from the current position (`from==1`), or from the end of the file (`from==2`).

The `truncate()` method is used to shorten the file. The call `f.truncate()` will set the file length to zero, but it will not set the current file position. The call `f.truncate(n)` will set the file length to integer `n`. You may have to set the current file position separately to make sure it is within the file.

Operating systems can achieve greater efficiency by performing file writes into buffers in main memory and writing the bytes out only when a buffer is full or the file is closed. The `flush()` method is used to force the buffers to be written out. This can be used for greater security, making sure that writes occur before the system crashes. It is particularly important when the file is really a stream through a pipe or socket to another program. If two programs are exchanging information, one of them must finish sending its message to the other before the other can respond.

The `close()` method will finish the file operations and write out any buffers that are necessary. The file object can no longer be used for any operations.

Python includes two rather specialized methods: The call `f.fileno()` will return the file descriptor number of open file `f` in a Posix (Unix or Linux or Windows) system. Call `f.isatty()` will return a nonzero value (i.e., true) if the file is a connection to an interactive terminal.

There are some kinds of files for which the current file position is not meaningful; for example, a socket connection to another process. The stream of bytes can only be read sequentially from an input file attached to a socket, or written sequentially to an output. You cannot seek to a position in a stream.

7.2   Execution Environment

7.2.1   Standard Input and Output

When a program runs in a Posix-compliant system, it has a standard input file open, and a standard output file, and a standard error output file. These files are available in the `sys` module as the initial values of `sys.stdin`, `sys.stdout` and `sys.stderr`. Python uses these for input and output. You can assign different files to them if you want to redirect the input or output of your program. The initial values are also stored in `sys.__stdin__`, `sys.__stdout__` and `sys.__stderr__`. You can use them to restore the initial values to `sys.stdin`, `sys.stdout`, and `sys.stderr` if you've changed them.

The built-in function `raw_input()` can be used to read a line from the standard input. You can optionally give it a prompt string, which it writes to the standard output:

```
>>> raw_input("so say it")
so say itHi
'Hi'
```

Notice that the prompt is written without trailing line termination and that the input line has its trailing line termination characters removed, *unlike* the file `readline()` method.

The built-in function `input()` is like, `raw_input()`, except that it evaluates the input as a Python expression; for example:

```
>>> input('expression: ')
expression: 1+2*3
7
>>> x=5
>>> input('expression: ')
expression: x**2
25
```

Be very careful with `input()`. The expression that a user puts in can do a lot of damage. For example, the `os` module has a function, `system(command)`, that creates a shell program and has it execute the *command* string. Here's a test:

```
>>> input('expression: ')
expression: os.system('echo Hello')
Hello
0
```

The `Hello` comes from the shell program. The `0` indicates the successful completion of the shell. What do you think would have happened if we had typed in `os.system('rm -r /')` to a Linux system? **No! Do not try this!**

7.2.2   Command Line Parameters

When you run a Python script, you can provide it with a list of command line parameters. These strings are available in list `argv` of the `sys` module: `sys.argv`. The first element, `sys.argv[0]`, is the name of the program being executed. Figure 7–1 shows a brief script, `argv.py`, that writes out its command line parameters. Here is an example run:

```
C:>python argv.py a b c d e f
['argv.py', 'a', 'b', 'c', 'd', 'e', 'f']
```

```
import sys
print sys.argv
```

Figure 7–1
argv.py.

7.2.3 Environment Variables

A program runs with a set of environment variables available. The environment variables have string names and string values. They are available in the dictionary `environ` in module `os`. Figure 7–2 shows a script, `environ.py`, that writes out the environment variables and their values. The following is a small part of what it printed out on my notebook:

```
C:>python environ.py
OS: Windows_NT
OS2LIBPATH: C:\WINNT\system32\os2\dll;
NUMBER_OF_PROCESSORS: 1
PROCESSOR_ARCHITECTURE: x86
SYSTEMDRIVE: C:
SYSTEMROOT: C:\WINNT
...
```

Both the names and the values are strings in `os.environ`. You can look up the value associated with name `k` using `os.environ[k]` or `os.environ.get(k)`.

You can also assign new values to environment variables or create new environment variables with a simple subscripted assignment:

```
os.environ[k]=v
```

These new environment variables and values are available to any subprocess you create. You can, for example, put a new directory on the operating system's search path with:

```
os.environ['PATH']=os.environ['PATH']+ \
    os.pathsep+dir
```

```
import os
for k in os.environ.keys():
    print k+":",os.environ[k]
```

Figure 7–2
environ.py.

The path to the new directory is the value of variable `dir`. The attribute `os.pathsep` is the string that separates directory paths in the PATH string, ":" on Linux and Unix and ";" on Windows.

Module `os` contains strings `os.curdir` and `os.pardir`, which are used to refer to the current and the parent directories, "." and "..". Using these named strings makes your code more system-independent.

7.3   Other Useful Modules

7.3.1   File Systems

The file systems under different operating systems have many things in common, and they have many differences. Python tries to make it easy to write both system-independent code and code that makes use of the facilities of particular systems. You can aim for portability or for efficiency. Here I concentrate on Unix/Linux and Windows.

The facilities you need are in various standard modules, but especially in modules `os` and `os.path`. Just import `os` and you will get both.

Generally, a filing system has text (or data) files and directories. The files and directories are contained in directories and are named with identifier strings. A path is an optionally empty sequence of directory names followed by a final file or directory name. The names along the path are separated by separator characters (or strings) that vary among the systems. Unix and Linux use forward slashes, "/", to separate the names along a path. Windows uses a backslash, "\".

There is typically a "current directory" that a program is executing in. Paths may be relative, starting at the current directory, or absolute, starting at a root of the file system. In Unix and Linux, the entire filing system is a single tree. The root is indicated by a single slash, "/". Paths that do not begin with a slash are relative.

In Windows, each disk is referred to by a letter (indicated by, e.g., `c:`) and may be viewed as a separate filing system. There is a current directory on each disk, and a current disk. The root directory on disk "c" is written `c:\`. The root directory on the current disk may be written "\". An absolute path on disk `c` begins `c:\`. A relative path on a disk begins `c:`*name* or *name*.

On Unix and Linux systems, the file names are case-sensitive. On Windows systems, they are not.

On Unix and Linux, the directory structure forms a tree, but regular files may be in more than one directory or in the same directory more than once with different names. Moreover, there is a special kind of file, a *symbolic link*, that contains a path to another directory or file. It is used to allow directories to be accessed as if they are contained in more than one directory.

7.3.2   os and os.path Modules

Table 7–2 shows the functions available in the `os.path` module. These manipulate and test paths. Table 7–3 shows some of the functions and attributes available in the `os` module. They manipulate directories and files. Examples of the operation of some of the functions as shown in Figure 7–3.

Table 7–2
Path manipulation in module os.path.

Function	Explanation
`dirname(path)`	Returns the directory part of the path: all of the path up to, but not including, the final name.
`basename(path)`	Returns the basename of the file, the last name on the path.
`split(path)`	Returns tuple `(dirname(path),` `basename(path))`
`splitext(path)`	Returns tuple `(path up to extension,` `extension)` The `extension` is the final dot-identifier of the base file name, usually used to tell the type of the file's contents.
`splitdrive(path)`	Returns tuple `(drive, rest of path)` For Windows, splits the drive part from the rest of the path.
`isabs(path)`	Returns true if the path is an absolute path (starting with "/" for Unix/Linux or "\" for Windows).

Table 7–2
Path manipulation in module os.path. (Continued)

Function	Explanation
`abspath(path)`	Converts path into an absolute path. It edits out backtracking sequences, for example, `id/..` on Linux.
`expanduser(path)`	Linux/Unix: Replaces an initial `~username` with the absolute path to the user's home directory.
`expandvars(path)`	Linux/Unix: Replaces `$envvar` and `${envvar}` in the path with the value of the environment variable `envvar`.
`normcase(path)`	In Windows, converts the characters in a path name into lowercase and converts forward slashes to backslashes. In Unix/Linux, returns the path unchanged.
`join(path1,` `    path2,...)`	Concatenates the paths into a single path, inserting separators ("/" or "\") where necessary.
`exists(path)`	Returns true if the path leads to a file.
`isdir(path)`	Tests whether the file is a directory.
`isfile(path)`	Tests whether the file is a normal file.
`islink(path)`	Tests whether the file is a symbolic link (Unix/Linux).
`getsize(path)`	Gives the size of a file.

Table 7–2
Path manipulation in module os.path. (Continued)

Function	Explanation
`getatime(path)`	Gives the time of last access of a file. This is a number, e.g., the number of seconds since the beginning of the day Jan. 1, 1970. See module `time` for conversion functions.
`getmtime(path)`	Gives the time of last modification of a file. This is a number, e.g., the number of seconds since the beginning of the day Jan. 1, 1970. See module `time` for conversion functions.
`samefile(path1, path2)`	Linux/Unix: Tests whether two paths lead to the same file.
`os.path.walk( path, visitorfunction, arg)`	Applies the `visitorfunction` to each directory tree rooted in the directory specified by `path`. The object specified by `arg` is passed to `visitorfunction` at each call, allowing it to accumulate information. The text gives more information.

Table 7–3
File and directory operations in module os.

Function or Variable	Explanation
`listdir(path)`	Yields a list of the base file names in the directory indicated by `path`.
`environ`	A dictionary-like object mapping environment variable, names (strings) into their values (also strings).
`os.sep`	Separates directories and files in a path; "/" on Linux and Unix, "\" on Windows.

Table 7–3
File and directory operations in module os. (Continued)

Function or Variable	Explanation
os.pathsep	Separates directory paths in the PATH environment variable; ":" on Linux and Unix and ";" on Windows. The PATH variable is used by the operating system to search for programs it is told to execute.
os.curdir	The string used by the operating system to refer to the current directory, ".", on Unix/Linux and Windows.
os.pardir	The string used by the operating system to refer to the parent directory, "..", on Unix/Linux and Windows.
W_OK R_OK X_OK F_OK	Used as a mode parameter for access(). W_OK–Is it okay to write? R_OK–Is it okay to read? X_OK–Is it okay to execute? F_OK–Does the file exist?
access(*path*, *mode*)	Checks whether a file or directory is accessible in the indicated mode. The mode is constructed by adding or *OR*ing together one or more of: W_OK, R_OK, X_OK, F_OK.
getcwd()	Returns a path to the current working directory.
mkdir(*path_to_new*)	Creates a directory.
chdir(*path_to_new_cwd*)	Changes the current working directory.
link(*srcfile*, *dst*)	Unix/Linux: Creates a link at the path dst to the file srcfile.

Table 7–3
File and directory operations in module os. (Continued)

Function or Variable	Explanation
symlink(*srcfile,dst*)	Unix/Linux: Creates a symbolic link at the path dst to the file or directory srcfile.
readlink(path)	Unix/Linux: Returns the absolute path to which the symbolic link at path points.
rename(*src,dst*)	Renames or moves the file indicated by the path src to the path dst.
remove(*path*) unlink(*path*)	Removes the file indicated by path.
rmdir(*path*)	Removes the empty directory indicated by path.
chmod(*path,* *permissions*)	Changes the permissions of the file or directory.
chown(*path, uid, gid*)	Changes the owner of the file or directory.
f=popen(*command*) f=popen(*command,mode*)	Runs the command (a string) as a separate process and returns a file that can be used to read its standard output (by default, or if mode is 'r') or to write text to the process's standard input (if mode is 'w').
stat(path)	Returns a tuple of information about a file. Module stat has constants and functions for analyzing the tuple.

```
>>> from os import *
>>> from os.path import *
>>> isabs("argv.py")
0
>>> abspath("argv.py")
'C:\\PPP\\argv.py'
>>> a=abspath("argv.py")
>>> isabs(a)
1
>>> dirname(a)
'C:\\PPP'
>>> basename(a)
'argv.py'
>>> split(a)
('C:\\PPP', 'argv.py')
>>> splitext(a)
('C:\\PPP\\argv', '.py')
>>> splitdrive(a)
('C:', '\\PPP\\argv.py')
>>> exists(a)
1
>>> isdir(a)
0
>>> isfile(a)
1

>>> islink(a)
0
>>> getsize(a)
32
>>> getatime(a)
981389526
>>> getmtime(a)
981323582
>>> listdir('.')
['argv.py', 'environ.py']
>>> mkdir('xxx')
>>> rename('argv.py',r'xxx\argv.py')
>>> listdir('.')
['environ.py', 'xxx']
>>> listdir('xxx')
['argv.py']
>>> rename(r'xxx\argv.py','argv.py')
>>> rmdir('xxx')
>>> listdir('.')
['argv.py', 'environ.py']
```

Figure 7–3
Examples of some os and os.path functions.

7.3.3   Function os.path.walk

The `walk()` function in module `os.path` has a functional programming flavor. It applies a function to every directory in a directory tree. It also resembles the *internal iterator* object-oriented design pattern.

You call `os.path.walk()` as follows:

```
os.path.walk(path, visitorfunction, arg)
```

Here `path` leads to the directory at the root of the directory subtree you wish to walk over. The `visitorfunction` will be called at each directory encountered during the walk. Object `arg` is an argument to be supplied to the function at each call. You typically make `arg` a mutable object so you can use it to accumulate information.

The form of the `visitorfunction` is:

```
def visitorfunction(arg,dirname,basenames):...
```

Here *arg* is the `arg` object passed into `walk`. The string *dirname* is the path to the directory. The list *basenames* contains base file names of the files and subdirectories in the directory. The `visitor` function is called before `walk` recurses into the subdirectories. You can remove subdirectory names from consideration by removing them from the *basenames* list.

7.3.4   File Copying

Copying a file can be as simple as this:

```
>>> f=open(src)
>>> g=open(dst,'w')
>>> g.write(f.read())
>>> f.close()
>>> g.close()
```

But Python provides the `shutil` module to make it even easier: `shutil.copyfile(src,dst)` or `shutil.copy(src,dst)`.

There are some subtle differences in how the two functions set file permissions. Module `shutil` contains several other useful functions as well, but it would require too lengthy a digression to discuss them here.

7.3.5   Temporary Files

Frequently you need to create temporary files, and it is important that their names not collide. The module `tempfile` exists to make the creation of unique temporary file names easier. The `mktemp()` function gives you a path to a temporary file with a new name. It will be in a directory that exists specifically for temporary files:

```
name=tempfile.mktemp()
name=tempfile.mktemp(suffix)
```

If you pass a suffix string, it appends that string to the unique file name. If, for example, you were generating a Python source file, you would use `mktemp('.py')`.

7.4 Wrap-Up

Here we looked into some of Python's facilities for creating, reading, writing, and manipulating files and directories. You will use these facilities extensively when you write system scripts. Files themselves are built into the Python system with operations for reading and writing by text lines or by characters, as well as some random access operations.

The `sys` module gives you access to the standard input and output and the command line arguments. The `os` library module gives you access to the environment variables and some system-specific data. It gives you the ability to manipulate directories and the ability to create subprocesses. The `os.path` module provides functions to manipulate the string paths to files and to get some information about the files, for example, the time the file was last modified. The `os.path.walk()` function allows you to process a directory recursively without having to write the recursive calls yourself. The `shutil` module has functions for file copying, and the `tempfile` module has functions for creating temporary files.

7.5 Exercises

7.1. Write an `echo` program that will write out its command line arguments.

7.2. Do a revised version of the `word count` program (Figure 2–4). It is to be given a list of file names on its command line. It will write out the numbers of characters, words, and lines in each file followed by the file names, one file per line, and then their sum on a final line.

7.3. Write a program that converts a text file's line termination characters to those of the system it is running on.

7.4. How is the `os.path.walk()` function like an internal iterator?

7.5. Write a program to recursively copy a directory.

7.6. Sometimes you have a copy of a file in more than one directory. It would be nice to find all the places you have it and determine which place has the most recent copy.

Write a program that will be given a list of directories. It will recursively search each directory. For each file name it finds, it will build a list of occurrences of the file name. At the end, it will write out a sorted list of the file names, and with each name, it will list the absolute paths to each file with that name and the time of last modification of the file. The paths and times of modification will be sorted by most recent modification first. See the `sort()` method for lists in Chapter 8, Section 8.3.1.

8

Sequences

Python has a number of sophisticated data types built into the language. Other object-oriented languages provide a smaller collection of built-in types, but make up for that by providing them in the standard libraries. Where the best place is to draw the line between built-in and library types is an open question; Python comes down on the side of more built-in types.

Python has the built-in container types: lists, tuples, and dictionaries, as well as strings and files that are arguably containers. The lists, tuples, and dictionaries can contain any other type of data object, whereas strings contain characters. Files at their lowest level contain characters, but can be used to implement databases that can contain other kinds of objects. (See Chapter 10, Section 10.3.)

The lists, tuples, and strings in Python are sequences, and they share a number of operations. The essence of a sequence in Python is that the elements have positions. The N elements in a sequence are in positions $0, 1, ..., N-1$. You can access the ith element of a sequence x by subscripting, x[i].

Here we look at the shared operations on sequences and look in detail at lists and tuples. Strings merit a chapter of their own, Chapter 9. Dictionaries are the subject of Chapter 10. Files have already been discussed in Chapter 7, although the use of files as simple, dictionary-like databases is covered in Chapter 10.

8.1   Common Sequence Operations

Some operations are common to all sequences–lists, tuples, and strings. They are shown in Table 8–1.

Table 8–1
Common sequence operators.

Operation	Explanation

`()`
`(e,)`
`(e_0, e_1, ..., e_{n-1})`
`(e_0, e_1, ..., e_{n-1},)`
	Tuple display. Creates a tuple containing the values of the expressions.

`[]`
`[e_0, e_1, ..., e_{n-1}]`
`[e_0, e_1, ..., e_{n-1},]`
	List display. Creates a list containing the values of the expressions.

`[e for ...]`	List comprehension. Creates a list whose initial contents are the values of the expression `e` for all values generated by the `for` and `if` phrases following. The syntax of list comprehensions is shown in Table 8–3.
`s + t`	Concatenation of sequences `s` and `t`, which must be the same type of sequence.
`s * n` `n * s`	`n` copies of sequence `s` concatenated together, where `n` is an integer.
`len(s)`	Length of the sequence `s`.
`min(s)`	The minimum element in the sequence.
`max(s)`	The maximum element in the sequence.

Table 8–1
Common sequence operators. (Continued)

Operation	Explanation
`s[i]`	The jth element of sequence `s`, where: `-len(s) <= i < len(s)`, and `j = i`, if `i>=0` `j = len(s)+i`, if `i<0`. It raises an `IndexError` if `i` is invalid. If `s` is a string, `s[i]` is a string of length one.

`s[i:j]`
`s[:j]`
`s[i:]`
`s[:]`
	The elements of `s` from element `m` up to but not including element `n`, where:
	`m = i`, if `i>=0`
	`m = len(s)+i`, if `i<0`
	`n = j`, if `j>=0`
	`n = len(s)+j`, if `j<0`.
	If `n<=m`, it yields an empty sequence.
	It does *not* raise an exception if `i` or `j` is invalid.
	If `i` is omitted, it defaults to `0`. If `j` is omitted, it defaults to `len(s)`.

`range(stop)`
`range(start, stop)`
`range(start, stop, step)`
	Returns a list of integers, `[start, start+step, start+2*step, ...]` up or down to but not including `stop`. `start` defaults to `0` and `step` defaults to `1`.

`cmp(s,t)`	Where `s` and `t` are the same type of sequence, compares the contents of the sequences `s` and `t` lexicographically, i.e., the comparison proceeds left to right, applying `cmp()` to the corresponding elements of `s` and `t` as long as the components are equal, and returns the results of the last element compare. If all elements are equal, returns `0`.

Table 8–1
Common sequence operators. (Continued)

Operation	Explanation
s < t s <= t s == t s != t s <> t s > t s >= t	For built-in sequences, these tests use cmp(s,t). How you can define them for your own sequence-like data types is discussed in Chapter 14 and Chapter 15.
s is t s is not t	Tests whether the two references are to the same object.
x in s x not in s	Tests whether object x is in sequence s. If s is a string, x must be a string of length one.
$x_0, x_1, \ldots, x_{n-1}$ = s	Unpacking, assigns x_i=s[i] for 0<=i<n where len(s)==n.

8.1.1   Indexing and Slicing

Indexing involves subscripting a sequence with a single expression, for example, s[i], accessing the single element of s at position i. Slicing involves providing two subscripts and accessing the elements between their positions:

```
>>> s=range(10)
>>> s[3]
3
>>> s[3:7]
[3, 4, 5, 6]
```

The slicing appears to be derived at least indirectly from the Icon programming language. My *Icon Programming Language Handbook* is available in PDF through the toolsofcomputing.com Web site. Slicing a sequence s from positions i to j is written as s[i:j]. You are selecting the elements from element i up to, but not including, element j. (Although, of course, when j is equal to the length of the sequence, technically there is no element j.)

The way to visualize the elements selected is to view the index positions as being between the elements. These are shown in Figure 8–1 for the string `spam`. Position zero is at the left, in front of the first character of the string `spam`, and the ascending integers are between successive pairs of characters. The length of the string corresponds to the position just beyond the right end of the string. The positions are also numbered –1, –2,..., from position -1 between the last two characters and moving toward the left.

In this numbering scheme, the leftmost position of a sequence has two numbers–*0* and the negative of the length of the sequence–and all the positions between elements have two numbers. But the position to the right of the rightmost element has only one number, equal to the length of the sequence.

When you subscript a sequence, `x[i]`, you are selecting the element immediately to the right of position `i`. When you slice a sequence, `x[i:j]`, all the elements between positions `i` and `j` are selected. In Python, if position `j` is to the left of position `i`, the sequence is considered to be empty. For example, using Figure 8–1:

```
>>> food="spam"
>>> food[0]
's'
>>> food[-1]
'm'
>>> food[1:-1]
'pa'
```

You can omit the first or second position in the slicing: `x[:j]`, `x[i:]` and `x[:]`. The positions default to the beginning and end of the

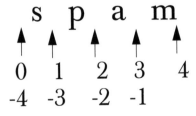

Figure 8–1
Index positions for slicing.

string. An invalid index will default to the closer of the beginning or
end of a sequence:

```
>>> x=[1]
>>> x[0:2]
[1]
>>> x[-10:2]
[1]
>>> x[20:22]
[]
```

8.1.2   Relational Operators and Comparisons

If you are interested in determining whether two sequences are the
same object or not, use the `is` and `is not` operators:

```
x is y
x is not y
```

You can also compare sequences with relational operators such as
`<` and `==`. All the relational operators use the built-in function `cmp(x,y)`,
which returns negative if `x` is less than `y`, zero if they are equal, and positive if `x` is greater than `y`. The `cmp()` function in Python compares
sequences lexicographically. Comparison of two sequences of the same
type proceeds from left to right, comparing their elements. As soon as
the elements are unequal, it can stop and report the results of the last
compare. If all the elements are equal, the sequences are equal. Two
sequences of different types are not equal.

```
>>> cmp([1,1],[1,0])
1
>>> cmp([1,1],[1,2])
-1
>>> cmp((1,1),(1,1))
0
>>> cmp((1,1),[1,1])
1
>>> cmp([1,1],[1,1])
0
>>> cmp([1,1],(1,1))
-1
```

If the sequences themselves contain sequences, those sequences
are compared in the same way.

```
>>> cmp([1,(1,1)],[1,(1,0)])
1
>>> cmp([1,(1,1)],[1,(1,2)])
-1
```

In Python versions prior to Python2, sequences were compared by a recursive function. It would run out of stack space and crash if the sequences contained themselves. With Python2, the comparison uses a better algorithm and can take recursive sequences. In this example, we create a list `x` composed of two elements, itself and one; and a list `y` composed of two elements, itself and one. The comparison `cmp(x,y)` terminates and returns zero, indicating that the lists are equal:

```
>>> x=[None,1]
>>> x[0]=x
>>> x
[[...], 1]
>>> y=[None,1]
>>> y[0]=y
>>> cmp(x,y)
0
```

8.1.3 Testing Contents

You can test whether a sequence contains an element with the `in` and `not in` operators. Most other languages do not provide these operators. Instead of `x in s`, you would probably call a function to do the check, or call a function to return the index of the `x` in sequence `s` and see if the value returned is a special, "not present" indication.

8.1.4 Critique of the Common Operations

The common operations across all sequences in Python represent an example of good design. The consistency makes the operations easy to remember. It is an aspect of the Principle of Least Astonishment, that elements of a design should fit people's expectations.

You may be wondering why you would wish to compare two lists lexicographically. You might not want to compare lists, but the `cmp()` function and relational operators are designed for strings and tuples. Their applicability to lists gives consistency. Obviously, you want lexicographical comparison of strings; many algorithms depend on it. Tuples themselves are used for keys in dictionaries, relational databases, and other associative data structures. As is the case with strings, comparison of their contents is required by the algorithms.

8.2   Tuples

You can create tuples with tuple displays:

$(e_0, e_1, \ldots e_{n-1})$

or

$(e_0, e_1, \ldots e_{n-1},)$ (Note the trailing comma.)

where each e_i is an expression. This could be ambiguous if you want a tuple of only one element, since `(e)` is also what you write for a parenthesized subexpression. In that case, you include a trailing comma and write `(e,)`. Without the comma, you would get the value of `e`.

There are contexts other than tuple displays for which you can create a tuple by listing its contents. On the right side of an assignment statement, for example:

`a,b=b,a`

In a dictionary subscript, for example:

`d[a,b]`

And in a return statement, for example:

`return height, width`

Again, in those contexts you can create a single-element tuple simply by following an expression with a comma. The only way to get an empty tuple is by writing an empty pair of parentheses, `()`.

Tuples differ from lists in that they are immutable. You cannot change the contents of a tuple once it has been created. If you cannot change it, what good is it? A major use for tuples is as keys in dictionaries. You want to be able to look things up in the dictionary by the contents of the key. With hash table dictionaries, that means the contents better not change, because if they did, the look-up wouldn't know where in the dictionary to start looking any more. Similarly, a binary search tree would become corrupted if a key changed. Tuples are marginally more efficient than lists, but lists are more flexible.

8.3   Lists

Lists are mutable sequences, unlike both tuples and strings. Therefore they have a number of operations beyond the common sequence operations. Table 8–2 shows the extra list operations.

8.3.1 Additional List Operations

With lists, you can assign to an element or a slice. When you assign to an element, you replace the current contents. When you assign to a slice, you must assign a list that replaces the slice. If the slice is an empty slice, assignment will insert the list. You can assign to an empty slice at the end of a list to extend it, for example:

```
>>> x
[1]
>>> x[1:1]=[2]
>>> x
[1, 2]
```

You can remove an element or a slice of a list with the `del` statement:

```
del L[i]
del L[i:j]
```

Other ways to add elements to a list include the methods `append()`, `extend()`, and `insert()`. Lists in Python have a number of methods. Method `L.append(x)` places x at the end of the list L. Method `L.extend(x)` splices the list x at the end of L. Method `L.insert(i,x)` inserts x at position i in list L. All elements of L at positions i or above are moved up one.

There are two methods to search lists. The method `L.index(x)` finds the first occurrence of x in list L. It will raise a `ValueError` exception if x isn't present. The method `L.count(x)` will count and return the number of occurrences of x in list L. If you are only interested in whether the number is zero or greater than zero, `x in L` will usually be faster.

There are two methods to remove elements from a list. The method `L.pop(i)` removes and returns the ith element of list L. All elements at positions greater than i are moved down one. When you omit the parameter i, `L.pop()` removes and returns the last element of list L.

The method `L.remove(x)` finds and removes the first occurrence of x in L. It is equivalent to the statement `del L[L.index(x)]`. It will raise an exception if x isn't present.

There are two methods that reorder lists. `L.reverse()` reverses the order of elements in list L. It doesn't return a value; it just modifies L.

Table 8–2
Additional list operations and methods.

Method	Description

`L[i]=x`	Replaces the jth element of list `L`, where `-len(L) <= i < len(L)`, and
	    $j = i$, if `i>=0`
	    $j = len(L)+i$, if `i<0`.

`L[i:j]=X`	Replaces the elements of `L` from element m up to but not including element n with list `X`, where
	    $m = i$, if `i>=0`
	    $m = len(L)+i$, if `i<0`
	    $n = j$, if `j>=0`
	    $n = len(L)+j$, if `j<0`.
	If `n<=m`, sequence `X` is spliced into list `L` at position m.
	If `i==len(L)`, `X` is concatenated onto the end of `L`.
	If `i` is omitted, it defaults to `0`. If `j` is omitted, it defaults to `len(L)`.

`del L[i]`	Deletes the jth element of list `L`, where `-len(L) <= i < len(L)`, and
	    $j = i$, if `i>=0`
	    $j = len(L)+i$, if `i<0`

`del L[i:j]`	Deletes the elements of `L` from element m up to but not including element n, where
	    $m = i$, if `i>=0`
	    $m = len(L)+i$, if `i<0`
	    $n = j$, if `j>=0`
	    $n = len(L)+j$, if `j<0`.
	If `i` is omitted, it defaults to `0`. If `j` is omitted, it defaults to `len(L)`.

`L.append(x)`	Places element `x` at the end of the list `L`, increasing the length of `L` by one. `L.append(x)` is equivalent to `L[len(L):]=[x]`.

Table 8–2
Additional list operations and methods. (Continued)

Method	Description
`L.extend(x)`	Places the list of elements x at the end of the list L, increasing the length of L by the length of x. `L.extend(x)` is equivalent to `L[len(L):]=x`.
`L.insert (i, x)`	Inserts item x at position i in list L. All items in L at positions i and above are moved to the right, i.e., their indices increase by one. `L.insert(len(L),x)` is equivalent to `L.append(x)`.
`L.pop()` `L.pop(i)`	Removes and returns an item from the list. If an index, i, is provided, `pop()` removes and returns the item at that position. If no index is provided, it removes and returns the last item, i.e., the index defaults to `-1`.
`L.remove(x)`	Removes the first item in L that is equal to x. It raises a `ValueError` exception if x doesn't occur in L.
`L.count(x)`	Counts the number of items in L that are equal to x.
`L.index(x)`	Returns the index of the first item in L that is equal to x. It raises a `ValueError` exception if x doesn't occur in L.
`L.reverse()`	Reverses the order of the elements of the list L in place.
`L.sort()` `L.sort(cmpfn)`	Sorts the elements of the list L in place into nondecreasing order. Function `cmpfn(x,y)` is called to compare x and y and return a negative integer if x precedes y in the desired ordering, 0 if they are to be considered equal, and a positive integer if x follows y. To sort into descending order, use: `def cmpfn(x, y): return -cmp(x,y)`

The method `L.sort()` sorts the elements of L into ascending order. As with `reverse()`, it doesn't return a value; it just modifies L.

8.3.2   Implementing Stacks and Queues

You can implement a stack on list `L` by using `L.append(x)` to push `x` on the stack, and using `x=L.pop()` to pop the top element of the stack into `x`.

You can implement a FIFO queue by using `L.append(x)` to enqueue `x` on `L`, and `x=L.pop(0)` to dequeue `x` from `L`. Or if you prefer, you can use `L.insert(0,x)` to enqueue and `L.pop()` to dequeue.

8.3.3   Example: Sestina Pattern Generator

As an example of permuting the elements of a list, consider sestinas. A sestina is a kind of poem that has six stanzas of six lines each. The six words that end the lines of stanza one also end the lines of the other stanzas, but are in a different order. The reordering is that the words ending lines 1 2 3 4 5 6 in one stanza will end lines 6 1 5 2 4 3 in the next. See Figure 8–2. There is usually a final three-line stanza, the envoi, which contains all six words, but we won't consider that here.

The code in Figure 8–3 is a generator for sestina patterns. When it is run with a list of six words on the command line, it writes out six lines containing the six words. Each line shows the order of end words in the corresponding stanza. For example, the end words of a sestina by Elizabeth Bishop give this output:

```
house grandmother child stove almanac tears
tears house almanac grandmother stove child
child tears stove house grandmother almanac
almanac child grandmother tears house stove
stove almanac house child tears grandmother
grandmother stove tears almanac child house
```

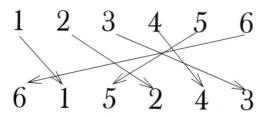

Figure 8–2
Reordering of end words in a sestina.

```
def shift(L):
    for i in range(0,len(L),2):
        L.insert(i,L[-1])
        del L[-1]
    return L
class SestinaGen:
    def __init__(self,L):
        self.firstL=L[:]
        self.L=L[:]
        self.more=1
    def hasMoreStanzas(self):
        return self.more
    def nextStanza(self):
        if not self.more: raise IndexError
        x=self.L[:]
        self.L=shift(self.L)
        self.more = self.L != self.firstL
        return x
import sys
if __name__=='__main__':
    L=sys.argv[1:]
    gen=SestinaGen(L)
    while gen.hasMoreStanzas():
        L=gen.nextStanza()
        for j in L: print j,
        print
```

Figure 8–3
Sestina generator.

The work of reordering the words is done in the function shift(). Function shift() takes a list L and reorders the words in it. It has been written to work for any length list of words, not just six. The underlying rule is that the words taken successively from the end of the list are to be placed in the even-numbered positions of the result list.

The body of shift() is a for loop that selects each even-numbered position i, inserts the last word of the list there, and then deletes the last word.

The rest of Sestina.py handles reading the end words from the command line and writing out the end words for each stanza, one stanza per line. The line:

```
if __name__=='__main__':
```

tests to see if the file is being run as a main program. The built-in variable __name__ is the name of the code that is running. If the code is in a module being imported, __name__ will have the name of the module. If the code is being run as a script, it will have the value '__main__'.

Assuming it is being run as a script, the line `L=sys.argv[1:]`gets the list of command line arguments except for the very first, which is the name of the program being run. We just assume the remaining arguments are the words to permute.

The class `SestinaGen` is a kind of external iterator. (See Section 5.4.3.) When created, it saves a copy of the list in `self.firstL`, and puts another copy in `self.L`.

Each time the `nextStanza()` method is called, it returns the list of end words for the next stanza. When `nextStanza()` method calls `shift()` to permute `self.L` into the list of end words for the following stanza, it compares `L` against `firstL` to see if there are more stanzas to generate. It saves the fact that there are more stanzas in attribute `self.more`. The method `hasMoreStanzas()` simply returns the value of `self.more`.

8.3.4 Constructing Lists

Lists can be constructed with list displays or with list comprehensions. The form of a list display is zero or more expressions in brackets. For example:

```
>>> []
[]
>>> [1]
[1]
>>> [1,]
[1]
>>> [1,2]
[1, 2]
```

Notice that the last expression in the list can be followed by a comma.

A list comprehension (the term comes from functional programming languages) is also contained in brackets. A list comprehension describes the contents of a list. It puts in a single expression the equivalent of a nest of `for` loops and `if` statements, appending elements to the list being constructed.

A list comprehension consists of a single expression followed by a list iterator. The list iterator is composed of two kinds of elements:

```
for varlist in sequence
```

and

```
if expression
```

The first of the elements in a list iterator must be a `for`. Thereafter they can be `for`s and `if`s in any order. The syntax is shown in greater detail in Table 8–3.

The behavior of a list comprehension is as if it were written as a group of nested `for` and `if` statements. For example, the following list comprehension will produce a list of tuples that represent Pythagorean triangles with integral sides *(x,y,z)*, where $1 \le x \le y \le 100$ and $z^2 = x^2 + y^2$:

```
>>> x=[ (x,y,z) for x in xrange(1,100) \
    for y in xrange(x,100) \
        for z in xrange(y,x+y) if z*z==x*x+y*y]
```

Table 8–3
List displays and comprehensions.

Syntax	Explanation

`[ ]`
`[ e`$_0$`, e`$_1$`, ..., e`$_{n-1}$` ]`
`[ e`$_0$`, e`$_1$`, ..., e`$_{n-1}$`, ]`
	A `list display` creates a list by listing expressions that compute the initial contents. It may be empty. It may have one or more expressions separated by commas. It may have a trailing comma, but only if it contains at least one expression.

`[ e for vars in e ... ]`	A `list comprehension` consists of an expression followed by a `for` iterator, which is followed by zero or more additional list iterators. List iterators are *for iterators* or *list ifs*.
`for vars in e`	The `for iterator` (`forIter`) looks like the header of a `for` statement, but it does not terminate with a colon.
`if expr`	A `list if` is like an `if` statement header, but is not terminated with a colon.

The assignment of the list comprehension is equivalent to:

```
L=[]
for x in xrange(1,100):
    for y in xrange(x,100):
        for z in xrange(y,x+y):
            if z*z==x*x+y*y:
                L.append((x,y,z))
x=L
```

The built-in function `range()` gives lists of integers. You can use that to create a list of a certain length; for example, `range(n)` would give you a list of length `n`. If you don't want the elements of the list initialized, you can use the replication operator, `[None]*n`. For example:

```
>>> [None]*5
[None, None, None, None, None]
```

Or you can use a list comprehension,

```
[None for i in xrange(n)].
```

For example:

```
>>> [None for i in xrange(5)]
[None, None, None, None, None]
```

8.3.5   Critique of Lists

Many languages provide arrays and then have their libraries implement lists using the arrays. Since Python's lists subsume arrays, Python can do without the arrays and simply use lists.

Considering the operations available on lists, it's a bit unfortunate that Python has no operator or method to give you the index without raising an exception if the item is not present. Frequently, you need to know the position of an item if it is present. For strings, there are methods to give you the position of a substring: `index()` raises an exception if one string is not a substring of the other, and `find()` returns a special value to indicate the absence. For lists, there is only one method, `index()`, that raises an exception if the element is not present. I frequently find myself writing something like:

```
if x in S:
    i=S.index(x)
    ...
```

which, alas, requires searching the sequence s twice. It would be nice to be able to write:

```
i=S.find(x) #alas, not available
if i!=NotPresent:
    ...
```

The presence of the `find()` method for strings, but not for lists, is an example of inconsistency across sequence types.

8.4 Wrap-Up

In this chapter we discussed the common operations of Python's sequence types: lists, tuples, and strings. Tuples are immutable, whereas the contents of lists can change. We examined lists in detail, including the methods available for lists that are not available for tuples. The list methods allow lists to be used as stacks, queues, and sets.

We gave an example of an iterator, SestinaGen, that generates lists of end words for sestina stanzas. We also looked at list comprehensions, ways to specify succinctly the contents of lists being created.

8.5 Exercises

8.1. Write a version of SestinaGen that will generate not lists of end words, but another external generator that will generate the end words with the methods `hasMoreEndWords()` and `nextEndWord()`. It can be used as follows:

```
gen=SestinaGen(L)
while gen.hasMoreStanzas():
    S=gen.nextStanza()
    while S.hasMoreEndWords():
      print S.nextEndWord(),
    print
```

8.2. What is the difference in speed between using the front of a list as the top of a stack, or using the end of the list as stack sizes grow large?

9

Strings

String processing is a particular strength of Python. In this chapter, we first examine strings themselves. For convenience, they may be written in any of several ways. You can choose whether to use conventional, byte-sized characters, or Unicode.

A large number of operators and built-in functions apply to or produce strings. Strings themselves have a large collection of methods for searching and editing. The % operator is especially powerful for string editing, using a string as a template and inserting edited values from your program into it.

We include as an example the splitter class, a kind of external *iterator* that can be cascaded as *decorators* and that uses the *state* pattern in its implementation.

9.1 String Literals

You can write string literals in any of several ways. You can enclose strings in single quotes or in double quotes as long as they occur on one line:

```
>>> 'aa'
'aa'
>>> "bb"
'bb'
```

It is permissible to continue the line by using a backslash as the last character on the line:

```
>>> 'b\
... b'
'bb'
```

Notice that the newline is not included in the string in this case. More generally, string literals have the forms shown in Figure 9–1.

A string can be surrounded by single or double quotes or by triple single quotes or triple double quotes. A string must begin and end with the same kind of quotes. The triple quotes allow the string to extend across multiple lines, whereas a single quote character forces the string to be completed on the same line on which it begins. The newlines in the multiline string are considered part of the string, for example:

```
>>> """<head>
... <title>Test page</title>
... </head>
... """
'<head>\012<title>Test page</title>\012</head>\012'
```

The backslash is an *incorporation* character, also known as an *escape* character. The backslash and the character(s) following it are referred to as an escape sequence. Within strings, except for "raw strings," the backslash character combined with certain other characters will be replaced by a single character. See Table 9–1.

```
' chars '                    u' chars '
" chars "                    u" chars "
''' chars '''                u''' chars '''
""" chars """                u""" chars """
r' chars '                   ur' chars '
r" chars "                   ur" chars "
r''' chars '''               ur''' chars '''
r""" chars """               ur""" chars """
```

Figure 9–1
Forms of string literals.

Table 9–1
Escape sequences in strings.

Escape Sequence	Means
\a	"attention," ASCII bell
\b	ASCII backspace
\f	ASCII form feed
\n	ASCII linefeed, also known as newline
\r	ASCII carriage return
\t	ASCII tab
\v	ASCII vertical tab
\\	\
\'	'
\"	"
\ (at the end of a line)	At the end of a line in triply-quoted strings, a backslash causes both itself and the newline character following it to be removed from the string. This prevents the new line from being included in multiline strings.
\ooo	The octal number of the character in the Latin1 character set. Up to three octal digits may be used.
\xhh	hh is two hexadecimal digits, the hexadecimal number of the character.
\uhhhh	In Unicode strings, the Unicode character with the number given by the hex digits hhhh.

If you write several strings in a row, separated only by white space, Python will concatenate them for you before the program runs:

```
>>> 'ab'   "cd"   'ef'
'abcdef'
```

This is one way to include quotes in strings:

```
>>> "Who dat say, "   '"Who dat say, '   "'Who dat?'"   '"'
'Who dat say, "Who dat say, \'Who dat?\'"'
```

However, most people would probably just use a backslash in front of an internal quote.

If you precede a string with the letter R in either upper or lower case, the string is interpreted as a "raw string." Backslashes and the following characters in the string are interpreted as themselves, not as an escape sequence:

```
>>> len('\\')
1
>>> len(r'\\')
2
```

You will want to use raw strings, as we will see in Chapter 21, for writing regular expressions. Note that a raw string cannot end in an odd number of backslashes. The string input routine in the Python compiler gathers the characters in strings before figuring out whether they are raw or Unicode or whatever. It includes the character following a backslash without examining it. A backslash in a sequence will always include the character following it in a string, even if that should have been a terminating quote. For file names under Windows, you might want to use a raw string, but be careful: Some Windows paths end in backslashes, and that will not work with raw strings.

Strings are normally in the 8-bit, Latin character set. In version 1.6, Python introduced Unicode strings. If you precede a string literal with a U character, in either upper or lower case, you get a Unicode string. You can include any Unicode character in the string by writing \uhhhh where hhhh is the hexadecimal number of the Unicode character. Raw Unicode strings are written ur"...", with any kind of quotes. We will generally ignore Unicode in this book.

9.2   Strings as Sequences

Strings are a built-in sequence type in Python. They implement the common sequence operators shown in Table 8–1.

Strings are immutable, like tuples; unlike tuples, which can have elements of any type, strings can contain only characters. However, when you subscript a string, you do not get a character; you get a string of length one. Python does not have a character data type.

Strings have more than just the common sequence operators. A complete list of the string operators is contained in Table 9–2. (The string formatting operator, %, is discussed later in the chapter.)

Table 9–2
String operators.

Operator	Meaning
s+u n*s s*n s[i] s[i:j] x_0, x_1, x_2, $\ldots$, $x_{n-1}=$s	See Table 8–1.
s % t	String formatting–Creates a new string by formatting values in tuple t and inserting them into specified places in string s. We discuss this later in the text.
s % d	String formatting–Creates a new string by formatting values in dictionary d and inserting them into specified places in string s. We discuss this in Section 9.5.
' e '	Converts the value of expression e into a string. Note: These are back-quotes. Regular quotes are used for string literals.
str(x)	Converts object x to a string to be understood by a human.

Table 9–2
String operators. (Continued)

Operator	Meaning
repr(x)	Converts x to a string. The intention is that, when possible, the string can be converted back to a copy of x.
hex(n)	Converts n to a hexadecimal string representation.
oct(n)	Converts n to an octal string representation.
int(s,base) int(s) long(s) float(s) complex(s)	Convert a string representation of a number to the numeric representation.

Putting back-quotes around an expression, `'e'`, is the same as calling repr(e). Function repr() is supposed to be the inverse of the built-in function eval(). With eval(), Python evaluates strings as expressions. The intent is that, when possible, eval(repr(x))==x.

The repr() built-in function converts numbers, strings, and None to strings that you can type into Python to get back to the same internal value. (Of course, floating-point numbers can only be guaranteed to come close.) Call these numbers, strings, and None "repr types." Then lists, tuples, and dictionaries are also repr types if they contain only repr types:

```
>>> `[1,[2]]`
'[1, [2]]'
```

As we will see in Chapter 14, you can create your own data types and specify how repr() should convert them to strings. If you write out a call of a constructor that will create a copy of your object, you have created a repr type according to our definition.

However, although repr() is supposed to convert all objects to strings, it cannot convert them all to expressions that eval() will convert back. For example, open files don't convert to expressions:

```
>>> repr(open("x.txt"))
"<open file 'x.txt', mode 'r' at 007B83D0>"
```

In addition to `repr()`, there are a number of other built-in functions that operate on or produce strings. They are listed in Table 6–3. Also, some of the functions in Tables 6–2 and 6–4 work on strings.

9.3   String Methods

Before Python2, the `string` module contained a large collection of functions for manipulating strings. Although the module is still there, the string functions have been made into methods of string objects. Table 9–3 lists these.

Table 9–3
Most important string methods.

Method (Python2)	Meaning

`s.endswith(suffix)`
`s.startswith(prefix)`
`s.startswith(sub,pos)`
	True if `s` ends with `suffix`, begins with `prefix`, or contains `sub` starting at position `pos`.

`s.find(sub)`
`s.find(sub,start)`
`s.find(sub,start,end)`
	Finds the first occurrence of `sub` in string `s` at or beyond `start` and not extending beyond `end`. Returns `-1` if it is not found. Parameter `end` defaults to the end of `s`, `start` to `0`.

`s.index(sub)`
`s.index(sub,start)`
`s.index(sub,start,end)`
	Like `find()`, but raises a `ValueError` if not found. I.e., finds the index of the first occurrence of `sub` in string `s` at or beyond `start` and not extending beyond `end`. Raises a `ValueError` exception if it is not found. Parameter `end` defaults to the end of `s`, `start` to `0`.

Table 9–3
Most important string methods. (Continued)

Method (Python2)	Meaning

`s.rfind(sub)`
`s.rfind(sub,start)`
`s.rfind(sub,start,end)`
	Finds the index of the last occurrence of `sub` in string `s` lying totally within the range beginning at `start` and not extending beyond `end`. Returns `-1` if it is not found. Parameter `end` defaults to the end of `s`, `start` to `0`.

`s.rindex(sub)`
`s.rindex(sub,start)`
`s.rindex(sub,start,end)`
	Like `rfind()`, but raises a `ValueError` if not found. I.e., finds the index of the last occurrence of `sub` in string `s` lying totally within the range beginning at `start` and not extending beyond `end`. Raises a `ValueError` exception if it is not found. Parameter `end` defaults to the end of `s`, `start` to `0`.

`s.split()`
`s.split(sep)`
`s.split(sep,maxtimes)`
	Returns a list of the substrings of `s` separated by string `sep`. If `sep` is `None`, or omitted, returns the substrings separated by white space. If `maxtimes` is present, returns no more than `maxtimes` substrings followed by the remainder of `s`, if any.

`sep.join(seq)`	Concatenates the strings in list or tuple `seq`. Puts string `sep` between each pair.
`s.lower()`	Returns a copy of `s` with all letters converted to lowercase.
`s.upper()`	Returns a copy of `s` with all letters converted to uppercase.
`s.strip()`	Returns a copy of `s` with all white space removed from both ends.

Table 9–3
Most important string methods. (Continued)

Method (Python2)	Meaning
`s.lstrip()`	Returns a copy of `s` with all white space removed from the left.
`s.rstrip()`	Returns a copy of `s` with all white space removed from the right.
`s.ljust(w)`	Returns a copy of `s` padded with blanks, left-justified in a field of width `w`. Returns `s` itself if it is as long as or is longer than `w`.
`s.rjust(w)`	Returns a copy of `s` padded with blanks, right-justified in a field of width `w`. Returns `s` itself if it is as long as or is longer than `w`.
`s.center(w)`	Returns a copy of `s` padded with blanks centered in a field of width `w`. Returns `s` itself if it is as long as or is longer than `w`.
`s.expandtabs()` `s.expandtabs(w)`	Returns a copy of `s` with tabs expanded into blanks. The tab stops occur each `w` characters, eight characters if `w` is omitted.

9.3.1 Comparing Substrings

There are three methods to see if a substring occurs in a particular place in another string. Method `s.startswith(prefix)` returns true if string `s` begins with the string `prefix`. Method `s.endswith(suffix)` returns true if `s` ends with the string `suffix`. Method `s.startswith(sub,pos)` returns true if `s` contains the string `sub` starting at position `pos`. Why "`startswith`"? You can think of it as meaning `s[pos:]startswith(sub)`. A different name could be more intuitive, but `s.startsWith(sub,pos)` is also used in Java.

9.3.2   Finding Substrings

Strings have a rich set of search methods for finding substrings. You can find a string or get a special value, -1, to indicate the string wasn't found. These methods include the word *find* in their names. Or you can have Python raise an exception if the substring is not found. These methods include the word *index* in their names. You can search left to right with `find()` and `index()`, or right to left with `rfind()` or `rindex()`. You can specify searching the entire string for the substring by default, or only part of it. When you specify a `start` or `start` and `end` for the search, they are interpreted as if specifying a slice. Negative offsets are allowed:

```
>>> 'abc'.find('b',-3,-1)
1
```

The `find()` method returns -1 if the substring is not found. This is fine if you are looking for only one string. If you are looking for the next occurrence of one of several strings, you might prefer it give the position at the end of the string. For example, suppose you want to find the first of two substrings, x or y, that occurs in a string. It would be convenient to be able to write `min(s.find(x), s.find(y))` and have it work even if one or both of x and y are missing; but since `find()` returns -1 for a missing substring, this will not work. Similarly, you often want to grab the next chunk of a string, s, from position k up to the next occurrence of some delimiter. If the delimiter doesn't occur, you usually want the rest of string s. It would be nice to write `s[k:s.find(delim,k)]` and have `find()` return the index of the end of the chunk you want, whether it is at a delimiter or at the end of the string. Again, this doesn't work in Python.

Figure 9–2 shows a function, `find()`, that is better for scanning. If it doesn't find the substring desired, it returns the value of `end`. The trick is in the modulus operator, `%`, in the `return` statement. We take the value returned by `s.find(sub,start,end)` modulus `end+1`. All the indices in the string s, from start through `end-1`, will be left alone. The -1 index modulus `end+1` becomes `end`.

```
def find(s,sub,start=0,end=None):
    slen=len(s)
    if end == None: end=slen
    elif end >= slen: end=slen
    elif end < -slen: end=0
    else: end+=slen
    return s.find(sub,start,end)%(end+1)
```

Figure 9–2
Function find() that returns the end position for "not found."

Here is an example of find() in action:

```
>>> e='a*b+c*d+e*f'
>>> len(e)
11
>>> e.find('-')
-1
>>> find(e,'-')
11
>>> find(e,'/',0,3)
3
>>> find(e,'/',0,0)
0
```

9.3.3 Split

There are alternatives to using s.find() to give you the next chunk of a string. The method s.split(delim) will give you a list of the substrings of s that are separated by a delimiter string, delim. You can default the delimiter to white space. Specifying None also chooses white space. You can specify the maximum number of times to split the string, leaving the rest of s as the final element of the list.

```
>>> "a b c d".split()
['a', 'b', 'c', 'd']
>>> "a b c   d".split()
['a', 'b', 'c', 'd']
>>> "a b c d".split('c')
['a b ', ' d']
>>> "a b c d".split(None,1)
['a', 'b c d']
```

To get the next chunk of a list to process, you might use:

```
chunk,s=s.split(delim,1)
```

but this will work only if s contains the delimiter. If the string does not contain the delimiter, split() returns a list with a single element, the entire string.

```
>>> 'a+b'.split('*')
['a+b']
```

9.3.4 Join

The join() method is the opposite of split(). It concatenates the strings in a list into a single string separated by a specified delimiter. The form is:

delimiter.join(listOfStrings)

It may feel a bit backward to call join for the delimiter string, rather than the list being joined, but it *is* a string operation rather than a list operation.

You can combine join() with split() to edit strings. For example:

```
>>> a='a\t \nb  c'
>>> a
'a\011 \012b  c'
>>> a.split()
['a', 'b', 'c']
>>> ''.join(a.split())
'abc'
>>> ' '.join(a.split())
'a b c'
```

That is, you can join using the empty delimiter, ''.join(a.split()), to squeeze white space from a string; or with a single blank as a delimiter, ' '.join(a.split()), to replace strings of white space with single blanks.

9.3.5 String Editing

There are several methods that deal explicitly with string editing. Although we usually talk of these methods as changing the contents of a string, they really leave the string as it is and construct a new string with the changes made.

The methods s.upper() and s.lower() convert all characters in s to uppercase or lowercase.

The method `s.strip()` removes white space from both ends of string `s`. The method `s.lstrip()` removes it from the left end and `s.rstrip()` from the right end.

The method `s.center(w)` returns `s` padded on both sides by blanks so that it is centered in a field `w` characters wide. If `len(s)` is greater than `w`, `s` is returned as is. Similarly, `s.ljust(w)` left-justifies `s` in a field `w` characters wide, padding with blanks on the right, and `s.rjust(w)` right-justifies `s`. Again, if `len(s)` is greater than `w`, `s` is returned unchanged.

The method `s.expandtabs(w)` will replace the tabs in `s` with blanks. Each tab from left to right is replaced with enough blanks to bring the length of the string to the next "tab column." The tab columns are `w` characters apart. If you omit `w`, the tab columns are eight characters apart.

9.4 Example: `Splitter`

A major problem with the `split()` method is that you can split on only a single delimiter. If you are trying to evaluate simple expressions, you might want to split a string at every operator and parenthesis. In that case you would need to know not only the parts separated by operators, but also the operators themselves. The `split()` method is not powerful enough to do this directly. Here we examine a class, `Splitter`, that overcomes these problems.

9.4.1 Features of `Splitter`

Figure 9–4 presents a class, `Splitter`, that allows us to split a string at multiple operators, giving us the operators and the strings they separate. Here is a list of the features we want in `Splitter`:

- We want to split strings by any number of separators.
- We want to retain the separators so we know which ones occur and where.
- We want to be sure we do not split the separators we have found if they contain other separators. For example, we might want to use "`==`", "`>=`", "`<=`", and "`=`" as separators, but we do not want the "`=`" to further split the first three.
- We want the separators to be easily distinguished from the surrounding strings.

- We want to omit empty strings between separators. Empty strings are an important part of the output of string's `split()` method, since we need to know how many separators occurred and where; but for `Splitter`, we are retaining the separators, so we do not need the empty strings.
- We want an external iterator interface, as discussed in Chapter 5. That will allow us to execute a loop iterating over each string and separator.
- We prefer not to construct an entire list of strings and separators at the beginning, but only the next item as we need it.
- We would like to be able to plug this into other iterators to be able, for example, to read its input from a file.

Here is an example of `Splitter` in action:

```
>>> import Splitter
>>> x=Splitter.Splitter('+','a+b*c+d*e+f*g')
>>> while x.hasMoreElements():
...     print x.nextElement()
...
a
('+',)
b*c
('+',)
d*e
('+',)
f*g
```

We create a `Splitter` object `x`, which is supposed to split the string `'a+b*c+d*e+f*g'` with the substring `'+'`. The method `x.hasMoreEle-ments()` will return true as long as `x` can return another substring or separator. The method `x.nextElement()` returns the next substring or separator. The separators are returned as single-element tuples, which distinguishes them from the strings.

The next example shows that we can plug more than one `Split-ter` to gather so that the output of one will be passed through the other, yielding a combined stream of strings and separators:

```
>>> x=Splitter.Splitter('*',
    Splitter.Splitter('+','a+b*c+d*e+f*g'))
>>> while x.hasMoreElements():
...     print x.nextElement()
...
a
('+',)
```

```
b
('*',)
c
('+',)
d
('*',)
e
('+',)
f
('*',)
g
```

The next two examples show the function Splitters() that builds a cascade of Splitter objects, one for each separator in a sequence. In the first example, the separators are given in a list:

```
>>> x=Splitter.Splitters(['+','-','*','/','(',')'],
    'a+b*c-d/(e+f)*g')
>>> while x.hasMoreElements():
...        print x.nextElement()
...
a
('+',)
b
('*',)
c
('-',)
d
('/',)
('(',)
e
('+',)
f
(')',)
('*',)
g
```

In this second example, the separators are the characters in a string:

```
>>> x=Splitter.Splitters('+-*/()','a+b*c-d/(e+f)*g')
>>> while x.hasMoreElements():
...        print x.nextElement()
...
a
('+',)
b
('*',)
c
('-',)
d
```

```
('/',)
('(',)
e
('+',)
f
(')',)
('*',)
g
```

9.4.2   Implementation of `Splitter`

Since `Splitter` objects can be cascaded as shown in Figure 9–3, they must be able to take their input from other objects with the `has-MoreElements()`/`nextElement()` interface. To simplify the design, we wrap the string being split in a `NonSplitter` object whose class definition begins Figure 9–4. `NonSplitter` is created with a string, `src`. When its `nextElement()` method is called, it returns the string. The next time the method is called, it will raise an `IndexError`. Method `hasMoreElements()` will return true before `nextElement()` is called and false afterward. `NonSplitter` remembers in attribute `done` whether `nextElement()` has been called yet, so `NonSplitter` is in one of two states depending on whether `done` is zero or one.

The function `Splitters(seps,src)` simply builds a cascade of `Splitter` objects for the separator strings in its `seps` parameter, left to right.

A `Splitter` object has these attributes:

- `src` is the object it is reading strings and separators from.
- `sep` is the separator it is using to split the incoming strings.
- `sepTuple` is the separator contained in a tuple to be returned at the places `sep` found in a string.
- `buf` is a buffer holding the string or separator tuple most recently read from `src`.
- `state` is an object indicating the current state of `Splitter`.

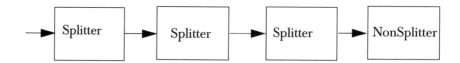

Figure 9–3
Cascading Splitter objects.

```
import types

class NonSplitter:
    def __init__(self,src):
      self.src=src
      self._done=0
    def nextElement(self):
      if self._done:
        raise IndexError
      self._done=1
      return self.src
    def hasMoreElements(self):
      return not self._done

class Splitter:
    def __init__(self,sep,src):
      self.sep=sep
      self.sepTuple=(sep,)
      if type(src) is types.StringType or \
        type(src) is types.UnicodeType:
        self.src=NonSplitter(src)
      else:
        self.src=src
      self.buf=''
      self.state=_getNext
    def hasMoreElements(self):
      return self.state.hasMoreElements(self)
    def nextElement(self):
      return self.state.nextElement(self)

def Splitters(seps,src):
    for x in seps:
      src=Splitter(x,src)
    return src

class _StringNextState:
    #here if splitter.buf contains more string to split
    def nextElement(self,splitter):
      if len(splitter.buf)==0:
        splitter.state=_getNext
        return _getNext.nextElement(splitter)
      x=splitter.buf.split(splitter.sep,1)
      if len(x)==1:
        splitter.state=_getNext
        return x[0]
      else:
        splitter.buf=x[1]
        if x[0]=='':
           #splitter.state remains _StringNextState
                  return splitter.sepTuple
        else:
                  splitter.state=_sepNext
```

Figure 9–4
Splitter.

```
                            return x[0]

    def hasMoreElements(self,splitter):
        if len(splitter.buf)>0:
          return 1
        else:
          return splitter.src.hasMoreElements()
_stringNext=_StringNextState()
class _SepNextState:
    #here if splitter.sep is next string to return
    def nextElement(self,splitter):
      splitter.state=_stringNext
      return splitter.sepTuple
    def hasMoreElements(self,splitter):
      return 1
_sepNext=_SepNextState()
class _GetNextState:
    #here if splitter.buf is exhausted, read from splitter.src
    def nextElement(self,splitter):
      splitter.buf=splitter.src.nextElement()
      if type(splitter.buf) is types.TupleType:
        #state remains _GetNextState
        return splitter.buf
      splitter.state=_stringNext
      return splitter.state.nextElement(splitter)
    def hasMoreElements(self,splitter):
      x=splitter.src.hasMoreElements()
      if not x:
        splitter.state=_done
      return x
_getNext=_GetNextState()
class _DoneState:
    #here if nothing more to return
    def nextElement(self,splitter):
      raise IndexError
    def hasMoreElements(self,splitter):
      return 0
_done=_DoneState()
```

Figure 9–4
Splitter. (Continued)

Splitter objects are implemented using the *state* design pattern.
(See Chapter 5, Section 5.4.9.) A Splitter object can be in one of four
states:

1. _DoneState. There are no more strings or separators to deliver. The
    method hasMoreElements() will return 0; nextElement() will raise
    an IndexError exception.
2. _StringNextState. The Splitter will split off and return a sub-
    string of buf the next time nextElement() is called.

3. `_SepNextState`. The `Splitter` will return a separator the next time `nextElement()` is called. The method `hasMoreElements()` will return true.

4. `_GetNextState`. The `Splitter` needs to read another item from its input to decide what to do next. The method `hasMoreElements()` will have to call the next stage's `hasMoreElements()` to find out if there are more elements to return. The method `nextElement()` will have to call the `src` object's `nextElement()` method to get a separator to return or a string to split and return.

Each state is represented by a state object. A method in the `Splitter` object delegates its behavior to the method with the same name in the current state object. For example, `hasMoreElements()` executes `return self.state.hasMoreElements(self)`.

The methods in the state objects take one more parameter than the same method in the `Splitter` object. They must be given a reference to the `Splitter` object so that they can access its attributes.

The state objects are singletons: They have no attributes of their own. Their methods manipulate the `Splitter` object that delegates to them, not their own object. One copy of each state object is created when the module is loaded.

_GetNextState

When a `Splitter` is created, it assigns its `state` attribute the instance `_getNext` of `_GetNextState`. This state says that the `Splitter` must read another element from its input before it can do anything else. When `hasMoreElements()` is called in `_GetNextState`, it checks to see if `src` has more elements. If not, it changes the `Splitter`'s state to `_DoneState`. In any case, it returns to its caller whatever its `src` object reports.

The method `nextElement()` in `_GetNextState` has to call `nextElement()` in the `src` object to get another separator to return or another string to split. It executes

```
splitter.buf=splitter.src.nextElement()
```

to read the next element into `buf`. If it is a tuple, it just returns it and remains in `_GetNextState`. However, if it is a string, then that string needs to be split and the substrings and separators returned. In this case, it changes the `Splitter`'s state to `_StringNextState` and delegates to that the splitting of the string in `buf` and the returning of what comes first.

_StringNextState

The `_StringNextState` is entered to split off and return the initial substring of the string that `buf` has in it. By our design decision that empty strings will not be returned, `hasMoreElements()` will return true (1) if `buf` has a nonempty string in it; but if `buf` is an empty string, `hasMoreElements()` will report true only if the `src` object can provide more elements.

The method `nextElement()` has a number of special cases to handle. It processes them in order.

1. If `buf` contains an empty string, we are not allowed to return it. We must read the next element from our `src` object. This is handled by changing our state to `_GetNextState` and letting that state handle the `nextElement()` call. Otherwise, we call `x=splitter.buf.split (splitter.sep,1)` to find the next separator in `buf`.
2. After step 1), if `x` is of length one, `sep` did not occur in `buf`. We must return the contents of `buf` as the next string, and change our state to `_GetNextState`. Otherwise, `buf` gets whatever tailed the separator and we go on to decide what to return next.
3. After step 2), if `x[0]` is an empty string, the separator occurred first in the buffer. We do not return empty strings, so we must return a reference to `sepTuple` next. We remain in `_StringNextState` because, having returned a separator, we need to look for a substring to return next.
4. If, however, `x[0]` is not an empty string, we return it and go to the `_SepNextState` to remember to return a separator next time.

_SepNextState

In `_SepNextState`, the `Splitter` is guaranteed to return a separator next. Therefore, `hasMoreElements()` will always return true and `nextElement()` will return a separator tuple. The next state is always `_StringNextState`, which will try to split the contents of `buf` following the separator.

9.5   String Formatting: The % Operator

The string formatting operator, `%`, gives you access to C-style output formatting. The string formatting operator is used as follows:

```
formatting_string % values_to_insert
```

For example:

```
>>> "%o:%d:%x" % (65,65,65)
'101:65:41'
```

The formatting string says there are three numeric fields to convert, separated by colons. These fields are supplied values from the tuple (65,65,65). The first formatting element, %o, says to convert an integer to an octal number; the second, %d, specifies decimal; the third, %x, specifies hexadecimal.

There are actually two ways to specify the values to insert: by a tuple or by a dictionary. We will look at tuples first.

Tuples

The formatting string contains formatting sequences, strings of characters that indicate that a value is to be converted and inserted. The formatting sequences have the form:

$$\% \ m \ f$$

where f is a formatting character and m is an optional modifier indicating such things as width and precision. The formatting characters are shown in Table 9–4.

Python makes a copy of the formatting string with the formatting sequences replaced with values converted from the tuple. The tuple must contain exactly as many values as are required by the formatting sequences.

Table 9–4
Formatting characters.

Character	Meaning
% m d	Decimal integer. The corresponding element of the tuple is converted to an integer and the integer is converted to a string in decimal format.
% m i	Decimal integer. The same as %d.

Table 9–4
Formatting characters. (Continued)

Character	Meaning

% *m* u	Unsigned integer. The same as %d, but the integer is interpreted as unsigned. The sign bit is interpreted as adding a large positive amount to the number, rather than a large negative amount.
	
	```>>> 0xc0000000```
	```-1073741824```
	```>>> '%u' % 0xc0000000```
	```'3221225472'```

% *m* o	Octal integer. The corresponding element of the tuple is converted to an integer and the integer is converted to a string in octal format.
	
	```>>> '%o' % 0xc0000000```
	```'30000000000'```

% *m* x	Hexadecimal integer. The corresponding element of the tuple is converted to an integer and the integer is converted to a string in hexadecimal format. Lowercase x uses lowercase letters for the values 10 through 15.
	
	```>>> "%x" % (-2)```
	```'fffffffe'```

% *m* X	Hexadecimal integer. Like x but uses uppercase letters for the values 10 through 15.
	```>>> "%X" % (-2)```
	```'FFFFFFFE'```

% *m* f	Floating-point format, with decimal point but without an exponent.
	```>>> "%f" % (0.5e-100)```
	```'0.000000'```

Table 9-4
Formatting characters. (Continued)

Character	Meaning

% *m* e	Floating-point format, with decimal point and an exponent (with a lowercase 'e').
	`>>> "%e" % (0.5e-100)`
	`'5.000000e-101'`

% *m* E	Floating-point format, with decimal point and an exponent (with an uppercase 'E').
	`>>> "%E" % (0.5e-100)`
	`'5.000000E-101'`

% *m* g	Behaves as either f or e depending on the size of the exponent, and additionally tries to minimize the number of digits shown.
% *m* G	Behaves as either f or E depending on the size of the exponent, and additionally tries to minimize the number of digits shown.

% *m* s	String, or any object converted to a string.
	`>>> "%s" % ([1,2])`
	`'[1, 2]'`

% *m* r	Like s, but uses `repr()` rather than `str()` to convert the argument (in Python 2).

% *m* c	A single character. The value to be converted can be either an integer that is the internal code for a character or a string of length one.
	`>>> "%c" % (88)`
	`'X'`
	`>>> "%c" % ("Y")`
	`'Y'`

%%	This does not match an element from the tuple. It is the way to incorporate a percent sign into the string.

As a degenerate case of a tuple, if there is only one value to be inserted, you needn't include it in a tuple:

```
>>> "|%d|" % 5
'|5|'
```

But note that there's a problem if you wish the single value to itself be a tuple:

```
>>> '%s' % (1,2,3)
Traceback (most recent call last):
  File "<stdin>", line 1, in ?
TypeError: not all arguments converted
>>> '%s' % ((1,2,3),)
'(1, 2, 3)'
```

The formatting characters are divided into several groups. Several formatting characters specify how to convert integers. Both %d and %i specify converting an integer to a decimal representation. Sequence %u also specifies decimal, but the integer is to be interpreted as unsigned. Sequence %o specifies converting to octal. Both %x and %X specify conversion to hexadecimal. The lowercase x tells Python to use lowercase letters a-f to indicate the values 10 to 15; uppercase X specifies using A-F.

There are five ways to tell how to convert a floating-point number: Format %f says to use a decimal point, but no exponent. Both %e and %E say to include an exponent with a lowercase or uppercase E, respectively. Sequence %g says to use format %f if the number can be represented that way and %e otherwise. Sequence %G says to use %f or %E.

The sequence %s says to include a string. If you pass some other Python object, x, to be included as a string, Python converts it with str(x). The sequence %r also tells Python to include a string, but to use repr(x) for any needed conversion. A one character string can be included with a %c format. Formatting an integer, i, with %c uses the value of chr(i).

Of course, sometimes you just want a percent sign. You include a percent sign with %%.

In a formatting sequence %mf, the modifier, m, is optional. If present, modifiers have the form a w .p, of which each part is optional. The a (alignment) may be any, all or none of a +, a -, or a 0, although - and 0 do not make sense together. The w (width) and p (precision) are numbers or asterisks. An asterisk means to read the number from the tuple of values. The interpretation of these modifier fields is shown in Table 9–5.

Table 9–5
Interpretation of format modifiers.

Modifier Pattern	Applied to Type	Means
+ w .p	numeric	Include + sign for positive values.
- w .p	any	Left align.
0 w .p	numeric	Zero fill.

a **w** .p	any	The integer w is the minimum field width.
		`>>> "|%4d|" % 5`
		`'|   5|'`
		`>>> "|%4d|" % 500000`
		`'|500000|'`

a w **.p**	string	The integer p is the maximum number of characters of a string that may be printed.
		`>>> "|%.3s|" % ("abcdef")`
		`'|abc|'`

a w **.p**	float	The integer p is the maximum number of digits following the decimal point.
		`>>> "|%.4f|" % (1.0/3.0)`
		`'|0.3333|'`

a w **.p**	integer	The integer p is the minimum number of digits to print.
		`>>> "|%4.2d|" % 5`
		`'|  05|'`

Table 9–5
Interpretation of format modifiers. (Continued)

Modifier Pattern	Applied to Type	Means
a * .p	any	Read the numeric value for the w field from the tuple.
a w .*	any	Read the numeric value for the p field from the tuple.

Dictionaries

You can use a dictionary instead of a tuple. You instruct Python what value to format by putting the key string in parentheses just after the opening %, inside the formatting sequence:

$$\% \text{ (key) m f}$$

For example:

```
>>> "|%(x)4.2d|" % {"x":5}
'|   05|'
```

However, with dictionaries you cannot use a variable width or precision. A "*" cannot specify which key in the dictionary has the precision, and "(key)" isn't accepted in the width or precision fields of a modifier.

```
>>> "|%(x)4.(p)d|" % {"p":2,"x":5}
Traceback (innermost last):
  File "<stdin>", line 1, in ?
ValueError: unsupported format character '(' (0x28)
>>> "|%(x)4.*(p)d|" % {"p":2,"x":5}
Traceback (most recent call last):
  File "<stdin>", line 1, in ?
TypeError: not enough arguments for format string
```

9.6 Wrap-Up

String processing is one of Python's great strengths. Here we looked at the operators, functions, and methods available for manipulating strings. Since strings are immutable sequences, all the basic sequence operations apply. A large number of built-in functions apply to or return strings. String objects have a large collection of methods for searching or editing them. Since they are immutable, the editing methods produce new strings. The most powerful string editing is done with the % operator that treats its left operand much like a format string in the C library.

The Splitter example showed a kind of external iterator/decorator class implemented with state objects. It provides a more powerful version of the split() method.

9.7   Exercises

9.1. Explain what is happening in the following:

```
>>> reduce(lambda x,y:y+x,'abcdef')
'fedcba'
```

9.2. Write a splitTree() function. When called for a string and delimiter, it will split the string at the delimiter and return a tree structure as if the delimiter were a left-associative operator. For example:

```
>>> e='a*b+c*d+e*f'
>>> splitTree(e,'+')
[['a*b', '+', 'c*d'], '+', 'e*f']
```

Function splitTree() gives you a tree structure in which every internal node is a list and every leaf is a string. When splitTree() is called for such a tree, it returns a tree of the same type by applying itself recursively to each subtree. Leaves in the original tree are replaced with subtrees returned by splitTree(). If they do not contain delimiters, they are unaltered; they remain strings. When they do contain delimiters, they are replaced with lists. For example:

```
>>> x=splitTree(e,'+')
>>> x
[['a*b', '+', 'c*d'], '+', 'e*f']
>>> y=splitTree(x,'*')
>>> y
[[['a', '*', 'b'], '+', ['c', '*', 'd']], '+', ['e',
'*', 'f']]
```

So by passing a string through several calls of `splitTree()`, you can break out several delimiters and retain the delimiter strings to tell you which delimiter occurred where.

9.3. We saw that we could not use formatting like `"|%(x)4.(p)d|"` `%` `{"p":2,"x":5}` to use values from a dictionary to specify precision. Can you rewrite the string as a string `s` such that `s` `%` `{"p":2,"x":5}` `%` `{"p":2,"x":5}` will take the precision from the dictionary?

9.4. Critique `Splitter`'s design and implementation.

Dictionaries

Dictionaries, also known as tables or maps, are some of the most useful high-level data types in any language. Dictionaries are mutable, associative containers. They map keys into values and, unlike the indices of lists, the keys can be structured values, such as strings or tuples. Dictionaries allow us to attach attributes to objects without modifying the objects themselves. Dictionaries allow us to form associations among objects.

We will make extensive use of dictionaries later in this book. In this chapter we demonstrate their use in implementing the union-find algorithm for disjoint sets.

Dictionaries can be viewed as "in-memory databases." Dictionaries are also used as models for database access, as we examine in "Persistence and Databases."

10.1 Dictionary Operations

First we look at the operations defined for dictionaries. Dictionaries have the operations shown in Table 10–1.

10.1.1 Displays

You can create an empty dictionary by writing empty braces:

$$\{\}$$

You can create a dictionary initialized with certain keys and values by putting a list of key-value expression pairs separated by commas

Table 10–1
Operations on Dictionaries.

Operator, Function, Method	Explanation
`{key:value,...}`	Creates a dictionary with the given key-value pairs. This is a dictionary display. Unlike lists, there are no "dictionary comprehensions."
`d[k]`	Returns the value associated with key `k` in dictionary `d`. It is an error if the key is not present in the dictionary. See methods `has_key()` and `get()`.
`d[k]=v`	Associates value `v` with key `k` in dictionary `d`. The key must be "hashable," that is, the `hash()` function must return a value for it.
`del d[k]`	Deletes key `k` and its associated value from dictionary `d`. It is an error if the key doesn't exist.

`cmp(d1,d2)` `d1<d2` `d1<=d2` `d1==d2` `d1!=d2` `d1>=d2` `d1>d2`	`cmp(d1,d2)` compares the contents of two dictionaries. The comparison is lexicographical. The comparison works as if implemented by:
	 `c1=d1.items()`
	 `c1.sort()`
	 `c2=d2.items()`
	 `c2.sort()`
	 `cmp(c1,c2)`
	 That is, the contents of each dictionary are placed in a list of `(key,value)` pairs, the lists are sorted by key, and the sorted lists of `(key,value)` pairs are compared with a normal list comparison.
	 The relational operators are implemented using `cmp()`.

`str(d)` `repr(d)`	Converts dictionaries to string representations.
`len(d)`	Returns the number of associations in the dictionary.

Table 10–1
Operations on Dictionaries. (Continued)

Operator, Function, Method	Explanation
`id(d)`	Returns an integer giving the identity of the dictionary.
`type(d)` `isinstance(d,t)`	The type of a dictionary is `types.DictType`. A dictionary is an instance of `types.DictType`.
`hash(key)`	Gives an error if applied to a dictionary. Dictionaries use the `hash(key)` function to compute from a `key` where to start searching in their dictionaries. If an object does not have a hash value, it cannot be used as a key in a dictionary. Mutable built-in objects, such as lists and dictionaries, do not have hash values.
`d.clear()`	Removes all key-value pairs from dictionary `d`.
`d.copy()`	Creates a copy of dictionary `d`. This is a *shallow* copy: The dictionary itself is copied, but none of the key nor value objects it contains are copied.
`d.get(k)`	Returns the value associated with key `k` in dictionary `d`. If `k` isn't present in the dictionary, it returns `None`.
`d.get(k,v)`	Returns the value associated with key `k` in dictionary `d`. If `k` isn't present in the dictionary, it returns `v`.
`d.has_key(k)`	Returns true (1) if dictionary `d` contains key `k` and false (0) otherwise.
`d.items()`	Returns `[(k,v),...]`, a list of all the key-value pairs currently in the dictionary `d`. The key-value pairs are tuples of two elements, (*key*, *value*).

Table 10–1
Operations on Dictionaries. (Continued)

Operator, Function, Method	Explanation
`d.keys()`	Returns a list of all the keys currently in dictionary d.
`d.update(m)`	Adds all the key-value pairs from dictionary m to dictionary d. Any key in d that is the same as a key in m has its value reassigned.
`d.values()`	Returns a list of all the values currently in dictionary d.

`d.setdefault(k)`
`d.setdefault(k,`
    `x)`
	Python2. Combining get() with initialization. As if defined:
	`def setdefault(self,k,x=None):`
	`    if self.has_key(k):`
	`        return self[k]`
	`    else:`
	`        self[k]=x`
	`        return self[k]`

`d.popitem()`	Removes and returns an arbitrary (*key*,*value*) pair from dictionary d. This is new in version 2.1.

within the braces. Each key is separated from its value by a colon. For example:

```
>>> i=5
>>> d={'a':i,i+1:'b'*3}
>>> d
{6: 'bbb', 'a': 5}
```

10.1.2   Subscripting

You can subscript a dictionary the same way you subscript a list, by placing an expression in brackets following a dictionary reference. You can use subscripting to look up the value associated with a key, to add a new key and associated value, to assign a new value to a key, and to delete a key and its value. Continuing the example:

```
>>> d['a']
5
>>> d['a']=(1,'c')
>>> d
{6: 'bbb', 'a': (1, 'c')}
>>> d[1,2]=3
>>> d
{(1, 2): 3, 6: 'bbb', 'a': (1, 'c')}
>>> del d[6]
>>> d
{(1, 2): 3, 'a': (1, 'c')}
```

Notice the assignment d[1,2]=3. You can use a tuple as a key, and you can create the tuple by listing its elements between the opening and closing brackets. This has the appearance of subscripting a multidimensional array.

When you subscript with a key that is not present, Python raises an exception:

```
>>> d['b']
Traceback (most recent call last):
  File "<stdin>", line 1, in ?
KeyError: b
```

Often you want to use a distinctive value to indicate the key isn't present. For this you want to use the get() or setdefault() method. The get() method has two forms:

- d.get(k) will return d[k] if dictionary d has the key k, and the value None otherwise.
- d.get(k,v) will return d[k] if dictionary d has the key k, and the value of v otherwise.

But neither version of get() will add a key and value to the dictionary. For example:

```
>>> d.get('b')==None
1
>>> d.get('b',"abc")
'abc'
>>> d['b']
Traceback (most recent call last):
  File "<stdin>", line 1, in ?
```

```
KeyError: b
```

If you not only want to do a `get()` but to add the key and value to the dictionary if the key is not already present, use `setdefault(k)` or `setdefault(k,v)`:

```
>>> d.setdefault('b')==None
1
>>> d['b']==None
1
>>> d.setdefault('c','abc')
'abc'
>>> d['c']
'abc'
```

You can test whether a dictionary has a key with the `has_key()` method:

```
>>> d
{'b': None, (1, 2): 3, 'c': 'abc', 'a': (1, 'c')}
>>> d.has_key('c')
1
>>> d.has_key('e')
0
```

10.1.3   Other Methods

You can get a list of the keys in a dictionary with the `keys()` method. The `values()` method gives you the values, and the `items()` method gives you a list of key value pairs in two-element tuples:

```
>>> d.keys()
['b', (1, 2), 'c', 'a']
>>> d.values()
[None, 3, 'abc', (1, 'c')]
>>> d.items()
[('b', None), ((1, 2), 3), ('c', 'abc'), ('a', (1, 'c'))]
```

The built-in function `len()` gives you the number of key-value pairs in the dictionary, which is also the length of the above lists.

```
>>> len(d)
4
```

Two dictionaries can be compared. Function `cmp(d1,d2)` behaves as if implemented as:

```
c1=d1.items()
c1.sort()
c2=d2.items()
c2.sort()
... cmp(c1,c2) ...
```

The `d1.update(d2)` method allows you to put all the key value pairs in dictionary `d2` into dictionary `d1`. If a key, `k`, is in both dictionaries, its value is replaced in `d1` with `d2[k]`.

```
>>> d1={'a':'x','b':'y'}
>>> d2={'a':'b','c':'d'}
>>> d1.update(d2)
>>> d1
{'b': 'y', 'c': 'd', 'a': 'b'}
```

Method `update()` is much the same as:

```
>>> for k in d2.keys():
...      d1[k]=d2[k]
```

You can create a copy of a dictionary with the `copy()` method. It creates a shallow copy of the dictionary, that is, it copies the dictionary itself, but not the keys or values in it. Here we put a list as a value in dictionary `d1`, assign a copy of `d1` to `d2`, change the contents of the list via `d1`, and show the change via `d2`.

```
>>> d1={'a':[0,1]}
>>> d2=d1.copy()
>>> d2
{'a': [0, 1]}
>>> d1['a'][0]=10
>>> d2
{'a': [10, 1]}
```

Requirements for Keys

Here's what dictionaries require of their keys:

- The keys need to have hash values: `hash(k)` must be defined.
- Keys must not change their hash values.
- Python must be able to compare keys, since `lookup` requires looking for an equal key. The `cmp()` function must work for them.
- Keys that compare `equal` must have equal hash codes, although equal hash codes do not imply equal keys.

Python generally computes hash codes from the contents of keys and compares keys based on their contents, as opposed to using the identity of the object. We want equal strings to be the same key, even if they were computed at different times and hence are different objects. So as a rule, Python requires that keys be objects of built-in immutable types or instances of classes that provide __hash__() methods. Strings and tuples can be used as keys, but lists and dictionaries cannot. Suppose you use a list as a key in a dictionary, and then you change the contents of the list and try to look it up again. Now the different contents will give a different hash value, which is almost certain to make Python start looking for the list at a different place in the dictionary. If you could change the contents of a key, you would be able to put the key into the dictionary and then you would not be able to find the same key again.

10.2   Example: Union-Find Algorithm

As an example of the use of dictionaries, consider the unionfind module shown in Figure 10–2 that implements the *union-find* algorithm. The algorithm allows you to gather objects into disjoint sets. An example will help you understand how it works and why it is useful. Suppose you have a huge wiring diagram and you want to make sure everything is connected. It is too large to just look at it and figure it out.

Here's what you can do: Give a code to each device and each junction of wires. Put into a computer the pairs of codes of junctions and devices that are directly connected by a wire. Now have a program go through the list of pairs of codes. These pairs tell you not only that the two devices and junctions are connected, but also that all things connected to either of them are connected.

Viewed as sets, every code starts off in its own singleton set. For every pair of codes, you merge the sets that each code is in. At the end, you check whether all codes are in the same set. If there exist at least two codes in different sets, the devices are not all connected.

10.2.1   Union-Find Algorithm

Here are the requirements for the union-find algorithm: You should be able to find the set an item is in, and you should be able to merge two sets into a single set.

We implement the union-find algorithm in a class, DisjointUnion. Each instance of the class is a separate collection of sets. The requirements are expressed as two methods:

- `find(x)`—Finds what set item `x` is in.
- `union(x,y)`—Puts items `x` and `y` in the same set by combining their sets into a single set. It performs no operation if `x` and `y` are already in the same set.

At first glance, the `find(x)` part looks easy. Just keep the name of its set for each item. A dictionary would be fine. The `union(x,y)` part, however, looks expensive. It looks as if you would have to find all the items in one set and change the name of the set they belong to.

But there a is a way to do it much faster than that. Build a tree for each set with the edges pointing rootward, as shown in Figure 10–1, which corresponds to the tree after the following operations:

```
>>> x=unionfind.DisjointUnion()
>>> x.union(1,2)
>>> x.union(3,4)
>>> x.union(5,6)
>>> x.union(7,8)
>>> x.union(2,3)
```

A single item in each set is at the root of the tree. This item represents the set. To find what set an item is in, just follow the path until you find the root. To form the union of two sets, point the root of one of them to the root of the other. This alone makes the `union()` much faster, but it could make `find()` much slower. It is possible for each set to end up as a chain rather than a bushy tree.

So there are two optimizations to speed up the algorithm: First, in the `union()` function, point the root of the smaller tree to the root of the

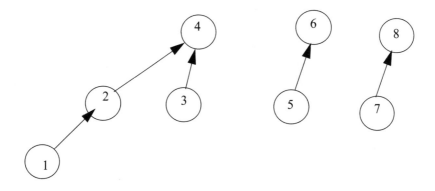

Figure 10–1
Example tree representation of sets in the union-find algorithm.

larger one. This means that when searching for the root of the tree, you now have to search one step further for the items that were in the smaller tree; but if you did it the other way around, you would be searching further for more items. To implement this, you need to keep a count of the number of items in the tree with the root of each tree. This is no problem. When you first add an item, it is the root of its own tree and has a count of one. When you form the union of two trees, add their counts together and store that result with the root of the combined tree.

The second trick is in the `find()` algorithm. When you follow the path from a node to the root of its tree, go along the path twice. First, find the root. Then, make every node on the path point directly to the root. This shortens all paths that go through any but just the last node.

How fast does this make the algorithms run? It cannot run faster than a linear algorithum. If you are processing N items, you have to look at each of them costing on the order of N. This algorithm is not quite linear, but it comes *very* close. You won't notice any difference in run-time with any data set size you are likely to use.

10.2.2   Implementation of Union-Find

Our implementation of the `union-find` algorithm (Figure 10–2) provides these operations:

- `find(x)`—Finds the set that `x` is a member of. The sets are indicated by a representative element. If `x` has not been encountered before, it is inserted into a set of its own and becomes its own representative element.
- `union(x,y)`—Merges the sets that `x` and `y` belong to into a single set. As with `find()`, `x` and `y` do not have to be known to the algorithm before the union.
- `in_same_set(x,y)`—Returns true if `x` and `y` are in the same set, false otherwise. Again, `x` and `y` do not have to be known before the test is performed, but they will be known to the algorithm after the test.
- `clear()`—Resets the algorithm. No elements are known to the algorithm afterward.

There is no requirement that the items used in the algorithm be integers. The only requirement is that they be hashable and that any two objects that compare as equal are considered to be the same element. These requirements mean, of course, that we are using dictionaries. We use two dictionaries:

- parent[x] is the parent of item x in the tree. The roots do not have parents.
- count[x] is the number of items in the set rooted at x. Items that are not roots do not have counts.

The behavior of union(x,y) is relatively simple. It finds the roots of the trees containing x and y. The find() method will create these trees if x or y has not been encountered before. If the roots are the same, x and y are already in the same set, so nothing further need be done. If the roots are not the same, the root of the tree with fewer elements is pointed to the root of the tree with the larger number (choosing arbitrarily if they are equal). The number of elements in the merged tree is placed in the count of the new root, and the count is deleted for the element that is no longer a root.

The behavior of find(x) is a bit more complex. If x has neither a count nor a parent, it is a new element. It is made into the root of its own tree by giving it a count of one.

Otherwise, we need to find the root of the tree containing x and make all the elements along the path from x to its root point directly to the root. We save x in y and then run through the path through its parents until we find the root. Now x points to the root of the tree. We start at y and follow the same path, making each element on the path point directly to the root, using z as a temporary pointer to the next element on the path.

Here is a run of the algorithm:

```
>>> import unionfind
>>> x=unionfind.DisjointUnion()
>>> x.find(1)
1
>>> x.union(1,2)
>>> x.union(3,4)
>>> x.union(5,6)
>>> x.union(7,8)
>>> x.union(2,3)
>>> for i in range(1,9): print x.find(i),
...
4 4 4 4 6 6 8 8
>>> x.in_same_set(1,4)
1
>>> x.in_same_set(1,5)
0
```

```
class DisjointUnion:
    def __init__(self):
      self.count={}
      self.parent={}
    def union(self,x,y):
      x=self.find(x)
      y=self.find(y)
      if x == y: return
      if self.count[x]>self.count[y]:
        x,y=y,x
      self.parent[x]=y
      self.count[y]=self.count[y]+self.count[x]
      del self.count[x]
    def find(self,x):
      if not self.count.has_key[x]        \
         and not self.parent.has_key(x):
        self.count[x]=1
        return x
      y=x
      while self.parent.has_key(x):
        x=self.parent[x]
      while y != x:
        z=self.parent[y]
        self.parent[y]=x
        y=z
      return x
    def in_same_set(self,x,y):
      return self.find(x) == self.find(y)
```

Figure 10–2
Union-find.

10.2.3 Critique

The unionfind module implements a useful algorithm. Its advantage is that it can handle arbitrary objects without putting parent or count fields within the objects themselves, without encoding the objects as integers and using a list to hold the parent and count fields, and without knowing the objects beforehand.

There is a function missing. We would like to be able to get a list of all the items that are in the sets. At the moment, we can get the list with x.parent.keys()+x.count.keys(), but that uses too much knowledge about the implementation. It could easily break if we decide to make changes to the module. It would be wise to have a function to give us the list.

10.3   Persistence and Databases

A dictionary is a pattern for a number of Python objects. One important example is databases. On Unix and Windows, you can use the BSD db library and the Python modules that are built using it. However, since these are based on dictionaries rather than on relational databases, they will be unsatisfying to people with serious database work to do.

10.3.1   `dbhash`

Module `dbhash` provides the ability to create and open databases that use hashing to look up information. Call the `open()` function `dbhash.open(path,flag)` or `dbhash.open(path,flag,mode)` to open a database file.

The `path` is the file name, a string giving an operating system path to the file. The `flag` is a string indicating what you want to do with the database:

- '`r`'–Open it only for reading.
- '`w`'–Open it for reading and writing.
- '`c`'–Open it for reading and writing and create it if it doesn't already exist.
- '`n`'–Always create a new database.
- '`rl`', '`wl`', '`cl`', or '`nl`'–If the BSD db library on your machine supports locking, use locking.

The mode specifies the Unix/Linux mode bits that should be set if the file is created (masked by your process's current mask).

The function `open()` returns a database object that behaves as a kind of dictionary. Database objects have at least the operations shown in Table 10–2. Unlike dictionaries, all the keys and values in the database must be strings.

Table 10–2
Operations on database objects.

Operation	Explanation
`db[x]`	Returns the value associated with key `x` in the database. Raises a `KeyError` if `x` is not a key in the database.
`db[x]=y`	Assigns the key `x` the value `y` in the database.

Table 10–2
Operations on database objects. (Continued)

Operation	Explanation
del db[x]	Removes the key x and its associated value from the database. Raises a KeyError if x is not a key in the database.
db.close()	Closes the database file.
db.has_key(x)	Returns true (1) if the database has the key x, false (0) otherwise.
db.keys()	Returns a list of the keys in the database.
db.first()	Returns the pair (key, value) of the first item in the database. It sets the *cursor* to this first item. With a hashed database, there is no particular order of the keys, so it is arbitrary which key comes first.
db.next()	Moves the cursor to the next item in the database and returns its (key,value) tuple. Raises a KeyError if the cursor is at the end of the database.
db.sync()	The intent is to synchronize the database to disk, i.e., flush the buffers from memory. On some systems it doesn't do anything, forcing you to close the database to flush the changes.

Notice that the database objects have a mixture of operations from different kinds of objects. They are opened and closed like files, of course, since they are built upon files. Like dictionaries, they have subscripting for lookup, insertion, and deletion, and they have the methods keys() and has_key(). Unlike dictionaries, they do not have the items() method to return all the key-value pairs in the database. That may be too large for memory. However, you can iterate over all the key value pairs with something like this:

```
try:
    key,value=db.first()
```

```
    while 1:
        #process key and value
        ...
        key,value=db.next()
except KeyError: #no more items
    ... #handle it
```

The `first()` and `next()` will raise a `KeyError` exception when you fall off the end of the database. Exceptions are discussed in Chapter 11.

10.3.2   Nonstring Keys and Values

A problem with databases built using `dbhash` is that the keys and values must be strings. What if they aren't strings? Maybe you can use `repr()` and `eval()` to convert to and from strings. For example:

```
>>> d[('a',1)]=('A',1)
Traceback (most recent call last):
  File "<stdin>", line 1, in ?
TypeError: bsddb key type must be string
>>> d[repr(('a',1))]=('A',2)
Traceback (most recent call last):
  File "<stdin>", line 1, in ?
TypeError: bsddb value type must be string
>>> d[repr(('a',1))]=repr(('A',2))
>>> d[repr(('a',1))]
"('A', 2)"
>>> eval(d[repr(('a',1))])
('A', 2)
```

10.3.3   `pickle`

The `repr()` function does not translate all objects into strings that will be converted back to the object by `eval()`. A more effective conversion is available in the `pickle` module. "Pickle" denotes "shrink and preserve" as opposed to "a difficult situation." The `pickle` module converts objects into strings and converts the strings back into objects. The string representation is not chosen to be human-readable. For example:

```
>>> import pickle
>>> d[pickle.dumps(('a',1))]=pickle.dumps(('A',2))
>>> d[pickle.dumps(('a',1))]
"(S'A'\012p0\012I2\012tp1\012."
>>> pickle.loads(d[pickle.dumps(('a',1))])
('A', 2)
```

The statement `y=dumps(x)` converts object `x` to a string `y`, and `z=loads(y)` converts `y` back into an object `z` equal to `x`. The `pickle` module can handle linked structures, including circularly linked structures:

```
>>> x=[1]
>>> x.append(x)
>>> x
[1, [...]]
>>> pickle.dumps(x)
'(lp0\012I1\012ag0\012a.'
>>> pickle.loads(pickle.dumps(x))
[1, [...]]
>>> x is pickle.loads(pickle.dumps(x))
0
>>> x == pickle.loads(pickle.dumps(x))
1
```

It deserves mention here, although it is not relevant to our database discussion, that the `pickle` module also has functions `dump(x,f)` that writes the encoded object `x` to file `f`; and `load(f)` that reads and decodes an object from file `f`. There is also a module, `cPickle`, containing an implementation of `pickle` that is written in `c` code and runs more quickly.

10.3.4   shelve

If you want to store arbitrary Python objects, having to call `pickle.dumps()` and `pickle.loads()` yourself can be a nuisance. Python's `shelve` module makes it easy. The statement `shelve.open(path,flag)` behaves like the open method of `dbhash` (although it does not neccessarily use `dbhash`). It returns a database object with most of the operations shown in Table 10–2. However, it is missing the `first()` and `next()` methods.

The big difference between `dbhash` and `shelve` is that, although the keys are required to be strings, the values in `shelve` can be arbitrary Python objects. The `shelve` module uses `cPickle` to convert the values to and from strings.

10.3.5   bsddb

Underlying the `dbhash` module is the `bsddb` module, a more direct connection to the BSD db system available with Unix and Windows. The module `bsddb` provides two organizations of databases that are of interest.

Hashed databases can be opened with `bsddb.hashopen(path,flag)`, which is the same as `dbhash.open(path,flag)`. B-tree databases can be opened with `bsddb.btopen(path,flag)`. B-trees are like binary search trees, except they are multiway trees with the nodes stored on the disk. They have an advantage over hashed databases in that the keys are in sorted order. You can go through the keys in ascending order with the `first()` and `next()` methods. You can visit them in descending order with methods `last()` and `previous()`. You can also set the cursor to an arbitrary record with the `set_location(key)` method. The additional methods for B-tree databases are shown in Table 10–3.

Table 10–3
Additional methods for B-tree databases.

Method	Meaning
`db.first()`	Returns the pair (`key, value`) of the first item in the database. It sets the *cursor* to this first item. With a B-tree database, this will have the smallest `key` value in sorted order.
`db.next()`	Moves the cursor to the next item in the database and returns its (`key,value`) tuple. With a B-tree, this key will be the next larger in sorted order.
`db.last()`	Returns the tuple (`key, value`) of the last item in the database. It sets the *cursor* to this last item. With a B-tree database, this will have the largest `key` value in sorted order.
`db.previous()`	Moves the cursor to the previous item in the database and returns its (`key,value`) tuple. With a B-tree, this key will be the next smaller in sorted order.
`db.set_location(key)`	Sets the cursor to the item in the database with the specified key and returns its (`key,value`) pair. You can move forward or backward in the database with the `next()` and `previous()` methods.

Here is an example showing how a B-tree database functions:

```
>>> import bsddb
>>> db=bsddb.btopen("xyz.db","n")
>>> db.keys()
[]
>>> db['a']="A"
>>> db['b']="B"
>>> db['d']="D"
>>> db['c']="C"
>>> db.keys()
['a', 'b', 'c', 'd']
>>> db.first()
('a', 'A')
>>> db.next()
('b', 'B')
>>> db.last()
('d', 'D')
>>> db.previous()
('c', 'C')
>>> db.set_location('b')
('b', 'B')
>>> db.next()
('c', 'C')
```

10.3.6 bsddb errors

You can get two classes of exceptions from database operations:

- KeyError—The specified key is not present.
- bsddb.error—The class of error raised for other kinds of errors. This is also raised by databases opened by dbhash, since it is simply a front end on bsddb. You can also refer to it as bdhash.error.

We discuss how to handle errors in Chapter 11.

10.4 Wrap-Up

Dictionaries are important containers, and it is a great convenience that they are built into Python. Dictionaries make up a form of in-memory database that allows fast lookup. They allow attributes to be associated with objects without altering the objects themselves. The two requirements are that the keys of the dictionaries must be hashable and comparable.

We devoted a section of this chapter to an implementation of the union-find algorithm in a class DisjointUnion. The DisjointUnion is itself a container that is important for a number of algorithms, as will be seen in several exercises throughout this book. The implementation of `DisjointUnion` demonstrated the use of dictionaries.

Dictionaries provide the pattern for Python's database access. Indeed, for a restricted set of operations, an open database may be substituted for a dictionary. A major restriction on most databases is that the keys and values must be strings, although databases opened with the `shelve` module can convert values to and from strings automatically. The `pickle` and `cPickle` modules provide functions to convert a wide variety of data structures to and from strings.

We will return to databases in our discussions of transactions in Chapter 19 and transaction run-queues in Chapter 20.

10.5 Exercises

10.1. Add a method `has(x)` to `DisjointUnion` that will return true if the item x is present without adding x.

10.2. Add a method `copy()` to `DisjointUnion` that will return a copy of the `DisjointUnion` object.

10.3. Add a method `items()` to `DisjointUnion` that will return a list of all the elements of the sets it contains.

10.4. Add a method `sets()` to `DisjointUnion` that will return a dictionary mapping the representative elements of the sets into lists of the elements in the sets.

10.5. Critique the use of a dictionary as a model for a database.

10.6. Use `DisjointUnion` in a program to create random rectangular mazes. Initially, the rectangle is composed of square cells. Each cell has four walls. Except along the edges, a wall is shared by two cells. Two cell walls are removed along opposite edges of the rectangle for entry and exit. Remove walls between cells. These walls are chosen randomly with the constraints that:

1. Exactly N-1 walls are removed if there are N cells in the rectangle. (This gives a "tree" if you view the cells as nodes and the removed walls as edges.)

2. No wall may be removed if the cells on both sides are already connected. (This is where union-find comes in.)

3. No more than three walls may be removed from any cell.

   There are random number generators in the Python library that you can use.

11

Exceptions

Errors can occur that make it impossible for a program to continue executing. In Python these errors cause a program to *raise exceptions*. The Python system itself raises some of the exceptions: for example, when you divide by zero or try to apply operators to the wrong type of operands. You yourself raise other exceptions when you discover that something has gone wrong.

The default behavior for an exception is to stop execution and write out a message and a trace of the call stack up to the place where the exception was raised. With the `try-except` statement, you can catch the exceptions and handle them yourself.

11.1 Exception Classes

There are two versions of exceptions. The preferred way of handling exceptions uses instances of classes to represent the exceptions. There is an older way that uses strings to name the exceptions. We are mainly concerned with using class instances for exceptions. The class indicates the type of exception and is used to select code to execute when we handle an exception ourselves. The instance can contain additional data to explain the exception.

The built-in exception classes are shown in Figure 11–1. The subclasses are to the right of and connected to their superclasses. Most of these classes are fairly obvious, but they deserve some remarks. The class `Exception` is a superclass of all exceptions. If you wish to create exception classes of your own, they should be descendents of `Excep-`

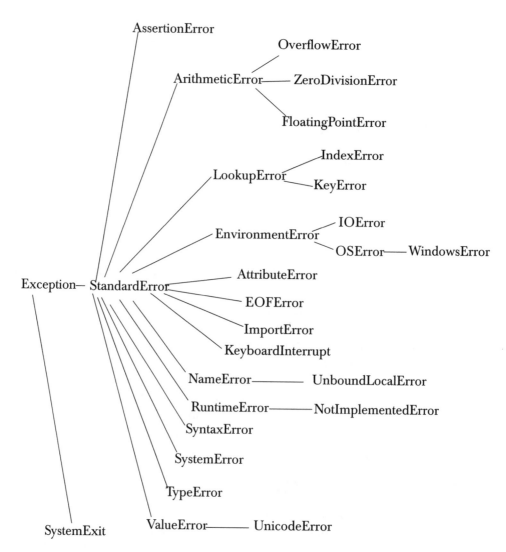

Figure 11-1
Built-in exception class hierarchy.

tion in the class hierarchy. They should probably be subclasses of `RuntimeError`, which is a catch-all for errors that do not fit into the other classes. The `NotImplementedError` is such an exception class. Programmers raise `NotImplementedError` in abstract classes to indicate that a method was supposed to be implemented in a subclass, but has not been.

The `AssertionError` is used by the `assert` statement. A `Lookup-Error` is given when a lookup fails in a list, tuple, string (`IndexError`), or dictionary (`KeyError`).

You can get an `IOError` when a file operation fails. An `EOFError`, however, applies only to the built-in functions `input()` and `raw_input()`. The various file `read()` methods return empty strings on end of file. In general, the `EnvironmentError`s are the results of conditions in the surrounding system, not within Python itself. The `Keyboard-Interrupt` also comes from the surrounding environment, but it is not actually an error; it simply means the user is trying to get the program's attention.

`AttributeError` is raised when access to a qualified name, an attribute, fails, whereas `NameError` is raised when an unqualified name, in other words, a variable, is not found. A special case is made for a local variable in a function that has not been assigned a value yet; in that case you get an `UnboundLocalError`.

The `ImportError` occurs when a requested module is not found, or a requested name in the module is not found. Importing a module can also give a `SyntaxError` if the Python code in the module is malformed. Similarly, the `input()`, `eval()`, or `execfile()` functions or `exec` statements also raise a `SyntaxError` when they encounter malformed code.

The `TypeError` is raised when the operands are of the wrong type for an operation. The `ValueError` is raised when the type is appropriate, but the value of the operand is not. It is only raised when a more specific exception class, such as `ZeroDivideError` or `IndexError`, is not available.

A `SystemError` is given for an error in the Python system implementation, at least for one that does not appear serious enough to terminate the system. A `SystemExit` is raised in the function `sys.exit()` to terminate execution. It allows resources to be freed in `try-finally` statements (see Section 11.9). Naturally, you should not try to handle this exception and recover, but just pass it on; the point is, after all, to terminate.

11.2 Minimal Exception Handling

The minimum syntax required to raise an exception yourself is `raise class`, which will create an instance of the given exception class and raise it as an exception. The class is used for selecting an `except` clause to handle the exception. The minimum syntax required to handle exceptions is a `try` statement of the form:

```
try:
    statements
except:
    statements
```

The statements between the `try` and the `except` are executed, and if an exception occurs within them, the statements nested following the `except` are executed. If an exception does not occur within the statements between `try` and `except`, the statements following the `except` are not executed. Actually, we should be saying "unhandled exception." The `try-except` statements do not have to handle all exceptions. Another form of `try` statement is:

```
try:
    statements
except classExpr:
    statements
```

Here the `classExpr` is an expression that yields a class, x. The statements following the `except` will be executed only if the exception is of class x or any subclass of x. If the exception is not of class x, Python goes on to the next dynamically surrounding `try` statement, and on and on until the exception is handled by a matching `except` clause. By "dynamically surrounding," we mean `try` statements that have been entered and not yet exited. The exception can be raised in the statements between the `try` and the `except`, but they can also be raised in functions called from those statements.

You can use more than one `except` clause in a `try` statement to catch and handle different classes of exceptions. You can also list several exception classes in a tuple in the `except` clause to specify that the code should handle any of them. For example:

```
try:
    statements
except (ImportError,SyntaxError):
    statements
except StandardError:
    statements
```

has two `except` clauses. The first one will handle `ImportErrors` and `SyntaxErrors`, the kind of errors that can occur when import statements are executed. The second one will handle all other built-in exceptions except `Exception` and `SystemExit`. Python will try the `except` clauses in order, executing the first that matches. Therefore, the later clauses should match more general categories of errors and the earlier clauses, the more specific; if a more general clause comes before the more specific, the specific clause will never be executed. Only the last clause, of course, can be "`except`," which matches anything.

11.3   Examining the Exception

The minimal exception handling described in the previous section does not use any information about the exception other than its class. Exceptions have three kinds of information: the class of the exception; extra data associated with the exception, which is contained in the instance object; and a traceback showing the call stack leading to the place in the program execution where the exception was raised.

You can get all three pieces of information from the function `exc_info()` in the module `sys`. The assignment `cl,inst,tb=sys.exc_info()` will assign the class of the exception to `cl`, the exception instance to `inst`, and a traceback object to `tb`. We consider how to use the `traceback` object in Section 11.5. Usually, you're just interested in the instance object, since that will tell you the exact class of the exception and whatever additional information was stored in it when the exception occurred.

If you want only the instance, you can use the form of an `except` clause that contains a target:

`except` *classExpr*, *target*: *suite*

The *target* variable is assigned the exception instance. You can get the exact class of the exception through the target's special `__class__` attribute. The class `Exception`, and hence all subclasses of `Exception`, has an attribute `args` that contains a tuple of the arguments used when creating the exception instance. Although you could provide your own initialization method for a subclass that does not assign its parameter list to `args`, to do so would violate the "contract" of the `Exception` class. Here's an example of printing the class and `args`:

```
>>> try:
...     raise RuntimeError("Hello")
```

```
...   except Exception,x:
...         print x.__class__,x.args
...
exceptions.RuntimeError ('Hello',)
```

11.4   Raising Exceptions

When your program detects an error, it can raise its own exception.
There are several ways to do this. You can create an instance of an
exception class and raise that:

<code>raise instance</code>

where `instance` is any expression that returns an instance of an exception class. You usually write this `raise` statement as:

<code>raise classname(args)</code>

In fact, that is the only form you really need. Because you can create a
class instance this way, the next form is totally unnecessary. You can
write:

<code>raise class, data</code>

to mean the something like:

<code>raise class(data)</code>

Actually, there are complications in specifying precisely how this
behaves. Python chooses the appropriate one of the following:

- `raise` `class()`—If data evaluates to `None`, the class is instantiated
  with no arguments.
- `raise` `class(data)`—If `data` does *not* evaluate to a tuple and
  does *not* evaluate to an instance of `class` or any subclass of it,
  the class is instantiated with a single argument that is the value
  of `data`.
- `raise` `data`—If `data` evaluates to an instance of `class`, this
  instance is raised as an exception.
- `raise` `class(*data)`—If `data` evaluates to a tuple, the class is
  instantiated with an argument list composed of the elements of
  the tuple.

You may be wondering why there is a "`raise class, data`" form
of the statement when "`raise class(data)`" would be easy enough to
write. This form of `raise` statement is vestigial. It was the required way
to pass back data when exceptions were indicated by strings. We look at
that in Section 11.7.

Note carefully: You can raise an exception specifying both an exception class and an instance, as follows:

```
raise class, instance
```

If the specified class is, or is a superclass of, the class of the `instance`, this is equivalent to `raise instance`. On the other hand, if the class is not the class of *instance* and not a superclass of it, it is equivalent to `raise class(instance)`; that is, Python creates an instance of the class with a single parameter. These two divergent behaviors may cause some confusion.

You can simply specify a class if you do not have any data about the exception to pass back. Python creates an instance with no parameters. If you write `raise class`, it is equivalent to writing *raise class()*.

11.5 Tracebacks

Recall that you can use the `exc_info()` function in the `sys` module to get three pieces of information about the exception currently being processed. The call `cl,inst,tb=sys.exc_info()` gives you the class of the exception, `cl`, the class instance, `inst`, and a traceback object, `tb`. It is the traceback object that Python uses to write out a trace of all the functions that were active when an exception occurred. You can use this traceback yourself. The structure of a traceback is shown in Figure 11–2. It should be noted that these objects have more attributes than are shown in the figure. A more complete discussion can be found in Chapter 12.

The variable `tb` will lead you to the first traceback object in a linked list. Each traceback object points to the next traceback object with its `tb_next` attribute. Each traceback object points to a stack frame (also known as "activation record") with its `tb_frame` attribute. The frames hold information for the functions that were active when the exception occurred.

The frames are kept in a linked *execution stack*. A frame is created when a function is called and pushed on the top of the stack and is linked to the frame of the caller through its `f_back` attribute. A frame is unlinked from the execution stack when the function returns. Python keeps a pointer to the top frame on the execution stack, since that is the frame of the function currently executing.

When the program raises an exception, Python creates a traceback object pointing to the top frame on the execution stack–the frame of the function that was executing when the exception occurred. As Python goes hunting for an except clause to handle the exception, it can leave one function and go back to the caller. Whenever Python falls off a function into its caller, it creates a traceback object for the caller's frame and links it in front of the previous traceback object, which gives a chain of traceback objects leading to the frame in which the exception occurred.

Each traceback object has attributes tb_lineno, which tells the line that was executing when the exception occurred, and tb_frame, which points to the frame object for the function. This frame object also has an attribute f_lineno indicating the line number of the code that most recently executed in the frame. This might not equal the tb_lineno value, since some code may have executed in except or finally clauses. The tb_lineno is guaranteed to be the line number of the instruction that was executing when the exception occurred. The frame object also has an attribute f_code that points to the code object for the function.

The code object has attributes co_name, giving the name of the function that was executing, and co_filename, the name of the file the function is defined in. The attributes tb_lineno and f_lineno are line numbers in this file.

Figure 11–2 shows the function toRaise(tb), which will write out a traceback along the traceback chain from the function handling the exception to the function in which the exception was raised. Figure 11–3 shows the function fromRaise(tb), which writes out the traceback in the reverse order, from the raise back to the current function.

```
def toRaise(tb):
    while tb!=None:
      f=tb.tb_frame
      c=f.f_code
      print ' line',tb.tb_lineno,'in',c.co_name,\
        'in file',c.co_filename
      tb=tb.tb_next
```

Figure 11–2
Writing a traceback to the frame where the exception occurred.

```
def fromRaise(tb):
    if tb!=None:
        fromRaise(tb.tb_next)
        f=tb.tb_frame
        c=f.f_code
        print ' line',tb.tb_lineno,'in',c.co_name,\
            'in file',c.co_filename
```

Figure 11–3
Writing a traceback from the frame where the exception occurred.

Figure 11–4 uses knowledge of traceback and frame objects to get the frame of a calling function. The call in function `f` of `caller=called-from()` assigns `caller` the frame of the function that called function `f`. You could use this in debugging to write all the places a function was called from. You might use that to find out what calls caused problems initially, since a traceback from an exception gives information only about the state of the computation when the error was detected, which can be much later than when the error actually occurred. Notice that `calledfrom()` raises an exception to get a traceback object for its own frame, from which it follows the `f_back` links to the frame of the caller of its caller. The "`del tb`" is to aid storage reclamation: If a frame points to a traceback object that points back to the frame, reference counting will not free the storage of either.

If you are *not* using threading (see Chapter 18), you can get the information about the class, value, and traceback of an exception from variables in the `sys` module: `sys.exc_type` for the class, `sys.exc_value`

```
def calledfrom():
    try:
        raise Exception
    except Exception:
        tb=sys.exc_info()[2]
        f=tb.tb_frame.f_back
        cf=f.f_back
        del tb
        return cf
```

Figure 11–4
Getting the frame of the caller of the calling function.

for the instance, and `sys.exc_traceback` for the traceback object. You should not use them in any code that might ever be used with multithreading. If two threads raise exceptions at about the same time, the second one will clobber the values set by the first. The function `sys.exc_info()` returns only the values for the exception that occurred in the thread that called it.

11.6 Re-Raising Exceptions

Suppose you've caught an exception in an `except` clause and then decide that you cannot handle it properly or completely. You need to

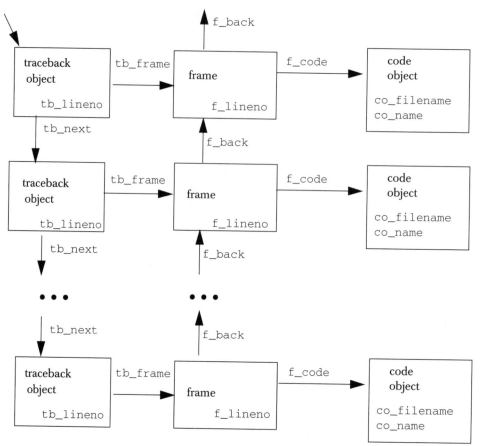

Figure 11–5
Traceback, frame, and code objects.

re-raise the exception to give some encompassing `try` statement the chance to handle it. The easiest way to do this is use an empty `raise` statement, thus:

```
raise
```

The `raise` that does not specify any operands will raise the current exception again, using and extending the current traceback. This is almost always what you need. You can use it, for example, to have a `try` statement process a general category of exception but not certain sub-classes of it, for example:

```
try:
    ...
except subclass: raise
except superclass: ...
```

If for some reason you wish to change the class of the exception or the data the exception instance contains, but still have the traceback indicate where the original exception occurred, you can use one of these forms:

```
raise class, data, tracebackObj
raise instance, None, tracebackObj
```

Either one will raise a new exception object but continue to use the pre-existing traceback.

11.7   Raise with Strings

Although the approved way to handle exceptions in Python uses classes and class instances, there is an older way still available. In this older style, the exceptions are indicated by strings. To raise an exception, you would write:

```
raise stringname, data
```

To catch it you would write:

```
except stringname, var: ...
```

That is, it looks much the same, except that class names are replaced with names of strings. There are some subtle differences:

- The `except` clauses match by object identity. The clauses test using the `is` operator, *not* the `==` operator. Therefore, the strings must be specified by names–variables that contain the strings. Because the `except` clause is chosen with the `is` operator, a literal string in an `except` clause or a `raise` statement could not be matched.

- Strings do not fit into a class hierarchy. Therefore, there is no matching of an entire category of exception in an except clause.
- The data passed in the `raise` statement is assigned to the variable in the `except` clause, unlike the class-based version that wraps it in an instance object.

11.8 Try-Except-Else

A `try-except` statement may optionally have an `else` clause at the end to be executed only if no exception occurs. For example:

```
try:
... #suite A
except:
... #suite B
else:
... #suite C
```

If an exception occurs in `suite A`, the code in `suite B` will execute and `suite C` will be skipped. If no exception occurs in `suite A`, `suite B` will be skipped and `suite C` will execute. The general rule is that the code following the `else` is executed only if the code between the `try` and the first `except` was *not* exited due to an exception.

You may be wondering why you would not just write the code as follows:

```
try:
    ... #suite A
    ... #suite C
except:
    ... #suite B
```

The difference is that in this second form, any exception occurring in `suite C` would be handled by `suite B`; whereas in the first form, `suite B` would not be given the chance to handle exceptions in `suite C`. This might turn out to be useful if you are expecting `suite A` to raise exceptions and if its failure to do so is an error.

You might write this code:

```
try:
    search()
except:
    useSolution()
else:
    raise NotFoundError
```

where `search()` is a recursive search algorithm. The `search()` function is supposed to raise an exception if it finds an answer, allowing it to remove all the recursive function calls from the stack. Otherwise, we would have to write search functions to return a value that says the search has been successful, and every function would have to check the return values of the functions it calls to see whether it should also return success or continue searching. In this design, the `search()` function would return only if the search were unsuccessful, allowing the `else` clause to raise `NotFoundError` to report the failure. We do not want to raise `NotFoundError` in the `try` clause, since that would have the `except` clause try to use a nonexistent solution.

11.9 The `Try-Finally` Statement

An entirely different form of `try` statement is the `try-finally` statement. It has the form

```
try:
    ... #suite A
finally:
    ... #suite B
```

The rule is this: No matter how control leaves `suite A`, whether by normal exit, `return`, `break`, or exception, `suite B` is *always* executed. (There is, at the time of this writing, a documented "feature" of the implementation that does not allow a `continue` statement to exit `suite A`.)

The `finally` clause may not be used with `except` clauses. If you need both `except`s and a `finally`, nest a `try-except` statement within a `try-finally` statement.

A major use for `try-finally` statements is to be sure to release locks. We discuss locks in conjunction with threading in Chapter 18. The most common pattern for mutual exclusion in a method is:

```
def method(self,...):
    self.lock.acquire()
    try:
        ...
    finally:
        self.lock.release()
```

The method acquires (locks) the lock of its object, does its work in the code between the `try` and the `finally`, and releases the lock in the `finally` clause. The reason it releases the lock in a `finally` clause is that the lock must be released for any other threads to be able to execute methods in the class. By wrapping the code in a `try-finally` statement, the lock is guaranteed to be released when the code returns. It is easier to do it this way than to remember to put a release in front of every `return` statement.

This method will also guarantee to release the lock if the method is terminated by an exception. It is questionable whether this is a good idea. The exception may occur when the data in the object is only partially updated. Releasing the lock will allow other threads to access inconsistent data and create obscure bugs.

11.10 Wrap-Up

Exceptions provide a way to abandon computations that have gone wrong and either to recover or report the location and cause of the error. Things are certain to go wrong, since even if the program is correct, there are likely to be problems with the data or the environment. Therefore, exception handling is essential to writing robust programs.

If anything, Python offers an overabundance of options for exception handling. You can use strings or classes to categorize exceptions. You can pass data back from the `raise` statement, or not. You can select `except` clauses using class hierarchy or tuples of exception types or a match-all `except:` header. You can assign the data from the `raise` to a variable in the `except` header, or you can ignore it. You can re-raise an exception if you cannot handle it in the current clause. You can get traceback objects to examine the call chain at the point where the exception occurred. Fortunately, only a minimal amount of syntax is required to use exceptions.

11.11   Exercises

11.1. If your object raises an exception in the middle of updating its data structure, it could be left unusable. How would you use the memento design pattern to restore the object to a usable state before propagating the exception out of your method?

11.2. Which of the functions `toRaise()`, `fromRaise()`, and `calledfrom()` (Figures 11–2, 11–3, and 11–4) are provided in the library module `traceback`?

12

Types

Because python is an interpretive, interactive, dynamically-typed system, it must keep information about program objects at run-time that some other languages have available only at compile time. This information is available for your use and allows you to do metaprogramming, that is, to process programs themselves as collections of objects.

In this chapter, we examine the types of objects built into Python and the information they make available to you. At the end of the chapter, we look at an example of a program that uses this information to analyze class hierarchies. Metaprogramming techniques will be used again in Chapter 22, where we will call methods, functions, or other "callable" objects knowing only their names, and will examine them to find the number of parameters they take.

12.1 Type Objects

You can find the type of an object, x, with the built-in function `type(x)`, which returns a type object. There is one *type* object for each built-in type. You can find them in the module `types`. The names for these type objects are given in Table 12–1. Figure 12–1 shows the relationship of objects to types.

Table 12–1
Type objects.

Type Object	Used For
`TypeType`	The type of *type* objects.
`NoneType`	The type of `None`.
`NotImplemented`	The type `NotImplemented` has a single value accessible via the built-in name, `NotImplemented`. It exists to be returned by operators that do not apply to the operand types provided.
`IntType`	The type of integers.
`LongType`	The type of long integers.
`FloatType`	The type of floating-point numbers.
`ComplexType`	The type of complex numbers.
`StringType`	The type of strings.
`UnicodeType`	The type of UNICODE strings.
`TupleType`	The type of tuples.
`ListType`	The type of lists.
`DictType` `DictionaryType`	The type of dictionaries.
`FunctionType` `LambdaType`	The type of user-defined functions.
`CodeType`	The type of code objects returned by `compile()`.

Table 12–1
Type objects. (Continued)

Type Object	Used For
`ClassType`	The type of classes.
`InstanceType`	The type of instances of classes.
`MethodType` `UnboundMethodType`	The type of user-defined methods.
`BuiltinFunctionType` `BuiltinMethodType`	The type of built-in functions and methods.
`ModuleType`	The type of module objects.
`FileType`	The type of open file objects.
`XRangeType`	The type of objects returned by `xrange()`.
`SliceType`	The type of objects returned by `slice()` and by `x:y:z` in subscripts.
`EllipsisType`	The type of " . . .".
`FrameType`	The type of function activation records.
`TracebackType`	The type of traceback objects.

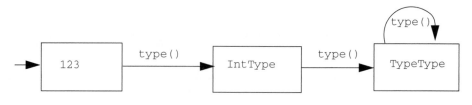

Figure 12–1
Objects and types.

12.2   Members and Methods

The built-in special attributes __members__ and __methods__ give the special data attributes and methods available with some, but not all, built-in types. We refer to these built-in special attributes as *members*. Those that they apply to are demonstrated in Table 12–2. In the table, the __members__ and __methods__ special attributes are tried for each built-in data type by the function show(), defined as follows:

```
>>> def show(x):
...     try:
...         print '__members__=',x.__members__
...     except: print 'not defined'
...     try:
...         print '__methods__=',x.__methods__
...     except: print 'not defined'
...
```

The table needs to be read sequentially, since some of the classes referred to are declared in preceding cells.

12.3   Numbers, Strings, Tuples, Lists, and Dictionaries

Integers, long integers, and floating-point numbers do not have methods or members. Complex numbers have the members real and imag for their real and imaginary components and the method conjugate(). (Of course, they also have the special members __members__ and __methods__ listing these.)

Table 12–2
Types with __members__ and __methods__.

Type Object	__members__ and __methods__

`TypeType`	```>>> show(type(None))```
	`__members__= ['__doc__', '__name__']`
	`__methods__= not defined`

`NoneType`	```>>> show(None)```
	`__members__= not defined`
	`__methods__= not defined`

`NotImplemented`	```>>> show(NotImplemented)```
	`__members__= not defined`
	`__methods__= not defined`

`IntType`	```>>> show(1)```
	`__members__= not defined`
	`__methods__= not defined`

`LongType`	```>>> show(1L)```
	`__members__= not defined`
	`__methods__= not defined`

`FloatType`	```>>> show(1.0)```
	`__members__= not defined`
	`__methods__= not defined`

`ComplexType`	```>>> show(1j)```
	`__members__= ['imag', 'real']`
	`__methods__= ['conjugate']`

`StringType`	```>>> show('')```
	`__members__= not defined`
	`__methods__= ['capitalize', 'center', 'count', 'encode', 'endswith', 'expandtabs', 'find', 'index', 'isalnum', 'isalpha', 'isdigit', 'islower', 'isspace', 'istitle', 'isupper', 'join', 'ljust', 'lower', 'lstrip', 'replace', 'rfind', 'rindex', 'rjust', 'rstrip', 'split', 'splitlines', 'startswith', 'strip', 'swapcase','title', 'translate', 'upper']`

Table 12–2
Types with __members__ and __methods__. (Continued)

Type Object	__members__ and __methods__
UnicodeType	```>>> show(u'')``` __members__= not defined __methods__= ['capitalize', 'center', 'count', 'encode', 'endswith', 'expandtabs', 'find', 'index', 'isalnum', 'isalpha', 'isdecimal', 'isdigit', 'islower', 'isnumeric', 'isspace', 'istitle', 'isupper', 'join', 'ljust', 'lower', 'lstrip', 'replace', 'rfind', 'rindex', 'rjust', 'rstrip', 'split', 'splitlines', 'startswith', 'strip', 'swapcase', 'title', 'translate', 'upper']
TupleType	```>>> show(())``` __members__= not defined __methods__= not defined
ListType	```>>> show([])``` __members__= not defined __methods__= ['append', 'count', 'extend', 'index', 'insert', 'pop', 'remove', 'reverse', 'sort']
DictType DictionaryType	```>>> show({})``` __members__= not defined __methods__= ['clear', 'copy', 'get', 'has_key', 'items', 'keys', 'setdefault','update', 'values']
FunctionType LambdaType	```>>> show(show)``` __members__= ['__dict__', '__doc__', '__name__', 'func_closure', 'func_code', 'func_defaults', 'func_dict', 'func_doc', 'func_globals', 'func_name'] __methods__= not defined (Pre version 2.1, __members__ does not include a __dict__ attribute.)

Table 12-2
Types with __members__ and __methods__. (Continued)

Type Object	__members__ and __methods__

CodeType	```>>> show(show.func_code)```
	```__members__= ['co_argcount', 'co_code', 'co_consts',```
	```'co_filename', 'co_firstlineno', 'co_flags',```
	```'co_lnotab', 'co_name', 'co_names', 'co_nlocals',```
	```'co_stacksize', 'co_varnames']```
	```__methods__= not defined```

ClassType	```>>> class C:```
	```... def M(self):pass```
	```...```
	```>>> show(C)```
	```__members__= not defined```
	```__methods__= not defined```

InstanceType	```>>> show(C())```
	```__members__= not defined```
	```__methods__= not defined```

MethodType
UnboundMethodType
	```>>> show(C.M)```
	```__members__= ['__doc__', '__name__', 'im_class',```
	```'im_func', 'im_self']```
	```__methods__= not defined```

BuiltinFunctionType
BuiltinMethodType
	```>>> show(max)```
	```__members__= ['__doc__', '__name__', '__self__']```
	```__methods__= not defined```

ModuleType	```>>> import scopes```
	```>>> show(scopes)```
	```__members__= not defined```
	```__methods__= not defined```

FileType	```>>> show(open('x.txt','w'))```
	```__members__= ['closed', 'mode', 'name', 'softspace']```
	```__methods__= ['close', 'fileno', 'flush', 'isatty',```
	```'read', 'readinto', 'readline', 'readlines', 'seek',```
	```'tell', 'truncate', 'write', 'writelines']```

Table 12–2
Types with __members__ and __methods__. (Continued)

Type Object	__members__ and __methods__

XRangeType	```>>> show(xrange(1,3,1))```
	```__members__= ['start', 'step', 'stop']```
	```__methods__= ['tolist']```

SliceType	```>>> class D:```
	```... def __getitem__(self,i):return i```
	```...```
	```>>> show(D()[1:3:1])```
	```__members__= ['start', 'stop', 'step']```
	```__methods__= not defined```

EllipsisType	```>>> show(D()[...])```
	```__members__= not defined```
	```__methods__= not defined```

FrameType	```>>> import TraceException```
	```>>> def myFrame():```
	```... return TraceException.calledfrom()```
	```...```
	```>>> myFrame()```
	```<frame object at 007B4A78>```
	```>>> show(myFrame())```
	```__members__= ['f_back', 'f_builtins', 'f_code',```
	```'f_exc_traceback', 'f_exc_type',```
	```'f_exc_value', 'f_globals', 'f_lasti', 'f_lineno',```
	```'f_locals', 'f_restricted',```
	```'f_trace']```
	```__methods__= not defined```

TracebackType	```>>> try:```
	```... raise```
	```... except:```
	```... import sys```
	```... show(sys.exc_info()[2])```
	```...```
	```__members__= ['tb_frame', 'tb_lasti', 'tb_lineno',```
	```'tb_next']```
	```__methods__= not defined```

Strings have the methods shown in Table 9–3. Lists have the methods shown in Table 8–2. Dictionaries have the methods shown in Table 10–1. Tuples do not have methods.

12.4 Modules

Module objects correspond to modules that have been imported. The command `import Mod` finds the module `Mod` (e.g., in file `Mod.py`), loads it, creates a module object for it, runs its initialization code, and assigns the module object to identifier `Mod`.

Table 12–3
Module members.

Member	Used For
`__dict__`	The dictionary containing the assignable attributes of the module.
`__name__`	The name of the module.
`__doc__`	The documentation string of the module.
`__file__`	The name of the file the module was loaded from.

The module object has the special members shown in Table 12–3. Perhaps the most important of these members is the `__dict__` member, which references a dictionary containing the user-defined, assignable attributes of the module. When the module's code is executed and assigns values to names, the names and values are placed in the `__dict__` dictionary.

The module object does not hold the code that was executed to initialize it, since that is not needed again once the module is loaded.

12.5 User-Defined Functions

A function object is created by executing a `def` statement. It has the members shown in Table 12–4. The `func_globals` member is the dictionary of the surrounding module.

Table 12–4
User-defined function members.

Member	Used For
__members__	The other member names in this table.
__dict__	A dictionary for attributes assigned by the program to the function object. (Appeared in Python version 2.1.)
__doc__ func_doc	The documentation string.
__name__ func_name	The name of the function.
func_defaults	The tuple of default values for arguments, or None if there are none. Because only the rightmost parameters can have default values, the length of this tuple, m, will be no longer than the number of positional parameters in the function, n, and the rightmost m of the positional parameters will have their values specified left to right by the elements of this tuple. The leftmost $n-m$ parameters do not have initial values. The code object, referenced by the func_code member, has members telling the number of parameters, the names of the parameters and local variables, and whether there are extra positional and keyword parameters. Section 12.16 shows how this information can be used.

Table 12–4
User-defined function members. (Continued)

Member	Used For
func_globals	The dictionary containing the global variables used by the function. This is the same as the __dict__ member of the module object of the module containing the function.
func_code	The code object of the function. The function object and its code object (see Section 12.6) together give a wide variety of information about the function. Several different function objects with their own func_defaults tuples can share the same code object, since the def statement is executable and can assign different default values to the parameters each time it is executed.

The func_defaults member is a tuple containing the default values for any defaulted parameters. If there are none, func_defaults will have the value None. The member func_code references the code object for the function. You can use the function object and the code object together to find a number of important things about the function; we look at the code objects in Section 12.6.

Here we iterate through all the defined members of a function, writing out each one:

```
>>> def f(a,b=1,*c,**d): e=2
...
>>> for x in f.__members__:
...     print x,getattr(f,x)
...
__doc__ None
__name__ f
func_code <code object f at 007B3F00, file "<stdin>", line 1>
func_defaults (1,)
func_doc None
func_globals {'f': <function f at 007B1ED4>, '__doc__': None, 'x':
'func_globals', '__name__': '__main__', '__builtins__': <module
'__builtin__' (built-in)>}
func_name f
```

12.6   Code Objects

Code objects are returned by the built-in function, `compile()`. They have the members shown in Table 12–5.

Table 12–5
Code object members.

Member	Used For
__members__	The other member names in this table.
co_name	The name of the function (if it is a function).
co_argcount	The number of positional arguments required, including defaulted positionals, but not including any extra positional (`*arg`) or extra keyword (`**arg`) argument. The presence of "extra" arguments is indicated by bits in the `co_flags` member.
co_nlocals	The number of local variables, including any arguments.
co_varnames	A tuple of variable names, including the arguments, in the order they were encountered in the code for the function. The arguments come first, in the order they appear in the function header.
co_code	The byte code in a string. (The string contains many unprintable characters.)
co_consts	A tuple of constants used by the byte code.
co_names	A tuple of names used by the code.
co_filename	A string indicating the source (e.g., the name of the file) from which the code was compiled.
co_firstlineno	The number of the first line of the code within the source file.

Table 12–5
Code object members. (Continued)

Member	Used For
`co_lnotab`	A string mapping byte code offsets into line numbers. (If you need this, read the interpreter documentation.)
`co_stacksize`	The amount of space required on the local stack.
`co_flags`	Flags for various uses. The two of interest are: Bit `0x04` is set if there is an extra positionals (`*arg`) argument. Bit `0x08` is set if there is an extra keywords (`**arg`) argument.

For example, here we create a function with a positional parameter, a defaulted parameter, an extra positional parameter, and an extra keyword parameter.

```
>>> def f(a,b=1,*c,**d): e=2
...
>>> f
<function f at 007B1ED4>
>>> f.__name__
'f'
```

We can get a tuple of the defaults:

```
>>> f.func_defaults
(1,)
```

Now we get the corresponding code object. Its `co_argcount` member gives the number of positional parameters, including the number of defaulted parameters, but not including the extra positionals nor the extra keywords parameters:

```
>>> f.func_code
<code object f at 007D7978, file "<stdin>", line 1>
>>> f.func_code.co_argcount
2
```

The member `co_nlocals` gives the total number of names defined in the function, including all the parameters and all the local variables assigned values in the function.

```
>>> f.func_code.co_nlocals
5
```

The names of the parameters and local variables are given in the tuple `co_varnames`. These are in order of occurrence in the function, so the names of the parameters come first in the order they are listed in the parameter list.

```
>>> f.func_code.co_varnames
('a', 'b', 'c', 'd', 'e')
```

The `co_flags` member contains an integer telling, among other uses, whether the function has an `*arg` (extra positionals) and/or a `**kwarg` (extra keywords) parameter. The expression `co_flags&0x4` is nonzero if there is an `*arg` parameter, and `co_flags&0x8` is nonzero if there is a `**kwarg` parameter.

```
>>> f.func_code.co_flags
15
```

We use this information in our example program in Section 12.16.

12.7 Classes

Class objects are created for each class statement executed. They have the members shown in Table 12–6. The member `__name__` is the name

Table 12–6
Class members.

Member	Used For
`__dict__`	The dictionary for class attributes.
`__name__`	The name of the class.

Table 12–6
Class members. (Continued)

Member	Used For
__doc__	The documentation string of the class, if any; otherwise, None.
__module__	The name of the module containing the class, a *string*.
__bases__	A tuple of the base classes of the class. The base classes are declared in parentheses following the class name. Their class objects are listed in this tuple in the same order they appeared, from left to right. The tuple is empty if there were no base classes in the declaration.

of the class. The member __doc__ is the documentation string, or None if there was no documentation string supplied. The member __module__ is the name of the module the class declaration appeared in. Note: It is the name—a string—not the module object.

The member __dict__ is a dictionary containing the normal, writable attributes of the class. When the class is created, the statements within the class declaration are executed and the names they assign are placed in the class's __dict__ dictionary. The member __bases__ is a tuple of the class objects of the superclasses, in the same order, left to right, as they were listed in the declaration. If no superclasses were listed, __bases__ is an empty tuple. An example of the relationship of classes, dictionaries, and bases is shown in Figure 12–2.

When Python looks for an attribute of a class, it searches in the class's __dict__ dictionary and then searches recursively through the __bases__, left to right, depth first.

Although classes are callable objects, they do not have a code object. If you need to know the parameters required to call a class, you need to look up the __init__() attribute of the class. From that function and its attached code object, you can decipher the parameters required; if there is no such function, you know the class takes no parameters.

```
class A(B,C):...
```

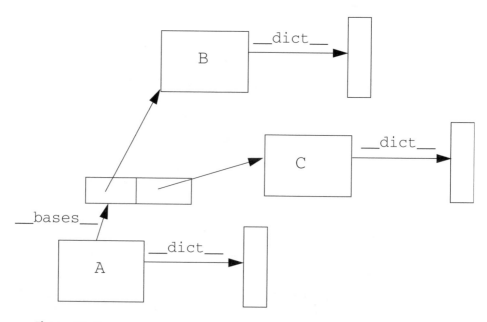

Figure 12–2
Structure of class inheritance.

12.8   Class Instances

Class instances are of type `InstanceType`. Their class is *not* their type. The relationship between instances, classes, and types is shown in Figure 12–3.

Instances have the special members shown in Table 12–7. The `__dict__` member is a dictionary containing the assignable attributes of the instance. We can write `x.__dict__['y']=z` instead of `x.y=z`. Using `__dict__` in this way is important for using the `__setattr__()` special method, as discussed at length in Chapter 14, Section 14.4.

The `__class__` member is a reference to the class object for the class of the instance. Since the class can be used to create an instance, you can use `x.__class__()` to create a new instance of `x`'s class.

```
>>> class A:pass
...
>>> a=A()
```

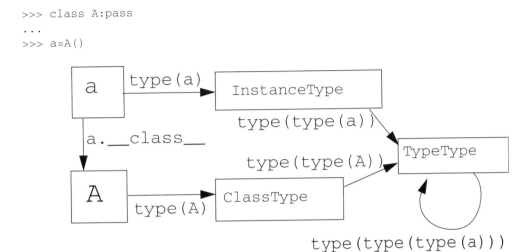

Figure 12–3
Relationships among instances, classes, and types.

Table 12–7
Class instance special members.

Member	Used For
__dict__	The dictionary containing the pool of attributes of the instance.
__class__	The class object of the instance.

12.9 User-Defined Methods

User-defined methods have the members given in Table 12–8. These MethodType objects are created only when function attributes are looked up in classes; see Figure 12–4. Given x.f where x is a class instance, Python tries to look up f in x's __dict__ dictionary. Not finding it, Python then looks in x's class and in x's superclasses, searching for f. When Python finds function object f in a class __dict__ dictionary, it creates a bound method object for it.

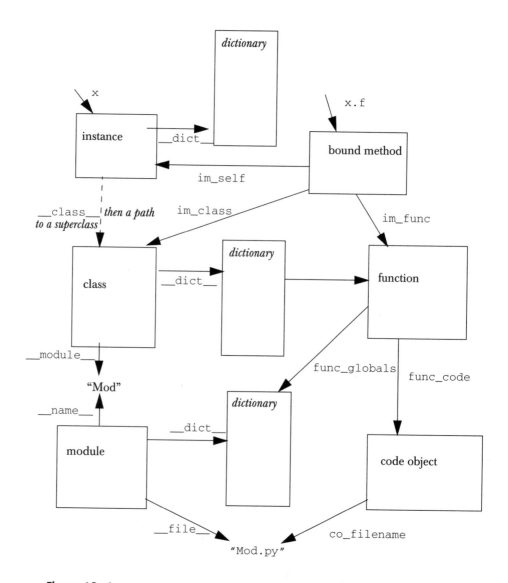

Figure 12–4
Relationship of methods, instances, classes, functions, modules, and code objects.

Python constructs an unbound method if it looks first in a class object, not in an instance. The unbound method object is the same as a bound method object, except it has `None` rather than an object instance in its `im_self` member.

Table 12–8
User-defined method members.

Member	Used For
__members__	The other member names in this table.
im_self	A reference to the instance object the method is bound to, or None if it is an unbound method.
im_func	The function object for the method. The function object itself points to the code object, as described in Sections 12.5 and 12.6.
im_class	The class the method is defined within. For a bound method object, this is either the class of im_self or an ancestor of it. For an unbound method, this tells Python what the class of the first operand must be.
__doc__	Same as im_func.__doc__.
__name__	Same as im_func.__name__.

A class instance, x, is a callable object if it has a __call__() method in its class or in some superclass. You can use the primitive function getattr(x,'__call__') to look up the call method. It will give you a method object for the __call__() method, if it exists, and it will raise an AttributeError if there is none.

12.10 Built-In Functions and Methods

Built-in functions and methods have the members shown in Table 12–9. The only difference between a built-in function and a built-in method object is that the method has an object reference in its __self__ member, and a built-in function has None.

Table 12–9
Built-in function members.

Member	Used For
__members__	The other member names in this table.
__doc__	The documentation string of the built-in function, if any; otherwise None.
__name__	The name of the built-in function.
__self__	If this is None, the object is a function. If it is a built-in method, this will reference an instance.

12.11   Slice

Slice objects are created for slices in subscript positions, in other words, x:y:z and sometimes x:y within subscripting brackets. They have the members shown in Table 12–10. How these members are assigned is described at greater length in Chapter 15.

Table 12–10
Slice object members.

Member	Used For
__members__	The other member names in this table.
start	The starting value of the slice.
stop	The stop value of the slice. The slice will go to, but not include, this.
step	The step size of the slice.

12.12 Xrange

An `xrange` object is created by the `xrange()` built-in function. It has `start`, `stop`, and `step` values for the range and a `tolist()` method to produce a list of the values in the range. See Table 12–11.

Table 12–11
XRange object members.

Member	Used For
__methods__	The `tolist()` method .
__members__	The other member names in this table.
start	The starting value of the range.
stop	The stop value of the range. The range will go to, but not include, this.
step	The step size of the range.
tolist()	Yields a list containing the values in the range: `xrange(i,j,k).tolist() == range(i,j,k)`

12.13 File

Open files have the members shown in Table 12–12. Files were discussed in Chapter 7.

Table 12–12
File object members.

Member	Used For
__methods__	File methods are shown in Table 7–1.
__members__	The remaining member names in this table.

Table 12–12
File object members. (Continued)

Member	Used For
closed	Used as boolean, true (nonzero), indicating the file is closed.
mode	The mode the file was opened with, the mode string passed to open().
name	The file name passed to open(). If the file was not opened with a call to open(), then some other string indicating the file.
softspace	A scratch member used by print to indicate whether it needs to insert a space character.

12.14 Frame

Frames are activation records for functions. An activation record is sometimes called a "stack frame," hence the name. When a function is called, a frame is allocated for it containing space for the parameters and local variables and for some control information, including a reference to the frame of the calling function. The members of a frame in Python are shown in Table 12–13. Frames and traceback objects are discussed more fully in Chapter 11.

Table 12–13
Frame object members.

Member	Used For
__members__	The remaining member names in this table.
f_back	A reference to the caller's frame. None if this is the bottom frame on the stack.
f_code	A reference to the code object the frame is executing.

Table 12–13
Frame object members. (Continued)

Member	Used For
f_locals	A dictionary used to look up the local variables.
f_globals	The dictionary for the global variables.
f_builtins	The dictionary for the built-in names.
f_restricted	A boolean indicating whether the frame is executing in the restricted mode.
f_lineno	The number of the line being executed.
f_lasti	The index in the byte code being executed.
f_trace	Either None or a function to be called when beginning to execute each source line.
f_exc_type f_exc_value f_exc_traceback	Have information on the most recent exception caught in this frame.

12.15 Traceback

Traceback objects are created automatically during exception processing. As Python searches for an except clause to handle an exception, it creates traceback objects and links them on a list. There is one traceback object created for each stack frame that it searches through. When you handle an exception, you can get a traceback object and follow a list linked through the tb_next members to the frame in which the exception was raised. The linked list of traceback objects and the frames are pictured in Figure 11–5. When the exception is raised, a traceback object is created for the frame that is executing. As Python tries to find an except clause to handle the exception, it may fall out of one function call and back into the caller. As it returns to the frame of its caller, it creates a traceback object for it and pushes that traceback on the front of the list. Each traceback object has a reference, `tb_frame`, to a corresponding frame. The frame points to the code object it was executing.

The traceback object has the line number, `tb_lineno`, and the byte code instruction index, `tb_lasti`, that were executing in the frame when the exception occurred. You can use this information to point precisely to where the error occurred. The `f_lineno` and `f_lasti` members in the frames may not still have this information when you get control in an `except` clause, since they reflect further executions after the exception occurred, such as in `finally` and `except` clauses of `try` statements that were executed. Traceback object members are shown in Table 12–14. Frames and traceback objects are discussed more fully in Chapter 11.

Table 12–14
Traceback object members.

Member	Used For
`__members__`	The remaining member names in this table.
`tb_next`	The next traceback object along a linked list from the point at which the exception is currently being processed to where the exception was raised.
`tb_frame`	The activation record frame object corresponding to the traceback object.
`tb_lineno`	The line number that was being executed by that frame when the exception occurred.
`tb_lasti`	The byte code instruction that was being executed when the exception occurred.

12.16 Example: `scopes`

In this section we present a program, `scopes`, that will analyze a module, a class hierarchy, or a class instance. It will list attributes, functions, classes, and methods. It will write out documentation strings. It will give warnings when, by Python's rules of multiple inheritance, a method in a superclass overrides a method in a subclass. (Its name should probably be "nameSpaces," since "scopes" is usually reserved for unqualified names.)

First, consider what it does with the module abcde used to demonstrate diamond inheritance in Chapter 4. The code for abcde is shown in Figure 12–5. When we execute the scopes program for module abcde, we get the output shown in Figure 12–6. It reports that there are five classes defined in the module and no functions. In Figure 12–7 we ask scopes to analyze the class E in the module abcde. In addition to the report on the module as a whole, scopes tells us that class E has no attributes and no functions. Then it runs through the superclasses and their superclasses in Python's depth-first, left-to-right search order.

Class C, it reports, has no attributes and no functions. C's superclass B has no attributes, but has the function f(self). B's superclass A has no attributes or functions. Backtracking, scopes finds that E's superclass D has no attributes, but does have a function, f(self), which is overridden in B; but B is not a subclass, which gives an inheritance anomaly. Then scopes encounters class B, which has already been encountered, so there is no reason to continue the search.

```
class A: pass
class B(A):
    def f(self): print "f() in B"
class C(B): pass
class D(B) :
    def f(self): print "f() in D"
class E(C,D) : pass
```

Figure 12–5
Module abcde.

```
C:\upcomingbooks\PPPBook\Code>python scopes.py abcde
Module abcde
 attributes:
    D : class abcde.D
    E : class abcde.E
    B : class abcde.B
    C : class abcde.C
    A : class abcde.A
 functions:
    no functions
```

Figure 12–6
Analyzing the module abcde.

```
C:\upcomingbooks\PPPBook\Code>python scopes.py abcde E
Module abcde
 attributes:
   D : class abcde.D
   E : class abcde.E
   B : class abcde.B
   C : class abcde.C
   A : class abcde.A
 functions:
     no functions
class abcde.E
 attributes of class:
     no class attributes
 functions:
   no functions
  class abcde.C
   attributes of class:
       no class attributes
   functions:
     no functions
    class abcde.B
     attributes of class:
         no class attributes
     functions:
       f(self)
      class abcde.A
       attributes of class:
           no class attributes
       functions:
         no functions
 class abcde.D
  attributes of class:
      no class attributes
  functions:
    f(self) overridden in abcde.B , NOT A SUBCLASS
   class abcde.B  -- already encountered
```

Figure 12–7
Analyzing the class E in module abcde.

Now we will look at the code in scopes.py. Passing scopes.py through itself, we get the report shown in Figure 12–8, beginning with the documentation string describing the usage of the module. The

```
C:\upcomingbooks\PPPBook\Code>python scopes.py scopes
Module scopes
      scopes.analyze(x)
where x is module, instance, or class
or execute the command line
```

Figure 12–8
Module scopes' analysis of itself.

```
python scopes.py module [class1, class2,...]
attributes:
  types : <module 'types' from
'c:\python20\lib\types.pyc'>
  os : <module 'os' from 'c:\python20\lib\os.pyc'>
  string : <module 'string' from
'c:\python20\lib\string.pyc'>
functions:
    analyze(c,cs=None,ms=None,d=0)
    analyzeInstance(c,cs,ms,d)
    analyzeClass(c,cs,ms,d)
    stringargs(code,defaults)
    analyzeFunctions(c,ms,d)
    analyzeFunction(m,c,ms,d)
    analyzeModule(c,cs,ms,d)
    showdoc(o,d)
```

Figure 12–8
Module scopes' analysis of itself. (Continued)

attributes of the module are the modules it imports: types, os, and string. The functions are analyze(), the entry function, and the functions it calls to do parts of the analysis and output. The functions are:

- analyze(c,cs=None,ms=None,d=0) is called to analyze an object. If the object is an instance, it is passed on to analyzeInstance; if a class, to analyzeClass; if a module, to analyzeModule; or if a function, to analyzeFunction. If the input to analyze() is none of these, its data type is written out.
  The defaulted parameters of analyze() are to force the creation of dictionary cs to hold the classes encountered so far, and ms to hold the methods encountered so far, and to initialize the depth, d, used for nesting the output.
- analyzeInstance(c,cs,ms,d) is called when c is an instance object. The function writes out its module and class names and attributes, and analyzes its class.
- analyzeModule(c,cs,ms,d) writes out the module's documentation string and attributes. The attributes are the items in the module's dictionary, __dict__. The listing of attributes omits those whose names begin with '_', which are assumed to be private. The classes are noted. The functions are skipped in the attribute listing and written out in a call to analyzeFunctions().
- analyzeFunction(m,c,ms,d) writes out a function header for function (usually method) m. It calls stringargs(), which converts the argument list to a string to be written out.

- analyzeFunctions(c,ms,d) **calls** analyzeFunction() **to write out all the functions in the module or class** c.
- analyzeClass(c,cs,ms,d) **writes out information about class** c. **If** c **has already been encountered, that fact is all that is written out. Otherwise, it writes out the attributes (in the** __dict__ **dictionary) other than those that are functions or whose names begin with "_" (those being private). Then it writes out the functions. Finally, it writes out the base classes, following the search path up the hierarchy.**
- stringargs(code,defaults) **writes out the argument list for the function with the code object** code **and the default argument values** defaults. **Since** defaults **is passed the function's** func_defaults **attribute, it may be** None. **If so, we assign it an empty tuple. From** code.co_argcount, **we can determine the number of positional arguments,** nargs. **Their names will be in** code.co_varnames[:nargs]. **The last** len(defaults) **of them will have default values, which are in** defaults. **Two bits in** code.flags **tell whether there are** *arg **and** **kwarg **parameters. If so, their names can be found as the next one or two items in** code.co_varnames.
- showdoc(o,d) **writes out the documentation string of object** o, **if any, with the nesting specified by depth** d.

```python
#!/usr/bin/python
"""scopes.analyze(x)
where x is module, instance, or class
or execute the command line
   python scopes.py module [name1 name2...]"""
import types,os,string
def analyze(c,cs=None,ms=None,d=0):
    #c - a class, instance, module, function, or data
    #cs - table of classes encountered so far
    #ms - table of methods encountered so far
    #d - how many recursive calls, indentation
    if cs==None: cs={}
    if ms==None: ms={}
    if type(c)==types.InstanceType:
        analyzeInstance(c,cs,ms,d)
        return
    if type(c)==types.ModuleType:
        analyzeModule(c,cs,ms,d)
        return
    if type(c)==types.ClassType:
        analyzeClass(c,cs,ms,d)
```

Figure 12–9
Module scopes.

```
      return
  if type(c)==types.FunctionType:
    class noClass:pass
    analyzeFunction(c,noClass,ms,d)
    return
  print c,type(c)
  return

def analyzeInstance(c,cs,ms,d):
  print "instance of %s.%s" % ( \
    c.__class__.__module__, \
    c.__class__.__name__)
  print " attributes:"
  for a in c.__dict__.items():
    if type(a[1])==types.ClassType:
      print "   ",a[0],": class",a[1]
    else:
      print "   ",a[0],":",a[1]
  analyzeClass(c.__class__,cs,ms,d+1)
  return

def analyzeModule(c,cs,ms,d):
  print "Module",c.__name__
  showdoc(c,d)
  print " attributes:"
  for a in c.__dict__.items():
    if a[0].startswith("_") :
      continue
    if type(a[1])==types.ClassType:
      print "   ",a[0],": class",a[1]
    elif type(a[1])!=types.FunctionType:
      print "   ",a[0],":",a[1]
  print " functions:"
  analyzeFunctions(c,{},d+1)
  return

def analyzeClass(c,cs,ms,d):
  print "%sclass %s.%s" % (
    "  "*d,c.__module__,
    c.__name__),
  if cs.get(c): #already encountered
    print " -- already encountered"
  else:
    print
    showdoc(c,d)
    cs[c]=c
    print "  "*d,"attributes of class:"
    count=0
    for a in c.__dict__.items():
      if a[0].startswith("_") :
        continue
      if type(a[1])==types.FunctionType:
        continue
```

Figure 12–9
Module scopes. (Continued)

```
                        count=count+1
                        print "   "*d,a[0],":",a[1]
                 if count==0:
                    print "   "*d,"      no class attributes"
                 print "   "*d,"functions:"
                 analyzeFunctions(c,ms,d)
                 for s in c.__bases__:
                    analyzeClass(s,cs,ms,d+1)
             return

def analyzeFunction(m,c,ms,d):
        n=m.__name__
        print "%s       %s(%s)" % (
           "   "*d,n,
           stringargs(m.func_code,m.func_defaults)),
        if ms.get(n):
           print "overridden in %s.%s" % (
              ms[n].__module__,
              ms[n].__name__),
           if not issubclass(ms[n],c):
              print ", NOT A SUBCLASS",
        else:
           ms[n]=c
        print
        showdoc(m,d)
def analyzeFunctions(c,ms,d):
        count=0
        for m in c.__dict__.values() :
           if type(m)!=types.FunctionType:
              continue
           count=count+1
           analyzeFunction(m,c,ms,d)
        if count==0:
           print "   "*d,"  no functions"

def showdoc(o,d):
        if not o.__doc__: return
        L=string.split(o.__doc__,os.linesep)
        for s in L:
           print "   "*d,"      ",s

def stringargs(code,defaults):
        if not defaults: defaults=()
        s=""
        nargs=code.co_argcount
        ndflts=len(defaults)
        firstdflt=nargs-ndflts
        for i in range(nargs):
          s=s+ code.co_varnames[i]
          if i>=nargs-ndflts:
            s=s+"="+repr(defaults[i-firstdflt])
          if i<code.co_argcount-1:
            s=s+","
```

Figure 12–9
Module scopes. (Continued)

```
         i=nargs
         if code.co_flags&0x4:
           if i>0: s=s+','
           s = s + "*" + code.co_varnames[i]
           i=i+1
         if code.co_flags&0x8:
           if i>0: s=s+','
           s = s + "**" + code.co_varnames[i]
         return s

if __name__=='__main__':
         import sys
         exec 'import '+sys.argv[1] + ' as x'
         analyze(x)
         for n in sys.argv[2:]:
           analyze(getattr(x,n))
```

Figure 12–9
Module scopes. (Continued)

The final section of code in `scopes.py` handles execution of the `scopes` program from the command line, rather than as a loaded module. The `__name__=='__main__'` tests whether it is being executed as a separate program. If it is being run as a separate program, built-in variable `__name__` will hold the string `'__main__'`; but if it is being executed as a module while being loaded, `__name__` will contain the string name of the module, '`scopes`'.

If `scopes` is being run as a program, it needs to load the module whose name is passed as its first argument, `sys.arg[1]`, analyze that, and then analyze the classes or functions within that module whose names are passed as arguments `sys.argv[2]`, `sys.argv[3]` .... Unfortunately, the command line arguments are strings, but `scopes.ana-lyze(c)` is called with the object, `c`, to analyze, rather than the string name of the object.

So we are forced to load a module whose name we are given, but the command `import mod` requires a name as its operand, `mod`, not a string-valued expression. What we have to do is create an import command as a string and tell Python to execute that:

```
         exec 'import '+sys.argv[1] + ' as x'
```

12.17 Wrap-Up

In this chapter we took a close look at built-in data types in Python, both those commonly used by programmers and those used by the implementation. We looked especially at the special members of data objects. These can be important when implementing diagnostic programs and when processing programs themselves at run-time. We gave an example of using this information in a diagnostic program, `scopes.py`, that analyzes modules and classes.

12.18   Exercises

12.1. Write a function `compatible(f,g)` where `f` and `g` are both functions. Function `compatible(f,g)` will return true if and only if `f` can be substituted for `g` wherever `g` can be called without any errors being detected during parameter passing. This means that whatever parameters will work for `g` will also work for `f`.

12.2. Python is dynamically typed, so you cannot count on inheritance telling you if one object can be substituted for another. Write a function `hasInterface(x,y)` that will return true if and only if `x`'s interface includes all of `y`'s. Both `x` and `y` are instance objects, or `x` is an instance and `y` is a class. All methods known in `y` must be available in `x`.

13

Programs and Run-Time Compilation

Python can compile programs at run-time, rather than in a separate phase before the program runs. This occurs in the interpreter, while modules are being imported, and under direct program command. In this chapter we look at how and when Python code is compiled and how run-time compilation can be used.

13.1   Python Interpreter Startup

You run the Python interpreter by executing the `python` command. Table 13–1 shows a number of forms of the command for invoking the Python interpreter. The `opts` are command line options, including those shown in Table 13–2. The `file` names a file containing Python code to execute. The executing code can access the command line arguments through the `sys.argv` list.

You can use '-' to have Python take its input from the standard input. You do not have to use the hyphen at all if you are not passing command line arguments. The Python interpreter will terminate when it comes to the end of the input, control-D in UNIX or control-Z in Windows.

You can redirect Python's input from a file rather than using the file name as the source of a program. The difference is that when you use "`python - <file`", the `input()` and `raw_input()` functions will take their input from the file. If you give Python the name of a file to execute, it will take its input from the standard input.

Table 13–1
Python command lines.

Command Line	Used For
`python opts file args`	Runs the Python program contained in the `file`, passing it the command line arguments `args` as strings in the list `sys.argv`. Element `sys.argv[0]` is the `file`.
`python opts - args` `python opts`	Runs Python, taking its input from the input and passing the command line arguments as strings in the list `sys.argv`. Element `sys.argv[0]` is '–'. If there are no command line arguments, you may omit the '–'.
`python opts -c cmd args`	If you use the `-c` `cmd`, the string `cmd` is executed as a command. You will probably need to quote `cmd`, since it may contain blanks.

Table 13–2
Command line options.

Flag	Meaning
`-h`	Print help message and exit.
`-i`	Enter interactive mode (i.e., take input from `stdin`) after executing the code in the file. Does not work when source is taken from the input, since ending the input will not allow more input to be taken from there.
`-O`	Produce optimized byte code.
`-OO`	`-O` plus eliminate the documentation strings.

Table 13–2
Command line options. (Continued)

Flag	Meaning
-S	Prevent inclusion of site-specific initialization code.
-t	Warn about inconsistent tab usage.
-u	Use unbuffered `stdout` and `stderr`.
-U	Treat string literals as UNICODE.
-v	Run in verbose mode, including tracing of `import` statements.
-V	Print Python version number and exit.
-x	Skip the first line of the source program, allowing non-Unix (non `#!`) commands.

13.2 Run-Time Compilation

Python does not force you to compile a program before running it. You can compile code just before executing it, the way the interactive Python system does it. As discussed in Chapter 3, if compiled versions are not already available, modules are compiled when they are imported.

It is necessary for some purposes to compile and execute Python code under program control. One of the most important purposes is constructing `import` statements for modules whose names you have as strings, as we will see in a moment. There are four ways to compile and execute code under program control: the `exec` statement, and the `eval()`, `execfile()`, and `compile()` functions. They are summarized in Table 13–3.

Table 13–3
Run-time compilation and execution statements and functions.

Statement or Function	Explanation
code = compile(string, fromWhence, kind)	*string* : The string to compile. *fromWhence*: A string identifying the source. For printing in error tracebacks. You can use `"<string>"`. *kind*: A string indicating the use of the compiled code: `"exec"` : To be used in `exec` statements; therefore, Python should expect to find a sequence of statements with newlines and tabs. `"eval"` : To be passed to the `eval()` function, therefore an expression. `"single"` : To be treated as a single statement. If it is an expression, the value it returns will be written out.
exec code exec *code* in *globals* exec *code* in *globals*, *locals* exec string exec string in *globals* exec string in *globals*,*locals*	Execute the statement(s) contained in the code or string. Execute it or them within the global and local environments indicated by the dictionaries' globals and locals. (If not provided, the environments are those of the exec statement itself.)

Table 13-3
Run-time compilation and execution statements and functions. (Continued)

Statement or Function	Explanation

`eval(code)`
`eval(code,globals)`
`eval(code,globals,locals)`
	Evaluate the expression contained in the code or string and return its value. Evaluate it within the global and local environments indicated by the dictionaries' globals and locals. (If not provided, the environments are those of the `eval()` function call.)

`execfile(name)`
`execfile(name,globals)`
`execfile(name,globals,`
`    locals)`
	Execute the statement(s) contained in the file of the specified name. Execute it within the global and local environments indicated by the dictionaries' globals and locals. (If not provided, the environments are those of the `execfile()` function call.)

13.2.1 `exec`

The `exec` statement compiles a string as a statement and executes it, or executes a code object returned by a call to the `compile()` function. Its forms are `exec` *code* and `exec` *string*.

The only difference is that the `code` option is the result of a `compile()` function call. One of the most common uses of `exec` is to execute an `import` statement. The `import` statement requires the module being imported to be named with an identifier, not a string; but sometimes we only have the string name of the module to load. We have to do something like this:

```
exec "import "+m + " as mod"
```

where `m` is a string containing the name of the module and `mod` is the variable you want to reference the module object through. An example of this use is shown in Section 12.16. When you execute code, it normally executes in your current scope, just as if the code being executed were there in place of the `exec` statement. You can explicitly give the *global* or both *global* and *local* environments in which it is to find and assign its variables. The options are as follows:

```
exec code
exec code in globals
exec code in globals, locals
```

where *code* in this case is either a string or a compiled code object, and *globals* and *locals* are dictionaries.

Be careful that you do not execute input from an arbitrary user. Suppose you read input into string s and execute it with exec s. The user could type:

```
import os;os.system("rm -R /")
```

which executes a command on a Unix system to delete as much of your file system as you have write permissions for.

13.2.2 eval

The built-in function eval() evaluates the code for a Python expression and returns its value. It has these forms:

```
eval(code)
eval(code,globals)
eval(code,globals,locals)
```

The code is either a string or a compiled code object. You can specify environments if you want to. The code needs to be an expression rather than a statement.

13.2.3 execfile

The built-in function execfile() executes a file. It is used as follows:

```
execfile(name)
execfile(name,globals)
execfile(name,globals, locals)
```

where *name* is the string name of the file. Again, you can provide an environment in which to execute the statements in the file.

13.2.4 `compile`

If you are going to execute the same string or file many times, it is more efficient to compile it first and then use the compiled version. `Compile` has the form:

compile(string, fromWhence, kind)

where

- *string* is the string to compile.
- *fromWhence* is a string identifying the source of the string for printing in error tracebacks. You can use `"<string>"`.
- *kind* is a string indicating the use of the compiled code:
  - `"exec"` says it is going to be used in `exec` statements, therefore Python should expect to find a sequence of statements. Newline characters and tabs are allowed in the string.
  - `"eval"` says it is going to be passed to the `eval()` function, therefore Python should expect to find an expression.
  - `"single"` says it should be treated as a single statement. If it is an expression, the value it returns will be written out.

Here is an example of the difference between `"exec"` and `"single"` compilation:

```
>>> exec compile("2*3","<string>","exec")
>>> exec compile("2*3","<string>","single")
6
```

Note that the `"exec"` form doesn't write out the result. The `"single"` form does.

Here is an example of compiling a class as a string and then creating an instance of it:

```
>>> c=compile('''class A:
...     def f(self):print 'hi'
...
...
... ''','<<<string>>>','exec')
>>>
>>> a=A()
Traceback (most recent call last):
  File "<stdin>", line 1, in ?
NameError: There is no variable named 'A'
```

```
>>> exec c
>>> a=A()
>>> a.f()
hi
```

Finally, here we compile a statement into a code object and iterate through its members, writing out each one. Notice that the co_code string contains a number of unprintable characters.

```
>>> f=compile('a=1','<<string>>','single')
>>> for x in f.__members__:
...     print x,getattr(f,x)
...
co_argcount 0
co_code ≠  ≠? d  Z  d? S
co_consts (1, None)
co_filename <<string>>
co_firstlineno 1
co_flags 0
co_lnotab
co_name ?
co_names ('a',)
co_nlocals 0
co_stacksize 1
co_varnames ()
```

13.3   Wrap-Up

In this chapter, we considered a number of things that are involved with the execution of Python code. First, we looked at the command-line options that control Python's execution of programs. Then we looked at statements and functions that call for compilation and execution of Python code while Python programs are executing.

The exec command is necessary to construct an import statement when the module name is available only in a string. It must be emphasized, though, that accepting any string from a user and then executing it is extremely unsafe.

13.4   Exercises

13.1. Is it safe to pass a string that a user types in to the function `eval()`?

13.2. Suppose we wish to save a data structure in a file in one program and recreate it from the file when we run another program.

The interface is to be:

- `writeStruct(x,f)` will write out the data structure `x` into file `f`.
- `y=readStruct(f)` will read in and return a copy of the data structure from file `f`.

We decide to have `writeStruct()` write executable Python code and to have `readStruct()` use `execfile()`. Figure out the rest of the implementation. You will probably need functions in the Python library's `new` module.

14

Abstract Data Types and Special Methods

You might think a data type, like integer, is a collection of values (for example, *0, 1, -1, ...*), but the set of values is only part of it. The data type also consists of the operations that can be performed on the values; for example, +, -, *,... in the case of integers.

A programming language provides a number of data types, but you can provide many more yourself. You create a class whose instances are values of your data type and whose methods are the operations on your data type. The attributes contained in the class instances provide the representation of your data objects. These data types are called *abstract data types* to distinguish them from the concrete data types built into the language.

In this chapter and the next, we explore abstract data types. Chapter 15 is devoted to container data types, or data types that contain other data objects. Python's built-in container data types are lists, tuples, and dictionaries. The code that comes with this book provides queue and set abstract container data types.

Python provides an important convenience for implementing abstract data types. You are able to make the built-in operators work for the new data types. You can provide your own implementation of binary operators like "x+y" and subscripting operators like "x[y]".

14.1 Special Methods

The way you define how operators work for your abstract data types is by the use of "special methods." Table 14–1 lists all the special methods, divided into categories. In this chapter, we examine all the categories other than the container operations, which are reserved for Chapter 15.

Table 14–1
Special method.

Method	Called by/to: Explanation
All Objects	
__init__(self,args)	Object creation, ClassName(args).
__del__(self)	The storage reclamation system when it is about to destroy the instance, not necessarily when a del statement is applied to the last reference to the instance.
__repr__(self)	repr(x) and 'x' to convert the object into a string. The string should be either a Python expression that will recreate the object if executed or a descriptive string if such an expression is not possible; for example: >>> repr(open('x.txt','w')) "<open file 'x.txt', mode 'w' at 007D2348>"
__str__(self)	str(x) and print statements; an informal string representation of the object.
__cmp__(self,x)	Compare self to object x; self<x yields a negative integer; self==x, 0; self>x, positive. This will be called for a relational operator if an appropriate one of the following six "rich comparison" methods is not defined.
__lt__(self,x)	self < x, new in Python 2.1
__le__(self,x)	self <= x, new in Python 2.1
__gt__(self,x)	self > x, new in Python 2.1
__ge__(self,x)	self >= x, new in Python 2.1

Table 14–1
Special method. (Continued)

Method	Called by/to: Explanation
`__eq__(self,x)`	`self == x`, new in Python 2.1
`__ne__(self,x)`	`self != x`, new in Python 2.1
`__hash__(self)`	Compute a hash value when the object is being placed in a dictionary. It is required that if `x.__cmp__(y) == 0`, then `x.__hash__() == y.__hash__()`. The hash value tells the dictionary where to start looking for the object. To find an equal object, the dictionary must start looking in the same place.
`__nonzero__(self)`	Test whether the object counts as true (nonzero) when used in `if` and `while` statements.
Arithmetic	
`__add__(x,y)` `__radd__(y,x)`	`x+y`
`__sub__(x,y)` `__rsub(y,x)`	`x-y`
`__mul__(x,y)` `__rmul(y,x)`	`x*y`
`__div__(x,y)` `__rdiv(y,x)`	`x/y`
`__mod__(x,y)` `__rmod(y,x)`	`x%y`
`__divmod__(x,y)` `__rdivmod__(y,x)`	`divmod(x,y)`

Table 14–1
Special method. (Continued)

Method	Called by/to: Explanation
__pow__(x,y) __rpow(y,x)	x**y, pow(x,y)
__lshift__(x,y) __rlshift(y,x)	x<<y
__rshift__(x,y) __rrshift(y,x)	x>>y
__and__(x,y) __rand(y,x)	x&y
__or__(x,y) __ror(y,x)	x|y
__xor__(x,y) __rxor(y,x)	x^y
__neg__(self)	-self
__pos__(self)	+self
__abs__(self)	abs(self)
__invert__(self)	~ self
__coerce__(x,y)	Binary arithmetic operation: Returns a tuple, (X,Y), of x and y converted to a common type, or None if the coercions are not possible.
__int__(self), __long__(self), __float__(self), __complex__(self)	int(self), long(self), float(self), complex(self), or in a mixed-mode context: Converts to the specified numeric type.

Table 14–1
Special method. (Continued)

Method	Called by/to: Explanation
`__oct__(self)`, `__hex__(self)`	`oct(self)`, `hex(self)`: To convert to an octal or hexadecimal string representation.
Operate-and-Becomes Operations	
`__iadd__(x,y)`	`x+=y`, the value returned is assigned to `x`.
`__isub__(x,y)`	`x-=y`, the value returned is assigned to `x`.
`__imul__(x,y)`	`x*=y`, the value returned is assigned to `x`.
`__idiv__(x,y)`	`x/=y`, the value returned is assigned to `x`.
`__imod__(x,y)`	`x%=y`, the value returned is assigned to `x`.
`__ipow__(x,y)`	`x**=y`, the value returned is assigned to `x`.
`__ilshift__(x,y)`	`x<<=y`, the value returned is assigned to `x`.
`__irshift__(x,y)`	`x>>=y`, the value returned is assigned to `x`.
`__iand__(x,y)`	`x&=y`, the value returned is assigned to `x`.
`__ior__(x,y)`	`x|=y`, the value returned is assigned to `x`.

Table 14–1
Special method. (Continued)

Method	Called by/to: Explanation
Attribute Operations	
`__getattr__(self,name)`	`self.name`: Called if the name attribute is not found by normal lookup. This allows some attributes to be computed.
`__setattr__(self,name, value)`	`self.name=value`. If present, Python calls this rather than doing the normal assignment to an attribute. You cannot use `self.name=value` within this method to directly assign values to attributes. You must use `self.__dict__[name]=value`.
`__delattr__(self,name)`	`del self.name`. It has similar restrictions to `__setattr__()`.
Function Call	
`__call__(self, args)`	When the instance is used as a function. Built-in function `callable(x)` will return true for an instance object `x` if its class has this method.
Container Operations	
`__len__(self)`	`len()`: Returns the number of objects in a container.
`__contains__(x,y)`	`y in x` (in Python2).
`__getitem__(self,key)`	`self[key]`: Returns the contained item associated with the key.
`__setitem__(self,key, value)`	`self[key]=value`: Assigns a value to the key in the container.

Table 14–1
Special method. (Continued)

Method	Called by/to: Explanation
`__delitem__(self,key)`	`del self[key]`: Deletes the item associated with the key from the container.
`__getslice__(self,i,j)`	`self[i:j]`. Requires `__len__(self)`: Negative indices have the length added before being passed in.
`__setslice__(self,i,j, seq)`	`self[i:j]=seq`. Requires `__len__(self)`: Negative indices have the length added before being passed in.
`__delslice__(self,i,j)`	`del self[i:j]`. Requires `__len__(self)`: Negative indices have the length added before being passed in.

To demonstrate a number of these methods, we will use the module `rationalmath` shown in Figure 14–1. The class `rational` represents rational numbers as two long integers, a numerator and a denominator. The denominator will always be a positive integer. The numerator can be positive, zero, or negative. The numerator and denominator are reduced by dividing them by their greatest common divisor, computed by function `gcd()`.

14.2   Methods for All Objects

There are some special methods that can apply to all objects.

14.2.1   Method __init__()

The `__init__()` method is used to initialize instances of objects. Python calls it just after an object has been created. For example, when you execute `x=className()`, Python will look up the `__init__` method for `className` and call it, passing the newly created instance as the first parameter.

In class rational (see Figure 14–1), the `__init__(self,*args)` method initializes the numerator and denominator to a value specified by the zero, one, or two argument. The call `rational()` will create a rational number zero with a numerator of `0L` and a denominator of `1L`.

The call `rational(x)`, where `x` is an integer or a long, creates the rational number with the value `long(x)/1L`. And of course, `rational(x,y)` creates the number with the value `long(x)/long(y)`. A floating-point number, n, is allowed only as a single argument: `rational(n)`. The initializer uses a function from the math module, `f,x=frexp(n)`, to split the floating-point number `n` into its fraction, `f`, and exponent, `x`. The numerator is set to the fraction multiplied by the large power of two and converted to a long, and the denominator is set to the same large power of two. The definition of the f and x parts is $n = f \cdot 2^x$, where $0.5 \leq f < 1.0$ unless f is zero. We take $2^{|x|}$ and multiply the numerator by that if $x \geq 0$, and we multiply the denominator by it if $x < 0$. Finally, we reduce the numerator and denominator by their greatest common divisor.

```
"""rational numbers"""
import types, math, hasher
def gcd(x,y):
    assert isinstance(x,types.IntType) or \
        isinstance(x,types.LongType)
    assert isinstance(y,types.IntType) or \
        isinstance(y,types.LongType)
    x=abs(x)
    y=abs(y)
    if y>x:
        x,y=y,x
    while y>0:
        x,y = y,x%y
    return x
class rational:
    def __init__(self,*args):
        if len(args)==0:
            self.numerator=0L
            self.denominator=1L
        elif len(args)==1:
            n=args[0]
            if isinstance(n,types.FloatType):
                f,x=math.frexp(n)
                self.numerator=long(f*2.0**64)
                self.denominator=2L**64
                if x<0: self.denominator*=2L**abs(x)
                else: self.numerator*=2L**x
            else:
                self.numerator=long(n)
                self.denominator=1L
        else :
            self.numerator=long(args[0])
            self.denominator=long(args[1])
        g=gcd(self.numerator,self.denominator)
        if g<=1:return
```

Figure 14–1
Rational numbers.

```
      self.numerator=self.numerator/g
      self.denominator=self.denominator/g
  def __add__(x,y):
    numr=x.numerator*y.denominator+ \
      y.numerator*x.denominator
    denom=x.denominator*y.denominator
    g=gcd(numr,denom)
    return rational(numr/g,denom/g)
  def __sub__(x,y):
    numr=x.numerator*y.denominator- \
      y.numerator*x.denominator
    denom=x.denominator*y.denominator
    g=gcd(numr,denom)
    return rational(numr/g,denom/g)
  def __mul__(x,y):
    numr=x.numerator*y.numerator
    denom=x.denominator*y.denominator
    g=gcd(numr,denom)
    return rational(numr/g,denom/g)
  def __div__(x,y):
    numr=x.numerator*y.denominator
    denom=x.denominator*y.numerator
    g=gcd(numr,denom)
    return rational(numr/g,denom/g)
  def __radd__(y,x): return x+y
  def __rsub__(y,x): return x-y
  def __rmul__(y,x): return x*y
  def __rdiv__(y,x): return x/y
  def __neg__(x):
    return rational(-x.numerator,x.denominator)
  def __float__(self):
    return float(self.numerator)/float(self.denominator)
  def __long__(self):
    return self.numerator/self.denominator
  def __int__(self):
    return int(long(self))
  def __repr__(self):
    return "rational("+repr(self.numerator)+ \
      ","+repr(self.denominator)+")"
  def __str__(self):
    return "("+str(self.numerator)+ \
      "/"+str(self.denominator)+")"
  def __cmp__(self,other):
    return cmp((self-other).numerator, 0L)
  def __hash__(self):
    x=hasher.hash1(hash(self.numerator))
    y=hasher.hash2(hash(self.denominator))
    return hasher.hash3(x-y)
  def __nonzero__(self):
    return self.numerator!=0
  def __coerce__(self,other):
    if isinstance(other,rational):
      return self,other
    return self,rational(other)
```

Figure 14–1
Rational numbers. (Continued)

14.2.2 Methods __str__ and __repr__

The __str__() method, if it exists, is called by the built-in function str() when it needs to convert the object to a string. The method __str__() overrides the default behavior that returns a string like:

'<module.classname instance at memory address>'

The __repr__() method allows you to provide your own behavior for the repr() built-in method. Its default behavior is the same for class instances as that of str().

In Figure 14–1, repr(x) for rational number x yields rational(x.numerator,x.denominator), which would give an equal rational number if executed. However, str(x) yields the form (x.numerator/x.denominator).

14.2.3 Del

The __del__() method is called as the garbage collector is deleting an object. It is not necessarily called when you execute a del statement. Here is an example where the del method writes out a good-bye message when an object is collected. When we execute the loop for i in xrange(10): ptr=C(), we create instances of class C and assign them to the variable ptr. Each time we assign a new value to ptr, the previous value becomes inaccessible, its reference count goes to zero, and Python collects it. As Python collects it, Python calls the object's __del__ method, which writes out a message. It appears that there are two objects that alternately have their __del__ methods called, but it is their *addresses* that are being recycled; the id() function returns the memory address of the object. When an instance is deleted, its memory becomes available and is reallocated to another instance of C.

```
>>> class C:
...       def __del__(self): print id(self),"says bye."
...
>>> for i in xrange(10): ptr=C()
...
<built-in function id> says bye.
8256420 says bye.
8250148 says bye.
8256420 says bye.
8250148 says bye.
8256420 says bye.
8250148 says bye.
8256420 says bye.
```

```
8250148 says bye.
8256420 says bye.
```

14.2.4 Cmp

The default behavior of cmp(x,y) is to compare the locations of the two instances. You can override it by supplying your own __cmp__(self,y). If it finds such a method for x's class, cmp(x,y) will call x.__cmp__(y). The __cmp__(self,y) method is to return a negative integer if self is less than y, zero if they are equal, and a positive integer if self is greater than y. If x's class does not have a __cmp__() method, but y's class does, Python calls y.__cmp__(x) and reverses the sense of the result. Unless there are rich comparison operators available (see Section 14.3), the relational operators, like ==, !=, >, <=, and so on are implemented by calls to cmp().

For rational numbers, the __cmp__(self,y) method subtracts y from self and compares the numerator to zero. We cannot just return the numerator of the difference, because that is a long int, and cmp() is supposed to return an int; we cannot just convert the numerator of the difference to an int, since it might be too large to represent.

14.2.5 Hash and cmp

The __hash__(self) method is called by built-in function hash() when you try to use the instance as a key to a dictionary.

By default, hash() returns an object's address–the value returned by id(). Similarly, the default behavior of cmp(x,y) is to compare id(x) to id(y). If you want different behavior, you need to define __hash__() and __cmp__() yourself. If you do want your objects to be used as keys, you need to make sure that any two instances of your class that are equal have the same hash value. That is, if x and y are instances of your class and cmp(x,y)==0, then hash(x) *must* equal hash(y). The reason is that dictionaries begin their search for a key at a position determined from the hash value of the key. Two different hash values will almost always cause the dictionary to look in different places. Even if two keys compare as equal, if the hash values are different, you will not be able to find one key if you try looking up the other.

Because of the requirement that equal values must have equal hash values, Python notices whether a class defines the __cmp__() method but not __hash__(). The default behavior of both cmp() and hash() is to use the address of the class instance. If cmp() no longer uses its default behavior, then the default hash value is no longer appropriate.

Python makes a class's instances unhashable if the class defines __cmp__() but not __hash__(), for example:

```
>>> class D: pass
...
>>> d=D()
>>> hash(d)
8291132
>>> id(d)
8291132
>>> class C:
...      def __cmp__(self,x): return 0
...
>>> c=C()
>>> hash(c)
Traceback (most recent call last):
  File "<stdin>", line 1, in ?
TypeError: unhashable instance
```

If you do not want instances of your class to be used as keys for dictionaries, you can make the __hash__ method raise an exception; for example:

```
def __hash__(self): raise NotImplementedError
```

Or you can simply define __cmp__() for it, but not __hash__().

In our rational numbers, two rationals are considered equal if they have the same numerator and the same denominator. Remember, the numerator and denominator are always reduced to their smallest values by dividing by the greatest common divisor, so there is a unique representation for a number. The __hash__() method for rational numbers computes its value solely from the numerator and denominator, so equal rational numbers will always return the same hash code.

The __hash__() method of rational deserves a bit of explanation. It uses the built-in hash() function on both the numerator and denominator to convert them to ints. For small values, this is the same as calling int(), but hash will also work for values outside the range of ints. Then the numerator and denominator are each passed through another hash function from our module hasher and their difference is passed through another. These functions are based on congruential random number generators. If you wanted random integers in the range one through maxint-1, inclusive, you could start with some value, *seed*, let the first hash value $h_0 = hash1(seed)$, and use $h_i = hash1(h_{i-1})$ to get the others. When used for hashing, you compute an int from the key and apply hash1(), hash2(), or hash3() to it. You can use other random number generators the same way. Pass in an `int` derived from your key as a seed and generate maybe the second random number of the sequence as the hash value. Experience with several random number generators, including those in our `hasher` module, indicates that generating only the first number in the pseudo-random sequence leaves too many bits in common among the hash values of keys in a sequence. (We will not go into an explanation of the hasher module here since an explanation of congruential pseudo-random number generators is beyond the scope of this book. It is available with the code for this book for your examination and use.)

14.2.6 Nonzero

The `__nonzero__()` method is called to test whether the object is to be considered as true in an `if` or `while` statement or with an `and`, `or`, or `not` operator. If you want to use your instances to control the execution of loops, you will need to implement the `__nonzero__` method to return some nonzero value if the instance should be considered `True`, and return zero if it is false. A rational number is considered to be nonzero when its numerator is not zero.

14.3   Operators

14.3.1 Arithmetic Operators

The unary and binary operators in Python have corresponding special methods. You can see some of these special methods at work in rational numbers defined in Figure 14–1. A rational number is represented as two long integers, numerator and denominator. The value of the rational number is the ratio of these. As you can see from Table 14–1, there are three special methods that correspond to each "arithmetic" binary operator. For example, the operator "`-`", has methods:

- `__sub__(self,x)` —for subtract `self-x`,
- `__rsub__(self,x)` —for reversed subtract, `x-self`, and
- `__isub__(self,x)` —for `self-=x`.

When we discuss the operators, we speak loosely of operator *op* having methods `__op__()`, `__rop__()`, and `__iop__()`. Obviously, you have to substitute the actual operator for *op* standing alone and the name for *op* in the methods, for example "`+`" and "`add`".

We will save the discussion of the combined operation and assignment operators, `__iop__()`, until the next section. Here, let us consider the differences between the regular and reversed operations. The rules get a bit complex, but here is a first cut at an explanation. If Python finds that the left operand of a binary operator *op* is an instance of a class that has an `__op__()` method, Python calls that method. Otherwise, if the right operand is a class instance with an `__rop__()` method, Python calls that method. Notice that the left operand takes precedence over the right operand in choosing the method to call.

This gets a bit more complex, because Python also allows objects of your abstract data types to be converted to compatible types, just as numeric operands are converted to a common type before being added. This forced conversion of operands to compatible types is called *coercion*. You can provide an optional method, `__coerce__()`, to do this conversion for your abstract data type. The call `x.__coerce__(y)` is supposed to return a tuple, `(X, Y)`, where x has been converted to X and y has been converted to Y. In Figure 14–1, the `__coerce__(self, other)` method can be called only if `self` is a rational number. It checks the `other` operand. If `other` is also a rational number, it simply returns the pair `(self, other)`. Otherwise, it returns the tuple `(self, rational(other))`.

Here is the sequence of things Python tries when given a binary operation, x *op* y, to evaluate:

1. **String formatting:** If the left operand is a string and the operator is "`%`", Python invokes string formatting.
2. **Left operand has method:** If the left operand is a class instance, Python tries these things:
   a. If x has a `__coerce__()` method, Python replaces x and y with the results of calling `x.__coerce__(y)`; however, if `__coerce__()` returns `None`, Python goes on to consider the right operand with rule 3.
   b. If after the coercion neither x nor y is a class instance, Python goes on to rule 4 to try to evaluate the operator for built-in types.
   c. If after step 2a, x is a class instance and has an `__op__()` method, Python returns the value of `x.__op__(y)`.
   d. Otherwise, Python restores x and y to their initial values and goes on to rule 3.
3. **Right operand has method:** If the right operand, y, is a class instance and either the left operand, x, is not a class instance or the rules in part 2 did not resolve the issue, Python tries these things:

a. If y has a __coerce__() method, Python replaces y and x with the result returned by y.__coerce__(x). Python reports an error if the __coerce__() method returns None.

b. If neither x nor y is a class instance after the coercion, Python goes on to rule 4.

c. If y after step 3a is a class instance and has an __rop__() method, Python calls and returns the value of y.__rop__(x).

d. If Python gets here, it has not been able to evaluate the operator, so it raises an exception.

4. **Neither operand is a class instance:** Python gets here when neither operand is a class instance. Python performs sequence concatenation, sequence repetition, or arithmetic depending on the types of the operands. If none of those apply, Python raises an exception.

These rules are detailed, but you need to know them if you are going to implement binary operators in your abstract data type. Let us consider some implications of the rules. To begin with, you do not need to provide a __coerce__() method. If your left operand has an __op__() method, Python will call that. Otherwise, if your left operand does not have an __op__() method but your right operand has an __rop__() method, Python will call that. You can have these methods do any conversions needed on the other operand. Indeed, you must have the __op__() and __rop__() methods do their own conversions in two situations:

1. The conversions required are different for different operators. Only one __coerce__() method is allowed, so it is only appropriate if the conversions are the same for all operators.

2. The required conversions are not commutative. By commutative I mean that no matter which operand is an instance of your class, you want to convert the other operand to the same type. There is *no* "__rcoerce__()" method. The __coerce__() method may be called for either the left or the right operand and it will not be told which. It has to do the same thing in both cases.

In the rational class, a __coerce__() method works. Whichever operand is a rational number, we want to convert the other operand to a rational. Now, you might think that because we have this __coerce__() method for rational numbers, we would not need the methods __radd__(), __rsub__(), and so on. After all, if the right operand converts the left to rational, then the left operand will have the __add__() or whatever method. However, that is not what rule 3 says. If __coerce__() is called for the right operand, Python will consider reverse operations only for the right operand. It does not go back to reconsider methods for the converted left operand. So in the `rational` class, we wrote:

```
def __radd__(y,x): return x+y
```

This method will only be called once the x operand has been converted to a `rational`, so the plus in the return statement will call `x.__add__(y)`.

Notice that there are no special methods for the comparison operators nor the logical operators and, or, and not. The relationals are handled by calls to __cmp__() or by the rich comparison operators discussed in the next section. The "and" and "or" operators are really control constructs. They are short-circuited, not evaluating their right operands if the left operand determines the result, whereas the regular binary operators evaluate both operands. The rules for coercion and the forward and reverse operations require that both operands have been evaluated so their types can be known. The logical operators are incompatible with regular operators and so do not have special methods.

The principle of least astonishment has implications for the design of these special operator methods. The binary and unary operators are defined for pure values. They do not have side effects, and they do not change the contents of their operands. People expect them to behave that way. It would be bad design to have these operators violate these assumptions. However, the __iop__() methods, like __iadd__() for +=, are permitted to make changes in their left operand. People are expecting that the left operand will be replaced, and it is not much of a leap, if the left operand is a mutable object, to allow its contents to be changed.

14.3.2   Augmented Assignment

The "operate and becomes" special method __iop__() is used for the augmented assignment statements op=. These __iop__() methods are not required in order to use augmented assignments. For example, the rational class does not have an __iadd__() method, but "+=" still works:

```
>>> x=rational(2)
>>> x
rational(2L,1L)
>>> x+=1
>>> x
rational(3L,1L)
```

This shows that x+=y will behave like x=x+y if there is no __iadd__()
method defined for x's class.

Why would you use the __iadd__() method? You would use it if
you want the augmented assignment to modify the contents of the left
operand. Remember, it would be very bad form to have x+y modify
the contents of x, since nobody is expecting + to behave that way; but
you can define a method __iadd__() to allow x+=y to modify x.

Consider the class stats in Figure 14–2 that is used to compute the
mean and standard deviation of a set of numbers by accumulating the
sum of the numbers, the sum of the squares of the numbers, and the
number of numbers and computing the statistics only when you ask for
them. You give it the numbers with the += operator, for example:

```
>>> import stats1
>>> s=stats1.stats()
>>> s+=1
>>> s+=1
>>> s+=1
>>> s+=2
>>> s+=2
>>> s+=2
>>> s.get_mean()
1.5
>>> s.get_std_dev()
0.5
```

When you call method get_mean() or get_std_dev(), the method computes the mean or standard deviation for the values seen up to that
time.

Notice that the __iadd__(self,x) method returns self. The value
it returns is assigned to its left operand. Hence x+=y behaves much the
same whether it is handled by the __iadd__() method or the __add__()
method; the value returned by the method is assigned to the variable on
the left-hand side of the assignment operator.

14.3.3 Rich Comparisons

"Rich comparison" operators are new to version 2.1 of Python. A relational operator will be interpreted as a call to one of these operators if
its left operand possesses an appropriate one. There are no reverse
operators; for example, there is *no* __rlt__. Instead, __gt__ is the
reverse of __lt__. The arguments to the rich comparisons are not
coerced, unlike the regular binary operators described earlier.

```
import math
class stats:
    def __init__(self):
      self.reset()
    def __iadd__(self,x):
      self.sumx+=x
      self.sumxsqd+=x*x
      self.N+=1
      return self
    def get_mean(self): return self.sumx/self.N
    def get_std_dev(self):
      mean = self.sumx/self.N
      return math.sqrt(self.sumxsqd/self.N-mean*mean)
    def get_N(self):return self.N
    def get_sum_x(self):return self.sumx
    def get_sum_x_sqd(self):return self.sumxsqd
    def get_all(self):
      return self.sumx/self.N,self.get_std_dev(),self.N, \
          self.sumx,self.sumxsqd
    def reset(self):
      self.sumx=0.0
      self.sumxsqd=0.0
      self.N=0
```

Figure 14–2
Module `stats1`, augmented assignment.

Rich comparison operators can return any type of value or raise an exception. You could implement a vector type whose __lt__ method will return a vector of element-wise comparisons; for example, `vector([1,2,3])<vector([2,2,2])` might yield `vector([1,0,0])`.

If there is no appropriate rich comparison operator available, Python will call a __cmp__ method if one is available.

14.4 Attribute Access

Python allows you to catch accesses to attributes and handle them in a special way. There are three special methods available. The method __getattr__(self,x) is called if the program attempts to fetch the value of an attribute that does not exist. Parameter x gets the string name of the attribute. The method __setattr__(self,x,y) is called if the program attempts to assign the value y to an attribute x. The method __delattr__(self,x) is called if the program attempts to delete the attribute x.

Consider the method __getattr__(self,x) first. The parameter x is passed a string containing the name of the attribute the program is attempting to fetch. Method __getattr__() is called if the instance does not contain the attribute; but if the object does have the attribute, the value of the attribute is returned and __getattr__() is not called. For example:

```
>>> class C:
...     def __getattr__(self,x):
...             print "trying to fetch",x
...
>>> c=C()
>>> c.z
trying to fetch z
>>> c.z=1
>>> c.z
1
```

You can use the __getattr__() method to make objects appear to have attributes that in reality are calculated as needed. Consider the second version of the stats class shown in Figure 14–3. It performs the same functions as the version shown in Figure 14–2, but it does not provide "get" methods. Instead of writing the call s.get_mean(), you would write an attribute access, s.mean. The real attributes are sumx, sumxsqd, and N. The __getattr__() method handles calculating and returning the mean, mean, the standard deviation, stdev, and a tuple of all statistics, all. It also handles the obvious synonyms sum_x, sum_x_sqd, and std_dev.

If x has a __setattr__() method, whenever you execute an attribute assignment, x.y=z, Python will call x.__setattr__(y,z). It is up to the __setattr__() method to assign z to the attribute y. The special method __delattr__(x,name) is called to override attempts to delete the attribute name from object x. Method __getattr__() is relatively straightforward, but the __setattr__() and __delattr__ methods are more problematic.

Here is the problem: "How can __setattr__() do the assignment?" If __setattr__() tries to do an assignment, self.y=z, that itself is an attribute assignment, and Python will call __setattr__() to handle it. The infinite recursion will exhaust stack space and raise a RuntimeError. What about calling the built-in function setattr(self,y,z)? It has the same problem. Function setattr() will call the object's __setattr__() method if one exists.

```
#stats2
import math
class stats:
    def __init__(self):
      self.reset()
    def __iadd__(self,x):
      self.sumx+=x
      self.sumxsqd+=x*x
      self.N+=1
      return self
    def __getattr__(self,a):
      if a == 'mean':
        return self.sumx/self.N
      elif a == 'stddev' or a == 'std_dev':
        mean = self.sumx/self.N
        return math.sqrt(self.sumxsqd/self.N- \
          mean*mean)
      elif a == 'sum_x': return self.sumx
      elif a == 'sum_x_sqd': return self.sumxsqd
      elif a == 'all':
        return self.sumx/self.N,self.std_dev,self.N,\
          self.sumx,self.sumxsqd
      else:
        raise AttributeError, a
    def reset(self):
      self.sumx=0.0
      self.sumxsqd=0.0
      self.N=0
    def __str__(self): return "stats2 @"+str(id(self))
```

Figure 14–3
Using __getattr__ to access computed attributes.

What you have to do is bypass attribute assignment to the object and go directly to the underlying representation. Class instances have a single pool of attributes in a dictionary. You can get the dictionary through the instance's special attribute __dict__ and assign to the attribute in it: self.__dict__[y]=z. Because self.__dict__ is an attribute reference that yields a dictionary, not an assignment, Python does not call __setattr__().

The __delattr__() method has the same problems. It cannot itself directly delete an attribute, as that would call it again. The same workaround is used. You have __delattr__(self,x) execute del self.__dict__[x].

Why would you ever use the __setattr__() method? You might use it for debugging, as shown in Figure 14–4. Suppose we are trying to use a stat object from the stat2 module and somewhere in the program one of its attributes is getting assigned a strange value. The question is, "Where is it getting clobbered?" To find out, we create a subclass that will catch all assignments to attributes and report what value is being assigned to what attribute and where in the program the attribute assignment occurred. The subclass defines a __setattr__() method, only the first and last statements of which are obvious: printing out the attribute assignment and performing the actual assignment. The code in between reports where the assignment is being done. It uses knowledge of some objects used in the Python implementation. The relationship of these objects is shown in Figure 14–5.

Here is the explanation: The try statement exists to get us a *traceback* object, which is the third element of the tuple returned by sys.exc_info(). A traceback object has a pointer, tb_frame, to the *frame* object of the function activation in which the exception occurred, which in this case is the __setattr__() method. A frame object has a pointer, f_back, to the frame of the function it was called from. That is the one we're interested in, since that is where the assignment to the attribute occurred. That frame object has two attributes of interest to us:

```
#stats3
import math,stats2
import sys
class stats(stats2.stats):
    def __setattr__(self,a,x):
        print 'stats.'+a+'='+str(x),
        try:
            raise Exception
        except Exception:
            cl,inst,tb=sys.exc_info()
            f=tb.tb_frame.f_back
            c=f.f_code
            print '; assigned at line',f.f_lineno,'in',\
                c.co_filename, ', function',\
                c.co_name,'()'
            del tb
        self.__dict__[a]=x
```

Figure 14–4
Reporting where attributes are being changed (stats3).

`f_lineno` is the number of the line that function was executing when it performed the assignment, and attribute `f_code` is the *code* object the function was executing. That code object itself has two attributes of interest: The attribute `co_name` is the name of the function that was executing, and the attribute `co_filename` is the name of the file the code was in. The line number in the frame is the line number in that file.

An example that uses all the attribute methods is the implementation of the object-oriented design pattern *decorator* shown in Figure 14–6. A decorator is an object that sits in front of another object, providing extra functionality. You could add functionality in a subclass, which adds some methods to those of its superclass or changes their behavior, but the decorator pattern uses a separate object that implements some methods itself and passes other accesses on to the object behind it, the *decoratee*, as shown in Figure 14–7. Users of a decorated object must be able to use it as if it had not been decorated. No methods must be removed or changed so much that they are unrecognizable. The decorator must handle at least all of the operations the decoratee handles.

Making the decorator a separate object allows decorations to be chosen at run-time. A combination of several different decorations can be added to the same object by chaining decorators together. Using subclasses to extend the functionality would not have the same advantages: Subclasses cannot be added dynamically, and creating combinations of subclasses would be problematic, since each combination would have

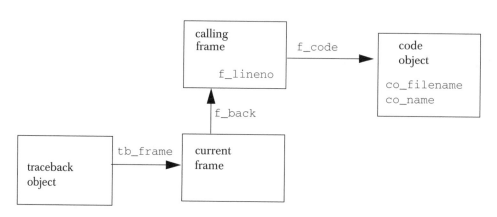

Figure 14–5
Traceback, frame, and code objects used in Figure 14–4.

to have its own class. Moreover, unlike the inheritance-based addition of methods, the object-based decorators can be attached to a variety of decoratee objects, not simply those of a particular class. The problem, though, is that all the methods known to the decoratee are called in the decorator objects, but not all methods are handled by the decorator. The decoratee should handle all those methods that the decorator does not.

Since the methods are called in the decorator, it would appear that it would have to define many of the methods of the decoratee with bodies that just pass on the call and pass back the result. However, the code in Figure 14–6 shows a base class for a decorator that automatically passes all accesses to the decoratee. Consider, for example, the following code in which we have created an instance, y, of the Decorator class with object x as its parameter:

```
y=Decorator(x)
y.f(z)
```

```
class Decorator:
    def __init__(self,x):
      self.__dict__['_decoratee']=x
    def __getattr__(self,name):
      return getattr(self._decoratee,name)
    def __setattr__(self,name,value):
      setattr(self._decoratee,name,value)
    def __delattr__(self,name):
      delattr(self._decoratee,name)
```

Figure 14–6
Base decorator.

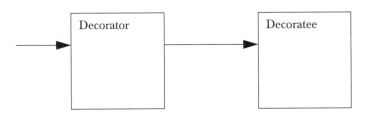

Figure 14–7
Decorator–decoratee relationship.

The attempt to call `y.f(z)` will first try to look up method `f` in class `Decorator`. Since `Decorator` does not provide a method `f()`, `Decorator`'s `__getattr__()` method will try to look up `x.f`. If `x`'s class does have a method `f`, `y`'s `__getattr__()` method will return it as `x.f`, a method bound to object `x`. Then the call will proceed as a call of `x.f(z)`.

The point of having class `Decorator` is that you can create subclasses that provide methods of their own. When you try calling one of those methods, it is called in your decorator object, but any method it does not provide is automatically passed on to its decoratee.

One problem with this base decorator class is that if you create a subclass of it, you cannot easily assign values to attributes of your decorator object. If the methods in your subclass of `Decorator` try assigning to attributes, the assignments will be made to attributes in the decoratee. Consider the code in Figure 14–8. We create a subclass of `Decorator`, class `D`, with one method, `f()`, that assigns its parameter to attribute `z`. We create an empty class `E`. Then we assign variable `x` an instance of `E` and assign `y` an instance of `D` decorating `x`. Initially, neither `x` nor `y` has an attribute `z`. Once we call `y.f(1)`, both `x` and `y` will report having an attribute `z` equal to one. The reason is that the assignment `self.z=z` in method `f(self,z)` of class `D` calls `self.__setattr__('z',1)`, which in turn executes `self._decoratee.z=1`. Thereafter we can see attribute `z` in `x` directly, and when we look for `z` in `y`, `y.__getattr__('z')` will return the value of `self._decoratee.z`.

14.5   Function Call Method

The special method `__call__()` allows you to use a class instance as a function. When your code tries to call the class instance, the `__call__()` method is executed. You can use this to implement a function that has a memory of its calls. Consider the prefix sum problem: You want to create a list of the sums of the initial numbers in another list,

$$x_i = \sum_{j=0}^{i} y_j$$

The class `sum` in Figure 14–9 gives you a function that you can use. An instance of `sum` is a function that on each call returns the sum of its

```
>>> class D(Decorator.Decorator):
...      def f(self,z):self.z=z
...
>>> class E:pass
...
>>> x=E()
>>> y=D(x)
>>> x.z
Traceback (most recent call last):
  File "<stdin>", line 1, in ?
AttributeError: 'E' instance has no attribute 'z'
>>> y.z
Traceback (most recent call last):
  File "<stdin>", line 1, in ?
  File "Decorator.py", line 5, in __getattr__
    return getattr(self._decoratee,name)
AttributeError: 'E' instance has no attribute 'z'
>>> y.f(1)
>>> y.z
1
>>> x.z
1
```

Figure 14–8
Demonstration of attribute assignment and lookup.

```
class sum:
    def __init__(self):
      self.acc=0
    def __call__(self,x):
      self.acc+=x
      return self.acc
```

Figure 14–9
Function with memory, class sum.

parameters for this and all previous calls. Using sum, you can produce a list of prefix sums using the map function:

```
>>> map(sum(),range(1,11))
[1, 3, 6, 10, 15, 21, 28, 36, 45, 55]
```

Another use for __call__() is to create partially bound functions. Suppose we want to create a function f that is the composition of two other functions, *g* and *h*, usually written $f = g \circ h$ and meaning $f(x) = g(h(x))$. We could write:

```
f=lambda x: g(h(x))
```

Now suppose instead of one of these, we want to create any number of compositions of pairs of functions. We would like to write a compose function that would take the two functions as parameters and return their composition, for example:

```
f=compose(g,h)
```

We could try:

```
compose=lambda g,h: lambda x,g=g,h=h:g(h(x))
```

This makes compose a function of two parameters, g and h, that returns a function of three parameters, x, g, and h, where g and h default to the g and h parameters passed to compose.

```
class compose:
    def __init__(self,g,h):
        self.h=h
        self.g=g
    def __call__(self,*x):
        return self.g(self.h(*x))
```

Figure 14–10
Composition of functions.

The problem with the above definition of compose is that after you create a composition f=compose(g,h), you can call f(a,b) and replace function g with b, which is probably not what you want. Figure 14–10 shows how to get around this by making compose a class. The class is instantiated with two functions that are saved in attributes. A call of the instance will use the functions the instance was created with. As an added benefit, the use of *x in both the parameter list of __call__(self,*x) and the argument list of self.h(*x) allows h to take more than a single argument.

14.6   Wrap-Up

In this chapter we looked at abstract data types and the special methods that support them. An abstract data type is a new data type with its own set of operations implemented in terms of other data objects. You implement an abstract data type in a class, whose methods provide the operations of the abstract data type, and whose instance attributes hold the data structure used for its implementation.

Python allows a much closer integration of abstract data types into the language than many other object-oriented languages do. We can use *special methods* to make the built-in operators apply to objects of our new data type. For example, we saw how to use special methods to implement a new numeric data type, `rational`, which can be used in mixed mode arithmetic with the usual operators, `+`, `-`, `*` and `/`.

We also studied the attribute access and function call special methods. The methods to override attribute access can be used for several purposes: to create attributes that are computed only when fetched, to observe accesses for debugging, and to automatically delegate operations to other objects. The function call special method makes a class instance behave like a function. You can use this to create functions with memories of previous calls and to create partially parameterized functions.

14.7   Exercises

14.1. Critique the implementation of rational numbers.

14.2. Critique the design of the `Decorator` class.

15

Abstract Container Data Types

Abstract container data type objects are used to contain other objects. They provide, in a way, a replacement for having to know data structures: Although they are implemented with a knowledge of data structures such as linked lists, trees, and hash tables, they may be used without such knowledge. In this chapter we consider how to implement container ADTs and examine the special methods that are used to access them. We include one container ADT, the doubly-ended queue (DEQueue) that you can use in your programs. Other ADTs are provided in Chapters 16 and 17.

We also reflect in this chapter on how to implement an N-dimensional array package that allows arbitrary lower bounds and trimming and slicing operations. This will make clear the subscripting operations possible in Python.

15.1 Special Methods for Container ADTs

The special methods are shown in Table 14–1. Those of greatest use for manipulating container ADTs are:

- __getitem__(self,key) for x[key],
- __setitem__(self,key,value) for x[key]=value,
- __delitem__(self,key) for del x[key].
- __getslice__(self,i,j) for x[i:j],
- __setslice__(self,i,j,value) for x[i:j]=value,
- __delslice__(self,i,j) for del x[i:j],

- __len__(self) for len(x), and
- __nonzero__(self) for use in if and while statements.

The "item" methods __getitem__(self,key), __setitem__(self, key,value), and __delitem__(self,key), are used in several situations:

- for single index or key value,
- for tuples used as keys,
- for slicing with a step size, i.e., using two colons: x[i:j:k],
- for slicing, x[i:j], if x has no "slice" method available.

The "slice" methods are more limited than the "item" methods, since they are called only when there is a single colon within the brackets. Here are some experiments to show how they work. We first create a class, show, that defines __getitem__() and __getslice__() methods that only return their parameters.

```
>>> class show:
...     def __init__(self,N): self.N=N
...     def __getitem__(self,i): return i
...     def __getslice__(self,i,j): return i,j
...     def __len__(self): return self.N
...
```

Note that __getitem__() returns a single value to be written out, while __getslice__() returns a tuple of length two. We needed to provide a __len__() method as well to make __getslice__() work, as we will see below.

We create an instance of show with a "length" of 10:

```
>>> s=show(10)
>>> len(s)
10
```

Now we try __getitem__(). No matter what number we pass in as a subscript, the parameter to __getitem__() gets that number unmodified.

```
>>> s[2]
2
>>> s[-2]
-2
```

Python also has a special value that can be used in subscripts, "...", "Ellipsis." It is available, but not currently used by Python.

```
>>> s[...]
Ellipsis
```

There is a slice object that you can use. You can create it with the slice() built-in function, or by writing it as *start*:*end*:*step*:

```
>>> s[1:5:2]
slice(1, 5, 2)
>>> s[-1:-5:-2]
slice(-1, -5, -2)
```

What happens is that a slice object is created and passed to __getitem__(), which returns it as a single value. However, if you use only a single colon, you call __getslice__():

```
>>> s[1:5]
(1, 5)
```

A slice object has three attributes, named start, stop, and step:

```
>>> dir(s[1:5:2])
['start', 'step', 'stop']
```

If you do not provide a bound, the call to __getslice__() uses zero for start and the maximum positive integer for stop:

```
>>> s[:]
(0, 2147483647)
```

However, an omitted value in the two-colon version is assigned None:

```
>>> s[::]
slice(None, None, None)
```

Now notice an important difference between __getitem__() and __getslice__(): A subscript passed to __getitem__() is unmodified and a component of a slice object is unmodified, but a start or stop position passed to __getslice__() is converted from a negative position to its positive equivalent:

```
>>> s[-3:-1]
(7, 9)
```

Remember, s has the length 10. The bounds -3 and -1 become 10-3 and 10-1. This is why we had to provide a __len__() method for show. Python uses it to convert the indices to the slice operation. Now let's create a class, showitem, that has no slice operation:

```
>>> class showitem:
...        def __getitem__(self,i):
...                return i
...
```

What happens when we use a single colon?

```
>>> x=showitem()
>>> x[1:2]
slice(1, 2, None)
```

Python creates a slice object and passes it to __getitem__(). The step was not provided, so Python gives it the value None. In fact, Python provides a value None for any component of a two-colon slice that is not specified:

```
>>> x[:1:2]
slice(None, 1, 2)
>>> x[1::2]
slice(1, None, 2)
```

But even though Python is going to produce a slice object to pass to __getitem__(), and even though slice objects can have negative bounds when they are created with two colons, if we try to use negative bounds for the single-colon version, we get an error, since showitem() does not have a length to modify them with:

```
>>> x[-1:2]
Traceback (most recent call last):
  File "<stdin>", line 1, in ?
AttributeError: 'showitem' instance has no attribute '__len__'
```

This will turn out to be a problem when we consider how to implement an N-dimensional array package.

A tuple of subscripts always calls __getitem__() and passes it a tuple. Negative values and negative bounds of slices in a tuple are passed to __getitem__() unaltered:

```
>>> s[1,2,3]
(1, 2, 3)
>>> s[1,-2,3]
(1, -2, 3)
>>> t=(1,2,3)
>>> s[t]
(1, 2, 3)
>>> s[-1:2,]
(slice(-1, 2, None),)
```

Although we have been talking in terms of __getitem__() and __getslice__(), the discussion applies to all the "item" and "slice" methods.

Circular, Resizable DEQueue

Problem: We need a FIFO queue, or a stack, or a queue in which items can be pushed back on the front.

Solution: A double-ended queue abstract data type. Use an array with head and tail pointers, or head and length. The elements of the queue are in the portion of the array indicated by these pointer or length fields. Provide methods to add or remove an item to either end. Wrap around from end to beginning or beginning to end. Reallocate upon attempts to add to a full queue.

Consequences: If the size is increased by a fraction of the previous size, e.g., double, the cost of insertion into and removal from the DEQueue will be constant. Insertion into or removal from the midst of the DEQueue is typically not available, or if it is, it is expensive.

15.2   DEQueue

15.2.1   Design

Figure 15–1 gives code for class DEQueue, a usable doubly-ended queue. It has the operations shown in Table 15–1.

Table 15–1
DEQueue operations.

Operation	Explanation
DEQueue(seq)	Creates a doubly-ended queue and initializes its contents to the elements of the sequence seq. Parameter seq defaults to an empty sequence.
q.put(x)	Puts x at the end of the queue q.
q.get()	Removes and returns the item at the head of the queue. Raises DEQueueEmptyError if q is empty.
q.push(x)	Puts x at the beginning of the queue. Methods push() and pop() can be used to implement a stack.
q.pop()	Equivalent to q.get(). It is used when the DEQueue is being used as a stack.
q.pull()	Removes and returns the last item in the queue. Raises DEQueueEmptyError if q is empty. The queue can be treated as a stack using put() and pull(). It can be treated as a queue using push() and pull() rather than put() and get().
q.copy()	Returns a copy of the queue.
len(q) q.__len__()	Returns the number of items in the queue.

Table 15–1
DEQueue operations. (Continued)

Operation	Explanation
repr(q) q.__repr__()	Returns a string containing a representation of the contents of the queue.
str(q) q.__str__()	Is the same as repr(q).
q[i] q.__getitem__(i)	Returns the ith item in the queue. The head of the queue is q[0]. The last item is q[len(q)-1], or q[-1].
q.__nonzero__()	Returns one (true) if the queue is not empty, and zero if it is empty. This is used in if and while statements, if q: and while q:.

```
""" DEQueue - double-ended queue """
class DEQueueEmptyError(LookupError):pass
class DEQueue:
    ""
    def __init__(self,stuff=()):
      self.rep=[None]*8
      self.hd=0
      self.size=0
      for x in stuff:
        self.put(x)
    def put(self,x):
      "Put at end of a DEQueue: q.put(x)"
      if self.size==len(self.rep):
        self.rep=self.rep[self.hd:]+  \
          self.rep[:self.hd]+  \
          [None]*len(self.rep)
        self.hd=0
      self.rep[(self.hd+self.size)%len(self.rep)]=x
      self.size=self.size+1
    def push(self,x):
      "Push at front of a DEQueue: q.push(x)"
      if self.size==len(self.rep):
        self.rep=self.rep[self.hd:]+  \
          self.rep[:self.hd]+  \
          [None]*len(self.rep)
```

Figure 15–1
DEQueue.

```
      self.hd=0
    self.hd=self.hd-1
    if self.hd<0:
      self.hd=self.hd+len(self.rep)
    self.size=self.size+1
    self.rep[self.hd]=x
  def get(self):
    "Get item from front of a DEQueue: q.get()"
    if self.size==0:
      raise DEQueueEmptyError
    x=self.rep[self.hd]
    self.rep[self.hd]=None
    self.hd=(self.hd+1)%len(self.rep)
    self.size=self.size-1
    return x
  def pop(self):
    "Pop item from front of a DEQueue: =q.get()"
    return self.get()
  def pull(self):
    "Get item from end of a DEQueue: q.pull()"
    if self.size==0:
      raise DEQueueEmptyError
    i=(self.hd+self.size-1)%len(self.rep)
    x=self.rep[i]
    self.rep[i]=None
    self.size=self.size-1
    return x
  def copy(self):
    "Copy of a DEQueue: q.copy()"
    x=DEQueue()
    x.rep=self.rep[:]
    x.hd=self.hd
    x.size=self.size
    return x
  def __getitem__(self,i):
    "Look at i-th item: q[i]"
    if i<0:
      i = self.size + i
    if i<0 or i>=self.size:
      raise IndexError
    return self.rep[(self.hd+i)%len(self.rep)]
  def __len__(self):
    return self.size
  def __nonzero__(self):
    return self.size!=0
  def __repr__(self):
    j=self.hd+self.size
    if j<=len(self.rep):
      s=self.rep[self.hd:j]
    else:
      s=self.rep[self.hd:]+ \
        self.rep[:j%len(self.rep)]
```

Figure 15–1

DEQueue. (Continued)

```
      return "DEQueue("+repr(s)+")"
  def __str__(self):
      return repr(self)
```

Figure 15–1
DEQueue. (Continued)

15.2.2 Implementation

The implementation of DEQueue is designed to be efficient. The queue itself is kept in a list, rep ("representation"), using a circular queue representation. Attribute hd is the index of the first element of the queue. Attribute size is the number of elements. When the size of the queue would exceed the length of rep, rep is reallocated twice as long.

The ith element of the queue is at self.rep[(self.hd+i)% len(self.rep)]; that is, the queue wraps around from the end of rep to the beginning. To put an item at the end of the queue, size is incremented and the appropriate element of self.rep is assigned the value. Similarly, when an item is pushed on the front of the DEQueue, hd is decremented modulus the size of rep, wrapping around from the front of rep to the end. Thus, very little overhead is encountered when adding items if the queue is not full. Even if the queue repeatedly overflows and is reallocated, the cost is small. Consider how many times items have been moved when the queue overflows. All items that were in the queue have to be moved to the new rep list. Because the size of the list doubles on each reallocation, one-half of the items being moved have been added since the last time the list was reallocated. Of those that were moved before, one-half were added since the previous reallocation, and so on. Multiplying the number of items being moved in the reallocation by the number of times they have been moved, we get $1\frac{1}{2} + 2\frac{1}{4} + 3\frac{1}{8} + 4\frac{1}{16} + \ldots < 2$ moves.

15.2.3 Critique

We have already seen that DEQueue is an efficient implementation. It offers an reasonable set of facilities. Indeed, it offers more facilities than may seem apparent. You can use a DEQueue in a for statement:

```
>>> import DEQueue
>>> q=DEQueue.DEQueue()
>>> q.put('a')
>>> q.put('b')
>>> q.put('c')
```

```
>>> for x in q: print x,
...
a b c
```

What is happening is that the `for` statement tries to assign `x` the values of `q[0]`, `q[1]`, and so on, and it succeeds until it tries to fetch `q[len(q)]`. When the fetch fails, the `for` statement stops executing.

Was it good design to have the methods `push()` and `pop()` insert and remove items on the front of the queue? Are these intuitive? Actually, they were taken from Icon, so they are intuitive to Icon programmers. But are they intuitive to Python programmers?

Alas, probably not. The problem is that Python already provides a `pop()` method for lists that removes and returns the last item. The `pop()` method for DEQueue removes and returns the first item. For Python, this is an efficiency issue: To remove the first item, the rest of the elements in the list must be moved. For DEQueue, there is no efficiency hit. The incompatibility would argue that `push()` and `pop()` be redesigned. If they were consistent with Python, they would be easier to remember. But here is a related consideration: Do we want the first element of a stack to be the top and the last be the bottom, or vice versa? The way DEQueue is designed, the top of the stack comes first. Suppose `stk` is a DEQueue. The statement `for x in stk:` will assign `x` the elements of the stack from the top to bottom; but if we redesigned to be consistent with Python's list `pop()` method, `x` would get the elements from the bottom to the top. We should consider which is more useful before redesigning DEQueue.

Do we need to be able to assign new values to elements of a DEQueue? Do we wish to delete them? If so, we should implement `__setitem__()` and `__delitem__()` methods. Of course, with the representation we have chosen, `__delitem__()` would not be particularly efficient. What about getting, setting, or deleting slices of queues? Those operations are not customarily a part of a queue, but if we needed them, we could implement the "`slice`" methods. What about concatenating queues? Do we want to implement `__add__()` or `__iadd__()`?

The question is: Would it be better to provide these facilities for the few occasions when they might be useful? Or is it better to keep the implementation clean and efficient? There is a good argument for clean and efficient design: Complex facilities probably have bugs, but if those facilities are not commonly used, the bugs usually will not be discovered until months or years after the software is completed and delivered. By then the original implementers may have moved on to other jobs, and even if they have not, they will have forgotten the details of the implementation. Trying to provide and maintain intricate features, given the few uses for them, is probably not cost-effective.

In the case of DEQueue, there is no convincing reason to allow slice operations, concatenation, or deletion. The built-in list type provides those, and indeed provides all the facilities of DEQueues. The only reason to provide DEQueue at all is its efficiency, so there would be no reason to use DEQueue if we were doing inefficient operations.

15.3 Multidimensional Arrays

In this section we reflect on the possibility of creating multidimensional arrays. We ask a number of questions about possible designs and implementations and consider the answers Python provides.

Q. Can we subscript more than one dimension in the same brackets, e.g., a[i,j], or must we use multiple brackets, a[i][j]?

A. As we saw in Section 15.1, if we put a sequence of expressions in the brackets separated by commas, then it passes to __getitem__() or either of the other "item" methods as a tuple. (In the following discussion, we will use __getitem__() when we mean any of the three "item" methods.) There should be no problem using multiple subscripts.

Q. Can we create a multidimensional array using square brackets around the dimensions, e.g., makeArray[3,4], or must we use parentheses around the dimensions, makeArray(3,4)? The brackets are more intuitive and more consistent with arrays in other languages.

A. Actually, yes, we can use brackets. The skeleton of the trick is shown in Figure 15–2. The trick uses two design patterns. First, we create a *factory* class, ArrayFactory. It has a __getitem__() method that allows us to use an instance of the class with parameters in brackets. The __getitem__() method then creates an instance of an array and returns it. Second, we use the singleton pattern. We create a single instance of ArrayFactory and assign it to makeArray. Whenever we want an array, we can write makeArray[...bounds...].

```
class ArrayFactory:
    def __getitem__(self,dims):
        ... #check dims?
        return Array(dims) #create and return the array
makeArray=ArrayFactory()
```

Figure 15–2
Skeleton of factory to create *n*-dimensional arrays.

Q.   Can we slice a multidimensional array? Slicing in this context has a different meaning from the Python slicing operation. Here "slicing" means that we specify subscripts for only some of the dimensions. If we have an *N*-dimensional array and we supply *m* subscripts, we get an *(N-m)*-dimensional array.

A.   Python allows us to use a colon in place of a dimension. In a multi-dimensional array, any dimension represented by a single colon in the code will have a slice object at its place in the tuple passed to __getitem__(). When our implementation of __getitem__() finds a slice object, it can return a subarray rather than an element. For example, suppose we have created a $3 \times 3 \times 3$, 3-dimensional array, a:

$$a=makeArray[3,3,3]$$

and filled it in row major order with the integers from zero to 26:

```
0  1  2
3  4  5
6  7  8

9  10  11
12  13  14
15  16  17

18  19  20
21  22  23
24  25  26
```

We get subarrays by slicing. For example, we can slice a along any of the three dimensions:

```
a[1,:,:]
9  10  11
12  13  14
15  16  17
```

```
a[:,1,:]
3 4 5
12 13 14
21 22 23

a[:,:,1]
1 4 7
10 13 16
19 22 25
```

Q. Can we have arbitrary lower bounds, not just zero?

A. There is no problem in creating such arrays. The `makeArray` factory can take array bounds using colons; for example:

$$x=\texttt{makeArray}[3,-1:3]$$

can create a 2-dimensional array with first-dimension indices 0, 1, 2 and second-dimension indices -1, 0, 1, 2. There is no problem subscripting, since a negative index in a tuple is passed in to __getitem__() unmodified.

Q. Can we trim a multidimensional array? "Trimming" arrays means something close to what Python documentation means by "slicing." To trim means to specify new bounds for a dimension that are a subrange of the previous bounds.

A. Trimming can use the same mechanism as slicing. The new bounds for a dimension can be specified as *lower:upper*, creating a `slice` object to be passed to __getitem__().

Unfortunately, one-dimensional arrays require special handling. Recall that a bare colon in a tuple of subscripts gives us a `slice` object with `start` and `stop` values of None. For example, `s[:,:]` passes the tuple `(slice(None, None, None), slice(None, None, None))` to `s`'s __getitem__() method. However, for a single dimension, we get a `slice` object with bounds already filled in: `s[:]` passes `slice(0, 2147483647, None)`. Note that for a single dimension, ":" gives us a `slice` object directly, not in a tuple, and instead of None, `start` and `stop` are assigned zero and the largest positive integer. Presumably this anomaly was considered helpful in processing data objects designed to resemble Python sequences. It is not helpful here.

As long as the array has more than one dimension, there is no problem trimming these dimensions. `slice` objects in a tuple of dimensions are passed in unaltered. If there is only one dimension and its lower bound is non-negative, again there is no problem. Zero and positive bounds in a `slice` are unaltered. However, if we try to slice a one-dimensional array with negative bounds on the slicing operator, the Python implementation will raise an exception if there is no `__len__()` method; and if there is a `__len__()` method, the implementation adds the subscript and the length and passes that value, not the actual value of the bound.

So, if we want negative bounds on single-dimensional arrays, what is our option? We could insist that a `slice` object containing bounds must be passed in a tuple. The user would have to write `s[-1:2,]` rather than `s[-1:2]`. We can enforce this, since `s[-1:2]` passes a `slice` object, whereas `s[-1:2,]` passes a tuple containing a single `slice` object. That will be annoying to the user, but it is the only thing that gives us exact information from Python's slice expression. On the other hand, this may be a good argument for restricting lower bounds to zero.

Q.   Are these arrays really implementable?

A.   They can be implemented using array descriptors that contain a reference to a list, *body*, containing the elements of the array, an integer *offset*, and to lists of the upper and lower bounds of each dimension and the *stride* of the dimension.

When presented with a subscripted reference:

$$A[i_0, i_1 \ldots i_{n-1}]$$

the array element is found at *body*[$offset + \sum_j i_j \cdot stride_j$].

This implementation allows slicing, trimming, transposition, reversal along a dimension, and changing the bounds of a dimension. The modified arrays share the same body and hence the same elements.

15.4 Class Versions of Built-In Data Types

Suppose we want to add a few features to a list. The normal way to do this would be to create a subclass of `list` with some extra methods. Unfortunately, *list* is not a class, so we cannot create a subclass of it; but Python does provide a way around this problem.

To make the problem concrete, suppose we wish to create a version of a list that can be used as a key for a dictionary. The list type cannot be used as an argument to hash(). Not having a hash value, lists cannot be used as keys for dictionaries. Moreover, it is not safe to use lists in the usual way. The hash() function computes a hash value for tuples from the hash values of their elements, and the cmp() function compares the elements of tuples. The problem with a list is that if we computed the hash value from its elements, used it as a key, and then changed its elements, we almost certainly would not be able to find it in the dictionary again. The new elements would give us a new hash value, so Python would start looking for the list in a different place.

How do we want to use lists as keys? Let us suppose that when we use a list as a key, we want to be able to look up the identical object, not another list with the same contents. This allows us to use the built-in id() function that gives a unique integer for each object (i.e., the memory address). We can use the id() value to compute the hash value and compare id() values to compare objects. The only problem is how to attach these meanings to a list.

The Python library gives us the module UserList, which contains a class UserList. (Python also provides UserDict and UserString classes to do for dictionaries and strings what UserList does for lists.) The UserList object behaves exactly as a list would. Indeed, it is a *wrapper* or *decorator*. It contains a list in its attribute data. It implements all list operations by passing them on to its data list. Being a class, UserList can be subclassed, which allows us to add to and change its behavior. Figure 15–3 shows how we use this to create a type of list we can use as a key in a dictionary. Our List class inherits all the methods of UserList and hence all list operations. We add a __hash__() method that returns the id() value of the underlying list object. We also have to override the __cmp__() method to compare the id() values of underlying lists. (If the other operand is not one of our Lists, we simply compare its own id() value to our data list's.)

```
import UserList
class List(UserList.UserList):
    def __hash__(self):
      return id(self.data)
    def __cmp__(self,other):
      if isinstance(other,List):
        return id(self.data)-id(other.data)
      else: return id(self.data)-id(other)
```

Figure 15–3
Hashable list.

15.4.1   Critique

The List class in Figure 15–3 does solve the problem of using lists as keys for a dictionary. Unfortunately, it breaks another part of a list's behavior. Two List objects are equal only if they are identical. For real lists, they are equal if their contents are the same. If L and M are two List objects, L==M is true only if they are identical, that is L is M. If we want to compare their contents, we could use L.data==M.data.

So here is a question: When we provided a different behavior for cmp(), did we violate the contract of the UserList class? If we did, it was a very bad decision. Users must be able to count on isinstance(x,C) returning true only if x adheres to the interface of class C.

The question becomes, "Does List adhere to the interface of UserList?" An argument in favor is that List does indeed have all the methods of UserList and they all do the same kind of thing. The argument against is that by changing the behavior of cmp(), List violates the principle of least astonishment by changing behavior that users have a right to rely on.

15.5   Wrap-Up

Abstract container data types make up one of the most important kinds of classes that you will be creating and using. They encapsulate data structures vital to efficient algorithms.

In this chapter we examined the container special methods in detail: __getitem__(), __setitem__(), __delitem__(), __getslice__(), __setslice__(), __delslice__(), along with __len__() and __nonzero__(). There are intricate interactions of the "item" and "slice" operations with simple subscript expressions and slices and tuples. To examine the interactions, we considered the opportunities and difficulties in implementing multidimensional arrays with the facilities Python provides, and we decided that it was possible except for some difficulties using the single-colon slice operator for a single-dimensional array.

We presented an implementation of a DEQueue or doubly-ended queue, an abstract container data type. Although Python's lists can perform the same functions, the DEQueue is likely to be significantly faster than the list for larger queues, since it does not move items in memory except when the underlying list overflows.

We also looked at the UserList class, which wraps a list in a class. Although lists cannot be subclassed, UserList can be, allowing us to build specialized variants of lists. There are also classes UserDict for dictionaries and UserString for strings.

15.6   Exercises

15.1. Does the appearance of rich comparison operators in Python version 2.1 change the special methods needed by the hashable list in Figure 15–3? Fix it, if necessary.

15.2. Add methods head() and top() to DEQueue. They are to return the value of the first item in the queue or the top item when it is being used as a stack. They are synonyms.

15.3. Implement multidimensional arrays as discussed in Section 15.3. Restrict lower bounds to be zero. Implement slicing and trimming operations.

15.4. Implement a RestrictedList class that behaves as a list, but restricts the items in the list to those that pass a test. The test is specified as a function that will return true if its argument is permitted in the list. The call RestrictedList(fn,init), where init is optional, will created a restricted list with the test function fn and the initial contents given by the sequence init. An attempt to put an item x into the list will raise a ValueError if f(x) returns false. Make it a decorator for a list. Have it inherit from UserList.

15.5. Do a decorator for DEQueue that puts and pulls at position zero and pushes, pops, and gets from the high end.

16

Priority Queues

A priority queue is a queue in which items are inserted in any order, but the higher priority items are removed before the lower priority items. They have a number of uses, including:

- scheduling tasks by urgency, deadline, or importance;
- searching for the cheapest or highest-profit solution;
- simulating discrete event systems, where the simulated time of the system is updated to the time of the next event.

We present two implementations that are based on differing answers to several questions: Do we want the item with the larger priority value to come first, or the item with the smaller value? What do we want to happen when the same item is inserted more than once? Do we want it to appear more than once in the queue and be removed more than once? Do we want it to be represented only once in the queue? If we want it to appear only once, then what do we do about its priority when it is inserted the second time? Do we want the second priority to override the first? Do we want the first priority to be preserved? Or do we want the maximum or minimum of the priorities or something else?

The priority queue is a commonly used data structure that has been missing from Python's module library. In addition to giving us an opportunity to look at lists and dictionaries in action and to use the *Strategy* design pattern, they represent a contribution to your arsenal of code.

349

16.1   Priority Queue Operations

Both our priority queues have the methods shown in Table 16–1. Module `prioque` is a priority queue implementation that can contain multiple copies of the same item. Module `prioqueunique` allows only a single copy of a particular item. When an attempt is made to insert an item again, it can change the priority of the item already present.

Table 16–1
Priority queue operations.

Operation	Explanation
`q.put(priority,item)`	Puts the `item` with the given `priority` into the queue. The priorities must be comparable values; e.g., `cmp()` is defined for the priorities.
`q.get()`	Removes and returns the first (highest priority) item in the queue. It raises an exception if the queue is empty.
`q.getPair()`	Removes and returns `(p,x)` where `x` is the first item in the queue and `p` is its priority. It raises an exception if the queue is empty.
`q.head()`	Returns the first item in the queue without removing it. It raises a `LookupError` exception if the queue is empty.
`q.headPair()`	Returns `(p,x)` where `x` is the first item in the queue and `p` is its priority. It does not remove `x`. It raises a `LookupError` exception if the queue is empty.
`len(q)` `q.__len__()`	Returns the number of items in the queue.

Table 16–1
Priority queue operations. (Continued)

Operation	Explanation
`q[i]` `q.__getitem__(i)`	Returns `(p,x)` where `x` is the `i`th item in the queue and `p` is its priority. The items are not in an obvious order.
`q.__nonzero__()`	Returns true if `len(q)>0`, false otherwise.
`q.remove(item)`	Removes the `item`. (In `prioqueunique` only).

`prioque.prioque(before)`
`prioque.prioque()`
	Creates a priority queue that allows multiple occurrences of an item. The `before(x,y)` function is to return true only if priority `x` is to precede priority `y`. The module contains these functions:
	    `prioque.smallerfirst` computes `x<y`.
	    `prioque.largerfirst` computes `y<x`.
	    Function `before()` defaults to `smallerfirst`.

Table 16–1
Priority queue operations. (Continued)

Operation	Explanation
`prioqueunique.prioque` `(before,newprio)` `prioqueunique.prioque` `(before)` `prioqueunique.prioque()`	Creates a new priority queue that does not allow multiple occurrences of the same item. The function `before(x,y)` is to return true only if priority x is to precede priority y. `prioqueunique.smallerfirst` is equivalent to $x<y$. `prioqueunique.largerfirst` is equivalent to $y<x$. Function `before()` defaults to `smallerfirst`. The function `newprio(x,y)` is to return the new priority to use when an attempt is made to insert an item already in the queue. Parameter x is the priority of the already enqueued copy; y is the priority of the copy being put in the queue. Those available are: `None` (the default) assigns `newprio` a function that chooses x if `before(x,y)` is true or y if `before(x,y)` yields false. `prioqueunique.minprio=min` `prioqueunique.maxprio=max` `prioqueunique.oldprio(x,y)` returns x. `prioqueunique.newprio(x,y)` returns y. `prioqueunique.sumprio=` `operator.add` Parameter `newprio` defaults to preserving the priority that comes earlier in the order given by the `before()` function.

The `__getitem__()` method exists to allow us to examine the contents of the queue without removing items. It allows us to write:.

```
for p,x in q: ...
```

However, the items are delivered in no particular order. The `__nonzero__()` method allows us to write:

Heap Data Structure

Problem addressed: You need a priority queue in which elements can be added in any order, but will be removed according to a precedence function.

Solution: A heap is a complete binary tree mapped onto an array, A, so that A[1] is the root of the tree, A[i/2] is parent of A[i] and A[i+1] for i>1, and all A[1]...A[N] are nodes of the tree if the heap has N elements. For a MAX heap, the value in a parent node is at least as large as the values in either of its children; or for a MIN heap, at least as small as either. By transitivity for a MAX heap, the value in a node is no smaller than any value in its subtree, and the value in the root is the largest value in the heap.

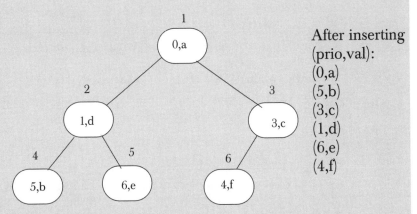

Figure 16–1
MIN Heap example.

Heaps are designed for arrays that begin with index one. If the first element of the array is at index zero, as with Python lists, you either waste the element at index zero, or you consistently subtract and add one, converting back and forth. In our implementation, we waste element zero.

A heap allows elements to be added and removed in logarithmic time. It may require reallocation if the number of items exceeds the size of the underlying array; but by multiplying the size of the space by a constant fraction each time (e.g., doubling), the cost of copying the elements can be kept to a constant factor.

```
                              if q:...
     or

                           while q:...
```

16.2   Priority Queue Implementation

Figure 16–2 shows the implementation of a priority queue that allows duplicate items. It is the obvious, heap implementation

A priority queue is an instance of class `prioque`. The instance has two attributes:

- `q`–a list containing the heap;
- `before`–a function to compare two priorities.

The function `before(x,y)` is to return true if priority `x` should come before priority `y`. It is an example of a *strategy pattern*. The module contains two strategies, the functions `smallerfirst()` and `largerfirst()`. When we create an instance of a priority queue, we can provide a strategy to enforce our preference by passing it as parameter `before`. If we don't specify otherwise, the policy defaults to "`smaller first`." If we prefer the other way, we can write:

```
q=prioque.prioque(before=prioque.largerfirst)
```

The items and their priorities are kept in `(priority,item)` tuples in the list `q`. The N pairs are kept in `q[1]` through `q[N]`, as the definition of a heap specifies. We waste `q[0]`, although we could subtract and add one in our code to fill in `q[0]` through `q[N-1]`. The saving in space did not appear to be worth the extra complexity.

The implementation uses a list for the underlying array. It appends an item being added to the queue and deletes the last element when an item is removed. This lets Python handle the reallocation of the list as the queue grows.

There are two internal methods, indicated by the double underscores at the beginnings of their names:

- `__siftHole(self,i)`–Moves the empty position in the midst of the heap to a leaf position by repeatedly promoting the higher-precedence child to fill the hole. It returns the position in which the hole finally ended up.
- `__siftRootwards(self,i)`–Moves the item in position `i` as far toward the root as it will go by repeatedly exchanging it with a parent that does not precede it in the ordering.

```
"""Priority queue
heap implementation"""
# these functions determine whether the first
# or second argument should be preferred.
# one of them is passed to parameter "first"
#when the queue is created
def smallerfirst(x,y): return x<y
def largerfirst(x,y): return y<x

class prioque:
    def __init__(self,before=smallerfirst):
      self.q=[(None,None)]
      self.before=before
    def __siftHole(self,i):
      j=i+i
      n=len(self.q)
      while j<n:
        k=j+1
        if k<n and \
            self.before(self.q[k][0],self.q[j][0]):
            j=k
        self.q[i]=self.q[j]
        i=j
        j=i+i
      return i
    def __siftRootwards(self,i):
      j=i/2
      while j>0:
          if self.before(self.q[j][0],self.q[i][0]):
          break
          self.q[i],self.q[j]=self.q[j],self.q[i]
          i=j
          j=j/2
      return i
    def put(self,prio,item):
      n=len(self.q)
      self.q.append((prio,item))
      self.__siftRootwards(n)
    def getPair(self):
      if len(self.q)<2: raise LookupError
      item=self.q[1]
      j=self.__siftHole(1)
      self.q[j]=self.q[-1]
      self.__siftRootwards(j)
      del self.q[-1]
      return item
    def get(self):
      return self.getPair()[1]
    def headPair(self):
      if len(self.q)<2: raise LookupError
      return self.q[1]
    def head(self):
```

Figure 16–2
Priority queue.

```
        if len(self.q)<2: raise LookupError
        return self.q[1][1]
    def __len__(self):
        return len(self.q)-1
    def __getitem__(self,i):
        return self.q[i+1]
    def __nonzero__(self):
        return len(self.q)>1
```

Figure 16–2
Priority queue. (Continued)

Insertion into the heap simply appends the new `(priority,item)` pair on `q` and then sifts it rootward. Removal of the highest priority element takes a copy of the root, `q[1]`, sifts the hole to a leaf, removes the last item from `q`, places it in the hole, and sifts it rootward.

16.3   Unique Elements

Figure 16–3 gives the code for a variation of the priority queue, module `prioqueunique`, with which you are allowed to change the priority of items already in the queue simply by inserting them again with a new priority. There are two consequences of this ability to change the priorities of items already in the queue:

1. The items may only appear in the queue once. If duplicates were allowed, it would be unclear which copy is having its priority changed.
2. It is possible to remove items from the queue. Since the queue already has to be able to find items, and since there is no real difference between the difficulties of removing the item at `q[1]` and removing the item at an arbitrary position, the cost of adding a `remove()` method was trivial.

The method call `pq.put(p,x)` either puts item `x` into the priority queue `pq` with priority `p`, or it changes the priority of `x` if `x` is already present. The way in which the priority changes is determined by a function. Because `put()` delegates part of its function to `newprio`, `newprio` is an example of a strategy pattern. The function attribute `newprio` of a `prioqueunique` object holds a function of two parameters. Function `newprio(x,y)` is called with `x` being the priority of the item already in the queue and `y` being the priority of the item passed to the `put()` method. The `newprio` function defaults to a function that will preserve the priority, either `x` or `y`, that comes before the other in the order

```
"""Priority queue, unique elements
heap implementation"""
import operator
#one of these will be called to choose the
# new priority when an item is reinserted.
#The first parameter will be the priority
# of the previous item, the second will be the
# priority of the new item.
minprio=min
maxprio=max
sumprio=operator.add
def oldprio(x,y): return x
def newprio(x,y): return y

# these functions determine whether the first
# or second argument should be preferred.
# one of them is passed to parameter "first"
 # when the queue is created
def smallerfirst(x,y): return x<y
def largerfirst(x,y): return y<x

class prioque:
    def __init__(self,before=smallerfirst, \
        newprio=None):
      self.q=[(None,None)]
      self.before=before
      if newprio==None:
        self.newprio=self.__beforeprio
      else:
        self.newprio=newprio
      self.loc={}
    def __beforeprio(self,x,y):
      if self.before(x,y): return x
      else: return y
    def __siftHole(self,i):
      j=i+i
      n=len(self.q)
      while j<n:
        k=j+1
        if k<n and \
            self.before(self.q[k][0],self.q[j][0]):
          j=k
        self.q[i]=self.q[j]
        i=j
        j=i+i
      return i
    def __siftRootwards(self,i):
      j=i/2
      while j>0:
        if self.before(self.q[j][0],self.q[i][0]):
          break
        self.q[i],self.q[j]=self.q[j],self.q[i]
```

Figure 16–3
prioqueunique.

```
            i=j
            j=j/2
      return i
  def __setLocs(self,lo,hi):
    i=hi
    while i>=lo:
      self.loc[self.q[i][1]]=i
      i=i/2
  def __delete(self,i):
    item=self.q[i]
    del self.loc[item[1]] #record item not present
    t=self.q[-1] #item from last position
    del self.q[-1] #reduce size
    if len(self.q)==1:
      #last item removed
      self.loc.clear()
      return item
    j=self.__siftHole(i) #sift hole from i to leaf
    self.q[j]=t #fill with old last item
    self.loc[t[1]]=j #record its new loc (?)
    k=self.__siftRootwards(j) #move to new position
    self.__setLocs(min(i,k),max(i,k)) #adjust table
    return item #return item removed

  def put(self,prio,item):
    if self.loc.has_key(item):
      #if inserting again
      i=self.loc[item]
      #get old priority
      oldprio=self.q[i][0]
      #calculate new priority to use:
      newprio=self.newprio(oldprio,prio)
      if newprio==oldprio:
        return
      t=(newprio,item)
      if self.before(newprio,oldprio):
        self.q[i]=t
        j=self.__siftRootwards(i)
        self.__setLocs(j,i)
      else:
        j=self.__siftHole(i)
        self.q[j]=t
        k=self.__siftRootwards(j)
        self.__setLocs(min(i,k),j)
      return
    #if new item
    n=len(self.q)
    self.q.append((prio,item))
    #self.loc[item]=n
    i=self.__siftRootwards(n)
    self.__setLocs(i,n)

  def remove(self,item):
```

Figure 16–3
prioqueunique. (Continued)

```
          if self.loc.has_key(item):
            return self.__delete(self.loc[item])
          else: return None
        def getPair(self):
          if len(self.q)==1:
            raise IndexError("empty priority queue")
          item=self.__delete(1)
          return item
        def get(self):
          return self.getPair()[1]
        def headPair(self):
          return self.q[1]
        def head(self):
          return self.q[1][1]
        def __len__(self):
          return len(self.q)-1
        def __getitem__(self,i):
          return self.q[i+1]
        def __nonzero__(self):
          return len(self.q)>1
```

Figure 16–3
prioqueunique. (Continued)

computed by the before() function. Several other functions are available in the prioqueunique module:

- prioqueunique.maxprio(x,y) returns the maximum of x and y.
- prioqueunique.minprio(x,y) returns the minimum of x and y.
- prioqueunique.oldprio(x,y) returns x, the priority already in the queue.
- prioqueunique.newprio(x,y) returns y, the priority passed to the put method. The priority already in the queue is replaced.
- prioqueunique.sumprio(x,y) returns x+y.

The code for prioqueunique (Figure 16–3) has several additions to the code for prioque (Figure 16–2). The attributes now include loc, a dictionary mapping items into their positions in the heap–their indices in list q. Attribute newprio holds the function that is used to compute the new priority of an item being reinserted into the heap.

The additional method, pq.remove(item), will remove the item from the queue. It returns the (priority,item) pair if the item is present. If the item is not present, remove() returns None.

Three additional internal methods are:

1. pq.__delete(i) removes the item at position i in the heap. The position of the first item in the heap is 1. The position of some other

       item being removed has been looked up in the `loc` dictionary before `__delete()` is called.

2. `pq.__setLocs(lo,hi)` reassigns positions in the `loc` dictionary to all the items between `lo` and `hi`. It is guaranteed that `lo` either equals `hi` or is the index of an ancestor of `hi` in the heap. The code simply follows the path from `hi` rootward to `lo`, assigning `loc[x]=i` to each item `x` at position `i` in the path. Its use is based on the observation that the operation `__siftRootwards()` or the `__siftHole()` and `__siftRootwards()` combination traverse a single path through the binary tree. Indeed, some of the items moved during `__siftHole()` may be moved back to their original positions later by `__siftRootwards()`. By keeping track of the endpoints of the path, the number of changes in the `loc` dictionary can be minimized.

3. `pq.__beforeprio(x,y)` is the method that `newprio` defaults to. This had to be a method in the class rather than a function, since it uses the `before` attribute.

16.4 Critique

These two versions of priority queues provide a reasonable set of methods. They are parameterized with functions to adapt their behavior. The ordering function is provided as parameter `before`. In the case of the priority queue with unique elements, the parameter `newprio` specifies how the priority of an item changes when it is reinserted.

Because they use a heap, the priority queues are efficient in insertion and removal of items, taking only logarithmic time in the number of items present. The dictionary `loc` used in `prioqueunique` makes lookup of items efficient, although it does require that the items be hashable.

Some priority queues do not have a separate priority, but just rank the items themselves. We didn't see the need for such queues, since one can write `pq.put(x,x)` instead of `pq.put(x)`. It might nonetheless be worthwhile to provide an option for `put()` that takes a single parameter as both item and priority.

Since the underlying algorithm is the same for both of these priority queues, we might wonder if we should have combined them into a single implementation, using either a subclass or another strategy to handle the differences. We might be able to do that, but it doesn't seem worth the effort. We have already implemented both of these versions. Combining them would force us to implement yet another version with two or three classes. For example:

- We could do a version that implements `prioque` and create a subclass for `prioqueunique`.
- We could do a version that implements common elements and contains template methods that are implemented in two subclasses, one for `prioque` and another for `prioqueunique`.
- We could do a version that implements common elements and delegates to one of two strategy objects the distinctive behavior of `prioque` or `prioqueunique`.

It might be worth doing one of these implementations if there were other versions of the priority queue that could then be implemented by simply writing a new subclass or a new strategy, but there do not seem to be any other versions of priority queues to implement. Could we have saved ourselves some work in writing these implementations if we had just used one of those designs from the beginning? It is unlikely we could have dispensed with one or both of the implementations and gone directly to a common one: We would not know what needed to be done to combine the versions without having prototyped them.

16.5 Wrap-Up

We devoted this chapter to building a priority queue abstract container data type. Indeed, we implemented two versions: `prioque`, which allows duplicate elements, and `prioqueunique`, which does not. The implementations use the usual heap, although the algorithm for updating the location table in `prioqueunique` is uncommon. These classes are adapted to varying uses with the strategy pattern. A function is used to determine which of two priorities comes first in the order, and in the priority queues with unique elements, to determine what the new priority will be when an element is reinserted. Aside from demonstrating abstract container data types and the use of strategy patterns, these priority queues are useful additions to your collection of Python modules.

16.6   Exercises

16.1. Implement an adaptor for priority queues that makes items their own priority: Items in the queue are themselves compared to determine their relative priority. Redefine `put(x)` to take a single argument. Remove `getPair()` and `headPair()`.

16.2. Implement an alternative to `prioque` using the library module `bisect`.

16.3. Implement a single-source, shortest path algorithm. Start with a directed graph with non-negative distances on its edges and a single `start` node. Initially, the `start` node is at distance zero and all the other nodes are at distance infinity (really, just use a large enough value). Put the `start` node in a priority queue of unique elements with the distance zero as its priority. Repeatedly remove the next node from the priority queue. Its priority will be the minimum distance to it from the `start` node. Add it to the set of nodes to which we know the distance. For every edge leaving the node, add the distance to the node and the length of the edge and put the destination node into the queue with that distance if it is not already known to have a smaller distance. Repeat until there are no nodes left in the queue. (If the graph does not have a path from the `start` node to some other node, we will terminate without having found a new distance to that node.)

17

$$\overline{\phantom{\text{Sets}}}$$

Sets

In this chapter we present: 1) an implementation of a `Set` abstract container data type; 2) a protection proxy, `PureSet`, that restricts a set to read-only access; and 3) a `SetEnumeration` class to deliver the elements of a set to loops. The classes we present give us the opportunity to discuss three object-oriented design patterns: the *Protection Proxy*, the *Iterator*, and the *Observer*.

17.1 Set Operations

The operations provided by our `Set` class are shown in Table 17–1. An empty set can be constructed by the call `Set()`. The call `Set(seq)` will create a set whose initial elements are the elements of the object `seq`. Generally `seq` will be a list or a tuple, although any type that can be used to control a `for` statement can be used. Due to its implementation, the elements of a set must be suitable keys for a dictionary.

Mathematical sets are pure values, but for efficiency, we allow sets to be modified. The method `s.insert(x)` will add element `x` to `s`, and `s.delete(x)` will remove `x` from `s`. Since sets do not allow duplicate elements, inserting an element already present performs no operation. Deleting an element that is not present also performs no operation. *No* exception is raised if the value is not present, unlike Python's `del x[k]` that raises an exception if `k` is not present in `x`. The read-only equivalents of `insert()` and `delete()` are `s.with(x)` and `s.without(x)`; they create copies of set `s` with `x` inserted or deleted.

Table 17–1
Operations on set.

Operation	Behavior
`s=Set()` `s=Set(seq)`	Creates a set. If `seq` is provided, the elements of `seq` are the initial elements of the set. The value of `seq` can be anything that can be iterated over in a "`for x in seq:`" statement, including another set.
`s.insert(x)`	Inserts x into set s, changing s's contents. No operation is performed if s contains x already.
`s.delete(x)`	Removes x from set s, changing s's contents. No operation is performed if s does not contain x.
`s.with(x)`	Creates a copy of set s with x inserted into it. No change is made to s. Behaves like `s.copy()` if x is already present in s.
`s.without(x)`	Creates a copy of set s with x deleted from it. No change is made to s. Behaves like `s.copy()` if x is not present in s.

`x in s`
`s.contains(x)`
`s.__contains__(x)`
	True (1) if x is a member of s and false (0) otherwise.

`s.members()` `s.items()`	Returns a list of the elements of s.
`s.elements()`	Returns a `SetEnumeration` object that will deliver the elements of set s one by one.

Table 17–1
Operations on set. (Continued)

Operation	Behavior
`s[i]` `s.__getitem__(i)`	Returns the `ith` item of `s`. The items are in arbitrary order. As long as no changes are made to the contents of `s` during the loop, `for x in s: ...` will iterate over all elements of `s`.
`s.copy()`	Returns a copy of set `s`.
`s.new()`	Returns a new, initially empty set.
`s|t` `s.__or__(t)`	Set union. Returns a new set containing all the elements that are in either `s` or `t`.
`s&t` `s.__and__(t)`	Set intersection. Returns a new set that contains all the elements that are in both `s` and `t`.
`s-t` `s.__sub__(t)`	Relative complement. Returns a set containing those elements of `s` that are not in `t`.
`s.issubsetof(t)`	Returns true (1) if all elements of `s` are also in `t`, otherwise returns false (0).
`s.ispropersubsetof(t)`	Returns true (1) if all elements of `s` are also in `t` but there are one or more elements of `t` that are not in `s`, otherwise returns false (0).
`s.equals(t)`	Returns true if all elements of `s` are in `t` and all elements of `t` are in `s`.

Table 17–1
Operations on set. (Continued)

Operation	Behavior
s<t s<=t s==t s!=t s.__cmp__(t)	s.__cmp__(t) returns -1 if s is a proper subset of t, 0 if s equals t, and 1 otherwise. Therefore: s<t is the same as s.ispropersubsetof(t). s<=t is the same as s.issubsetof(t). s==t is the same as s.equals(t). s!=t is the same as not s.equals(t). But s>t does *not* imply t<s and s>=t does *not* imply t<=s. This module was implemented before Python version 2.1's rich comparison methods, so it uses cmp() that can compare items in a chain, but not in a lattice.
s.arb()	Returns an arbitrary element of s.
len(s) s.__len__()	Returns the number of elements in s.
s.__nonzero__()	Equivalent to len(s)>0.
str(s) s.__str__()	Converts s into a string of the form { x_0, x_1, ..., x_{n-1} } for elements x_i.
repr(s) s.__repr__()	Converts s into a string of the form Set((x_0, x_1, ..., x_{n-1})) for elements x_i.

Method s.contains(x) tests x's membership in s. The special method s.__contains__(x) is identical to s.contains(x) and allows you to use the syntax "x in s" and "x not in s". Similarly, s.members() and s.items() are synonyms. Both return a list of all the elements in set s.

The method `s.elements()` returns a `SetEnumeration` object that resembles the Enumerations of Java. This is discussed in Section 17.4. It is used to iterate over the elements of the set, making it an alternative to the `members()`, `items()`, and `__getitem__()` methods.

You can create a copy of a set with the `copy()` method. You can create a new, empty set with the `new()` method. The `new()` method was put in to be compatible with the set examples in Chapter 4, but it is somewhat pointless here since there are no subclasses overriding it.

The union and intersection set operations use the bit-wise equivalent operations: `x|y` performs set union and `x&y` performs set intersection. Relative complement is written `x-y`. These operations create new sets and do not modify their operands.

There are methods to determine whether two sets are equal, and whether one is a subset of the other or a proper subset of the other. Expression `s.equals(t)` is true if sets `s` and `t` contain the same elements. Expression `s.issubsetof(t)` is true if all elements of `s` are also in `t`. Expression `s.ispropersubsetof(t)` is true if `s.issubsetof(t)`, but `s` is not equal to `t`.

In normal mathematical notation, `s.issubsetof(t)` is usually written $s \subseteq t$ and `s.ispropersubsetof(t)` is usually written $s \subset t$. It would be nice to have similar notation in Python, but the symbols are not available. What we have done is allow `s<=t` to be used for $s \subseteq t$; `s<t` for $s \subset t$; and `s=t` or `s!=t` for equality and inequality. This may have been a bad design decision when we implemented Sets before version 2.1 of Python. Before version 2.1, Python did not allow us to write special methods for `<`, `<=`, and `==`. Instead, we had to define `__cmp__()` so that it returns -1 for "`<`", zero for "`==`", and either -1 or zero for "`<=`". The problem is that set containment is a partial ordering, not a chain. If set `s` is not equal to set `t` and not all elements of set `s` are elements of set `t`, we cannot infer that all elements of `t` are in `s`. The way we have defined `s.__cmp__(t)`, it returns one if `s` is neither a subset of `t` nor equal to `t`. This makes `<`, `<=`, `==`, and `!=` work just fine, but `>=` and `>` do not have the expected meanings.

Since the release of Python 2.1 of course, we can correct this problem by using the "rich comparison" methods `__lt__()`, `__le__()`, and so on. We leave that as an exercise.

17.2   Implementation

The implementation of `Set` is shown in Figure 17–1. The implementation uses two attributes: `rep` and `cache`. The representation of a set, `rep`, is a dictionary. Every element of the set is a key in `rep` and is its own value, `rep[x]==x`. Attribute `cache` starts out `None`. When a list of the members of the set is needed, the list is saved in `cache` so that subsequent accesses do not have to recompute it. In particular, `__getitem__()` will save a list in `cache` so that `for x in s:` is nearly the same as `for x in s.members():`.

```
""" Set """
class SetEnumeration:
    def __init__(self,s):
      self.members=s.members()
      self.set=s
    def hasMoreElements(self):
      if len(self.members)>0:
        return 1
      self.set._removeObserver(self)
      return 0
    def nextElement(self):
      try:
        return self.members.pop()
      except:
        self.set._removeObserver(self)
        raise IndexError
    def __getitem__(self,i):
      return self.nextElement()
    __nonzero__=hasMoreElements
    def _delete(self,item):
      try:
        self.members.remove(item)
      except:
        pass
    def _insert(self,item):
      self.members.insert(0,item)

class Set:
    "Create a set: Set() or Set(seq)"
    def __init__(self,stuff=()):
      self.rep={}
      self.cache=None
      self.observers=[]
      for x in stuff:
        self.insert(x)
    def _registerObserver(self,observer):
      self.observers.append(observer)
```

Figure 17–1
Set.

```
            def _removeObserver(self,observer):
              try:
                self.observers.remove(observer)
              except:
                pass
            def insert(self,x):
              "Insert into a set: s.insert(x)"
              if not self.rep.has_key(x):
                self.cache=None
                self.rep[x]=x
                for ob in self.observers:
                  ob._insert(x)
            def delete(self,x):
              "delete an item: s.delete(x)"
              if self.rep.has_key(x):
                self.cache=None
                del self.rep[x]
                for ob in self.observers:
                  ob._delete(x)
            def with(self,i):
              t=self.copy()
              t.insert(i)
              return t
            def without(self,i):
              t=self.copy()
              t.delete(i)
              return t
            def contains(self,x):
              "Test for membership: s.contains(x)"
              return self.rep.has_key(x)
            __contains__=contains
            def members(self):
              "List members of set: s.members()"
              if not self.cache:
                self.cache=self.rep.keys()
              return self.cache[:]
            def items(self): return self.members()
            def elements(self):
              e=SetEnumeration(self)
              self._registerObserver(e)
              return e
            def copy(self):
              "Copy of a set: s.copy()"
              x=Set()
              x.rep=self.rep.copy()
              return x
            def new(self):
              "Create a new set like this one: s.new()"
              x=Set()
              return x
            def __or__(self,s):
              "Set Union: x|y "
              x=self.copy()
```

Figure 17–1
Set. (Continued)

```
      for y in s.members():
        x.insert(y)
      return x
    def __and__(self,s):
      "Set Intersection: x&y"
      x=Set()
      for y in self:
        if s.contains(y):
          x.insert(y)
      return x
    def __sub__(self,s):
      "Relative complement: s1 - s2"
      x=Set()
      for y in self:
        if not s.contains(y):
          x.insert(y)
      return x
    def issubsetof(self,other):
      if len(self)>len(other):
        return 0
      for x in self:
        if not other.contains(x):
          return 0
      return 1
    def ispropersubsetof(self,other):
      if len(self)>=len(other):
        return 0
      for x in self:
        if not other.contains(x):
          return 0
      return 1
    def equals(self,other):
      if len(self)!=len(other):
        return 0
      for x in self:
        if not other.contains(x):
          return 0
      return 1
    def __cmp__(self,other):
      """
        -1 if self is a proper subset of other
        0 if self == other
        1 otherwise
        Note: not symmetric """
      d = len(self)-len(other)
      if d>0: return 1
      for x in self:
        if not other.contains(x):
          return 1
      if d==0: return 0
      else: return -1
    def __getitem__(self,i):
      "Get i-th item, no particular order: s[i]"
```

Figure 17–1
Set. (Continued)

```
        if self.cache is None:
          self.cache=self.rep.keys()
        return self.cache[i]
    def arb(self):
        if self:
          return self[0]
        else:
          import SetExceptions
          raise SetExceptions.EmptySetException()
    def __len__(self):
        return len(self.rep)
    def __nonzero__(self):
        return len(self.rep)!=0
    def __str__(self):
        return "{"+str(self.rep.keys())[1:-1]+"}"
    def __repr__(self):
        s="Set(("
        for x in self.rep.keys() :
          s=s+repr(x)+","
        return s+"))"
```

Figure 17–1
Set. (Continued)

There are two differences, however, that result from clearing out the cache. Whenever the contents of the set are changed by `insert()` or `delete()`, cache is cleared out to None again. If no changes are made to the set, all subsequent occurrences of "`for x in s:`" will use the same cached copy, whereas "`for x in s.members():`" will create a copy of cache each time the `for` statement is entered. However, if the contents of the set are being changed in the loop, the "`for x in s:`" will rebuild the list after every change and perhaps miss some elements of the set or report some more than once; whereas "`for x in s.members():`" will build the list only at the beginning of the loop and will report precisely once every element occurs that was present when the loop was entered.

17.3 PureSet: A Protection Proxy

In theory, sets are pure values, but we allow their contents to change for purposes of efficiency. Copying an entire set as we add single elements would convert a linear time algorithm to a quadratic one. However, there are cases when we want to insist that sets be pure values, that the contents do not change. Suppose we want to default a parameter of a function to the empty set. If we just create a set when we define the function, e.g., def `f(s=Set()):`..., the function could mistakenly insert a value into it, so that subsequent calls would have their parameter default to a nonempty set.

Considerations such as these led to the creation of the `PureSet` proxy shown in Figure 17–2. A `PureSet` takes an underlying set and passes all set operations on to it except `insert()` and `delete()`. Since `insert()` and `delete()` are the only operations that modify sets in place, the `PureSet` proxy protects its underlying set from modification.

This proxy looks a lot like a *decorator* or *wrapper*. Decorators also sit in front of another object, accept the operations that object accepts, and pass many of them on to the underlying object to perform. That is what the `PureSet` proxy is doing, but here is the difference: A decorator adds functionality. Its collection of operations must be the same as or a superset of the operations the underlying object accepts. You must be able to use the decorator everywhere the underlying object can be used. `PureSet`, however, removes two operations. We might also think of this proxy as an *adapter*. An adapter converts from one interface to another. In this case, the conversion is from an interface to a subset of itself, so the term adapter does not apply very well.

```
""" PureSet: Adapter to treat a set as a pure value """
import Set,types
class PureSet:
    "Create  an immutable set: PureSet() or PureSet(seq)"
    def __init__(self,rep=None):
      if rep is None:
        rep=Set.Set()
      elif not isinstance(rep,Set.Set):
        rep=Set.Set(rep)
      self.with=rep.with
      self.without=rep.without
      self.contains=rep.contains
      self.__contains__=rep.__contains__
      self.members=rep.members
      self.items=rep.items
      self.elements=rep.elements
      self.__or__=rep.__or__
      self.__and__=rep.__and__
      self.__sub__=rep.__sub__
      self.issubsetof=rep.issubsetof
      self.ispropersubsetof=rep.ispropersubsetof
      self.equals=rep.equals
      self.__cmp__=rep.__cmp__
      self.__getitem__=rep.__getitem__
      self.copy=rep.copy
      self.new=rep.new
```

Figure 17–2
PureSet.

```
        self.arb=rep.arb
        self.__len__=rep.__len__
        self.__nonzero__=rep.__nonzero__
        self.__str__=rep.__str__
        self.__repr__=rep.__repr__

emptySet=PureSet(rep=Set.Set())
```

Figure 17–2
PureSet. (Continued)

A proxy stands in for another object and controls access to it. A protection proxy protects the object in some way–for example, by removing methods from the object's interface to deny certain kinds of accesses–and that is what PureSet does for Set.

The implementation of PureSet may look strange. It does not contain declarations of methods that pass on calls to the underlying set. It does not even contain an attribute referencing the underlying set. Instead, it creates methods bound to the underlying set object and stores them with the same name in its own instance.

Notice that PureSet passes the copy() method on to the underlying set. If you copy a pure set, you get a set you can modify. This is usually what we want. We want to make sure the recipient of a PureSet cannot clobber it; but if the recipients create copies of their own, there is no reason they shouldn't be able to modify these.

17.4 SetEnumeration

The class SetEnumeration shown at the beginning of Figure 17–1 is an example of an *Iterator*. An iterator is an object that delivers the elements of a container one at a time so they can be processed in a loop. By that definition, Set itself is an iterator, since it can deliver its own elements one at a time with its __getindex__() method; but SetEnumeration is a class devoted solely to iterating over the elements of a set. A SetEnumeration object is returned from Set's elements() method and has the methods shown in Table 17–2. SetEnumeration provides two kinds of methods. The public methods are those that allow the users of set enumerators to iterate over the elements of sets. The restricted methods are those called by the Set whose elements are being enumerated to report changes in its contents.

Table 17–2
SetEnumeration methods.

Method	Meaning
e.hasMoreElements()	Returns true if the enumeration has more elements to deliver. After returning false, the SetEnumeration is no longer active and will deliver no more elements.
e.nextElement()	Returns the next element in the enumeration. Raises IndexError if it is called when no more elements are present. After raising IndexError, the SetEnumeration is no longer active and will deliver no more elements.
e[i] e.__getitem__(i)	Equivalent to e.nextElement(). The parameter i is ignored.
e.__nonzero__() if e:... while e:...	Behaves the same as hasMoreElements().
Restricted Methods	
e._insert(x)	Called by Set when a new element, x, is inserted into the set. SetEnumeration will enqueue x to be reported after the elements already queued to be reported. This method will no longer be called after SetEnumeration has become inactive.
e._delete(x)	Called by Set when an element, x, is removed from the set. The element x will be removed from the elements still to be reported. This method will no longer be called after SetEnumeration has become inactive.

The two ways to use SetEnumerations are with while loops and with for loops. The while-loop version is based on Java's Enumeration interface. You create an enumeration object and loop while it has more elements, fetching and using the next element, thus:

```
e=s.elements()
while e.hasMoreElements():
    x=e.nextElement()
    . . .
```

Or, because SetEnumeration's __nonzero__() is the same as hasMoreElements():

```
e=s.elements()
while e:
    x=e.nextElement()
    . . .
```

The hasMoreElements() method returns true if there are more elements of the set to report. The nextElement() method returns the next. If no elements are added to or removed from the set during the loop, these loops will execute with x being assigned each element of the set. If new elements are inserted into the set while the loop is executing, they will also be returned by nextElement(). If an element is deleted from the set that has not yet been returned by nextElement(), it will not be. Of course, if it has already been reported, that cannot be undone. After hasMoreElements() reports false, the SetEnumeration object has become inactive. It will never report the presence of or return more elements. If nextElement() is called when there are no more elements to report, it raises IndexError. This will happen after hasMoreElements() returns false. It can also happen after hasMoreElements() returns true if the last element to be returned is deleted from the set before nextElement() is called.

The for-loop pattern is:

```
for x in s.elements():
    . . .
```

The for statement uses the __getindex__() special method. The loop asks the SetEnumeration object returned by s.elements() for item 0, item 1, and so on. The loop terminates when __getitem__() raises an IndexError. Actually, e.__getitem__(i) is implemented as a call to e.nextElement(). This does imply a strange behavior if you subscript the SetEnumeration object. If you write e[i], it will report the next item of the enumeration to you, whatever the value of `i`, or it will raise an `IndexError` if there are no more elements to report. Two occurrences of `e[i]` in a row will give different results. Thus subscripting will do unexpected things without any warning. So, should we have defined `__getitem__()` this way? It is required to make a `SetEnumeration` work in a `for` statement, and since an iterator is only supposed to be used to control loops, this implementation of `__getitem__()` appears justified.

The implementation of `SetEnumeration` is an example of the *observer* object-oriented design pattern. The `SetEnumeration` object contains a list of the elements that were in the set when it was created. The elements are returned from this list one at a time for each call to `nextElement()` or `__getitem__()`. However, when a new element is added to the set after it has been created, the `SetEnumeration` object is still supposed to report it, and if an element is deleted, `SetEnumeration` is not supposed to report it. This requires that a `SetEnumeration` object learn of changes in the set after its creation. We accomplished this by making `SetEnumeration`s observers of the set.

`Set` objects contain a list `observers`, initially empty. When a `SetEnumeration` is created by `elements()`, it is registered as an observer by appending it to the list of observers. Whenever an element that was not already present is inserted into the set, `insert()` runs through the list of observers, calling their `_insert()` methods to inform them of the presence of a new element. The `SetEnumeration _insert()` method queues up the new element in its own list to be reported later. Similarly, when an element is removed from a set, `delete()` calls the `_delete()` methods of all observers. The `_delete()` method will remove the element from its list, if present. Elements will not be present if they were already reported in the enumeration.

When an enumeration is exhausted–when `hasMoreElements()` reports false or `nextElement()` raises an `IndexError`–the `SetEnumeration` object removes itself from the list of observers. We do not want to accumulate a long list of inactive observers attached to a set.

17.5 Wrap-Up

In this chapter we examined a `Set` abstract container data type. Although the set is useful in its own right, the object-oriented design patterns shown in the chapter are more significant. We saw a protection proxy, `PureSet`, that obeys most of `Set`'s operations by passing them on to the underlying set object. What makes it a proxy rather than a decorator is that it does not implement *all* of the `set` methods. It omits `insert()` and `delete()`, the only methods that can change the contents of a set. Removing them converts sets into pure values.

We presented an iterator, `SetEnumeration`, that delivers elements of a set one at a time to loop iterations. An iterator is associated with an underlying container, allowing users to iterate over the contained elements without having to know the representation of the container. The iterator preserves encapsulation by hiding the implementation of the container.

`SetEnumeration` is also an example of the observer pattern. `SetEnumeration`s are registered with their underlying sets to be informed when elements are added or removed, so those elements can be included in or excluded from the enumeration.

17.6 Exercises

17.1. Rewrite `set` to use Python 2.1's rich comparison operators rather than `__cmp__()`, making `>` and `>=` work correctly.

17.2. `PureSet` does not keep a reference to the underlying set. Show how to get a reference to the underlying set using a special attribute of any of the methods. (See Chapter 12.)

17.3. What is the performance of this set implementation? Write some test programs to time it.

17.4. Look up the Python Enhancement Proposal 234 for iterators and redesign `set` (and `SetEnumeration`) based on it. (You can get to it via the python.org Web site.)

18

Concurrency

Concurrency involves having more than one part of a program in execution at the same time. Concurrency allows you not to have to specify the precise ordering of all activities in your program. Concurrency is particularly valuable when writing networked programs, since performance requires that several network operations proceed simultaneously.

In this chapter we look at the facilities provided by the `threading` module in the Python library. It allows us to create threads to execute parts of our program concurrently. We look at a number of problems involved with concurrent programs, in particular the need for mutual exclusion among threads that try to access the same data structure at the same time and the danger of deadlock caused by cycles of threads waiting for each other to release locks.

18.1 Threads

To use the threading facilities discussed here, you will need to import the `threading` module that provides the classes and functions shown in Table 18-1. The central class is the class `Thread`, whose operations are shown in Table 18-2. Python's Thread class is based on Java's Thread class. To create a concurrent "thread of control," you create a `Thread` object, telling it what code to execute, and then start it executing.

When you create a thread, there are two ways to tell it what code to execute. In the first method, you create a thread object, giving it a function to execute and the arguments to pass it. When the thread starts executing, it will call the function with the arguments specified. When

Table 18–1
Classes and functions provided by the threading module.

Objects and Functions	Explanation
Thread	A Thread object must be created for each thread.
Lock	A non-reentrant lock object. It is used for mutual exclusion. A thread can only acquire the lock once without releasing it; a subsequent attempt to acquire it will block because it is already locked.
Condition	A condition is attached to an underlying lock. A thread that has acquired a lock can wait for the condition to be true or notify waiting threads that the condition has become true.
RLock	A reentrant lock. This kind of lock allows a thread to acquire it more than once so one method that has locked its object can call another method that locks it.
Semaphore	Similar to a lock, but containing a count. A semaphore allows the number of threads given by the count to acquire it at the same time.
Event	A toggle that blocks threads until it has been set.
activeCount()	Returns the number of active threads as of the time of the call. By the nature of concurrency, the number could change immediately after the call.
currentThread()	Gives the Thread object for the thread that calls the function.
enumerate()	Gives a list of the active threads as of the time of the call. The set of active threads could change immediately after the call.

Table 18–2
Thread objects.

Operation	Explanation

`t=Thread (target=None, args=(), kwargs={}, name=None)`
 	
`Thread()`
	Creates a thread object. *Use only keyword parameters* when creating a thread. The `target` is the function for the thread to execute, `args` is a tuple of positional arguments for the function, and `kwargs` is a dictionary of keyword arguments for the function. If the `name` string is provided, errors during the thread's execution will be reported under that name.
	    The version with no parameters is to indicate that you can inherit from `Thread`. You override `Thread`'s `run()` method to specify the code to execute. In your `__init__()` method, you must call `Thread.__init__(self)`.

`t.start()`	Starts a thread executing.
`t.join()` `t.join(waittime)`	Waits for thread `t` to terminate. If a `waittime` is provided, it is a floating-point number specifying the number of seconds or fractions of seconds to wait before timing out and returning. A thread may not be joined before it is started.
`t.isAlive()`	Returns true if thread `t` has not terminated.

Table 18-2
Thread objects. (Continued)

Operation	Explanation
`t.setDaemon(yes)`	The program will run until all non-daemon threads have terminated. If you do not want a thread to keep the program running, make it a daemon before starting it. If the parameter, `yes`, is true, the thread is made a daemon thread; if false, a normal thread. If you do not call `setDaemon()`, a thread created by a daemon thread will be a daemon thread, and a thread created by a normal thread will be a normal thread.
`t.isDaemon()`	Returns true if thread `t` is a daemon thread.
`t.getName()`	Returns the string name of the thread.
`t.setName(name)`	Assigns the string name to the thread.
`t.run()`	To be overridden in a subclass of `Thread`. When you start a thread, it executes its `run()` method. The `run()` method in class `Thread` calls the `target` function.

the function returns, the thread "dies." Once the thread is dead, it can no longer execute; you cannot restart it.

The other way to tell the thread what to do is to create a subclass of the `Thread` class and provide a `run()` method. When the thread starts executing, it will execute the `run()` method and die when that method returns. We examine these two methods in more detail in the subsections that follow.

18.1.1 Thread Object with Target

The first way to create a thread is to create a thread object, passing it the function to execute in the keyword parameter, `target`. The code:

```
t=Thread(target=fn)
t.start()
```

creates a thread object and assigns it to `t`. The `start()` call will set the thread running. The thread will call the function `fn`, passing it an empty parameter list. You can provide positional and keyword arguments and a name for the function, thus:

```
t=Thread(target=fn,args=(a0,a1,...), \
    kwargs={n0:v0,n1:v1,...},name=str)
t.start()
```

The tuple `args` gives the positional arguments. The dictionary `kwargs` gives the keyword arguments. The string `name` gives the name of the thread, which will be included in diagnostic tracebacks if an error occurs in it. By default, `args` is an empty tuple and `kwargs` is an empty dictionary. Also by default, the `Thread` class makes up its own name for the thread.

The *states* a thread can be in are shown in Figure 18–1. If you have a reference, `t`, to a thread, you can find out if the thread is still alive with the method call `t.isAlive()`. If you want to wait for a thread to complete its execution, you can call `t.join()`, which will *block* you until thread `t` terminates. While a thread is alive, it will be runnable, running or blocked. While running, it will get a share of the processor, executing a few instructions at a time. A thread is blocked when it is waiting for some condition, as for example, `t.join()` waits for `t` to terminate.

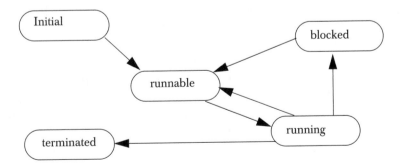

Figure 18–1
States of a thread.

Here is an example of running a subcomputation in a thread. We define a function loopBumping that will call bump() in a counter object (see Figure 4–2). It is told the counter object to "bump," the amount to be added each iteration, and the number of iterations. We create a counter object with an initial count of zero and a thread, up, that will call loopBumping, passing it the counter object, the amount to add (one), and the number of times to execute (100,000). We start the thread join() to wait for its completion, and write out the count: 100000, as expected.

```
>>> import threading
>>> import counterObj
>>> def loopBumping(counter,by,iterations):
...     for i in xrange(iterations):
...             counter.bump(by)
...
>>> iterations=100000
>>> counter=counterObj.counter()
>>> up = threading.Thread(target=loopBumping,  \
... args=(counter,1,iterations))
>>> up.start()
>>> up.join()
>>> counter.count
100000
```

18.1.2   Inheriting from Thread

The second way to specify the code a thread will execute is to create a subclass of thread and override Thread's run() method. When the thread starts executing, it executes its run() method. If you have not overridden it, it will execute the target function. If you override the run() method, the thread will execute your run() method and not try to call a target function.

Since your run() method is not passed any parameters, you will probably need to provide an __init__() method for your class to give it data to work on. However, Thread's __init__() method *must* be executed before you start the thread. The pattern for creating a thread by subclassing is shown in Figure 18–2.

That is:

1. You must inherit from Thread.
2. You must execute Thread's __init__() method.
3. You must override Thread's run() method.

```
class MyThread(threading.Thread):
    def __init__(self,...):
        threading.Thread.__init__(self)
        ...
    def run(self):
        ...
```

Figure 18–2
Pattern for creating a thread by subclassing.

```
import threading

times=100
delay=10000

class egoistThread(threading.Thread):
    def __init__(self,id,times,delay):
        threading.Thread.__init__(self)
        self.id=id
        self.times=times
        self.delay=delay
    def run(self):
        for i in xrange(self.times):
            print self.id,
            for j in xrange(self.delay): pass
egoists=[]
for c in 'abc':
    t=egoistThread(c,times,delay)
    egoists.append(t)
for t in egoists:
    t.start()
for t in egoists:
    t.join()
```

Figure 18–3
Egoist, inheriting from thread.

An example of inheriting from Thread is shown in Figure 18–3. The egoistThread class inherits from Thread. An egoistThread is created with a name, id, to write out; the number of times to write out its name; and the delay between occurrences of writing out its name. The delay is the number of iterations of an empty loop. We create three egoist threads with the names 'a', 'b', and 'c.' We set them running and then wait for them to terminate.

18.2   Race Conditions

Two outputs from executing the egoist threads are shown in Figure 18–4. As you can see, the results are not the same. Generally, concurrent execution is nondeterministic. The actual behavior of a program is determined by the relative speeds of the threads, so-called race conditions. This has two huge consequences for programming. One is that it is hard to understand what is occurring when the results of computation can change each run. With a program that has a single thread of control, you can at least in theory point to a particular place in the program and know what is supposed to be true when control reaches there. With even two threads of control, the situation becomes much more complex.

The second problem is that interference of threads can cause the program to produce incorrect answers or to crash. Programs perform their computations by making a series of small, incremental changes in data structures. It takes several changes to make a data structure go from one consistent state to another. If two threads are updating the data structure at the same time, one will overwrite some of the data the other is writing and leave the data garbled. If it doesn't crash the program immediately, it probably will later when some thread tries to use the data structure again.

Just how likely is it that this garbling will occur? Figure 18–5 shows another use of the `loopBumping` function from the previous section. In this case, we create two threads: one to increment the counter 100,000 times and the other to decrement it 100,000 times. Since the counter starts off at zero, adding and subtracting one the same number of times should leave it zero. Figure 18–6 shows the results of six runs. Sometimes we get zero, sometimes not.

How does the program get a nonzero result? The actual code in `counterObj` is `this.count+=by`. The translated code is not very long, but it is more than one bytecode instruction. What happens is that occasionally one thread fetches this count but, before it can store the new value, the other thread starts running. Suppose `count` is initially k. Thread A fetches it and subtracts 1, giving k-1. Before A can store this, thread B gets control, fetches k from count, adds 1 to it, and stores k+1 back in count. Now thread A regains control and finishes storing k-1 in

```
C:>python EgoistThread.py
a a a a a a a a a a b b b b b b b b b b b c c c c c a a a a
a a c c c c a a a a c c c c a a a a c c c c a a a a a c c c
c c c c c c a a a a a a a a a c c c c c c c c c a a a a a
a a a a c c c c c c c c c a a a a a a a a a c c c c c c c
c c a a a a a a a a a c c c c c c c c a a a a a a a a a c
c c c c c c c a a a a a a a a a a c c c c c c c c c c a a
a a a a a a a a c c c c c c c a a a a a a c c c b b b b
b b b b b b b b b b c c c c c b b b b b b b b b b b b b b b
b b b b b b b b b b b b b b b b b b b b b b b b b b b b b b
b b b b b b b b b b b b b b b b b b b b b b b b b b b b b b

C:>python EgoistThread.py
a a a a a a a a a b b b b b b b b b b b c c c c c a a a a c
c c c a a a a a c c c c c a a a a a a a a a c c c c c c c c
c a a a a a a a a a c c c c c c c c a a a a a c c c b b b
b b b c c c c c b b b b b c c c c c b b b b b c c c c c b b b b c
c c c b b b b b b c c c c c b b b b b c c c c b b b b b b b b b
b c c c c c c c c c b b b b b b b b b c c c c c c c c c b b
b b b b b b b c c c c c c c c c b b b b b b b b b c c c c c
c c c b b b b b b b b b b c c c b b b b b a a a a a a a a a
a a a a a a a b b b b b b b b b b a a a a a a a a a a a a a
a a a a a a a a a a a a a a a a a a a a a a a a a a a a a a
```

Figure 18–4
Two runs of `EgoistThread`.

count. Instead of the net effect of the two operations being zero, it is negative 1.

The code `this.count+=by` is called a *critical section*. It must be executed by only one thread at a time.

18.3   Locks and Mutual Exclusion

Critical sections of code require mutual exclusion among threads. At most one thread may execute a critical section at a time. While one thread is executing in the critical section, the other threads must be locked out. In Python's threading module, critical sections are protected by lock objects. There are two kinds of lock objects, of class `Lock` and

```
import threading
import counterObj

def loopBumping(counter,by,iterations):
    for i in xrange(iterations):
      counter.bump(by)

iterations=100000
counter=counterObj.counter()

up = threading.Thread(target=loopBumping, \
args=(counter,1,iterations))
down = threading.Thread(target=loopBumping, \
args=(counter,-1,iterations))

up.start()
down.start()

up.join()
down.join()

print 'result:',counter.count
```

Figure 18–5
upanddownCounter.

```
C:>python upanddownCounter.py
result: 0

C:>python upanddownCounter.py
result: -6128

C:>python upanddownCounter.py
result: 0

C:>python upanddownCounter.py
result: 0

C:>python upanddownCounter.py
result: -70983

C:>python upanddownCounter.py
result: 35602
```

Figure 18–6
Several runs of upanddownCounter.

class `RLock`. They both have the same methods, shown in Table 18–3. The class `Lock` gives `lock` objects that are faster but more limited, since a `lock` object makes it easy for you to deadlock with yourself. We discuss `lock` first.

Table 18–3
`Lock` and `RLock` operations.

Operation	Explanation
`lock=Lock()`	Creates a `lock` object. `Lock` objects are not "reentrant." A thread that tries to acquire a `lock` object twice without releasing it in between will be deadlocked with itself.
`lock=RLock()`	Creates a reentrant lock object. This is the preferred version for use in monitors. A thread may acquire a reentrant lock any number of times without blocking.
`lock.acquire(block=1)`	Acquires (locks) the `lock` object. If `block` is omitted or true, the executing thread will block and wait for the lock to be released by another thread before acquiring it. If `block` is false, `acquire` will return immediately, reporting true if the lock was acquired and false if the lock is in use by another thread. An `RLock` object can always be acquired again by the thread that holds it. A `Lock` object cannot be acquired more than once by any thread without being released.
`lock.release()`	Releases the lock. If the lock is a `Lock` object, another thread can acquire it immediately. If the lock is an `RLock`, it does not become available to other threads until the thread that holds the lock has released it as many times as it has acquired it.

A lock object is created simply by:

```
lock=threading.Lock()
```

The simplest pattern for mutual exclusion using a lock object is:

```
lock.acquire()
... #critical section
lock.release()
```

When a thread executes the `lock.acquire()`, it locks the `lock`. When it executes `lock.release()`, it unlocks it. When a thread tries to execute `lock.acquire()` and the lock has been acquired by some other thread, the thread is blocked until the lock is released. It is vitally important that if a thread acquires a lock, it also releases it. If the lock remains locked, other threads will block trying to acquire it and never wake up. It is an unimpressive bug, since you do not actually see anything wrong happening. It just looks like the program is taking forever to finish executing.

To make sure a lock is released, you can use the following pattern:

```
lock.acquire()
try:
    ... #critical section
finally:
    lock.release()
```

Here, no matter how you leave the critical section, the lock will be released, including if the critical section raises an exception. Although this does guarantee that other threads can enter the critical section, it itself is somewhat unsafe. If the critical section is left by an exception, the data structure may be only partially updated, which can cause another thread to crash when it tries to use the garbled data. If there is any chance of an exception leaving the critical section before the update is complete, you might want to use the pattern shown in Figure 18–7.

```
lock.acquire()
try:
    try:
        ... #critical section
    exception:
        ... #restore the data structure
        raise
finally:
    lock.release()
```

Figure 18–7
Full pattern for mutual exclusion.

Figure 18–8 shows how a critical section can be used to protect the critical section in counter. This module, threadsafeCounter, acquires and releases a lock around the update of count. Six executions of it are shown in Figure 18–9, all giving the desired answer, zero.

```
import threading

class counter:
    "creates counter objects"
    def bump(this,by=1):
        self.lock.acquire()
        try:
            this.count+=by
            return this.count
        finally:
            self.lock.release()
    def __init__(self,val=0):
        self.count=val
        self.lock=threading.Lock()
```

Figure 18–8
threadsafeCounter.

```
C:>python upanddownThreadsafe.py
result: 0

C:>python upanddownThreadsafe.py
result: 0

C:>python upanddownThreadsafe.py
result: 0

C:>python upanddownThreadsafe.py
result: 0

C:>python upanddownThreadsafe.py
result: 0

C:>python upanddownThreadsafe.py
result: 0
```

Figure 18–9
Testing `threadsafeCounter`.

18.4   Monitor Pattern

Unfortunately, critical sections can be more complicated than shown earlier. Although we talk about "the" critical section, there are often several for the same data structure, some protecting threads that are reading the data, some protecting updates. All have to lock the same lock. This leads naturally to the idea of a *monitor*, a shared data structure protected in an object with a lock attribute. The pattern for a monitor is shown in Figure 18–10. The various critical sections become methods. They all lock the object, perform their read or update, unlock it, and return.

There is a further complexity. Suppose one thread puts data into the object, and another thread removes it and uses it. Clearly, the second thread can fetch only data that is present. If it locks the object and looks for the data, what is it to do if the data is not yet present?

One thing it cannot do is hold the lock and loop waiting for the other thread to put the data in. As long as it holds the lock, the other thread cannot get into a method to deposit the data. It could loop outside the critical section, locking the object, checking whether the data is available, and if not, unlocking the object and repeating the loop. This

```
class monitor:
   def method(self,...):
     self.lock.acquire()
     try:
       try:
         ...
         while not condition:
           self.cnd.wait()
         ...
         if condition:
           self.cnd.notify()
         ...
       except:
         ... #restore object to a consistent state
         raise
     finally:
       self.lock.release()
   def __init__(self,...):
     self.lock=RLock()
     self.cnd=Condition(self.lock)
     ...
```

Figure 18–10
Monitor pattern.

busy waiting is usually a bad idea. It burns up machine cycles that could be better devoted to the thread that is producing the data.

This consideration led to the creation of *condition* objects. You create condition objects attached to lock objects, thus:

```
self.lock=RLock()
self.cnd=Condition(self.lock)
```

The RLock, reentrant lock, object is better to use for monitors than Lock objects are, for reasons we discuss below. All the methods of the monitor protect their code by acquiring and releasing lock. The Condition class has the operations shown in Table 18–4.

The idea behind Condition objects is that sometimes threads in a monitor must wait for certain conditions to become true before they can proceed. Condition objects allow these conditions to be given names. When a thread needs to wait for a condition, cnd, to become true, it executes self.cnd.wait(). The wait() method does two things simultaneously: It gives up the monitor lock, and it blocks the thread that executed it. Because the monitor is no longer locked, another thread can get in and make the condition true.

Table 18–4
Condition operations.

Operation	Explanation
`cnd=Condition()` `cnd=Condition(lock)`	Creates a condition object bound to an underlying lock. If you do not specify the lock, Condition creates an `RLock` object.
`cnd.acquire()` `cnd.acquire(block)`	`acquire()` on a condition object performs the acquire on the underlying lock.
`cnd.release()`	`release()` on a condition object performs the release on the underlying lock.
`cnd.wait()` `cnd.wait(timeout)`	`wait()` will block the thread that executes it and fully release the underlying lock object. The thread will remain blocked until the time-out period has expired or some other thread has called `notify()` or `notifyAll()` on the condition. Parameter `timeout` is a floating-point number giving the maximum number of seconds and fractions of seconds the thread is to wait. Once the caller of `wait()` has been unblocked, it will reacquire the lock before it returns from the `wait()`. Other threads may acquire and release the lock before it runs again, so the condition that prompted the notify may no longer be true.
`cnd.notify()`	If any threads are waiting on the condition, `notify()` unblocks precisely one of them. If there are no threads waiting, `notify()` performs no operation.
`cnd.notifyAll()`	If any threads are waiting on the condition, `notifyAll()` unblocks *all* of them. If there are no threads waiting, `notifyAll()` performs no operation.

When a thread makes condition `cnd` true, it should execute `self.cnd.notify()`. If any threads are blocked waiting for condition `cnd`, one of them will be awakened. If there are none waiting, the `notify()` performs no operation. When you wait for a condition or notify a waiting thread that the condition is now true, you must hold the underlying lock.

A thread that has been waiting for a condition will reacquire the monitor lock before returning from the `wait()` call. The thread executing `notify()`, however, does not immediately give up the monitor lock, so the waiting thread does not get control immediately. This is why you usually put the `self.cnd.wait()` in a loop. While the condition is not true, you wait. You will be awakened by another thread that has made the condition true, but before you start running again, the condition can again have become false. You have to check again, and you may have to wait.

You can have any number of conditions represented by any number of `Condition` objects. As a special case, if there is only one condition, you do not have to create the monitor lock separately. If you call `cnd=Condition()` without any parameters, it creates an `RLock` object and attaches the `Condition` object to that. You can then lock and unlock the monitor by calling `cnd.acquire()` and `cnd.release()`.

An example of a monitor is the `Latch` class shown in Figure 18–11. A `Latch` object can hold a single piece of data at a time. A datum is placed in the `Latch`, x, by a call to the `x.put(y)` method and is removed by a call to `x.get()`. When `x.put(y)` is called, it cannot place y in x unless x does not currently have any contents. The attribute `contents` is used both to hold the data and to indicate whether a datum is present. When `x.put(y)` is called, it checks to see if the object has a `contents` attribute. If it does, `put()` cannot store y yet, so it waits for `self.empty`, the condition that the `Latch` is empty. Similarly, `get()` cannot return the contents unless attribute `contents` is present. If `get()` is called and there is no `contents` attribute, it waits for the condition `full`.

When `x.put(y)` is allowed to store y in x, it calls `full.notify()` to wake up a waiting `get()`. Similarly, when it removes the contents of x, `x.get()` deletes `x.contents` to indicate that x is empty and calls `empty.notify()` to wake up a waiting `put()`.

```
import threading
class Latch:
    def __init__(self):
      self.lock=threading.Lock()
      self.empty=threading.Condition(self.lock)
      self.full=threading.Condition(self.lock)
    def put(self,x):
      self.lock.acquire()
      try:
        while hasattr(self,'contents'):
          self.empty.wait()
        self.contents=x
        self.full.notify()
      finally:
        self.lock.release()
    def get(self):
      self.lock.acquire()
      try:
        while not hasattr(self,'contents'):
          self.full.wait()
        x=self.contents
        del self.contents
        self.empty.notify()
        return x
      finally:
        self.lock.release()
```

Figure 18–11
Latch monitor.

18.5   Producer-Consumer

We can test the `Latch` class with a simple program that uses the producer-consumer pattern. The producer-consumer pattern is an abstraction of customers queueing up in a single line to be served by several bank tellers, or several computers on a network submitting files to be printed by any of several printers.

The producer-consumer pattern has one or more threads producing data and placing them in a buffer object while one or more consumer threads remove and use the data. The consumers cannot run ahead of the producers, of course. Since the buffer has a limited capacity, the producers are limited in how far they can run ahead of the consumers.

In this test code, there is one producer and one consumer. The producer and the consumer are implemented as functions that take a `Latch` object as their single parameter. Each is run as a thread. The producer puts the integers from 0 through 9 into the shared latch followed by a None value. The consumer removes values from the latch and writes out their values, stopping when it gets the value None. Here is the code:

```
import threading
import Latch
def producer(shared):
    for i in xrange(10):
        shared.put(i)
    shared.put(None)
def consumer(shared):
    x=shared.get()
    while x is not None:
        print x,
        x=shared.get()
shared=Latch.Latch()
p=threading.Thread(target=producer,args=(shared,))
c=threading.Thread(target=consumer,args=(shared,))
c.start()
p.start()
```

The output is simply the numbers the producer placed in the latch:

```
C:>python testLatch.py
0 1 2 3 4 5 6 7 8 9
```

The Latch class, containing only a single value at a time, is not the most flexible buffer. Usually one uses a queue with a limited capacity. The Python library provides a bounded queue for use in producer-consumer systems. It is *not* contained in the threading module, but rather the Queue module. The Queue module provides the classes and methods shown in Table 18–5.

Redoing our test of Latch to use Queue, we make the following changes:

```
import threading
import Queue
... #defs of producer and consumer the same
shared=Queue.Queue(3)
p=threading.Thread(target=producer,args=(shared,))
c=threading.Thread(target=consumer,args=(shared,))
p.start()
c.start()
p.join()
c.join()
```

Table 18–5
Queue module.

Facility	Explanation
`q=Queue(maxsize)`	Creates a `Queue` object with the capacity specified by `maxsize`. If `maxsize` is a positive integer, the queue can hold at most `maxsize` elements at one time. If `maxsize` is zero or negative, the queue can hold an unlimited number of elements.
`Empty`	An exception class. An `Empty` exception is raised if a thread attempts to perform a nonblocking `get()` on an empty queue.
`Full`	An exception class. A `Full` exception is raised if a thread attempts to perform a nonblocking `put()` on a full queue.
`q.put(item,block=1)`	Puts code in `Queue` q. If `block` is specified and false, it raises a `Full` exception if the queue does not have any remaining capacity. If `block` is not specified or is true, it will wait until the queue has enough capacity for the item to be placed in it.
`q.put_nowait(item)`	Equivalent to `q.put(item,0)`.
`q.get(block=1)`	Removes and returns the first item from the queue. If `block` is not specified or is true, it will wait for the queue to contain an item to be removed. If `block` is false, it will raise an `Empty` exception if the queue is empty.
`q.get_nowait()`	Equivalent to `q.get(0)`.
`q.qsize()`	Returns the number of items in the queue at the instant `qsize()` is called.

Table 18–5
Queue module. (Continued)

Facility	Explanation
`q.empty()`	Returns true if the queue is empty at the instant it is called.
`q.full()`	Returns true if the queue is full at the instant it is called.

We created a queue with a capacity of three items. Since the `get()` and `put()` methods for `Latch` and `Queue` are compatible, we didn't need to change the producer or consumer functions. We started the producer first to give it a chance to fill up the queue before the consumer even starts, although we are not guaranteed that that is what actually happens. Running it gives:

```
C:>python testQueue.py
0 1 2 3 4 5 6 7 8 9
```

A major use for `Queue`s is processing network traffic, handling requests and data transmissions. For input, the producer is the part of the program connected to the network receiving requests and data. Its job is solely to receive the requests and data, not to process them. The consumer actually handles the requests. The network sometimes makes heavy demands on the producer, sometimes light. A `Queue` allows the producer to handle bursts of activity without having to wait for the consumer to process them.

18.6   Deadlock

One of the big risks of multithreaded systems is deadlock. Deadlock consists of a collection of threads that are trying to acquire locks that are held by other threads in the collection. No thread can proceed without acquiring the next lock, and no thread will give up the locks it has already acquired. For example, thread A has acquired lock x and thread B has acquired lock y. Then A executes `y.acquire()` and B executes `x.acquire()`. A will be blocked until it gets lock y and B will be blocked until it gets lock x. Since neither of them is running, neither of them will release the lock it holds.

Deadlock is an unimpressive error. It does not raise any exceptions. It does not do anything. It just looks like the program is running very slowly. In fact, the part of the program that is deadlocked is not making and cannot make any progress at all.

Dijkstra provided a metaphor for a deadlocking system: Imagine that there are a number of philosophers eating spaghetti together around a table (Figure 18–12). Each philosopher has a plate of spaghetti and there are forks between the adjacent plates. Philosophers are in one of two states, thinking or eating. When a philosopher finishes thinking, he takes a fork from each side of his plate and eats for a while. Done eating, the philosopher replaces the forks at each side of his plate. If all the philosophers try to start eating at about the same time, they may all pick up one fork, the left fork say, and deadlock waiting to pick up the right fork.

We will simulate this with the philosophers being threads and the forks being locks. Figure 18–13 gives code for an implementation of the

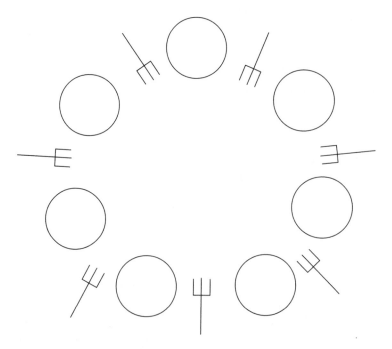

Figure 18–12
Dining philosophers table settings.

```python
import threading
import random
import sys

numPhilosophers=7
iterations=100
forks=[None]*numPhilosophers
for i in range(numPhilosophers):
    forks[i] = threading.Lock()
state=['.']*numPhilosophers

showlock=threading.Lock()
def showState():
    showlock.acquire()
    try:
      s = "".join(state)
      print >>sys.stderr, s
      return s
    finally: showlock.release()

def delay(t):
    timer=threading.Condition()
    timer.acquire()
    timer.wait(t)
    timer.release()

class Philosopher(threading.Thread):
    def __init__(self,num):
      self.num=num
      threading.Thread.__init__(self)
    def run(self):
      leftFork= self.num
      rightFork= ((self.num+1)%numPhilosophers)
      for iternum in xrange(iterations):
        state[self.num]='<'; showState()
        forks[leftFork].acquire()

        delay(1*random.random())

        state[self.num]='>'; showState()
        forks[rightFork].acquire()

        state[self.num]=str(self.num); showState()
        delay(2*random.random())

        forks[rightFork].release()
        forks[leftFork].release()
        state[self.num]='.'; showState()
        delay(2*random.random())

def start():
    for i in range(numPhilosophers):
```

Figure 18–13
Dining philosophers, with deadlock.

```
                p=Philosopher(i)
                p.start()
        start()
```

Figure 18–13
Dining philosophers, with deadlock. (Continued)

dining philosophers problem, `DiningPhilosophs1.py`. Here we set the number of philosophers to seven. The forks are `Lock` objects. We keep a list, `state`, in which each philosopher places a character to indicate his current state: '.' for thinking, '<' for trying to pick up the left fork, '>' for trying to pick up the right fork, and his own number for eating. The `Philosopher` class gives the code for the philosophers. Since `Philosopher` inherits from `Thread`, the `run()` method provides the program the philosophers execute. If the philosophers get through a specified number of iterations, they terminate normally.

An additional point of interest is the `delay()` function. It creates a `Condition` variable, `timer`. We do not specify a lock for the condition, so the call to `Condition` creates an `RLock` object on its own. The `delay()` function acquires the underlying lock by calling `acquire()` on the condition and then waits on the condition with a timeout. The `wait(timeout)` method for `Condition`s will wait at most the amount of time given by `timeout`, a floating-point number specifying a number of seconds and fractions of seconds. After the timeout period is exhausted, if the condition has not been signaled, the thread is reawakened anyway and returns from the `wait()` call.

The `delay()` function allows us to suspend a thread for an amount of time. Its use here is to allow an amount of time to pass without burning up processor cycles in a delay loop.

The following is a run of `DiningPhilosophs1`:

```
C:>python DiningPhilosophs1.py
<......
<<.....
<<<....
<<<<...
<<<<<..
<<<<<<.
<<<<<<<
<><<<<<
<><><<<
<><><><
<><><>>
```

```
>><><>>
>>>><>>
>>>>>>>
```

The final state shows each philosopher thread, having acquired its left fork, trying to pick up the right fork. The program stopped running at this point, but did not terminate. Python is not programmed to determine that the threads are deadlocked.

Deadlock is not an unusual or exotic occurrence. Deadlock is common in concurrent programs. We need to consider what can be done about deadlock.

18.6.1   RLock versus Lock

It is possible for a thread to deadlock with itself. Suppose we have created a lock, x:

```
x=threading.Lock()
```

If a thread tries to acquire it twice,

```
x.acquire()
..
x.acquire()
```

the second attempt will block because the lock is unavailable. You may wonder whether you are likely to write code like that. It is, in fact, very common. You have every method in a monitor acquire a lock on entry and release it on exit. Suppose you want one method to call another. The `acquire()` at the beginning of the second method would block.

For this reason, the threading package provides RLock, "reentrant lock," objects. A thread can acquire the same RLock object any number of times without blocking, allowing one monitor method to call another without worry. This is why the code in Figure 18–10 creates an RLock for the monitor.

A reentrant lock keeps the identity of the thread that holds it, a count of the number of times it has been acquired by that thread, and an underlying primitive lock. When a thread acquires an RLock for the first time, the `acquire()` method itself acquires the underlying lock and then sets the owner to the calling thread and the count to one. When a thread calls `acquire()` for the same lock again, the count is incremented. When the thread releases a lock, its count is decremented. Only when the count goes to zero is the underlying lock actually released. `Conditions` attached to `RLocks` have to save the count and owner and release the underlying lock. When they are notified or they timeout, they reacquire the underlying lock and restore the owner and count.

18.6.2   Conditions for Deadlock

There are four conditions required for deadlock to occur. If we can eliminate any one of them, our system will not deadlock. The conditions are:

1. mutual exclusion—only one thread may acquire a lock at a time;
2. hold and wait—a thread can hold one lock while waiting to acquire another;
3. no preemption—a thread must release a lock itself; and
4. circular wait—there must be a cycle of threads, each waiting to acquire the held by the next thread in the cycle.

Which of these conditions can we eliminate to prevent deadlock? We cannot eliminate mutual exclusion. The whole point of locking things is to provide mutual exclusion. Without mutual exclusion, race conditions can cause our programs to produce wrong answers or to crash. The no-preemption condition is also difficult to eliminate. There are no good facilities to force one thread to give up a lock, or to wrest the lock away from a thread. That leaves hold and wait and circular wait as candidates for elimination.

18.6.3   Deadlock Avoidance Strategies

Eliminating Hold-and-Wait

It is possible to eliminate the hold-and-wait. The call `lock.acquire(0)` is nonblocking. If it does acquire the `lock`, it returns true (1). If it does not acquire it, it returns false (0). We can eliminate the hold-and-wait condition by using only nonblocking `acquire()` calls. If we do not acquire the lock, we can give up all the locks we hold and start to acquire them again.

There are a few mechanics of this approach that may make it more efficient. We can create an exception type, say `LockUnavailableError`, and raise it if an acquire returns false. We can use this to force us to restore data structures to their previous states and release the locks we have acquired previously. Eventually, we catch the `LockUnavailable-`

Error and restart the process of acquiring locks. It would also be a good idea to wait a bit of time before starting the process again, to give another thread the chance to complete its processing. If we are not careful, we might have something like thread A trying to acquire locks x, y, and z in order, and thread B trying to acquire z, y, and x. They could continually restart, acquiring x and z. One of them would get y, but then they would both find a lock unavailable, back off, and restart.

To minimize the effects of this problem, we can use the delay() function in Figure 18–13. In choosing the delay time, good options are random back-off and exponential back-off. Random back-off means waiting a random amount of time before trying again. Exponential back-off means waiting twice the amount of time each time the Lock-UnavailableError brings control back to the start. Random back-off would address the example of threads A and B acquiring x, y, and z. Whichever thread gets the smaller random delay would have a chance to get all the locks before the other thread starts up again. The exponential delay can reduce the contention for a bunch of heavily used locks.

It would also be better not to give up immediately if a lock is unavailable. We might want to try something like:

```
def lockorfail(lock):
    if not lock.acquire(0):
        delay(timeout)
        if not lock.acquire(0):
            raise LockUnavailableError
```

Another way to eliminate hold-and-wait is to use *transactions*, which we discuss in Chapter 19. In their simplest implementation, transactions use a single lock for an entire database. Transactions may read records from a database one at a time, acquiring the single lock for the duration of each read. They lock the entire database at the end to *commit* all their changes at once. If at the commit they find they have used data that has changed since they read it, they back up and restart their access.

Ordering Locks to Break Circular Wait

The circular wait condition is often the easiest one to eliminate. A trick is to give a unique number to each of the locks. The rule then is that a thread can only acquire a lock with a higher number than any it already owns. Consider the cycle pictured in Figure 18–14. Suppose x's number is less than y's number and y's number is less than z's. The

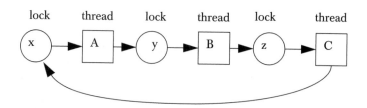

Figure 18–14
Cycle of threads and locks.

only way to have a cycle like that is for some thread, in this case, C, to hold the highest-numbered lock and be waiting for a lower-numbered lock. But by our rule, thread C is not permitted to wait for x, a lower-numbered lock than z, which it holds.

In the case of the dining philosophers code, philosopher reaches for fork i first, and then `(i+1)%numPhilosophers`. If we used the ordering rule, philosopher number *(numPhilosophers-1)* would have to reach for fork zero first, then fork *(numPhilosophers-1)*.

It is usually easy to use this approach. When you have to lock a group of objects, you lock them in a particular order.

18.6.3.1 Using Semaphore to Limit Entry

Another approach to eliminating the circular wait condition is to have more resources than the threads need. Suppose that there are seven philosophers, but only six are allowed to try to eat at the same time. This will make an extra fork available so that at least one philosopher can get two forks and eat. For example, suppose philosopher two is not allowed to eat because all the others are trying to eat. Philosopher two will not try to pick up fork two, which makes it available to philosopher one. If everybody has picked up his left fork, philosopher one is guaranteed to be able to pick up his right fork and eat. Then when philosopher one finishes eating, he will put down fork one, allowing philosopher zero to pick it up and eat, and so on.

A way to limit the number of threads accessing a set of resources at the same time is to use a semaphore. The `threading` module's `Semaphore` class is described in Table 18–6. A semaphore is like a lock, but it can allow more than one thread to acquire it at the same time. A semaphore contains a nonnegative integer count. When a thread acquires a semaphore, it decrements the count. When it releases the semaphore, it increments the count. However, because the count is restricted to being

Table 18–6
Semaphore.

Operation	Explanation
`s=Semaphore(init=1)`	Creates a semaphore object with its count initialized to nonnegative integer `init`.
`s.acquire(block=1)`	Decrements the count and returns if the count is positive. If `block` is omitted or is true and the count is zero, it will block until the count becomes positive and hence can be decremented. It returns immediately if `block` is false. It returns one if the count was decremented successfully. It returns zero if it was called with `block` false and the count zero.
`s.release()`	Increases the count of the semaphore. The semaphore is made available for other threads to acquire it.

nonnegative, a thread cannot acquire the semaphore if its count is zero. If you do not pass it a parameter, the `acquire()` method will block until the count is greater than zero, permitting it to be decremented. When you pass a parameter to `Semaphore`'s `acquire` method, it will block only if the parameter is true. If it is false, it will return immediately. Whether the parameter is true or false, `acquire()` returns true if it decremented the count, and false if it did not block and the count was zero and hence has not been modified.

18.7 Example: Future

A *future* is an assign-once variable that can be used to pass results back from concurrent subroutines. Figure 18–15 gives the code for `Future`, an implementation of a future object. The operations on futures are given in Table 18–7.

A future can be assigned a value precisely once. Future, `f`, has three operations: The method `f.set(x)` will assign `x` as the future's contents. If `f` already has its contents assigned, the `set()` method will raise

```
import threading

class StateError(StandardError):pass

class Future:
    def __init__(self,*arg):
      self.lock=threading.RLock()
      self.full=threading.Condition(self.lock)
      if len(arg)>0:
        self.contents=arg[0]
    def isSet(self):
      self.lock.acquire()
      try:
        return hasattr(self,"contents")
      finally:
        self.lock.release()

    def set(self,x):
      self.lock.acquire()
      try:
        if self.isSet():
          raise StateError("Future already set")
        self.contents=x
        self.full.notifyAll()
      finally:
        self.lock.release()
    def get(self):
      self.lock.acquire()
      try:
        if not self.isSet():
          self.full.wait()
        return self.contents
      finally:
        self.lock.release()
```

Figure 18–15
Futures.

Table 18–7
Future operations (`Future.py`).

Operation	Explanation
f=Future() f=Future(val)	Creates a Future. If specified, sets the future's contents to val.
StateError	An exception subclass of StandardError. Raised if an attempt is made to reassign the contents of a Future.

Table 18–7
Future operations (`Future.py`). (Continued)

Operation	Explanation
`f.set(value)`	Sets the contents of the `Future` f to value. Raises a `StateError` if f already has contents assigned.
`f.get()`	Gets the contents of the `Future` f. Blocks until the contents are assigned.
`f.isSet()`	Returns true if f's contents are set, false otherwise.

a `StateError` exception. The call `f.get()` will return the contents of f, blocking until f has its contents assigned. The call `f.isSet()` will return true if f has already had its contents assigned. By the nature of concurrency, `isSet()` can return false and f can have its contents set immediately thereafter.

One way to use futures is to return them from a concurrent function. The function creates a thread to calculate the value and store it in a `Future`. The function returns the `Future`, and the caller gets the value out of the future when it needs it.

```
f=concurrentFunction(...)
...
...f.get()...
```

A `Future` can be created with its contents already set. This may seem pointless, but if a function can calculate the value immediately, rather than starting a thread to do it, it should return the future already set.

Note in the implementation that both methods `set()` and `get()` call method `isSet()`. We have to use an `RLock` object here to avoid deadlock. Another point is the use of `Condition` method `notifyAll()`, which awakens all waiting threads. Any number of threads can get the value out of a `Future`, and they all need to be notified when the value is assigned.

18.8   Wrap-Up

We examined how to provide concurrency in a Python program using the `threading` module. We saw two ways of creating threads. We saw two kinds of locks that can be used to provide mutual exclusion when threads are accessing the same data structure. We saw how to use locks and conditions to implement monitors.

We examined the danger of deadlock and how to prevent it from occurring. Ways to prevent deadlock include using timeouts on `acquire()` calls, numbering resources to prevent circular waits, and using semaphores to limit the number of threads contending for resources at one time.

We looked at the producer-consumer pattern and the `Queue` module that provides a bounded buffer to link producers to consumers. We showed a `Latch` class to give a bounded buffer with a capacity of one as an example of a monitor. We provided a `Future` class that can be used to pass results back from a concurrent subroutine.

18.9   Exercises

18.1. Modify Figure 18–7 to use the *memento* pattern to restore the data structure.

18.2. Implement your own version of `Semaphore`. You will need an integer count attribute and a `countPositive` condition attribute.

18.3. Implement your own version of `Queue`. You can start with `Latch` and use an underlying `DEQueue` object.

18.4. Change the body of the `delay()` function in Figure 18–13 to use a single function from the `time` module.

18.5. Implement a `Barrier` class. A `Barrier` object is used by a collection of *n* threads to synchronize. It is created by:

```
b=Barrier(n)
```

where n is an integer. Thereafter, each thread calls `b.gather()` and is delayed until all *n* threads have called `gather()`, whereupon all resume executing. The barrier resets itself so that the *n* threads can gather at it repeatedly.

19

Transactions

Database accesses can be a problem. Throughput requires that we handle more than one request at a time, so we need concurrency. With concurrency comes the need to protect the data from being corrupted, either from race conditions or from partial updates due to abnormal termination. Since the order of accesses to records in the database can be data-dependent, the usual way of providing mutual exclusion–locking objects in order–will not work.

We are concerned with two aspects. We want the transactions to execute correctly and we want them not to deadlock. By "transaction," we mean a self-contained collection of accesses to the database, reading and updating its contents as a response to a single request. As to "correctly," let us agree that transactions are correctly executed if they produce the same results as if they ran one at a time, in a single thread, in an arbitrary order.

Here we examine a simple transaction-based system that allows concurrent access to a database where the database is updated only at the end of a series of reads and writes, when a transaction *commits* its changes. We want the updates to the database to be the same as if the transactions executed in the order they successfully committed their changes. Transaction A's attempt to commit changes will be unsuccessful if any of the data transaction A is using has been changed by another transaction, B, after transaction A has read it and before A completes. Because A is trying to commit its changes after B, it must produce the same results as if it had started running after B completed, and hence would only see the data values B had written. If A cannot successfully commit its changes, it is forced to "roll back," or restart its transaction.

These transactions prevent deadlock by eliminating the hold-and-wait requirement. Threads lock a single lock on the database for the duration of a read or the duration of writing all their changes back at once. However, they may be susceptible to *starvation*. Although threads are not deadlocked, they may not be able to get their work done at any reasonable rate. They might spend inordinate amounts of time re-executing transactions, being forced repeatedly to roll back after unsuccessful commits.

In our system, the shared databases sit in front of Python databases as a kind of protection proxy. As with Python's databases, our shared databases can be opened and closed and records can be accessed by subscripting with keys.

We should pause to emphasize that while the code presented here may be useful for coordinating several threads accessing the same database or dictionary, it is not a production quality system. It is not adequate for mission-critical applications, since it does not protect the database against program or machine crashes.

19.1 Shared Database Operations

Figure 19–1 gives a picture of the objects involved in a shared database. There is a database object that is being shared. In front of it sits a `SharedDB` object that functions as a monitor, coordinating access to the database. Each thread accesses the shared database through a `Transaction` object. The `Transaction` object is a protection proxy for the database.

The operations on `SharedDB` objects are shown in Table 19–1, and the operations on `Transaction` objects are shown in Table 19–3. These accesses can raise the shared database exceptions shown in Table 19–2. The order of operations for a shared database is:

1. The database is opened. It can be a dictionary or a database, as shown in Section 10.3:

```
db=dbhash.open(path,flag) #or however the database is #opened
```

or

```
db={} #or some other dictionary
```

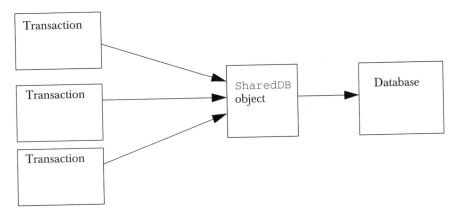

Figure 19–1
Structure of SharedDB.

Table 19–1
Operations on SharedDB.

Operation	Explanation
Public	
sdb=SharedDB(db)	Creates a SharedDB object to provide transaction-based shared access to db, a database-like object (or a dictionary).
sdb.open()	Creates a Transaction object for accessing the database protected by sdb.
sdb.close(force=0)	Closes the shared database if there are no Transaction objects currently using it. If force is provided and is true, the shared database object is closed even if there are Transactions using it. It also closes the underlying database that was passed to the SharedDB constructor.

Table 19–1
Operations on SharedDB. (Continued)

Operation	Explanation
For Use by Transaction Only	
sdb.get(key)	Reads the value of the key from the database and returns the tuple (*value*, *timestamp*).
sdb.commit(stamps, changes)	Tells SharedDB the transaction is closing. The parameter stamps is a dictionary of time stamps of the keys read from the database. If any of the keys has a fresher time stamp in SharedDB, commit() does not update the database but raises a CommitError. If stamps passes the test, the keys and values in dictionary changes are written to the database.
sdb.closeTransaction (stamps)	Called to indicate the transaction is closing and no longer has an interest in the keys in dictionary stamps.

Table 19–2
SharedDB exceptions.

Class	Explanation
SharedDBError	Base class for the SharedDB exceptions.
CommitError	The attempt to close a transaction and commit its changes failed because the transaction was discovered to be using stale information.
ClosedError	Raised on an attempt to use a closed Transaction or SharedDB object.
InUseError	Raised on an attempt to close a shared database while there are still Transactions using it.

Table 19–3

Operations on `Transaction`.

Operation	Explanation
`t[key]` `t.__getitem__(key)`	Looks up the value key in the underlying database, `db`. This will pass back any exception `db[k]` raises.

`t[key]=value`
`t.__setitem__`
`(key,value)`
	Assigns a new value to key in the underlying database. Subsequent accesses to `t[k]` will see the change, but that is only using the transaction `t`. The change will not be seen anywhere else until `t.close()` is called. Then, if the commit is successful, the changes will be written into the underlying database.

`t.abandon()`	Abandons the updates, closes the transaction.
`t.close()` `t.close(okay=1)`	Closes the transaction. If the parameter, `okay`, is omitted or is true, `close()` will try to commit any value assignments back to the database and will raise a `CommitError` if the `Transaction` read values that were subsequently changed in the database by another transaction's `close()`. If `okay` is false, `close()` will close the transaction without writing any changes back to the database and will raise a `CommitError`.

2. A `SharedDB` object, `sdb`, is created with a reference to the database opened in step 1:

```
sdb=SharedDB(db)
```

3. When a thread needs to read or update the database, it creates a transaction object by calling:

```
t=sdb.open()
```

4. The thread reads data with

$$t[key]$$

It writes data with:

$$t[key]=value$$

After writing data at a key, the thread will be able to read back the data by executing `t[key]`, but no other thread will be able to see the changes yet.

5. When a thread has successfully finished its accesses and updates, it executes `t.close()` to try to commit the changes it has made to the underlying database. After the `close()` returns normally, other threads will be able to see the changes this thread made with its assignments to keys. However, if any of the keys this thread was using have changed between the time it fetched the data and the time it closes the transaction, the `close()` raises a `CommitError` and does not change the database. Whether the `close()` returned or raised a `CommitError`, the transaction object is closed and may not be used again.

6. If the thread discovers that it cannot properly update the database, for example because an account does not have enough money in it, it can execute `t.abandon()`, which behaves similarly to a `close(0)` in that it closes the transaction without writing any changes back to the database; unlike `close(0)`, it does *not* raise a `CommitError`.

The `SharedDB` objects must be created with an underlying database that has the operations `db[key]` to fetch a value and `db[key]=value` to assign one. The database may have a `close()` method, although it is not obligatory.

`SharedDB` objects provide two methods to general users. The `open()` method creates a `Transaction` associated with the database. The `close()` method will close the `SharedDB` if there are no open transactions using it. If there are open transactions, `close()` will raise an `InUseError`. To force the closure of a shared database that still has open transactions, call `close(true)`—pass any nonzero argument to `close()`.

The transaction, `t`, itself behaves like a restricted database object. It has only the database operations `t[key]`, `t[key]=value`, `t.close()`, and `t.abandon()`. Looking up a value, `t[key]` will read the value of the key from the underlying database if this is the first access the transaction has made to it. The values are kept in a write-back cache, so subsequent accesses will use the cached value.

Assigning a new value to a key stores only the value in the cache. Subsequently, when the thread accesses the key, it will see the changes it has made; but because this is a write-back cache, other threads will not see the changes yet.

When the thread closes the transaction, the `t.close()` call first checks that no keys in the underlying database have had their values changed later than the time it first fetched the value. If any have, the thread has performed computations based on invalid, out-of-date data. In this case the `t.close()` call does not write back the cache contents, but raises a `CommitError`. If the data are valid, `t.close()` will write back the contents of the transaction's cache. In either case, the transaction object, `t`, is closed and cannot be used again.

Calling `t.close(0)`, or passing an argument false to `close()`, does not check on the validity of the data or try to write back the cache. It always closes the transaction, and it *always* raises a `CommitError`. A `Transaction` object has an additional method, `t.abandon()`, that closes the transaction without writing any changes back to the database.

19.2   Example: Dining Philosophers

As an example of threads synchronizing using a shared database, see the code for the dining philosophers problem in Figure 19–2. The forks are represented by a `SharedDB` object that contains an initially empty dictionary. We open a transaction and assign each fork its initial value, -1. Negative one indicates the fork is available. The N forks are named with strings 'fork$i$' for $0 \le i < N$. (The variable N's name is `numPhilosophers`.)

```
import threading
import SharedDB
import random

numPhilosophers=7
iterations=50
timer=threading.Condition()
forks=SharedDB.SharedDB({})
d=forks.open()
for i in range(numPhilosophers):
    d['fork%d' % i] = -1
d.close()
state=['.']*numPhilosophers

def showState():
```

Figure 19–2
`DinersSDB.py`, dining philosophers synchronized through a `SharedDB`.

```
        print "".join(state)

def delay(t):
    timer.acquire()
    timer.wait(t)
    timer.release()


class Philosopher(threading.Thread):
    def __init__(self,num):
        self.num=num
        threading.Thread.__init__(self)
    def run(self):
        leftFork='fork%d' % self.num
        rightFork='fork%d' % ((self.num+1)%numPhilosophers)
        for iternum in xrange(iterations):
            #get forks
            while 1:
                d=forks.open()
                try:
                    left=d[leftFork]
                    right=d[rightFork]
                    delay(random.random())
                    if left == right == -1:
                        d[leftFork]= \
                            d[rightFork]=self.num
                        d.close()
                        break
                    d.close()
                except SharedDB.CommitError:
                    #print '('+str(self.num)+")"
                    delay(random.random())
                    pass
            state[self.num]=str(self.num); showState()
            delay(1*random.random())
            d=forks.open()
            d[leftFork] = d[rightFork] = -1
            state[self.num]='.'; showState()
            d.close()
def start():
    for i in range(numPhilosophers):
        p=Philosopher(i)
        p.start()

if __name__=='__main__':
    start()
```

Figure 19–2

DinersSDB.py, dining philosophers synchronized through a SharedDB. (Continued)

Each simulated philosopher is a thread. The code for the philosophers is in class Philosopher that inherits from Thread and overrides the run() method. The N philosopher threads are numbered $0 \le i < N$.

Philosopher *i* needs to acquire forks *i* and *(i+1) modulus N*. The way a philosopher acquires a fork is by writing his own number into the database as the value for the fork's name.

Each philosopher thread executes the following loop `iterations` times:

1. The philosopher tries to acquire his forks. He opens a transaction for the forks `SharedDB` and reads the values associated with his two forks. If both forks have the value `-1`, they were free as of the time the philosopher got their values, so the philosopher writes his own number as the value for each and closes the transaction. If the `close()` raises a `CommitError`, a neighboring philosopher has just acquired a fork, so this philosopher delays for a random fraction of a second and tries again.

   When the philosopher looks at the forks, if they do not both have the value `-1`, he knows they are in use. The philosopher closes the transaction and loops to try again.

2. When the philosopher gets out of the loop in step 1, he has acquired the forks. He delays a random amount of time to simulate eating.

3. To give up the forks, the philosopher opens a transaction and writes `-1` as the value for each of his forks. This cannot raise a `CommitError` since the philosopher does not read the values first; hence the values written cannot depend on obsolete data, and in any case, no one else can assign a new value to either of the forks, since this philosopher stored his number in them.

Figure 19–3 shows a portion of a run of `DinersSDB.py`, this implementation of the dining philosophers problem. It should be read column-wise.

19.3 Implementation of `SharedDB`

The code for the `SharedDB` module is shown in Figure 19–4. To understand it, let us consider what facilities we need and then ask questions about how the code provides those facilities. What we need are:

1. a reference to the underlying database;
2. a representation of time;
3. memory of when keys in the database have been reassigned;
4. memory of when keys have had their values read from the database;

. . . .	0 . 2	. . . .	. . . 3 . . .	. . . . 4 . .
. . . . 4 . .	0	. . 2	. . . .	. . . .
. . . .	0 . . . 4 . .	. . . .	. . . . . 5 .	. . 2 . . . .
0	. . . . 4 . .	. . . . 4 . .	0 . . . . 5 .	0 . 2 . . . .
0 . . . 4 . .	. . 2 . 4 . .	0 . . 3 . 5 .	0 . . 3 . 5 .	0 . . . . . .
. . . . 4 . .	0 . 2 . 4 . .	0 . . 3 . . .	0 . . 3 . . .	. . . .
. . . .	. . 2 . 4 . .	. . . 3 . . .	0	0 . . . . . .
0	. . 2	. . . 3 . 5 .	0 . . . . 5 .	. . . .
0 . . . 4 . .	. . . .	. . . 3 . . .	0 . . 3 . 5 .	. . . . . 5 .
0 . 2 . 4 . .	. . . . 4 . .	0 . . 3 . . .	0 . . . . 5 .	. . . .
. . 2 . 4 . .	. . 2 . 4 . .	0 . . 3 . 5 .	. . . . . 5 .	0 . . . . . .
. . 2	. . 2 . 4 . 6	0 . . . . 5 .	0 . . . . 5 .	0 . . 3 . . .
0 . 2	. . . . 4 . 6	0 . . 3 . 5 .	0	0 . . . . . .
0 . 2 . . 5 .	. . . . 4 . .	0 . . 3 . . .	. . . .	0 . . 3 . . .
0 . . . . 5 .	. . 2 . 4 . .	0	. . . . 4 . .	
. . . . . 5 .	. . 2	0 . . . . 5 .	. . 2 . 4 . .	
. . . .	. . 2 . . . 6	. . . . . 5 .	0 . 2 . 4 . .	
. . 2	 6	. . . 3 . 5 .	0 . 2	
0 . 2	. . . . 4 . 6	0 . . 3 . 5 .	0 . 2 . 4 . .	
0 . 2 . 4 . .	 6	0 . . 3 . . .	0 . . . 4 . .	

Figure 19–3
Fragment of a run of `DinersSDB.py`.

```
"SharedDB shared database"
import threading

class SharedDBError:pass
class CommitError(SharedDBError):pass
class ClosedError(SharedDBError):pass
class InUseError(SharedDBError):pass

class SharedDB:
    def __init__(self,db):
      self.db=db
      self.time=0
      self.numOpen=0
        #num Transactions open
      self.amOpen=1
      self.stamp={}
        #key->timestamp
      self.numUsers={}
        #key->num Transactions using it
      self.lock=threading.RLock()
    def _timeStamp(self):
      if not self.amOpen: raise ClosedError
      self.time+=1
```

Figure 19–4
`SharedDB` module.

```
      return self.time
def get(self,key):
    self.lock.acquire()
    try:
        if not self.amOpen: raise ClosedError
        v=self.db[key]  #may raise exception
        if not self.stamp.has_key(key):
                ts=self.stamp[key]=self._timeStamp()
        else: ts=self.stamp[key]
        if self.numUsers.has_key(key):
                self.numUsers[key]+=1
        else: self.numUsers[key]=1
        return v,ts
    finally:
        self.lock.release()
def closeTransaction(self,stamps):
    self.lock.acquire()
    try:
        if not self.amOpen: raise ClosedError
        for k in stamps.keys():
                self.numUsers[k] -= 1   #moved from above
                if self.numUsers[k]==0:
                        del self.numUsers[k]
                        del self.stamp[k]
        self.numOpen-=1
    finally:
        self.lock.release()

def commit(self,stamps,changes):
    self.lock.acquire()
    try:
        if not self.amOpen: raise ClosedError
        error=0
        for k in stamps.keys():
                if stamps[k]<self.stamp[k]:
                        error=1
                        break
        if not error:
            for k in changes.keys():
                    self.db[k]=changes[k]
                    if self.stamp.has_key(k):
                            self.stamp[k]=self._timeStamp()
        self.closeTransaction(stamps)
        if error: raise CommitError
    finally:
        self.lock.release()
def open(self):
    self.lock.acquire()
    try:
        if not self.amOpen: raise ClosedError
        self.numOpen+=1
        return Transaction(self)
    finally:
```

Figure 19–4
SharedDB module. (Continued)

```
        self.lock.release()
    def close(self,force=0):
        self.lock.acquire()
        try:
            if not self.amOpen: raise ClosedError
            if self.numOpen>0 and not force: raise InUseError
            self.amOpen=0
            try: self.db.close()
            except: pass
        finally:
            self.lock.release()
class Transaction:
    def __init__(self,shared):
        self.shared=shared
        self.values={}
        self.changed={}
        self.stamps={}
        self.amOpen=1
    def close(self,okay=1):
        if not self.amOpen: raise ClosedError
        self.amOpen=0
        if okay:
            self.shared.commit(self.stamps,self.changed)
        else:
            self.shared.closeTransaction(self.stamps)
            raise CommitError
    def __getitem__(self,key):
        if not self.amOpen: raise ClosedError
        if not self.values.has_key(key):
            self.values[key],self.stamps[key]= \
                self.shared.get(key)
        return self.values[key]
    def __setitem__(self,key,val):
        if not self.amOpen: raise ClosedError
        self.values[key]=self.changed[key]=val
    def abandon(self):
        self.shared.closeTransaction(self.stamps)
```

Figure 19–4
SharedDB module. (Continued)

5. memory of which keys and values a transaction has written; and

6. an indication whether the transaction or database is open or closed.

Now let us consider how the SharedDB and Transaction classes are implemented.

Q. How do we keep track of the underlying database?

A. SharedDB keeps a reference to it in attribute db. Transaction keeps a reference to its SharedDB object in attribute shared, but does not access the database itself.

Q.   How do we represent time?

A.   We use time stamps. In `SharedDB`, the attribute `time` keeps an integer count. The method `_timeStamp()` increments it and returns the new value. We simulate the flow of time, numbering the sequence of significant events, which are:
- when a key is first looked up in the database, and
- when a key has its value changed.

Q.   How do we keep track of when a key has been read from the database?

A.   We need to do that both in `SharedDB` and in `Transaction`. When we call `Transaction`'s `__getitem__()` method, typically by `t[key]`, and it has not read or written the key before, it calls `SharedDB`'s `get()` method, which returns a value and a time stamp. `Transaction` keeps the values in its dictionary attribute `values` and keeps the time stamps for keys in dictionary attribute `stamps`. Otherwise, if `__getitem__()` finds the key in `values`, it uses that value and leaves the time stamp alone. Attribute `stamps` is set only the first time a value is accessed, and only if it is read from the database.

SharedDB itself keeps time stamps associated with keys in dictionary attribute `stamp`. It assigns a time stamp to a key when 1) the key is read from the database, and 2) `stamp` does not have an entry for it. If it is already in dictionary `stamp`, its time stamp is not modified. `SharedDB` also assigns a new time stamp to `stamp[key]` when the `key` has been assigned a value by a transaction committing its changes.

Q.   How does a transaction keep track of the keys that have been changed?

A.   `Transaction` has a dictionary attribute `changed`. When its `__setattr__()` method is called to give a new value to a key, it assigns the value to the key in both the dictionaries `values` and `changes`. Subsequent accesses to the key will find it in `values`. No time stamp is kept for any key that has only been assigned a value but has not been read from the database.

Q.   How are these dictionaries used to commit changes to the database or to raise a `CommitError`?

A.   A call to `close()` in `Transaction` in turn calls `self.shared.commit(self.stamps,self.changed)`. The `commit(stamps,changes)` method in `SharedDB` checks validity by comparing `stamps[k]` to `self.stamp[k]` for each key, k, in `stamps`. If `self.stamp[k]>stamps[k]`, a new value has been assigned to key k after the transaction fetched the value. Since the transaction is not using the most up-to-date value, `commit()` raises a `CommitError`.

If the transaction has used the freshest value for each key, `commit()` writes the values in changes back to the database and allocates a new time stamp for each one that has a time stamp in the `stamp` dictionary.

Q.   Why not assign a time stamp to a key being assigned a value, even if it was not already in the `stamp` dictionary?

A.   The `stamp` dictionary has time stamps for those keys that were read from the database that we still need to keep track of. If the key is not in the `stamp` dictionary, no active transaction has read the value, so we do not need to know the value has changed when a transaction later tries to commit.

Q.   How do we know which keys we still need to keep track of in `SharedDB`'s stamp dictionary?

A.   We keep track of how many transactions have read a key from the database in `SharedDB`'s dictionary attribute `numUsers`. The first time a key, k, is read from the database, `numUsers[k]` is set to one. Subsequent times, `numUsers[k]` is incremented. When a transaction closes, it passes its `stamps` dictionary to `SharedDB`. The only keys in the stamps dictionary are those that were read from the database. They will have been counted in the `numUsers` dictionary. `SharedDB`'s `closeTransaction()` method goes through the keys in the `stamps` dictionary, decrementing the counts of all the keys in `numUsers`. If the count goes to zero, it removes the key from both the `numUsers` and the `stamp` dictionaries. If the key is read again later, a new time stamp will be assigned.

Transaction's `__getitem__()` method must help `SharedDB` keep track of the number of transactions interested in keys by looking up keys in its own cache, `values`, and calling `get()` only if the key is not present. It must call `get()` at most once for any key.

19.4   Wrap-Up

We have examined a simple transaction-based system for sharing a database composed of two classes. The `SharedDB` class is a monitor, allowing a number of threads to share the database. The `Transaction` class provides a protection proxy. A transaction can use the shared database without hold-and-wait, and hence without deadlock, because it locks the entire database each time it reads a record or commits its changes. It will receive a `CommitError` exception on closing if it used stale information. The shared database is updated as if 1) the transactions that terminated normally executed one at a time, and 2) the transactions that received `CommitError` did not execute at all.

We included an example of using a `SharedDB` to implement a Dining Philosophers program without deadlock. The `SharedDB` coordinated access to the simulated forks.

19.5   Exercises

19.1. `SharedDB` does not try to force database changes to disk (in the event it is attached to a real database object). Change it to try to do so, but to ignore the exceptions where there is no `sync()` method available or working for the underlying `db` object.

19.2. In Exercise 7.6, you were asked to write a program to recursively search directories, finding files with the same name and writing out lists of their occurrences. Convert that program to use more than one thread. Have the threads share a database in which they record the files they find and synchronize via a `SharedDB` object.

19.3. Critique `SharedDB`.

19.4. Would keeping time stamps in the database work better? Redesign `SharedDB` so that the key maps into a (`timestamp`, `value`) pair in the underlying database. Would this work? Would this give greater concurrency? Compare the book's design to yours.

20

Run Queues

Creating threads can be expensive. It would save processing time to reuse thread objects. Once they have finished running one function, it would be nice to be able to reassign them to another, rather than having to create a new thread each time.

Here we present a class, RunQueue[*], that recycles threads. You enqueue a "runnable" object in a run queue, that is, an object which has a run() method. The run queue will allocate a thread to call the object's run() method. When one object's run() method returns, the thread queues up again to run another object. New threads are created only when an object is enqueued and there are no waiting threads. The RunQueue is an implementation of what may also be known as a "thread pool," whereby the idea is that threads are allocated from a pool as needed; or as a "thread farm," whereby the idea is that jobs are "farmed" out to threads.

20.1 **Simple** RunQueue

Table 20–1 lists the operations on RunQueues. Python's threading package provides two ways to create threads: Provide a function and arguments when creating a Thread object, or inherit from Thread and override its run() method. RunQueue requires yet a third way. You create a RunQueue object and put objects with run() methods in it, as shown in Figure 20–1.

---

[*] The RunQueue class is based on the version in Christopher and Thiruvathukal, *High-Performance Java Platform Computing* (Prentice Hall PTR, 2000).

```
class X:
    def __init__(self,...):...
    def run(self):
        ...#code for the thread to execute
rq=RunQueue()
t=X(...)
rq.run(t)
```

Figure 20–1
Runnable objects: declaring and running them.

There are three equivalent names for the method to put runnables into the queue: `enq()`, `put()`, and `run()`. The name `put()`, of course, is consistent with `DEQueue` and `prioque`. The name `run()` corresponds to how we usually think of the run queue functioning; we are asking it to run an object.

The default behavior of a run queue is as follows:

- Runnable objects, or objects with `run()` methods, are placed in the `run` queue.
- A thread removes the object from the queue and calls its `run()` method.
- When one runnable's `run()` method terminates, the thread loops back to `dequeue` and runs another runnable.
- When there are no runnables in the queue, the threads wait for more runnables to be enqueued.
- When a runnable is enqueued and there are no threads waiting, another thread is created.

Because threads are reused, not as many threads usually need to be created over the course of program execution. The number of threads is only the maximum required at one time, not the count of all required.

When you no longer need the run queue, you can call its `terminate()` method to terminate all the threads that are waiting to, or subsequently try to, `dequeue` another runnable. Threads executing runnables will not be terminated until their `run()` methods return. If you need a run queue again later, you must create another one.

There are a number of ways to customize run queues. The `RunQueue` initializer takes several optional keyword parameters. Two of them are of some interest to general users of run queues, and two others are of interest only to implementers of specialized run queues. We discuss the specialized methods along with `TransactionQueue` in Section 20.4.

Table 20–1
RunQueue operations.

Operation	Explanation

`rq=RunQueue()`
 	
`rq=RunQueue(`
`  maxthreads=N,`
`  queue=Q,`
`  runstrategy=RS,`
`  threadfunction=TF)`
	Creates a run queue. The optional keyword parameters specify the following:
	    `maxthreads`—The maximum number of threads to create. By default, the number is unbounded.
	    `threadfunction`—The function to remove and execute runnables, it is called by `threadfunction(rq,RS)` where `rq` is the run queue and `RS` is the run strategy. It defaults to a loop, removing runnables from the queue and calling `runstrategy` to execute them.
	    `runstrategy`—A function that will run a runnable. By default, it calls the runnable's `run()` method and then returns. Transaction queues use the `transactionRunStrategy` that resubmits a runnable if its execution terminated with a `CommitError`. A run strategy takes two parameters: `runstrategy(runnable,rq)`, where `runnable` is the object to run, and `rq` is the run queue (allowing the runnable to be resubmitted).
	    `queue`—The underlying queue object to use. It defaults to `DEQueue`. Any object, `Q`, with `Q.put(arg,...)` and `Q.get()` methods may work.

`rq.enq(*runnable)`
`rq.put(*runnable)`
`rq.run(*runnable)`
	All these functions are synonyms. The default queue requires they be called with a runnable object, but substitution of a different queue may require more parameters to be passed; e.g., a `prioque` object requires `rq.run(priority,runnable)`.

`rq.terminate()`	Tells the run queue to terminate execution. All threads terminate when they try to dequeue and run a new runnable.

Normally, a run queue will create a new thread whenever a runnable is enqueued and there are no threads waiting. You can limit the number of threads created by passing a `maxthreads` parameter. `RunQueue(maxthreads=N)` will create a run queue that will create no more than integer *N* threads. If you are creating a large number of runnables, this parameter can prevent filling up memory with a similarly large number of threads.

There is a danger in specifying `maxthreads`. If runnables block, waiting for other runnables later in the queue to produce results, you can get deadlock. The blocked runnables will not give up their threads until later runnables finish, and the later runnables will not run because there are no threads for them. However, if your runnables run to completion without blocking except for mutual exclusion, you can save some memory and processing time by limiting the number of threads that can be created.

You can provide your own queue for the `RunQueue` object to use. Normally, the `RunQueue` creates a `DEQueue` to use. If you want priority scheduling, you could pass it a `prioque`:

```
RunQueue(queue=prioque.prioque())
```

The only requirements for a different queue are:

1. It must have a `get()` method to return the next item in the queue.
2. It must have a `put()` method to put items into the queue. The put method may take any number of positional parameters: `RunQueue`'s `enq()`/`put()`/`run()` method passes all its parameters on to the underlying queue unaltered.
3. It must have unbounded capacity.
4. It must have a `__len__()` method giving the number of runnables in the queue.

20.2   Implementing RunQueue

The code for `RunQueue` is shown in Figure 20–2. First consider the `RunQueue` class. Its `__init__(self,**kwargs)` method requires keyword arguments. We judged that the parameters would be used so infrequently that their positions would not be reliably remembered.

```
from threading import *
import DEQueue,sys

class TerminateException(Exception): pass

import traceback

def simpleRunStrategy(runnable,rq):
    runnable.run()

def Xeq(runQueue,runStrategy):
    while 1:
      try:
        r=runQueue.deq()
        runStrategy(r,runQueue)
      except TerminateException:
        runQueue.numThreads-=1
        return
      except:
        traceback.print_exc()

class RunQueue:
    def __init__(self,**kwargs):
      self.runStrategy=kwargs.get('runstrategy', \
        simpleRunStrategy)
      self.maxThreads=kwargs.get('maxthreads', \
        sys.maxint)
      self.numThreads=0
      self.numThreadsWaiting=0
      self.rq=kwargs.get('queue')
      if self.rq is None: self.rq=DEQueue.DEQueue()
      self.lock=RLock()
      self.awaitWork=Condition(self.lock)
      self.stop=0
      self.makeDaemon=1
      self.threadfunction=kwargs.get( \
        'threadfunction',Xeq)
    def enq(self,*r):
      self.lock.acquire()
      self.rq.put(*r)
      if self.numThreadsWaiting>0:
        self.numThreadsWaiting-=1
        self.awaitWork.notify()
      elif self.numThreads<self.maxThreads:
        t=Thread(target=self.threadfunction, \
          args=(self,self.runStrategy))
        t.setDaemon(self.makeDaemon)
        self.numThreads+=1
        t.start()
      self.lock.release()
    put=run=enq
    def deq(self):
```

Figure 20–2
RunQueue.

```
        self.lock.acquire()
        while len(self.rq)==0:
          if self.stop:
            self.numThreads-=1
            self.lock.release()
            raise TerminateException
          self.numThreadsWaiting+=1
          self.awaitWork.wait()
        if self.stop:
          self.numThreads-=1
          self.lock.release()
          raise TerminateException
        r=self.rq.get()
        self.lock.release()
        return r
      get=deq
      def terminate(self):
        self.lock.acquire()
        self.stop=1
        self.awaitWork.notifyAll()
        self.numThreadsWaiting=0
        self.lock.release()
```

Figure 20–2
RunQueue. (Continued)

To some extent, a run queue fits the producer-consumer pattern. Runnables are placed in the queue by users calling `enq()` by any of its names. Threads call `get()` or `deq()` to take out the runnables and run them. There are some complications caused by the need sometimes to create threads.

First, how do we know whether to create a thread when a runnable object is enqueued? We keep an attribute, `numThreadsWaiting`, which has a count of the number of threads that are blocked on condition `awaitWork`, waiting for runnables. If the count is greater than zero, all we have to do is call `awaitWork.notify()` to wake one of them up and decrement the `numThreadsWaiting` count. It is important to decrement the count here, rather than having the thread decrement it itself when it falls out of its `awaitWork.wait()` call. As soon as we have notified the thread to wake up, there is one fewer thread available. We need to know this immediately. Suppose there is one thread waiting and two calls are made to `enq()`. The first call will wake up the thread. If we didn't decrement `numThreadsWaiting`, the second call would think there is another thread available and would call `notify()`; but the call will be ignored, since there are no threads waiting. The second `enq()` call should have created a new thread.

If there are no threads waiting when we call `enq()`, we should create one, but we are only permitted to create a thread if we haven't reached the limit `maxThreads`. We keep a count of the number of threads we have created in `numThreads` and compare it to `maxThreads`. As long as it is less, we can create another thread. We create the thread by constructing an instance of a `Thread` object. We make its target the function that we have in our `threadfunction` attribute. By default, that will be the `Xeq` function. We pass it a reference to our run queue and a `runstrategy` function. We will call these threads Xeq threads, based on their default function.

We make the Xeq thread a daemon thread. The only difference between a daemon thread and a normal thread is that the program will not terminate as long as there are any normal threads in existence, but it will terminate if the only threads are daemons. The differences between making the Xeq threads daemons and making them normal threads include the following:

- By making the Xeq threads daemons, we do not have to call the run queue's `terminate()` method before ending the program. If they were normal threads, just by sitting at the run queue, they would keep the program from terminating.
- On the other hand, since they are daemons, we cannot have our program just drop some items into the run queue and let them do all the work. A normal thread must wait for them to finish processing. If we just drop runnables into the run queue and terminate, the program will terminate before the computation is done.

The Xeq function simply loops, pulling runnables off the run queue and calling the `runstrategy` to execute them. The default `runstrategy` is the `simpleRunStrategy` function, which as you can see merely calls the runnable's run method and returns. We will see why we use this strategy rather than just calling `run()` directly when we examine the `TransactionQueue` later. The Xeq function runs the runnable in a try-except statement. If the call `r=runQueue.deq()` raises a `TerminateException`, the thread has been asked to terminate, so it returns, ending the thread. Other exceptions cause it to print out a traceback.

Runnables are removed from the run queue by the threads calling `deq()` or `get()`. A thread loops while the underlying queue is empty, waiting for notification that there is something to run. It has to wait in a loop, since even if it is awakened by a `notify()`, the queue may be empty by the time it gets control; another thread can call `deq()` later but acquire the lock sooner. An Xeq thread increments the count `numThreadsWaiting` before executing `self.awaitWork.wait()`, so a call to `enq()` will know there is a waiting thread to notify.

In two places the `deq()` method checks the flag attribute `stop`. If set, the `RunQueue` has been requested to terminate, so the thread exits by raising a `TerminateException`. The `stop` attribute is set by the `terminate()` method. To make sure the waiting threads terminate, the `terminate()` method calls `notifyAll()` to wake them all up so they can see the `stop` flag.

20.3   Detecting Termination of an Object on the RunQueue

Since the threads created by a run queue are daemon threads, they will not keep a program executing. You will need to have some normal thread wait for the completion of all the processing you start in a run queue. The obvious way is to explicitly wait for each one of the runnables to terminate, just as you could use `join()` to wait for threads to terminate. Unfortunately, `join()` does not work with runnables, only with threads. We need a facility like `join()`—a way for a thread to wait for a runnable to terminate. The runnable has to do something to inform others that it is done. Two ways are `Future` and `Event`.

20.3.1 Future

The `Future` class, discussed in Chapter 18, allows a thread to wait for another thread to store a value in the `Future`. To report completion, you could use something like this:

```
class runnableX:
    def __init__(self,...):
        self.done=Future()
        ...
    def run(self):
        ...
        self.done.set(None)
rq=RunQueue()
r=runnableX(...)
rq.put(r)
...
r.done.get()
```

We have a runnable class, runnableX, whose instances have an attribute, done, that contains a Future. Just before terminating, the runnable will set the Future to an arbitrary value. When we create an instance of runnableX and put it in a run queue, we keep a reference to it. Before we terminate, we wait for the instance's done Future to have a value by calling its get() method.

20.3.2   Event

The threading module provides the Event class, which can also be used for termination detection. An Event object is a toggle, initially in a *cleared* state. The set() method changes the toggle to *set*. The method wait() will wait until the event is set. If the event is already set when wait() is called, its call will return immediately. The reason for the name Event is that the setting of the toggle corresponds to an event occurring. The wait() method allows us to wait until the event has occurred. The code to use it is approximately the same as for a Future:

```
class runnableY:
    def __init__(self,...):
      self.done=Event()
      ...
    def run(self):
      ...
      self.done.set()
rq=RunQueue()
r=runnableY(...)
rq.put(r)
...
r.done.wait()
```

As with Conditions, there is a timeout option on waits that allows code to be more robust: A failure in one part of the system will not necessarily block another part forever. In addition, an isSet() method will report if the event has occurred yet.

Another method is difficult to use safely. The clear() method will set the toggle to its cleared state. Its existence might tempt you to try to use it in a loop, with one thread setting it each iteration and another waiting for its next occurrence. Unfortunately, the thread setting the event could run ahead of the thread waiting for it, or vice versa; and since the event has no memory, an occurrence could be lost, no matter which thread has the responsibility for clearing the event. For example, thread A sets an event x and thread B waits for it. If A sets the event and then clears it, and if B was not already waiting on the event, B will block rather than continue to execute when it does wait. Or suppose A sets the event x, and B waits on it and then clears it. A could set x, loop, and set x again before B clears x. The second set would be lost. As a rule, never clear an Event.

Table 20–2
Event operations.

Operation	Explanation
e=Event()	Creates an event object, initially in a *cleared* state.
e.set()	Puts the event into a *set* state. If it was not already in the set state, there may be threads waiting, so it awakens them.
e.wait() e.wait(timeout)	Waits for the event to be in the *set* state, If the event is already in the set state, it simply returns. If a (floating-point) timeout is given, it returns from the wait after that many seconds and fractions of seconds have occurred, even if the event has not been set.
e.isSet()	Returns true if the event is in the *set* state and false if it is in the *cleared* state.
e.clear()	Puts the event into the *cleared* state. It is difficult to use this correctly.

20.4   TransactionQueue

In this section, we show a variety of RunQueue, a transaction queue, that exemplifies several object-oriented design patterns. The transaction queue is not a separate class. It is a RunQueue parameterized with a different run strategy, transactionRunStrategy, an example of the *Strategy* pattern. The name TransactionQueue is the name of the module and the factory function that creates these queues. The runnables placed in the transaction queue are examples of the *Command* pattern. The runnables are expected to update a database. The transactionRunStrategy tries to run a command; but if the command raises a CommitError, it did not terminate successfully, because the data it was using was updated by another thread. On CommitError, the transactionRunStrategy resubmits the command to the run queue to be tried again later. To be able to restart the command, it must be put back in the state it was in at the beginning. This is accomplished by use of the *memento* pattern: A memento (a copy of the state) of the command is saved before trying to execute the command. If the command fails with a CommitError, the memento is used to reinitialize it before it is resubmitted to the transaction queue. The methods that a transaction strategy must provide are shown in Table 20–3.

Table 20–3
Methods a transaction runnable must provide.

Method	Explanation
t.run()	Executes the transaction, t. It returns normally on success. If it raises a CommitError, the transaction must be reinitialized and re-executed.
m=t.getMemento()	Creates a memento object that can be used by t to reinitialize its state later, if it needs to be run again due to a CommitError. The memento can be None if t does not modify its state during calls to the run() method.
t.setMemento(m)	Restores t to the state it was in when m=t.getMemento() was called.

The code for the module TransactionQueue is shown in Figure 20–3. The factory function TransactionQueue creates a RunQueue with its runstrategy specified as transactionRunStrategy. Figure 20–4 shows what is involved in running a transaction. A RunQueue has created a number of Xeq threads, that is to say, threads that are running the Xeq function (see Figure 20–2). The Xeq functions have been created with a reference to the queue and a reference to the transactionRunStrategy function. In Figure 20–4, Xeq thread A has taken the runnable command X off the RunQueue and passed it to the transactionRunStrategy function. The transactionRunStrategy function was

```
import RunQueue
import threading
import SharedDB
import sys

def transactionRunStrategy(r,rq):
    c=r.getMemento()
    try:
      r.run()
      return
    except SharedDB.CommitError:
      r.setMemento(c)
      rq.enq(r)
      return
    except:
      cl,ex,tb=sys.exc_info()
      print >>sys.stderr, cl,ex
      import traceback
      traceback.print_tb(tb)
      return

def TransactionQueue():
    return RunQueue.RunQueue(
      runstrategy=transactionRunStrategy)
```

Figure 20–3
TransactionQueue.

passed a reference to the run queue and a reference to the command to run. It creates a memento of object x.

The Xeq function's code, shown in Figure 20–2, is executed by a thread created by the RunQueue when a new runnable object is enqueued and there is no thread waiting to run it. The Xeq function is given two parameters: a reference to the run queue and a strategy function encapsulating the algorithm to run an object. The Xeq thread uses its reference to the run queue to dequeue objects to run and uses its runStrategy function to actually run them.

A RunQueue normally provides a function, simpleRunStrategy, that simply calls the run() method of the command object. When created by TransactionQueue, the RunQueue gives the Xeq threads the transactionRunStrategy function.

A run strategy function is called with a reference to the command object it is to execute and with a reference to the run queue the object was taken from. The transactionRunStrategy performs the following operations on runnable object r:

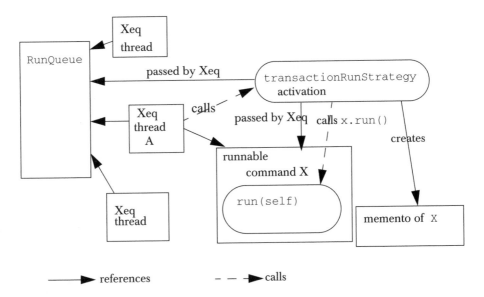

Figure 20–4
Running a transaction.

- It creates a memento of the command object by calling `c=r.getMemento()`. What `getMemento()` is supposed to return is enough data in object `c` so that later on, `r.setMemento(c)` can restore `r` to its state at the time `c` was created.
- It calls `r.run()` to execute the command the object represents.
- If `r` returns normally, `transactionRunStrategy` returns normally.
- If `r` raises a `CommitError`, it could not complete its execution due to a race condition with another command. The `transactionRunStrategy` resets `r`'s state by calling `r.setMemento(c)` and puts it back on the run queue with `rq.enq(r)`, to be tried again later.
- If `r` raises any other exception, `transactionRunStrategy` writes out the exception and a traceback and returns.

A strategy pattern involves an object delegating part of its behavior to another object. It allows encoding a family of algorithms with one general algorithm and several specific parts. In this case, the general algorithm for removing and running commands from a run queue is in function Xeq. The additional functions, `simpleRunStrategy` and `transactionRunStrategy`, adapt the behavior.

A command pattern involves putting the code to perform a command in an object with the data it needs when the code is executed. The command object allows you to delay executing the operation and allows some code other than the code that created the command object to execute it. There can be several reasons for creating a command object rather than executing the operation immediately. There are two motivations for its use here:

1. We want the command to be executed concurrently, so we hand it to a thread to execute.
2. We want to be able to restart the command if it fails, so we want to be able to create and set a memento.

A memento pattern involves saving data from the object so that it can be restored later to the current state. The memento pattern allows code in the object itself to choose the representation of its state and how to save and restore it. This preserves encapsulation, since code outside the object does not need to know anything about the object's implementation.

20.5   Example of `TransactionQueue`: Dining Philosophers

Figure 20–5 shows an implementation of the dining philosophers problem using a transaction queue. As in Figure 19–2, the philosopher threads coordinate through a shared database, `forks`. Variable `tq` is a transaction queue that is used to run the philosopher threads and the transactions they use to pick up and release forks. The class `Philosopher` contains the main loop for the philosophers in its `run()` method. To pick up the forks, a philosopher thread creates a `startEating` object, deposits it in the transaction queue, and waits for it to set its `done` Event. Similarly, to put down the forks, the philosopher creates a `stopEating` command, drops it in the transaction queue, and waits for it to set its `done` Event. The `startEating` and `stopEating` transactions will not signal that they are done until they have successfully picked up or put down the forks. The `Philosopher` class has `getMemento()` and `setMemento()` methods simply because it is placed in a transaction queue. Method `getMemento()` is called before the `run()` method is executed. Method `setMemento()` is never called, because the `Philosopher`'s `run()` method never terminates with a `CommitError`.

```
import threading
import SharedDB
import random
import TransactionQueue
import Future

numPhilosophers=7
iterations=50
timer=threading.Condition()
forks=SharedDB.SharedDB({})
d=forks.open()
for i in range(numPhilosophers):
    d['fork%d' % i] = -1
d.close()
state=['.']*numPhilosophers

tq=TransactionQueue.TransactionQueue()

def showState():
    print "".join(state)

def delay(t):
    timer.acquire()
    timer.wait(t)
    timer.release()

class startEating:
    def __init__(self,num,leftFork,rightFork):
      self.num=num
      self.done=threading.Event()
      self.leftFork=leftFork
      self.rightFork=rightFork
    def getMemento(self): return None
    def setMemento(self,x): pass
    def run(self):
      leftFork=self.leftFork
      rightFork=self.rightFork
      d=forks.open()
      left=d[leftFork]
      right=d[rightFork]
      if left != -1 or right != -1:
        d.close(0) #raises CommitError
      d[leftFork]=d[rightFork]=self.num
      delay(random.random())
      d.close()

      state[self.num]=str(self.num); showState()
      self.done.set()

class stopEating:
    def __init__(self,num,leftFork,rightFork):
      self.num=num
```

Figure 20–5

TransactionQueue implementation of dining philosophers.

```
            self.done=threading.Event()
            self.leftFork=leftFork
            self.rightFork=rightFork
        def getMemento(self): return None
        def setMemento(self,x): pass
        def run(self):
          leftFork=self.leftFork
          rightFork=self.rightFork
          d=forks.open()
          d[leftFork] = d[rightFork] = -1
          delay(random.random())
          d.close()
          state[self.num]='.'; showState()
          self.done.set()

    class Philosopher:
        def __init__(self,num):
          self.num=num
          self.leftFork='fork%d' % self.num
          self.rightFork='fork%d' %
            ((self.num+1)%numPhilosophers)
          self.iterations=iterations
          self.done=Future.Future()
        def getMemento(self): return None
        def setMemento(self,x): pass
        def run(self):
          try:
                for iternum in xrange(iterations):
                  num=self.num
                  leftFork=self.leftFork
                  rightFork=self.rightFork
                  cmd=startEating(num,leftFork,rightFork)
                  tq.run(cmd)
                  cmd.done.wait()

                  delay(1*random.random())

                  cmd=stopEating(num,leftFork,rightFork)
                  tq.run(cmd)
                  cmd.done.wait()

                  delay(2*random.random())

          finally:
            self.done.set(None)

    diners=[]
    def start():
        for i in range(numPhilosophers):
          p=Philosopher(i)
          diners.append(p)
          tq.run(p)
```

Figure 20–5

TransactionQueue implementation of dining philosophers. (Continued)

```
if __name__=='__main__':
    start()
    for p in diners:
        p.done.get()
```

Figure 20–5
`TransactionQueue` implementation of dining philosophers. (Continued)

The `startEating` and `stopEating` classes are similar, so we will only look at the `startEating` class. Methods `getMemento()` and `setMemento()` do nothing, because the `startEating` class does not change its state during its operation. The `run()` method opens a transaction, d, in the `forks` database and reads the values for the left and right forks. If they are not both -1, then at least one of them is in use, so it calls `d.close(0)`, which closes the transaction without writing any changes back (indeed, there have been none) and raises a `CommitError` exception. If both forks have -1 as their values, they were available as of the time their values were read. The transaction assigns both of them its philosopher's number and closes d. If the forks have not been acquired by another philosopher between the time this transaction read the forks' values and closed d, writing the new values back, the forks get the number of this philosopher and `d.close()` returns normally. However, if a fork has had a new value assigned in the meantime, `d.close()` does not write the new values into the database, but raises a `CommitError`. Therefore, the `d.close()` is a bit deceptive. It looks like it returns and control goes on executing in the `run()` method, but sometimes it and the `run()` method exit with a `CommitError` exception that takes control back to the `transactionRunStrategy` function of the `TransactionQueue` module. The method `transactionRunStrategy` calls `startEating`'s `setMemento()` to restore its state and then resubmits it to the transaction queue to try again later.

20.6 Wrap-Up

We have looked at a `RunQueue` class that allows code to be run in threads without having to create a new thread for each. Runnable objects—objects with `run()` methods—are dropped into run queues. Threads wait for runnables to be enqueued, remove them, and call their `run()` methods. When the `run()` methods return, the threads queue up again to wait for another runnable to execute. These threads are created as needed when runnables are enqueued, so the total number of threads will not be greater than the maximum number of runnables enqueued or executing at one time.

We looked at the implementation of a `RunQueue`. Run queues are monitors. It is a bit tricky to keep a count of the number of threads waiting for runnable objects. The number is needed to decide whether to create another thread or to wake up a waiting thread.

The threads in `RunQueues` are made daemon threads so that the program will terminate even if there are threads waiting at a run queue. Unfortunately, this means that even if the threads are executing runnables, they will not be able to keep the program running. You need to have a normal thread in existence until all the runnables are done with their work.

Because runnables are not themselves threads, you cannot wait for them to complete with a `join()` method call. The threads have to signal their completion, e.g., by assigning values to `Futures` or setting `Events`.

We examined a variant of the `RunQueue`, the kind of run queue returned by function `TransactionQueue`, that runs transactions, reinitializing them and resubmitting them to the transaction queue if they raise a `CommitError`.

A number of object-oriented design patterns are used in this code. The runnable objects placed in run queues can be considered examples of the *command* pattern. The runnables placed in transaction queues participate in the *memento* pattern: They implement the method `getMemento()` to save a copy of their state and `setMemento()` to restore it. The implementation of `RunQueue` uses the *strategy* pattern to specify how to run an object. The only difference between a transaction queue and a simple run queue is the method that handles running objects.

20.7   Exercises

20.1. Write an `isTerminated()` method for `RunQueue`. It is to return 1 if the `RunQueue`'s `terminate()` method has been called, and 0 otherwise.

20.2. Design and implement a `PriorityRunQueue` that schedules higher-priority runnables before lower-priority ones. Choose either `prioque` or `prioqueunique` to use in the implementation, if possible.

20.3. Add methods to `RunQueue` to allow the processing to be suspended:

- `suspend(block=1)` will cause processing to be suspended: No Xeq threads will be allowed to dequeue runnables until the processing has been resumed. If `block` is true, this function will not return until all Xeq threads are waiting in the `RunQueue`, or until no Xeq threads are still executing runnables. Multiple calls to `suspend` are permissible.
- `resume()` will allow the Xeq threads to resume dequeueing and executing runnables.

20.4. Critique `RunQueue`.

21

Regular Expressions

Regular expressions are patterns that match strings. They can be used for searches, matching substrings, splitting, and substitution. Although they can be complex, it is usually easier to use them than to write code to do the pattern matching.

Python handles regular expressions in its `re` module. In this chapter we examine some of the facilities provided by the `re` module. Tables provide a more complete listing of the facilities available.

Finally, we provide an example of using regular expressions to write a scanner, a class that returns the next token (significant substring) from a file on each call to its `scan()` method. We use the scanner in Chapter 22, where we implement an interpreter for a simple expression language.

21.1 Overall Behavior of `re` Module

A regular expression is written as a string. To use it for pattern matching, you compile it into an efficient representation called a pattern object. You can do this directly, using `re.compile()`, or you can do it implicitly, using one of the other `re` functions that both compiles the pattern string and uses it.

Once you have compiled a regular expression, you can use it to try to match its pattern at a particular place in a string using its `match()` method; or you can search for the first occurrence of a matching substring using `search()`. There are other, more specialized methods for the pattern objects, such as splitting a string, getting a list of

447

non-overlapping occurrences of a pattern, or performing substitutions on matching substrings.

In regular expressions, most characters match themselves. The pattern 'xyz' will match the string 'xyz'. Other characters have other meanings. For example, '[xyz]' will match precisely one of the characters 'x', 'y', or 'z'. The brackets group sets of characters. Similarly, '+', '*', and '?' specify the number of occurrences of the preceding pattern element; 'x+y*z?' will match one or more 'x's followed by zero or more 'y's, followed optionally by a 'z'.

If a match or a search is successful, it returns a match object. If it is unsuccessful, it returns None. The match object has attributes and methods to allow you to find the beginning and ending positions of the substring that matched and the beginning and ending positions and contents of substrings that match parts of the regular expression.

21.2   re **Syntax**

In regular expression strings, most characters, and all letters and digits, match themselves. The characters and character sequences with special meanings are listed in various tables. Table 21–1 lists the most common special characters and syntactic constructs. Table 21–3 lists sequences that refer to classes of characters or kinds of positions in the string. For example, \s will match any white space character, but \b matches only the empty string at the beginning or end of a word. Table 21–4 gives some extra syntax for a variety of uses, such as giving names to substrings or looking ahead.

21.2.1   Basic re Syntax

We demonstrate regular expressions using a little program that asks for expressions and then for each input string, tells all the places it matches, each followed by a tuple of the substrings that match parenthesized subexpressions in it. We will see the code later, in Figure 21–1.

Literals

A character that does not have special significance is an expression element. It matches itself. An expression element is an expression, but we need to distinguish it from a more general expression. Certain operators apply to the preceding expression element.

Table 21–1
Regular expression elements.

Element	Matches in Normal Mode
c	Itself, where c is an ordinary character, i.e., none of the special characters.
.	Any character other than newline. (Mode flag S allows it to match newline as well.)
\c	c unless c is one of: A, b, B, d, D, s, S, w, W, Z, or a digit. For these characters, see Table 21–3.
[list]	Any character in list. Ranges of characters can be indicated by forms such as a-z, A-Z, and 0-9.
[^list]	Any character *not* in list. Ranges of characters can be indicated by forms such as a-z, A-Z, and 0-9.
^	The empty string at the beginning of a line.
$	The empty string at the end of a line.
(e)	The strings matched by expression e. The matched string can be referred back to later as a "group"; see \n.
(? ...)	Extension notation. See Section 21.2.3.
e?	Zero or one occurrences of expression element e. This will match the longest sequence, i.e., one if possible.
e*	Zero or more occurrences of expression element e. This will match the longest sequence.
e+	One or more occurrences of expression element e. This will match the longest sequence.

Table 21–1
Regular expression elements. (Continued)

Element	Matches in Normal Mode
e*? *e*+? *e*??	These are like e?, e*, and e+, but will match the shortest possible sequence.
e f	An occurrence of expression e followed by an occurrence of expression f.
e | f	An occurrence of expression e or an occurrence of expression f.
e{ *n*} e{ *n*, *m*} e{ *n*, }	Exactly n occurrences of expression e, or between n and m occurrences of expression e, or n or more occurrences of expression e.
\ *n*	The string previously matched by the *n*th parenthesized expression, where *n* is a decimal number in the range 1 to 99.
\ 0*n* \ *n*	The character whose representation is the octal number n, where n is composed of octal digits beginning with a zero or of length at least three digits long.

Table 21–2
re operator precedence.

Precedence	Operators
1 lowest	x | y
2	x y

Table 21–2
re operator precedence. (Continued)

Precedence	Operators
3	x*
	x+
	x?
	x*?
	x+?
	x??
	x { ...}
4 highest	\ x
	[...]
	(....)
	c

```
regular expression:x
input string:xyzxyz
results:
0..1: ()
3..4: ()
```

The i..j means the pattern matches from character position i up to but not including j. The following empty tuple means there are no parenthesized groups in the expression.

Groups

If x is an expression, (x) is an expression that matches what x matches. It can group a more complicated expression into a single expression element; hence, parenthesized subexpressions are referred to as *groups*. A group has the additional property that substrings that match parenthesized elements can be referred to later by a number that is the order in which its opening parenthesis occurs in the expression. The groups are numbered from one, not zero, when referenced later in the regular expression. After the match, you can get a tuple of the substrings matched by the groups; in that case, because they are in a tuple, they are indexed from zero.

```
regular expression:(x)
input string:xyzxyz
```

```
results:
0..1: ('x',)
3..4: ('x',)
```

Sequence

If x and y are expressions, xy is an expression that matches what x matches followed by what y matches.

```
regular expression:xy
input string:xyzxyz
results:
0..2: ()
3..5: ()
```

In this example, you see three groups and the substrings they match:

```
regular expression:((x)(y))
input string:xyzxyz
results:
0..2: ('xy', 'x', 'y')
3..5: ('xy', 'x', 'y')
```

An empty string is a regular expression that matches an empty string.

```
regular expression:(x())
input string:xyzxyz
results:
0..1: ('x', '')
3..4: ('x', '')
```

Alternation

If x and y are expressions, x|y is an expression that matches what x matches or what y matches. The | operator has lower precedence than concatenation, so wx|yz groups as (wx)|(yz); of course, the parenthesized form creates groups that can be referred to numerically later, and the unparenthesized form does not.

```
regular expression:((x)|(y))
input string:xyzxyz
results:
0..1: ('x', 'x', None)
1..2: ('y', None, 'y')
3..4: ('x', 'x', None)
4..5: ('y', None, 'y')
```

The alternatives separated by vertical bars are ordered so that the first alternative that both matches and allows the rest of the pattern to match is the one used. Here, for example, the (xx) alternative is never used:

```
regular expression:((x)|(xx))
input string:xyzxxxyyyz
results:
0..1: ('x', 'x', None)
3..4: ('x', 'x', None)
4..5: ('x', 'x', None)
5..6: ('x', 'x', None)
```

But here, the following y forces the second alternative to be selected:

```
regular expression:(((x)|(xx))y)
input string:xyzxxxyyyz
results:
0..2: ('xy', 'x', 'x', None)
4..7: ('xxy', 'xx', None, 'xx')
5..7: ('xy', 'x', 'x', None)
```

Repetition

If x is an expression element, x* will match zero or more occurrences of x. It will match the longest sequences of x's that allow the overall expression to match.

```
regular expression:(x*)x
input string:xyzxxxyyyz
results:
0..1: ('',)
3..6: ('xx',)
4..6: ('x',)
5..6: ('',)
```

If x is an expression element, x+ will match one or more occurrences of x. It will match the longest sequences of x's that allow the overall expression to match.

```
regular expression:(x+)x
input string:xyzxxxyyyz
results:
3..6: ('xx',)
4..6: ('x',)
```

If x is an expression element, x? will match zero or one occurrences of x. It will match one occurrence of x if that allows the overall expression to match.

```
regular expression:(x?)x
input string:xyzxxxyyyz
results:
0..1: ('',)
3..5: ('x',)
4..6: ('x',)
5..6: ('',)
```

The patterns x*, x+, and x? give you the longest match possible. If you want the shortest match that will let the overall match succeed, use x*?, x+?, or x??:

```
regular expression:(x*?)y
input string:xyzxxxyyyz
results:
0..2: ('x',)
1..2: ('',)
3..7: ('xxx',)
4..7: ('xx',)
5..7: ('x',)
6..7: ('',)
7..8: ('',)
8..9: ('',)

regular expression:(x+?)y
input string:xyzxxxyyyz
results:
0..2: ('x',)
3..7: ('xxx',)
4..7: ('xx',)
5..7: ('x',)

regular expression:(x??)y
input string:xyzxxxyyyz
results:
0..2: ('x',)
1..2: ('',)
5..7: ('x',)
6..7: ('',)
7..8: ('',)
8..9: ('',)
```

Match All

Dot, '.', matches any single character other than a newline (and even that can be modified by a flag). It is often combined with a `*`, `+`, `?`, `*?`, `+?`, or `??` operator.

```
regular expression:x.*x
input string:xyzxxxyyyz
results:
0..6: ()
3..6: ()
4..6: ()

regular expression:x.*?x
input string:xyzxxxyyyz
results:
0..4: ()
3..5: ()
4..6: ()
```

Sets of Characters

Brackets enclosing a set of characters form a pattern element that matches any of the characters in the set. For example, `[ xy]` will match either an `x` or a `y`, the same as `x|y`. The basic rules are:

- Special characters lose their special meanings within brackets, except for `^`, `-`, `]`, and `\`. To include one of them, you can put a `\` in front of it.
- The special sequences `\w` and `\W` can be used in character sets to mean alphanumerics and non-alphanumerics. Backslashes in front of other letters are used to include control characters as in Python strings. A backslash in front of an octal number incorporates the character with that ordinal value.
- Sets must have at least one character listed; therefore, `[]]` represents the set containing just the character ']'.
- You can specify a range of characters by using a hyphen between the first and last character in the range. For example, `[ a-zA-Z]` matches any lowercase or uppercase Latin letter. You can put the hyphen first or last to include it in the set.
- To make a set of all except for certain characters, put a `^` first in the brackets. For example, `[ ^0-9]` will match any character other than a digit. A `[ ^-]` will match any character except a hyphen.

21.2.2   Special Sequences

The special character sequences starting with a backslash are shown in Table 21–3. There are several kinds of special sequences. Some of them represent sets of characters. The rule for these is that a backslash in front of a lowercase letter represents a set and a backslash in front of the uppercase letter represents the complement of the set. So, \d matches a decimal digit, and \D matches any character except a decimal digit; \s matches any white space character, and \S matches any character except a white space; \w matches a letter, a digit, or an underscore, and \W matches any character \w does not match.

Table 21–3
Special sequences.

Special Sequence	Meaning
\A	Matches the empty string at the start of the string.
\b	Matches the empty string at the start or end of a word. A word is a string of alphanumeric characters.
\B	Matches the empty string *except* at the start or end of a word. A word is a string of alphanumeric characters.
\d	Matches any decimal digit. It is equivalent to [0-9] .
\D	Matches any character except a decimal digit. It is equivalent to [^0-9] .
\s	Matches any white space character. It is equivalent to [\t\n\r\f\v] .
\S	Matches any non white space character. It is equivalent to [^ \t\n\r\f\v] .
\w	Will match any alphanumeric character or underscore, equivalent to [a-zA-Z0-9_] . This behavior can be modified by the LOCALE and UNICODE flags.

Table 21–3
Special sequences. (Continued)

Special Sequence	Meaning
\W	Will match any non-alphanumeric character or underscore, equivalent to [^a-zA-Z0-9_]. This behavior can be modified by the LOCALE and UNICODE flags.
\Z	Matches the empty string at the end of the string.
\\	Matches the backslash character.
\n	If number n is between 1 and 99 inclusive, this will match group number n, which is the string matched by the nth parentheses. Parentheses are numbered from one by the order of occurrence of the open parenthesis. If n begins with a zero or n is three digits long, this will be treated as the character with octal number n.

The sequences that match the empty string in particular contexts are used to test for those contexts. The beginning of the string matches \A, and the end matches \Z. The beginning or the end of a word matches \b, and any other position matches \B.

We have already seen how parenthesized regular expressions not only match strings, but save the matched string to be examined later. A backslash followed by a decimal integer, *n*, where *n* is in the range 1 through 99 and does not begin with a zero, matches the substring matched by "group" *n*. The open parentheses are numbered from one and the substrings are numbered by the open parenthesis of the expression that matched. So for example, the pattern (.)\1 will match an adjacent pair of any character other than newline:

```
regular expression:(.)\1
input string:xyzxxxyyyz
results:
3..5: ('x',)
4..6: ('x',)
6..8: ('y',)
7..9: ('y',)
```

The `\n` element does not match if the group number `n` has not matched. In the expression, `((x)|(y))\2`, group 2 is `(x)`. Although `((x)|(y))` will match either an `x` or a `y`, the `\2` will fail unless `x` matched, so the overall pattern matches only "xx".

```
regular expression:((x)|(y))\2
input string:xyzxxxyyyz
results:
3..5: ('x', 'x', None)
4..6: ('x', 'x', None)
```

21.2.3   Extension Notation

The `re` package allows you to use a so-called extension notation for a variety of things. The elements in extension notation begin with "`(?`" and end with "`)`". The kinds of uses are described next.

Pragmats

Pragmats are comments to control the expression matching. The `(?` followed by any collection of the letters 'i', 'L', 'm', 's', 'u', or 'x' will set the corresponding mode flags as discussed in Section 21.6.

Comments

Comments may be written as `(?# comment)`. They are treated as the empty string by the pattern matching.

```
regular expression:(x(?#comment)y)
input string:xyzxxxyyyz
results:
0..2: ('xy',)
5..7: ('xy',)
```

Nongrouping Parentheses

Form `(?:regex)` makes the regular expression `regex` an expression element, but not a group.

```
regular expression:((?:x)|(?:y))
input string:xyzxyz
results:
0..1: ('x',)
1..2: ('y',)
3..4: ('x',)
4..5: ('y',)
```

Named Groups

Form `(?P<name>regex)` behaves as `(regex)`; that is, it creates a numbered group. It also gives the group the *name* which must be a valid Python identifier. Form `(?P=name)` refers back to the substring previously matched by the group with the given *name*.

```
regular expression:((?P<A>.)(?P=A))
input string:xyzxxxyyyz
results:
3..5: ('xx', 'x')
4..6: ('xx', 'x')
6..8: ('yy', 'y')
7..9: ('yy', 'y')
```

Look-Aheads

Form `(?=regex)` will match the empty string if the initial part of the remaining string matches *regex*. It does not move past the string that matches *regex*. Form `(?!regex)` will match the empty string if the remaining string does not begin with a substring that matches *regex*.

```
regular expression:(x(?=x))
input string:xyzxxxyyyz
results:
3..4: ('x',)
4..5: ('x',)
```

```
regular expression:(x(?!x))
input string:xyzxxxyyyz
results:
0..1: ('x',)
5..6: ('x',)
```

Look-Backs

Form `(?<=regex)` will match the empty string if the part of the string preceding its position matches *regex*. Form `(?<!regex)` will match the empty string if the part of the string preceding its position does not match the pattern *regex*. In both of these, *regex* must match a fixed sized string.

```
regular expression:((?<=x)x)
input string:xyzxxxyyyz
results:
4..5: ('x',)
5..6: ('x',)
```

```
regular expression:((?<!x)x)
input string:xyzxxxyyyz
results:
0..1: ('x',)
3..4: ('x',)
```

Table 21–4
Extension notation.

Notation	Explanation
(? iLmsux)	Set the mode flags for the regular expression. The mode flags are discussed in Section 21.6.
(? : regex)	Makes the regular expression *regex* into an expression element, but does not make it into a numbered group.
(? P<*name*> *regex*)	Like (*regex*), that is makes *regex* into a numbered group, and assigns the group the name *name*.
(? P=*name*)	Like \ *k*, where *k* is the number of the group previously matched by (? P<*name*> *regex*).
(? #*comment*)	Is ignored by the pattern match.
(? =*regex*)	Matches the empty string if the following characters match *regex*.
(? ! *regex*)	Matches the empty string if the following characters do not match *regex*.
(? <=*regex*)	Matches the empty string if the preceding characters match *regex*. The regular expression *regex* must match a fixed sized string.
(? <! *regex*)	Matches the empty string if the preceding characters do not match *regex*. The regular expression *regex* must match a fixed sized string.

21.3   Functions in re **Module**

The re module provides the functions listed in Table 21–5. The basic function is compile(pattern), where pattern is a regular expression. The compile() function returns a regular expression object. The actual class of the regular expression object will vary depending on the implementation of the re package being used.

The other functions—search(), match(), findall(), split(), sub(), and subn()—are all shorthand notation for compiling a pattern and immediately calling a method of the same name, so we save our discussion until we talk about the pattern object methods. The call,

```
patobj=re.compile(r'[A-Za-z_][A-Za-z0-9_]*')
```

creates a pattern object that matches an identifier composed of a letter or underscore followed by zero or more letters, digits, and underscores. The reason we make this a "raw string" (see "String Literals") is that the backslash character is used extensively in regular expressions, and it is a good habit to make all patterns raw strings.

The escape() function simply converts a string into a version that can be used as a literal pattern to compile(). There are a number of special characters that the re module uses in patterns. If you need to match one of the special characters, you can put a backslash in front of it in a pattern. The escape() function inserts backslashes in front of all characters other than letters and digits so that they will be matched literally and will not be interpreted as control characters. For example:

```
>>> re.escape('1234567890!@#$%^&*()qwertyuiop[]')
'1234567890\\!\\@\\#\\$\\%\\^\\&\\*\\(\\)qwertyuiop\\[\\]'
```

(Note that the output doubles backslashes since it is not a raw string.)

The optional flags argument contains one or more of the attributes shown in Table 21–8, ORed together, for example "re.I|re.S". These flags influence the pattern matching and are discussed in Section 21.6. To avoid explanations full of special cases, we first discuss the functions and methods as if none of these mode flags are specified.

Table 21–5
Functions in `re` module.

Function	Explanation
`p=compile(pat)` `p=compile(pat,flags)`	If `pat` is a regular expression string, `compile()` compiles it into a pattern object p. If `pat` is already a pattern object, it just returns it. The flags are discussed in Section 21.6.
`m=search(pat,string)` `m=search(pat,string,flags)`	Returns a match object m if `pat` can be found in `string`, or `None` if it cannot. This is equivalent to `m=compile(pat,flags).search(string)` See Table 21–6.
`m=match(pat,string)` `m=match(pat,string,flags)`	Returns a match object m if `pat` can be found at the beginning of `string`, or `None` if it cannot. This is equivalent to `m=compile(pat,flags).match(string)` See Table 21–6.
`L=split(pat,string)` `L=split(pat,string,maxsplit)`	Returns a list of the substrings of `string` separated by occurrences of pat. This is equivalent to `m=compile(pat,flags).split(string)` See Table 21–6 and Section 21.7.
`L=findall(pat,string)`	Returns a list of all the non-overlapping substrings of `string` that match pat. This is equivalent to `m=compile(pat,flags).findall(string)` See Table 21–6 and Section 21.7.

Table 21–5
Functions in `re` module. (Continued)

Function	Explanation

`s=sub(pat,repl,string)`
`s=sub(pat,repl,string,count)`
	Returns a string with all the non-overlapping substrings of `string` that match `pat`, replaced with `repl`. This is equivalent to
	`m=compile(pat,flags). \`
	    `sub(repl,string)`
	Template `repl` can be a string. Substrings of the template of the form `\g<n>` are replaced with the substring that matched group n, the nth parenthesized subexpression of `pat`. If `repl` is a function, it is called with the match object for each match found in the `string`, and the string it returns replaces the matched substring.
	If `count` is specified to be an integer greater than zero, only `count` substitutions will be made.
	Empty matches are separated by at least one character.
	See Table 21–6 and Section 21.7.

`s=subn(pat,repl,string)` `s=subn(pat,repl,string,count)`	Returns `(sub(pat, repl, string, count),n)` where n is the number of substitutions made.
`s=escape(string)`	Returns a string with all the non-alphanumeric characters preceded with backslashes. It converts a string into a pattern that will match it.

21.4   Pattern Objects

The pattern objects returned by `compile()` have the methods shown
in Table 21–6. We are most interested in `match()` and `search()` in this
section.

Table 21–6
Methods in pattern objects.

Method or Attribute	Explanation

`m=p.search(string)`
`m=p.search(string,pos)`
`m=p.search(string,pos,endpos)`
	Returns a match object m if `pat` can be found in the substring of `string` from `pos` up to but not including `endpos`, or `None` if it cannot. Parameter `endpos` defaults to the end of the string, and `pos` defaults to zero.

`m=p.match(string)`
`m=p.match(string,pos)`
`m=p.match(string,pos,endpos)`
	Returns a match object m if `pat` can be found beginning at position `pos` in `string` and not including the character at `endpos`, or `None` if it cannot. Parameter `endpos` defaults to the end of the string, and `pos` defaults to zero.

`L=p.split(string)` `L=p.split(string,maxsplit)`	Returns a list of the substrings of `string` that are separated by occurrences of `pat`. If `maxsplit` is passed a positive integer, at most `maxsplit` occurrences of `pat` are used, and the remainder of `string` is the last component of the list. If `maxsplit` is omitted or zero, all occurrences of `pat` are found. If parentheses are used in `pat`, all the strings matching the groups (parenthesized subexpressions) are placed as components in the list between the separated substrings. See Section 21.7.

Table 21–6
Methods in pattern objects. (Continued)

Method or Attribute	Explanation
`L=p.findall(string)`	Returns a list of all the non-overlapping substrings of `string` that match `pat`. If one group (parenthesized subexpression) appears in the pattern, `findall()` returns a list of the substrings that match that group. If more than one group appears, `findall()` returns a list of tuples, where the components of each tuple are the substrings that match each group. See Section 21.7.
`s=p.sub(repl,string)` `s=p.sub(repl,string,count)`	Returns a string with all the non-overlapping substrings that match `pat` replaced with `repl`. Template `repl` can be a string. Substrings of the template of the form `\g<n>` are replaced with the substring that matched group (parenthesized subexpression) n, which must have matched. If `repl` is a function, it is called for each match found in the string with the match object as its parameter. The string that `repl` returns replaces the matched substring. If `count` is specified to be an integer greater than zero, only count substitutions will be made. Empty matches are separated by at least one character. See Section 21.7.

Table 21–6
Methods in pattern objects. (Continued)

Method or Attribute	Explanation
`s=p.subn(repl,string)` `s=p.subn(repl,string,count)`	Returns `(sub(pat, repl, string, count),n)` where n is the number of substitutions made.
`p.flags`	Contains the mode flags the pattern was compiled with.
`p.groupindex`	Contains a dictionary mapping group names into their corresponding group numbers. If there were no named groups, it is empty.
`p.pattern`	Contains the string pattern the pattern object was compiled from.

Both `match()` and `search()` return `None` if their pattern does not match. They return match objects if the pattern does match. We can look in the match object to find information about where the match begins, where it ends, and what substrings match parts of the pattern.

The method call `m=p.match(s)` will try to match the pattern object `p` at the beginning of the string `s`, returning either a match object or `None`. If you want to see if it matches starting at position `j`, call `p.match(s,j)`. If you do not want a match that extends beyond the substring of `s` from position `j` up to but not including `k`, call `p.match(s,j,k)`.

If you want to find the first matching substring, use `m=p.search(s)`.

21.5 Match Objects

Calling match or search on a pattern object, `m=p.match(s)` or `m=p.search(s)`, will return `None` if the pattern, `p`, was not found in string `s`. It will return a *match object* if pattern `p` *was* found. The match object gives information about the match. You can get the bounds and contents of the substring that matches the overall pattern. You can get the bounds and contents of each group in the pattern. See Table 21–7.

The call m.group(g) will give the substring that matches group g. If g is numeric, it refers to the group numbered g. If g is an identifier, it refers to the group given that name by (?P<g>regex). If g is zero, it refers to the string that matches the entire pattern. Parameter g defaults to zero. To find the starting and ending positions of the group, you can call m.start(g), and m.end(g), or you can call m.span(g) to get a tuple containing both.

You can get a tuple of all matching groups by calling m.groups(), but there is no element for the entire matching string: m.groups()[0] gives group one, m.groups()[g] gives group *g+1*. The groups that did not match are represented by None unless you provide a default value by calling m.groups(default).

You can get a dictionary of all named groups by calling m.groupdict(). Every name, *g*, given in a (?P<g>regex) form will have an element in the dictionary. By default, a named group that did not participate in the pattern match has its name mapped to None. You can specify an alternative default with m.groupdict(default).

The method m.expand(template) will return the template string with group references replaced with the contents of the group. A group reference is written \g<*n*> where *n* is the number or name of a group.

Table 21–7
Methods and attributes of re match objects.

Methods and Attributes	Explanation
m.group(g) m.group(g1,g2,...)	m.group(g) returns the string matching group g, or None if group g did not match. Argument g can be either a number or a name. If more than one argument is provided, m.group(g1,g2,...), it returns a tuple as if it were written (m.group(g1),m.group(g2),...). The argument 0 refers to the entire matching substring.
m.groups() m.groups(default)	Returns a tuple of all groups, where m.groups()[i]==m.group(i+1). If a default is provided, it is used for all groups that did not match. If it is not provided, None is used.

Table 21–7
Methods and attributes of `re` match objects. (Continued)

Methods and Attributes	Explanation
`m.groupdict()` `m.groupdict(default)`	Returns a dictionary for the named groups, mapping the name into the matching string. The name of any group that did not participate in the match is mapped into `None` or `default` if it is provided.
`m.start()` `m.start(g)`	`m.start()` gives the start position of the entire matching substring, as does `m.start(0)`; and `m.start(g)` gives the starting position of the substring matching group g. Returns -1 if group g did not participate in the match.
`m.end()` `m.end(group)`	`m.end()` gives the end position of the entire matching substring, as does `m.end(0)`; and `m.end(g)` gives the end position of the substring matching group g. Returns -1 if group g did not participate in the match. As is the custom in Python, the end position is the next index beyond the last character of the substring.
`m.span()` `m.span(g)`	`m.span(g)` is equivalent to `(m.start(g),m.end(g))`. Argument g defaults to zero, so `m.span()` is equivalent to `(m.start(),m.end())`.
`m.pos`	The value of `pos` passed to `match()` or `search()`.
`m.endpos`	The value of `endpos` passed to `match()` or `search()`.
`m.re`	The regular expression whose `match()` or `search()` was called.

Table 21–7
Methods and attributes of `re` match objects. (Continued)

Methods and Attributes	Explanation
`m.string`	The string passed to `match()` or `search()`.
`m.expand(template)`	The `template` is a string containing references to groups. `m.expand(template)` returns a string derived from `template` by replacing the group references with the matching strings. The reference `\g<n>` refers to the group with name or number n.

Figure 21–1 gives the code for the test program we have been using to see if a pattern matches at a particular position. It prompts for regular expressions, reads a sequence of lines, and for each line writes out the start and end positions at which the pattern matches as well as a tuple of the groups that match.

```
import sys, re
while 1:
    pat=re.compile(raw_input('regular expression:'))
    line=raw_input('input string:')
    while len(line)>1:
        print 'results:'
        col=0
        while 1:
            if col>=len(line): break
            r=pat.match(line,col)
            if r==None:
              col+=1
              continue
            print str(col)+'..'+str(r.end())+':',r.groups()
            col+=1
        line=raw_input('input string:')
if len(line)==0: break
```

Figure 21–1
`Test_re.py`.

21.6   Other Modes

There are alternate ways the `re` module can handle expressions and pattern matching. You can specify them by ORing together mode bits for the flag parameter to `compile()`, `search()`, or `match()`. The modes are shown in Table 21–8.

Table 21–8
Mode flags.

Flag	Meaning
I IGNORECASE (?i)	Treat uppercase and lowercase letters as equivalent.
L LOCALE (?L)	Make the special sequences \b, \B, \w, and \W (alphanumeric character sets and word boundaries) accord to the locale.
M MULTILINE (?m)	Allow multiline matching. If set, ^ will match at the beginning of the string and the beginning of each line in it (i.e., following a newline), and $ will match at the end of each line and the end of the string.
S DOTALL (?s)	If set, the dot pattern, ".", will match any character, including a newline.
U UNICODE (?u)	Set the special sequences \b, \B, \w, and \W (alphanumeric character sets and word boundaries) according to the UNICODE database.
X VERBOSE (?x)	Ignore white space in the patterns except in character sets or escaped. Treat # to the end of a line as a comment unless the # appears in a character set, is escaped, or appears in the header of a (?#...) comment.

The modes can also be specified directly in the regular expression with the form (?*letters*), where `letters` is a list of one or more mode letters. If included in the regular expression, the (?*letters*) should come at the very beginning of the pattern. The mode letters are case-sensitive. They are also shown in Table 21–8.

The `re.X` flag allows you to write more readable patterns. With it, you can include blanks and comments in your regular expression. You will almost certainly wish to use raw multiline strings, `r"""..."""` or `r'''...'''`. With the `re.X` flag, white space within a regular expression is ignored unless it is in a character set (between '[' and ']') or escaped with a backslash in front of it. A Python-like comment begins with a '#' character and extends to the end of the line unless the '#' is in a character set, is preceded by an odd number of backslashes, or is in a `(?#...)` comment. An example of the VERBOSE (x) mode is shown in Figure 21–4.

Two modes help with processing multiline strings. The M flag allows ^ to match at the position just after a newline character, whereas it usually matches only at the beginning of the entire string. Similarly, the M flag allows $ to match at the end of a line as well as at the end of the entire string. The S flag allows '.' to match the newline character. Normally, dot matches any character except newline. The reason for the usual restriction on '.' is that it prevents '.*' from unexpectedly gobbling up all the lines in the entire rest of the string.

The I (IGNORECASE) flag has the `re` module treat uppercase and lowercase Latin characters as equivalent. It is not modified by the internationalization features.

There are two internationalization flags. The L flag tells the pattern match to make the meanings of `\w`, `\W`, `\b`, and `\B` depend on the locale, in other words, what character codes are considered to be letters. The U flag makes `\w`, `\W`, `\b`, and `\B` depend on the Unicode database.

21.7 Other Methods and Functions

21.7.1 split

The regular expression `split` method and function are similar to the string `split()` method. The calls

```
L=split(p,s)
L=split(p,s,maxsplit)
L=p.split(s)
L=p.split(s,maxsplit)
```

return a list of the substrings of string s separated by occurrences of the pattern p. The ways that the re module's split() differs from the string split() method are:

1. A regular expression, not a string, is used to separate the substrings.

```
>>> re.split(r"\s?,?\s?","a, b, c, d , or e")
['a', 'b', 'c', 'd', 'or', 'e']
```

2. If the regular expression has groups, the groups are included in the resulting list.

```
>>> re.split(r"\s* (<<|>>|<|>|\+|-|\*|/|\ (|\))) \s*","a<<b+c<(d+e)")
[ 'a', '<<', 'b', '+', 'c', '<', '', '(', 'd', '+', 'e', ')', '']
>>> re.split(r"(\s*) (<<|>>|<|>|\+|-|\*|/|\ (|\)) (\s*)","a<< b+c < (d +e)")
[ 'a', '', '<<', ' ', 'b', '', '+', '', 'c', ' ', '<', ' ',
        '', '', '(', '', 'd', ' ', '+', '', 'e', '', ')', '', '']
```

As with string's split() method, if maxsplit is passed a positive integer, at most maxsplit occurrences of pat are used, and the remainder of string is the last component of the list. If maxsplit is omitted or zero, all occurrences of pat are found.

```
>>> re.split("\s?,?\s?","a, b, c, d , or e",1)
[ 'a', 'b, c, d , or e']
```

21.7.2 findall

The findall() function and method

```
L=findall(p,string)
L=p.findall(string)
```

return a list derived from all the non-overlapping substrings that match a pattern. The exact behavior depends on the number of groups (parentheses) in the patterns:

- If there are no groups in the pattern, they return a list of all the non-overlapping substrings of string that match the pattern.
- If one group appears in the pattern, they return a list of the substrings that match that group.

- If more than one group appears, they return a list of tuples, where the components of each tuple are the substrings that match each group.

```
>>> re.findall(r"\w|[-+=/*%()]",'(a + b*c/d*(e-f)')
['(', 'a', '+', 'b', '*', 'c', '/', 'd', '*', '(', 'e', '-', 'f', ')']
>>> re.findall(r"(\w)|[-+=/*%()]",'(a + b*c/d*(e-f)')
['', 'a', '', 'b', '', 'c', '', 'd', '', '', 'e', '', 'f', '']
>>> re.findall(r"(\w)|([-+=/*%()])",'(a + b*c/d*(e-f)')
[('', '('), ('a', ''), ('', '+'), ('b', ''), ('', '*'), ('c', ''), ('',
'/'), ('d', ''), ('', '*'), ('', '('), ('e', ''), ('', '-'), ('f', ''),
('', ')')]
```

21.7.3 sub

The sub() function and method

```
s=sub(pat,repl,string)
s=sub(pat,repl,string,count)
s=p.sub(repl,string)
s=p.sub(repl,string,count)
```

return a string with all the non-overlapping substrings of string that match pat replaced with the strings specified by repl.

Template repl can be a string.

```
>>> re.sub(r"\w+",'_','(ax + by*c/d*(e-f)')
'(_ + _*_/_*(_-_)'
```

Substrings of the template of the form \g<n> are replaced with the substring that matched group n. It is an error if group n did not match.

```
>>> re.sub(r"(\w)(\w)",r'\g<2>\g<1>','(ax + by*c/d*(e-f)')
'(xa + yb*c/d*(e-f)'
```

If repl is a function, it is called with the match object for each match found in the string. The string repl returns and replaces the matched substring.

```
>>> re.sub(r"(\w)(\w)",lambda
x:x.group(2)+x.group(1),'(axyz + bpqr*c/d*(e-f)')
'(xazy + pbrq*c/d*(e-f)'
>>> re.sub(r"(\w)(\w*)(\w)",lambda
```

```
x:x.group(1)+x.group(2).translate('.'*256)+x.group(3),'(axy
+ bpqr*c/de*(e-f)')
'(a.y + b..r*c/de*(e-f)'
```

If `count` is specified to be an integer greater than zero, only `count` substitutions will be made.

Empty matches are separated by at least one character.

```
>>> re.sub(r"",'.','(ax + by*c/d*(e-f)')
'.(.a.x. .+. .b.y.*.c./.d.*.(.e.-.f.).'
```

21.7.4   subn

The `subn()` functions and methods

```
s=subn(pat,repl,string)
s=subn(pat,repl,string,count)
s=p.subn(repl,string)
s=p.subn(repl,string,count)
```

return the pair (`sub(pat, repl, string, count)`,n) where n is the number of substitutions made.

21.8   Example: Scanner

In Chapter 22 we show the implementation of a simple calculator language. We need a scanner for it. A scanner is an adapter that reads a sequence of lines from a file and delivers a sequence of tokens to its caller. The position of the scanner in the entire implementation is shown in Figure 21–2. The scanner's job is, so to speak, to find the words on the input, while the parser's job is to find the phrases. The job of the semantics is to assign meanings to the phrases. In the case of our calculator, the semantics interprets the expressions and assignments. Here we consider the scanner and the tokens it produces.

A token is a significant substring, for example, an identifier, a number, or an operator. For our purposes, we represent a token by an object with the attributes and methods shown in Table 21–9. Every token has a `body`, the characters that comprise the token, and every token has a `type`, a string that identifies the kind of token. In our scanner, identifiers all share a single type, "id". Our numbers share type "num". Our operators have types identical to their bodies–"+" has type "+", and so on. If we had keywords in our calculator, they would, like

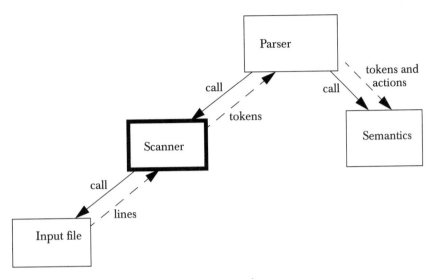

Figure 21–2
How the scanner fits into the calculator implementation.

our operators, have types identical to their bodies. In other scanners, operators might be classified by precedence level, for example, "mulop" for "*", "/", "%".

In addition to this essential information, our tokens have three attributes to identify their source. Attribute `line` is the number of the line that contained the token, and `column` is the position of the token in the line. Attribute `source` identifies the source file. These can be used to point to the exact location of an error.

Table 21–9
Attributes and methods of `Token`, `ErrorToken`, and `ActionToken`.

Attribute or Method	Meaning
t.body	The characters that comprise token.
t.type	The token type, a string that identifies the kind of token.

Table 21–9
Attributes and methods of `Token`, `ErrorToken`, and `ActionToken`.

Attribute or Method	Meaning
`t.line`	The number of the line that contained the token. This can be used to point to the exact location of an error.
`t.column`	The position of the token in the line.
`t.source`	An identification of the source file.
`t.recycle()`	Equivalent to `Token.recycle(t)`, returns the token to a pool for reallocation.
`t.copy()`	Creates a copy of token `t`.
`repr(t)` `t.__repr__()`	Yields a string representation of token `t`.
`str(t)` `t.__str__()`	Equivalent to `repr(t)`.

Tokens are handled by module `Token`, which has the classes and methods shown in Table 21–10. To create a token, we call:

```
t=Token.mkToken(type,body,line,column,source)
```

It is possible to pass fewer parameters. The `type` is required because the parser needs it. We almost always pass a `body` as well, because the semantics subsystem needs it, and the position of the token in the input so error recovery can point to the position where the error was discovered.

We call a factory function `mkToken()` rather than creating a `Token` object directly because the `Token` module has the ability to recycle tokens. When we are done with a token, `t`, we can call `t.recycle()`, or equivalently, `Token.recycle(t)`, and the token will be placed in a pool for reallocation later. This is not necessary, but it should speed up allocations by requiring neither storage allocation nor reclamation of most tokens.

Table 21–10
`Token` module.

Class or Method	Explanation
`Token.Token`	Regular token, returned by the scanner.
`Token.ErrorToken`	Error token, generated by the parser during error recovery.
`Token.ActionToken`	Action token, not used in this book.

`t=Token.mkToken(type,`
`   body="",line=0,`
`   column=0,source=None)`
	Returns a token. The scanner uses this to allocate the tokens it returns to the parser.

`t=Token.mkErrorToken`
`   (type,body="",line=0,`
`   column=0,source=None)`
	Returns an error token. The parser creates `ErrorToken`s during error recovery.

`t=Token.mkActionToken`
`   (type,body="",line=0,`
`   column=0,source=None)`
	Returns an action token. They are not used in this book.

`Token.recycle(t)`	Recycles token `t` for `mkToken()`, `mkErrorToken()`, `mkActionToken()` to reallocate later.

There are two subclasses of `Token`: `ErrorToken` and `ActionToken`. `ErrorToken`s are created by the parser and the semantics subsystem during error recovery. The `ActionToken`s are not used in this book.

The code for `Token` is shown in Figure 21–3. The code for the classes is relatively straightforward, except for `copy()` in `Token`. It looks up the class of this token in the dictionary `makeForClass` and finds the factory function to allocate another token of this type.

```
class Token:
    def __init__(self,type,body="",line=0, \
        column=0,source=None):
      self.type=type
      self.body=body
      self.line=line
      self.column=column
      self.source=source
    def __repr__(self):
      return "Token("+repr(self.type)+","+ \
        repr(self.body)+","+ \
        repr(self.line)+","+ \
        repr(self.column)+","+ \
        repr(self.source)+")"
    def __str__(self): return repr(self)
    def recycle(self):recycle(self)
    def copy(self):
      return makeForClass[self.__class__] \
        (self.type,self.body, \
        self.line,self.column,self.source)

class ErrorToken(Token):
    def __repr__(self):
      return "Error"+Token.__repr__(self)

class ActionToken(Token):
    def __repr__(self):
      return "Action"+Token.__repr__(self)

TokenPool=[]
ErrorTokenPool=[]
ActionTokenPool=[]
pools={Token:TokenPool, \
    ErrorToken:ErrorTokenPool, \
    ActionToken:ActionTokenPool}
def mkToken(*args):
    if TokenPool:
      t=TokenPool.pop()
      t.__init__(*args)
    else:t=Token(*args)
    return t
def mkErrorToken(*args):
    if ErrorTokenPool:
      t=ErrorTokenPool.pop()
      t.__init__(*args)
    else:t=ErrorToken(*args)
    return t
def mkActionToken(*args):
    if ActionTokenPool:
      t=ActionTokenPool.pop()
      t.__init__(*args)
    else:t=ActionToken(*args)
```

Figure 21–3
Token module.

```
        return t
def recycle(*tokens):
    for t in tokens:
        pools[t.__class__].append(t)

makeForClass={Token:mkToken,ErrorToken:mkErrorToken, \
    ActionToken:mkActionToken}
```

Figure 21–3
Token module. (Continued)

Each "make" factory function tries to find a token of the appropriate class in a "pool" implemented as a list. If it finds the appropriate list is not empty, the factory pops a token from it and calls the token's __init__() method. If the list is empty, the factory method has to allocate a new token.

We keep a dictionary pools that maps each token class into its pool list. We need this for the recycle() function to be able to append token t into the proper pool for its class.

The code for our scanner is shown in Figure 21–4. It recognizes the following kinds of tokens:

- identifiers, composed of a letter followed by a string of letters and digits;
- numbers, decimal integers;
- operators, single characters, "+", "-", "*", "/", "%" or "=";
- punctuation, single characters, " (", ") ", and "; ";
- EOL, end of line; and
- EOI, end of input.

```
#Scanner for Calc, simple calculator
import Token,re
pat=re.compile(r"""((?x)([a-zA-Z][a-zA-Z0-9]*)|
        ([-=+*/%();])|
        ([0-9]+)|
        \Z)""")
whitespace=re.compile(r"\s*")
class CalcScanner:
    def __init__(self,src,srcname):
        self.src=src
        self.srcname=srcname
        self.line=None
        self.lineno=0
        self.col=0
```

Figure 21–4
Calc scanner.

```
            self.eof=None
    def scan(self):
        while 1:
        if self.eof: return self.eof.copy()
        if self.line is None:
        self.line=self.src.readline()
        self.col=0
        self.lineno+=1
      r=whitespace.match(self.line,self.col)
      self.col=r.end()
      if self.col==len(self.line):
        if self.line=='':
          self.eof=Token.mkToken( \
            "EOI","EOI", \
            self.lineno,self.col, \
            self.srcname)
          return self.eof.copy()
        self.line=None
        return Token.mkToken("EOL","EOL", \
            self.lineno,self.col, \
            self.srcname)
      r=pat.match(self.line,self.col)
      if r==None:
        print "bad character '"+ \
            self.line[self.col]+"' at", \
            self.lineno,self.col
        self.col+=1
        continue
    #print r.groups()
    gs=r.groups()
    try:
      if gs[1]:
        return Token.mkToken("id",gs[1], \
            self.lineno,self.col,self.srcname)
      elif gs[2]:
        return Token.mkToken(gs[2],gs[2], \
            self.lineno,self.col,self.srcname)
      elif gs[3]:
        return Token.mkToken('num',gs[3], \
            self.lineno,self.col,self.srcname)
    finally: self.col=r.end()
```

Figure 21–4
Calc scanner.

The parser calls the scanner's `scan()` method. A `scan()` method can be written following this general pattern:

1. Loop through the following rules until the scanner returns a token.
2. If the scanner has already returned an end-of-input, EOI, token, return another one. EOI means the scanner has come to an end-of-file on its input. Look-ahead in the parser may make it look beyond

the end of input. Instead of crashing, the scanner should give as many EOI tokens as the parser needs.

3. If the scanner needs a new line, read one in, increment the line number, set the column to zero, and go to the next step to scan the new line for tokens. This is a good place to check for end of file and return an EOI token; however, we do that in Step 5.

4. Look in the line starting at the column position, and move the column position past any white space.

5. If the column position is at the end of the line, set the indication that the scanner needs to read in a new line. This is where we check for end of file and create an EOI token, although it would fit as well or better in Step 3.

   If we did not detect an empty line indicating end of input, our scanner returns an EOL token to indicate the end of the line. If the scanner was supposed to ignore the ends of lines, we would loop back to Step 1 to continue looking for tokens.

   The reason we do not read in the next line here is that we want to use our scanner interactively. If it read the next line before returning the end of this one, the user would have to type an extra line before the calculator would respond.

6. We get here only if we have a line, the column position is not at the end of the line, and the character at the column position is not white space. We try to match a token beginning at the column position in the line. The only way this can fail in our case is for the character at that position to be illegal. If it is, we write out an error message, move the column past it, and loop to try to find a token starting at the next position.

   Otherwise, we return a token appropriate for the kind of token we have matched, saving the column position just beyond it to start searching at next time.

21.9 Wrap-Up

Most of this chapter was devoted to the regular expression, re, module. We looked at the functions available in the module and the pattern and match objects and their methods. Regular expressions are written as strings and may be compiled into pattern objects. The pattern objects can be used in matching and searching of strings. Upon successful match or search, we get a match object that gives us information about the section of the string that matched the regular expression pattern. In addition, parenthesized parts of the regular expressions create groups. The `match` object can tell us which groups matched what substrings.

We ended the chapter with an example scanner that we will need for the calculator implementation in Chapter 22. We looked at the representation of tokens and the factories with recycling we can use to allocate them. We considered the general organization of scanners and how our implementation follows and departs from it.

21.10   Exercises

21.1. Write a regular expression to match a quoted string with the following requirements:

- The string begins and ends with either single-quote characters or double-quote characters.
- The string cannot extend across lines.
- The incorporation character, backslash, includes itself and the single character following it in the string.

21.2. Write a regular expression that will recognize Python floating-point numbers.

21.3. Extend the CalcScanner (Figure 21–4) to allow the operators '&', '|', '^', and '~'.

21.4. Extend the CalcScanner (Figure 21–4) to allow floating-point numbers.

21.5. If your scanner needs to recognize keywords and identifiers, which of the following is better? 1) Have your regular expression match both the keywords and the identifiers. 2) Have your regular expression match only an identifier, and then have your code look up the identifier in a dictionary to see if it is a keyword. Compare the advantages and disadvantages of the two choices.

21.6. Design and implement a scanner that can be told what token patterns it is to recognize. Use `CalcScanner` (Figure 21–4) as a starting point. You will have to design the methods to specify the patterns yourself, but here are some suggested examples:

```
scan=Scanner() #create instance
scan.num(r'0(x|X)[0-9a-fA-F]+','hexint') #hex integers
scan.num(r'0[0-7]+','octint') #octal integers
scan.num(r'\d+','decint') #decimal. Integers must be in this order
scan.id(r'[_a-zA-Z]\w*',"ident") #identifiers
scan.keyword('if') #keyword, a kind of identifier
scan.strings(['+=','**']) #strings that are their own types
scan.chars('+-*/%()=') #characters that are their own types
```

22

Parser

This chapter presents a work in progress, the retargeting and porting of the TCLLk parser generator and parser classes to Python. The "LLk" in the name TCLLk stands for LL(k) parsing: going left-to-right through the input finding a "leftmost derivation" and looking at most k symbols ahead. The "TC" stands for either "Tools of Computing" or the name of the author. The object-oriented design patterns we discuss here include *Interpreter, Strategy, Chain of Responsibility, Builder, Visitor,* and *Façade.* The overall parser is a framework: The provided classes are in charge and the user of the system must write classes to be plugged in to them.

We use the system to implement a simple expression calculator with variables and assignments. We do not, of course, need an expression evaluator, since we could just use Python; but expressions and assignments are easily understood, so there is no learning curve for the application area. The system presented here can be used to implement special-purpose languages in other application areas.

22.1 Overview of the Process

One of the first program designs worked out was for compilers. The design technique was called *Syntax-Directed Compiling.* It breaks a compiler into three components, as shown in Figure 22–1. The division of responsibilities is as follows:

- The scanner reads in the input and delivers a stream of tokens to the parser. Each token is a significant chunk of characters, for example, an identifier, a keyword, a number, or an operator.

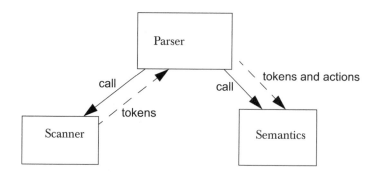

Figure 22–1
Syntax-directed compiling.

The scanner classifies the tokens by type, since the parser needs that information.

- The parser is in charge of finding the phrases in the input. It gets tokens from the scanner as it needs them, and calls the semantics routines to deal with the meanings of the phrases it finds.
- The semantics routines do all the rest of the work, maintaining symbol tables and generating object code or interpreting the input directly.

The design is called "syntax-directed" because the parser, which deals with the syntax, is in charge, calling the other routines. The design is not well-balanced. The scanner is trivial. The parser can be complex, but can often be generated from a grammar and so does not require significant programming. The semantics can be huge for an optimizing compiler.

TCLLk is an LL(k) parser generator and a collection of classes including a parser and error recovery classes. It is used as shown in Figure 22–2. The parser generator, TCLLk, is given a grammar file, G.grm. If there are no errors in the grammar, it generates a file of tables, G.llk. The tables are translated to a Python module, G_Tables.py, that executes code to build the tables as Python data structures and assign them to local variables. The program using the parser imports the module G_Tables and passes it to the parser, which then consults the tables as it looks for phrases in the input.

The components of a compiler in the TCLLk system are shown in Figure 22–3. The parsing is directed by an instance of class LLkParser. It uses the tables in a module that the TCLLk parser generator builds from a grammar. When it needs tokens, it reads them from a scanner

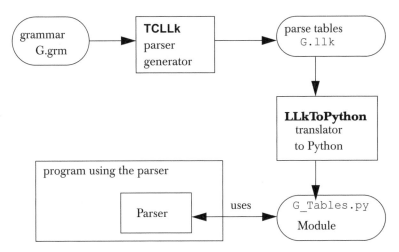

Figure 22–2
Parser generation.

object. As it recognizes tokens, it writes them to a semantics object. The `ActionSemantics` class is a base class for user-written semantics routines. When the parser detects a syntax error, it calls a method in a strategy object to recover and continue parsing. The error recovery can be a chain of specialized recovery object. The `PanicMode` object shown at the end of the chain is an instance of a panic-mode error repair class that comes with the system. The `ErrorOutput` object is a trivial error-reporting object that can be replaced for specific purposes.

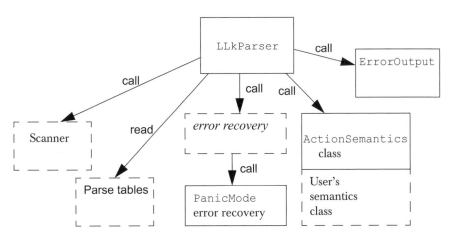

Figure 22–3
Components of TCLLk parser.

Since syntax-directed compiling places the parser in control and TCLLk provides the parser, the classes provided by TCLLk constitute a *framework*. A framework is a collection of classes that implement a particular program design. The classes provide the higher-level control. You plug classes into the framework to specialize the processing for your application area, in this case, for the language you are implementing. A framework contrasts with a *toolkit*, a collection of classes that you can use in a program. With a toolkit, your program is in charge.

22.2   Implementing a Calculator

22.2.1   What the Calculator Is to Do

Now let us consider a calculator implemented with the TCLLk system. As we type expressions in, they are evaluated and their values are written out. We can type in assignments, for example, a=b+c. The right-hand side of the assignment is evaluated and the value is assigned to the variable name on the left-hand side; but unlike with expressions, the value is not written out. The expressions and assignments are separated by either semicolons or newlines. A semicolon or newline not preceded by an expression or assignment is a null statement and is ignored; for example:

```
a=1;  b=2

a+b
3
```

A run of the calculator for the input file given in Figure 22–4 is shown in Figure 22–5. The first line in the file contains an error, causing the parser to write out (via the ErrorOut class) the message about the unexpected token and to ignore the assignment.

```
a=;
a=1;  a;
a=a+1;  a;
12/(12/3);
a*a;
a+12/(12/3);
10-4;
```

Figure 22–4
Test code for the calculator.

```
17%10;
(a+a)*a;
(a+1)*(7%4);
1+2--3--4;
```

Figure 22–4
Test code for the calculator. (Continued)

```
>python CalcEval.py CalcTest.txt
Token(';',';',1,2,'CalcTest.txt') : unexpected input
1
2
3
4
5
6
7
8
9
10
```

Figure 22–5
Output for the test program of Figure 22–4.

22.2.2   Grammar

Form of the Grammar

A grammar for this calculator is shown in Figure 22–6. Grammars have the following syntax:

- A symbol is indicated by either a quoted string or an identifier.
- In the grammars, the symbol in front of the equal sign, '=', is defined by the expression that follows it. The definition ends with a period. The symbol in front of the equal sign is called a nonterminal.
- Quoted strings are enclosed in either single or double quotes.
- A sequence of items in the grammar means the strings they describe are concatenated: xy means an x will be immediately followed by a y.
- White space may not be included in any token except a character string.
- The vertical bar, '|', separates alternatives: x | y means you will find an x or a y, but not both.
- The parentheses, '(' and ')', group alternatives.

```
start= STARTL!
   {e EXPRSTMT! endstmt  DOPENDINGACTIONS! STMT!
   | a endstmt STMT!
   | endstmt  NULLSTMT! }.
a = id "=" e ASGN! DOPENDINGACTIONS!  .
e = e "+" t ADD! | e "-" t SUB! | t.
t = f {"*" f MPY! |  "/" f DIV! |  "%" f MOD!}.
f = num CVTNUM! | id LOOKUPID! | "-" f NEG! | "(" e ")" PARENS!  .
endstmt = ";" | EOL.
fiducials: ";" EOL .
```

Figure 22–6
Calc grammar.

- The braces, '{' and '}', group items that can appear zero or more times.
- The brackets, '[' and ']', group items that are optional, or that can appear zero or one times.
- The identifiers followed by exclamation points are *action symbols*. They are names of semantic action routines to be called. You have to provide these routines yourself when you use the system.
- A symbol that is neither a nonterminal or an action symbol is a terminal symbol. The terminal symbols correspond to the token types reported by the scanner.
- EOI is a terminal symbol created by the parser generator to allow the scanner to indicate the end of the input.
- The nonterminal start is the start symbol of the grammar. The language is the set of programs derived from start.
- The *fiducial symbols*–the symbols following fiducials:–are terminal symbols used in panic mode error repair. EOI is automatically a fiducial symbol.

Action Symbols

The action symbols behave like suffix Polish operators. There is a semantics stack. As tokens are recognized, they are pushed on the semantics stack. When the parser comes to an action symbol, it pops a number of items off the semantics stack, passes them as parameters to a function or method with the same name as the action symbol, and pushes the value returned back on the semantics stack. The number of items popped depends on the action function, but it is a fixed number for each function and the value it returns is always pushed back on the stack. A function that takes no arguments will therefore leave one more item on the semantics stack than was there before; a function that takes a single argument will replace the top item on the stack; a function that takes two arguments replaces two items with one, and so forth.

To see how this works, consider first the definitions of nonterminal f:

- num CVTNUM!—The num is a token whose body is a string representation of a number. The CVTNUM function takes the token as its single parameter and writes back the number converted from a string to an integer.
- id LOOKUPID!—The id is a token containing the string name of a variable that should already have a value assigned. The function LOOKUPID looks up the value of the variable and replaces the token with the value.
- "-" f NEG!—The function NEG takes two parameters, the token "-" and the value of the f subexpression, and returns the negative of the value of f. The "-" and f are removed from the semantics stack, and the value NEG returns is pushed back in place of them.
- "(" e ")" PARENS!—The function PARENS gets three arguments: the parenthesis tokens and the value of the subexpression e in between them. It returns the value of expression e to be pushed in place of the three.

In the case of all the definitions of f, you can view the operation of the action routine as taking the meanings of all the symbols in the definition and returning the value of the nonterminal being defined. It would always be the case that you were defining the semantics of a nonterminal by the semantics of the symbols defining it if you wrote only productions (definitions) of the form:

```
nonterminal = r1 r2 ... rn action.
```

Here each ri is a terminal or nonterminal symbol on the right-hand side and action is the only action symbol. The process is pictured in Figure 22–7. Unfortunately, the metalinguistic symbols such as braces and brackets make it more difficult to understand what is going on.

For binary operators, first consider the definitions of nonterminal e:

- e "+" t ADD! says function ADD gets three arguments: the value of subexpression e, the "+" token, and the value of subexpression t. It returns the sum of the values of e and t to be placed on the semantics stack in place of the three items.

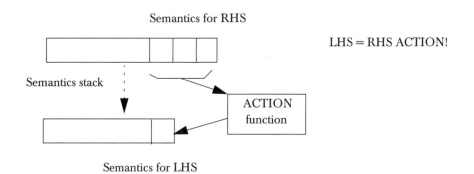

Figure 22–7
The effect of action functions on the semantics stack.

- `e "-" t SUB!` is like "+".
- `t` says that an `e` can be the same thing as a `t` and the semantic values (integers in this case) are the same.

The definitions of `t` parallel those of the definitions of `e`, but they use braces to indicate zero or more repetitions. The action functions `MPY`, `DIV`, and `MOD` take three arguments and produce one result, just as `ADD` and `SUB` do, but they are preceded in the braces by just two symbols. The trick is the `f` in front of the braces. The definitions say that a `t` is an `f` followed by zero or more `+f`, `/f`, or `%f`'s. Consider this expression:

```
3*4/2
```

The `3` is the value of the first `f` in the definition of `t`. That is followed by `* 4`, so the semantics stack will be:

```
xxx 3 * 4
```

(The stack grows to the right. The *xxx* represents the elements lower on the stack.) Function `MPY` is called with arguments `3`, `'*'`, and `4` and returns `12`. The semantics stack now contains:

```
xxx 12
```

The `/` and `2` are placed on the stack, giving:

```
xxx 12 / 2
```

The `DIV` function is called and passed `12`, `'/'`, and `2`. It returns `6`, which is placed on the stack in place of the three items, giving:

```
xxx 6
```

The braces can be thought of as a kind of loop. Each of the MPY, DIV, and MOD functions take as their first argument either the value of the initial f or the value left by the function called in the previous iteration of the loop.

The definition of start in the Calc grammar says that a Calc program is a sequence of expression statements, assignment statements, and null statements. Specifically:

- The braces say "sequence of."
- The a endstmt STMT! is used for an assignment statement. Nonterminal a is defined as an assignment, and endstmt is defined as an end-of-statement token, either ";" or EOL for end of line.
- The STMT! is an action we perform when we come to the end of a statement. If it were written without braces, it would be in a production something like:

```
statement_list = statement_list statement endstmt STMT!.
```

That is, the STMT function's first argument is the value left on the semantics stack by processing all the previous statements; the second argument is the item left by processing the most recent statement; and the third argument is the end-of-statement token, either ";" or EOL. It returns the item to leave on the semantics stack to represent the statement list up to and including the most recent statement. The value None works fine as a value for the initial statement list when we are directly evaluating the expressions. In a later section, we will be building a tree, and the semantic values for statements and statement lists will be trees.

- As with the initial f in the definition of t, STARTL! starts the statement list. The function STARTL takes zero arguments and leaves one result that represents the initial empty statement list.
- The endstmt NULLSTMT! says that a statement may be an end-of-statement token without anything in front of it. It corresponds to a production:

```
statement_list = statement_list endstmt NULLSTMT!.
```

In other words it takes two arguments and leaves one result.

- The e EXPRSTMT! endstmt DOPENDINGACTIONS! STMT! says a statement can be an expression followed by an endstmt (';' or EOL) token. The action EXPRSTMT! writes out the value of the expression in front of it. The DOPENDINGACTIONS! action tells the parser to make sure the preceding actions are executed before it continues.

22.2.3   Instantiating the Parser

The main program and semantics routines for our calculator are shown in Figure 22–8. The parser is created by the lines:

```
errorout=ErrorOutput.ErrorOutput()
p=LLkParser.LLkParser(CalcScanner.CalcScanner(f,name),
    Calc_Tables,CalcSemantics(),errorout,
    Discard.Discard("EOL",PanicMode.PanicMode()))
```

The `LLkParser` object is created with these arguments:

1. the scanner;
2. the parsing tables produced from the grammar by TCLLk;
3. the semantics object (whose class needs to inherit from the `ActionSemantics` class and have every action symbol of the grammar represented by a method or a function attribute);
4. an error output object to write, or otherwise deal with, messages about syntax errors; and
5. error recovery strategy objects to be used when the parser discovers a syntax error.

The `LLkParser` object is an example of the façade pattern. It hides the details of the scanning, parsing, error recovery, and semantics. All one need do is call its `parse()` method and use the value it returns as the semantic value of the file it processed. The value returned by `parse()` in the `CalcEval` example in Figure 22-8 is not significant; but in the `CalcTree` example, in Figure 22-12, it will be.

The scanner is an instance of class `CalcScanner`, whose implementation was discussed in Chapter 21. Its two parameters are the file, `f`, from which it is to read the commands it is interpreting, and `name`, identifying the source of the expressions and assignments. The name is not of any vital importance; it is mentioned in the tokens as the "source."

```
#main program for simple calculator using TCLLk in Python
# includes semantics class

import LLkParser, Token, ActionSemantics, ErrorOutput
import CalcScanner, Calc_Tables, sys, Discard, PanicMode
import operator
```

Figure 22–8
CalcEval.

```
def isError(x):
    return isinstance(x,Token.ErrorToken)

def anyError(*L):
    for x in L:
      if isError(x):
        return x
    return None

def doBop(x,op,optoken,y):
    try:
      return op(x,y)
    except Exception, e:
      errorout.error(optoken, 'arithmetic error')
      return Token.mkErrorToken("num",str(e))
class CalcSemantics(ActionSemantics.ActionSemantics):
    def __init__(self):
      ActionSemantics.ActionSemantics.__init__(self)
      self.vars={}
    def STARTL(self): return None
    def EXPRSTMT(self,e):
      if not isError(e):
        print e
    def STMT(self,s,semi):
      Token.recycle(semi)
      return None
    def NULLSTMT(self,semi):
      Token.recycle(semi)
      return None
    def ASGN(self,L,eq,R):
      e=anyError(L,R)
      if e: return e
      Token.recycle(eq)
      self.vars[L.body]=R
    def ADD(self,L,op,R):
      e=anyError(L,R)
      if e: return e
      Token.recycle(op)
      return doBop(L,operator.add,op,R)
    def SUB(self,L,op,R):
      e=anyError(L,R)
      if e: return e
      Token.recycle(op)
      return doBop(L,operator.sub,op,R)
    def MPY(self,L,op,R):
      e=anyError(L,R)
      if e: return e
      Token.recycle(op)
```

Figure 22–8
CalcEval. (Continued)

```
          return doBop(L,operator.mul,op,R)
      def DIV(self,L,op,R):
        e=anyError(L,R)
        if e: return e
        Token.recycle(op)
        return doBop(L,operator.div,op,R)
      def MOD(self,L,op,R):
        e=anyError(L,R)
        if e: return e
        Token.recycle(op)
        return doBop(L,operator.mod,op,R)
      def CVTNUM(self,t):
        try:
          v=eval(t.body)
        except:
          errorout.error(t, 'conversion error')
          v=Token.mkErrorToken("num",t.body)
        Token.recycle(t)
        return v
      def LOOKUPID(self,t):
        if isError(t): return t
        try:
            try:
                return self.vars[t.body]
            except:
                errorout.error(t, 'unknown variable')
                return Token.mkErrorToken(t.type,t.body)
        finally:
            Token.recycle(t)
      def NEG(self,minus,e):
        if isError(e): return e
        try:
            try:
                return -e
            except Exception, ex:
                errorout.error(minus,str(ex))
                return Token.mkErrorToken('num',str(ex))
        finally:
            Token.recycle(minus)
      def PARENS(self,Lpar,e,Rpar):
        Token.recycle(Lpar,Rpar)
        return e

if len(sys.argv)>1:
    name=sys.argv[1]
    f=open(name)
else:
    name='stdin'
```

Figure 22–8
CalcEval. (Continued)

```
      f=sys.stdin
  errorout=ErrorOutput.ErrorOutput()
  p=LLkParser.LLkParser(CalcScanner.CalcScanner(f,name), \
      Calc_Tables,CalcSemantics(),errorout, \
      Discard.Discard("EOL",PanicMode.PanicMode())))

  p.parse()
```

Figure 22–8
CalcEval. (Continued)

The error output can be as simple as the code shown in Figure 22-9. All it requires is a method or function error(token,message) that takes an optional token identifying the place in the input where the error occurred (usually the token that was the problem) and a string message to further identify the problem.

22.2.4   Error Recovery

Error recovery is invoked when the parser encounters a token it was not expecting. It calls the recoverFromError() method in the error recovery strategy to recover:

```
a+*b
Token('*','*',7,2,'stdin') : unexpected input
```

```
#Error output for TCLLk in Python
#

class ErrorOutput:
    def error(self,token,message):
      print token,message
```

Figure 22–9
Simple error output.

By default, the error recovery strategy is an instance of class `PanicMode` in the module of the same name. `PanicMode` writes out the message that the token was not expected, replaces part of the input, and resumes parsing at a fiducial token, one listed in the fiducials rule in the grammar file. The intent of fiducial symbols is that they delimit large portions of the input. `PanicMode` repairs the error by throwing away input tokens up to the fiducial symbol and replacing them with others that would legitimately have come between the point of error and the fiducial symbol. These replacement tokens are `ErrorToken` objects. The presence of an error token tells the action functions to omit evaluating their operands, since they were not part of the input or had some other error.

The `PanicMode` object is not the only error recovery object. There is a `Discard` object plugged in front of it. It is a trick to allow error recovery to do something that the grammar did not do and maybe could not do.

We want to be able to extend expressions beyond the end of a line. As long as an end of line cannot end the statement, we want it not to. We want to be able to write:

```
a=1
b=2
a+
b
```

and have the calculator respond:

```
3
```

But we do not want semicolon to behave the same way; for example:
```
a+;b
Token(';',';',8,2,'stdin') : unexpected input
2
```

That is what the `Discard` error recovery object does (see Figure 22–10). It is instantiated with a terminal symbol, in other words, a token type, `symb`, and another error recovery strategy, `next`. When called for error recovery, it checks the current token in the parser. That token is the one that was not expected. If it has the type `symb`, `Discard` removes it by reading the next token into the parser and then returns. If the token has some different type, `Discard` calls the next error recovery strategy and lets that handle the error.

```
class Discard:
    def __init__(self,symb,next):
      self.symb,self.next=symb,next
    def recoverFromError(self,parser):
      if parser.currentToken.type==self.symb:
        parser.getToken()
        return 1
      return self.next.recoverFromError(parser)
```

Figure 22–10
Discard class.

Because we pass `Discard.Discard("EOL",PanicMode.Panic-Mode())` as the error recovery parameter, any erroneous `EOL` token will be discarded without a message or any further processing. That is how

```
a+
b
```

works. The end of line following `a+` gives an EOL token. The EOL cannot come after an operator, so the parser detects an error; but the `Discard` object throws the EOL away, and so the `b` is read as the right operand of the plus.

By chaining error recovery objects, we have converted the *strategy* pattern into the *chain of responsibility* pattern. A chain of responsibility allows each object in a chain to try to handle a request until one is found that succeeds.

22.2.5 `ActionSemantics`

The action routines are methods in the class `CalcSemantics`. `CalcSemantics` is a subclass of `ActionSemantics` because that class handles gathering the tokens that the parser recognizes and passing them to the action methods when the parser comes to an action symbol. The code for `ActionSemantics` is shown in Figure 22–11.

```
import Token
import DEQueue
import Semantics
import types
import sys
```

Figure 22–11
ActionSemantics.

```
class ActionSemantics(Semantics.Semantics):
    def __init__(self):
      self.__semStk=DEQueue.DEQueue()

    def outToken(self,t):
      self.__semStk.push(t)


    def outError(self,t):
      self.__semStk.push(t)

    def outAction(self,t):
      f,n=self.actionRoutineInfo(t)
      L=[] #was [self]
      for i in range(n):
        L.insert(0,self.__semStk.pop())
      try:
        x=apply(f,L)
      except:
        cl,exc,tb=sys.exc_info()
        x=Token.mkErrorToken(str(cl),str(exc))
      self.__semStk.push(x)

    def close(self):
      self.__semStk.pop() #the EOI
      return self.__semStk.pop()

    def actionRoutineInfo(self,t):
      m=getattr(self,t)
      if isinstance(m,types.MethodType):
        f=m.im_func
        n=f.func_code.co_argcount-1
      elif isinstance(m,types.FunctionType):
        f=m
        n=f.func_code.co_argcount
      elif isinstance(m,types.ClassType):
        try:
          f=m.__init__.im_func
          n=f.func_code.co_argcount-1
        except:
          n=0
      elif isinstance(m,types.InstanceType):
        try:
          f=m.__call__.im_func
          n=f.func_code.co_argcount-1
        except:
          n=0
      else:
        raise TypeError("action "+t+" not callable")
      return m,n
```

Figure 22–11
ActionSemantics. (Continued)

The parser passes the tokens it recognizes to method `outToken()`, which pushes them on the semantics stack, `__semStk`. When the parser encounters an action symbol, it calls `outAction()`. The method `outAction()` calls `actionRoutineInfo()` to look up information about the action function: its callable object and the number of parameters it requires. Then `outAction()` pops the required number of items off the semantics stack, passes them to the action function, and pushes its result back on the stack.

The function `actionRoutineInfo()` is worth examination for the way it determines the number of parameters required for an action routine. The `m=getattr(self,t)` looks up the function. Generally, as is the case in `CalcSemantics`, the routines are methods of a subclass of `ActionSemantics`, but they could be callable attributes. So it must consider several cases: If the action routine is a method, it requires all its parameters but one, `self`, to be popped off the semantics stack. If it is a function, it requires all its parameters to be supplied from the semantics stack. If it is a class instance, then we have to look at the parameters required by its `__call__()` method, and if it is a class, the parameters required by its `__init__()` method, if any. The number of positional arguments is in the `co_argcount` attribute of the (method's) function's code object.

The action routines in Figure 22–8 do three things:

1. They check to see if any important arguments are error tokens. If any are, the program will not try to evaluate the expression, but will return an error token to represent that the result of the expression is not meaningful.
2. The action routine tries to calculate the value of the expression.
3. The action routine returns the value of the subexpression, or an error token if the calculation encountered an error.

Consider ADD:
```
def ADD(self,L,op,R):
   e=anyError(L,R)
   if e: return e
   Token.recycle(op)
   return doBop(L,operator.add,op,R)
```

The call `e=anyError(L,R)` will return either `L` or `R`, whichever one of them is an error token. If neither is an error token, it returns `None`. If one of the subexpressions is in error, ADD returns it. ADD uses `doBop()` to evaluate the operator. It passes the operands, the function from the operator module that performs the operation, and the operator token. The operator token is used to write out the location of the error.

The `doBop()` method tries to calculate the value of the expression and returns either that or an error token if the evaluation fails:

```
def doBop(x,op,optoken,y):
    try:
        return op(x,y)
    except Exception, e:
        errorout.error(optoken, 'arithmetic error')
        return Token.mkErrorToken("num",str(e))
```

The error tokens are created by factory function `mkErrorToken()` since that allows recycling. The call to `Token.recycle(op)` occurs a bit too soon, since we are not quite done with `op` yet, but that does not cause problems here.

Here are some examples of errors:

```
9999999*999999999
Token('*','*',1,7,'stdin') arithmetic error
99999999999999999999
Token('num','99999999999999999999',2,0,'stdin') conversion
error
a
Token('id','a',3,0,'stdin') unknown variable
```

22.3 Building a Tree

Now we look at another, noninteractive implementation of the calculator. `CalcTree`, shown in Figure 22–12, builds a tree for the calculator statements. The nodes in the tree can be evaluated or written out in suffix Polish order.

The tree nodes are instances of classes:

- `Bop`. Binary operators and ';' which combines statements into statement lists.
- `Nothing`. The initial empty statement list. The result of action symbol `STARTL`.
- `Var`. A variable.
- `Number`. A number.
- `Neg`. The unary minus operator.
- `Asgn`. The assignment operator.

- `ExprStmt`. An expression statement. The value of an expression needs to be written out.

```
#main program for simple calculator using TCLLk in Python
# includes semantics class

import LLkParser, Token, ActionSemantics, ErrorOutput
import CalcScanner, Calc_Tables, sys, operator

def isError(x):
    return isinstance(x,Token.ErrorToken)

def anyError(*L):
    for x in L:
      if isError(x):
        return x
    return None

class WriteOut:
    def __call__(self,node):
      getattr(self,node.__class__.__name__)(node)
    def Bop(self,node): print node.op,
    def Var(self,node): print node.name,
    def Neg(self,node): print '.-',
    def Number(self,node): print node.n,
    def Asgn(self,node): print node.id+'=',
    def ExprStmt(self,node): print "print",
    def Nothing(self,node): print 'Nothing',

class Nothing:
    def walk(self,f):
      f(self)
    def eval(self,d):
      return None

class Bop:
    opr={'+':operator.add,'-':operator.sub, \
      '*':operator.mul,'/':operator.div, \
      '%':operator.mod,';':lambda x,y:None}
    def __init__(self,x,op,y):
      self.left=x
      self.op=op
      self.right=y
    def walk(self,f):
      self.left.walk(f)
      self.right.walk(f)
      f(self)
    def eval(self,d):
      L=self.left.eval(d)
      R=self.right.eval(d)
      return self.opr[self.op](L,R)
```

Figure 22–12
CalcTree.

```
def BOP(x,op,y):
    e=anyError(x,op,y)
    if e: return e
    return Bop(x,op.body,y)

class Var:
    def __init__(self,name):
      self.name=name.body
    def walk(self,f):
      f(self)
    def eval(self,d):
      return d[self.name]

class Neg:
    def __init__(self,minus,e):
      self.e=e
    def walk(self,f):
      self.e.walk(f)
      f(self)
    def eval(self,d):
      return - self.e.eval(d)

class Number:
    def __init__(self,n):
      self.n=n
    def walk(self,f):
      f(self)
    def eval(self,d):
      return self.n

class Asgn:
    def __init__(self,id,op,e):
      self.id=id.body
      self.e=e
    def walk(self,f):
      self.e.walk(f)
      f(self)
    def eval(self,d):
      d[self.id]=self.e.eval(d)
      return None

class ExprStmt:
    def __init__(self,e):
      self.e=e
    def eval(self,d):
      v=self.e.eval(d)
      print v
      return v
    def walk(self,f):
```

Figure 22–12
CalcTree. (Continued)

```
            self.e.walk(f)
            f(self)

    class CalcSemantics(ActionSemantics.ActionSemantics):
        def __init__(self):
            ActionSemantics.ActionSemantics.__init__(self)
            self.ADD=BOP
            self.SUB=BOP
            self.MPY=BOP
            self.DIV=BOP
            self.MOD=BOP
            self.NEG=Neg
            self.STARTL=Nothing
        def STMT(self,sl,s,semi):
            if isinstance(s,Token.ErrorToken):
                return sl
            return Bop(sl,';',s)
        def NULLSTMT(self,sl,semi): return sl
        def PARENS(self,Lpar,e,Rpar):
            return e
        def ASGN(self,var,op,e):
            err=anyError(var,op,e)
            if err: return err
            return Asgn(var,op.body,e)

        def LOOKUPID(self,t):
            if isError(t): return t
            return Var(t)
        def CVTNUM(self,n):
            if isError(n): return n
            return Number(eval(n.body))
        def EXPRSTMT(self,e):
            if isError(e): return e
            return ExprStmt(e)

    if __name__=='__main__':
        if len(sys.argv)>1:
            name=sys.argv[1]
            f=open(name)
        else:
            name='stdin'
            f=sys.stdin
        csem=CalcSemantics()
        #print dir(csem)
        p=LLkParser.LLkParser(
            CalcScanner.CalcScanner(f,name),Calc_Tables, \
            csem,ErrorOutput.ErrorOutput())

        t=p.parse()
```

Figure 22–12
CalcTree. (Continued)

```
#print "semantics:",t
if t is not None: t.walk(WriteOut())
print

if t is not None: t.eval({})
```

Figure 22–12
CalcTree. (Continued)

CalcTree demonstrates several object-oriented design patterns, as discussed in the following four subsections.

22.3.1   Builder

The line t=p.parse() shows that the LLkParser's parse() method not only parses the input, but returns the "semantic" result, in this case, the tree. The ActionSemantics class (Figure 22–11) and its subclass Calc-Semantics in the CalcTree module are examples of the *builder* design pattern. The tree is not built all at once, but rather is constructed bottom-up, a part at a time. The parser passes tokens to the ActionSemantics outToken() method one at a time, where they are placed on a stack. The parser calls outAction() with action symbols, which in turn calls action routine methods in CalcSemantics to construct the internal tree nodes.

All the tree nodes have two methods in addition to their __init__() methods:

1. Tree.eval(d) evaluates the subtree and returns the value. Dictionary d is used to hold the values of the variables.
2. Tree.walk(f) walks over the tree, applying function f to each node in postfix order.

22.3.2   Interpreter

The eval() method is part of the *interpreter* pattern. The interpreter pattern does two things:

- Designs a representation for commands. Most commonly, one uses a tree representation for commands that can be described syntactically. This is, of course, precisely what we have done here.

- Provides a method in the representation to interpret the command. For a tree representation, the interpretation method calls itself recursively in subnodes. This is what the `eval()` does.

22.3.3   Internal Iterator

The command in the test code `t.walk(WriteOut())` calls the `walk()` method on the root to walk over the tree, applying the callable instance object to each node. The output for the test code in Figure 22–4 is:

```
Nothing 1 a= ; a print ; a 1 + a= ; a print ; 12 12 3 / /
print ; a a * print ; a 12 12 3 / / + print ; 10 4 - print
; 17 10 % print ; a a + a * print ; a 1 + 7  4 % * print ;
1 2 + 3 .- - 4 .- - print ;
```

The `walk()` method is an example of an *internal iterator* pattern (as discussed in Section 5.4.3). An internal iterator is a method associated with a container or other data structure. It is called with a function argument and it applies the function to each item in the container or component of the data structure. If the data structure is recursive, like the tree for the calculator, the internal iterator is typically a recursive method that calls itself in neighboring nodes to visit all the elements of a data structure. Since the iteration is handled totally by methods in the components of the data structure, it is called internal.

By way of contrast, an example of an external iterator is the `Enumeration` class associated with the `Set` class we examined in Section 17.4. It is a separate object whose methods are called to deliver elements of the set one at a time.

Both forms of iterator are based on loops that perform one iteration for each element of the data structure. In the case of the external iterator, the iterator object would be used in a conventional loop. It would be consulted at the top of the loop to determine whether more elements are available, and it would deliver the next element when asked.

The internal iterator removes the loop construct. What would be the body of the loop is converted into a function, and the iterator method takes the responsibility for executing it for each element of the data structure.

22.3.4   Visitor

The `WriteOut` class is an example of the *visitor* pattern solving the problem of writing out a representation of the tree. The obvious way to write out the tree is to provide a recursive method in each node class, say "show()", that would call itself recursively as eval() does, and write out a representation of the node. The entire recursive call would write out a representation of the tree. A question, though, is "Just how many of these recursive methods are we going to need?" As we need more methods to walk over the tree, we will find ourselves providing more and more recursive methods. Every time we need another one, we have to modify all the node classes again. Worse, we will not need all of them in every program, but their code will always be loaded.

The visitor pattern provides a way of adding special-purpose methods to nodes without putting them in the nodes themselves. It is used as follows:

- An instance of WriteOut is passed to the walk() iterator to be called at each node in the tree.
- The WriteOut instance's __call__(self,node) method is called for each node. It takes the name of the node's class and passes the call on to the method with that name.
- The class WriteOut has one internal method named for every class of node in the tree. This method will be called when a node of that type is passed to the instance.

So, instead of writing a WriteOut method for every node class, we wrote one WriteOut class with methods for every node class. The number of methods required was the same, but they are packaged differently. We did not have to clutter up the tree nodes with methods. We do not have to load them if we do not need them.

22.4 Wrap-Up

In this chapter we looked at two related examples: 1) direct evaluation of a calculator language and building, and 2) evaluation of a tree representation of a calculator program. Both of these used LLkParser, an LL(k) parser provided with the TCLLk system. This parser and related classes form a framework: a set of classes that are in control of the processing. The programmer using the system has to create other classes to be used by the framework classes to specialize the processing.

The examples show a number of object-oriented design patterns. The parser's error recovery used a *chain of responsibility* pattern, whereby each object in the chain tries to handle the error and passes the responsibility on to the next object if it cannot handle the error itself.

The example that builds a tree shows numerous patterns: The `ActionSemantics` and `CalcTree` classes comprise a *builder*. The `eval()` method in the tree nodes is an *interpreter*. The `walk()` method is an *internal iterator*. The `WriteOut` class is a *visitor*. The `LLkParser` class is a kind of *facade*: It provides an interface to scanning, parsing, error recovery, and semantic processing.

The `outAction()` method in `ActionSemantics` provides a good example of metaprogramming, using a run-time representation of the program within the program. The `outAction()` method has to look up the action routine by name in the current object, find out how many parameters it requires, and call it.

22.5   Exercises

22.1. Implement a `Visitor` for the expression trees in Figure 22–12 that evaluates and writes out the values of expression trees the same as `eval()`. Hints: `eval()` uses a dictionary to keep track of the values of names. It could also be used to keep track of the values of subtrees, or you could keep the values of subtrees on a stack.

22.2. Redo the expression trees of Figure 22–12 using the `Composite` pattern discussed in Section 5.3.4, as modified in Exercise 5.1.

22.3. Add exponentiation to `CalcEval`. This will require adding the "**" operator to the scanner discussed in Section 21.8, changing the grammar in Figure 22–6 and rebuilding the parser, and changing the `CalcSemantics` class in Figure 22–8. You will need a right-recursive definition for exponentiation to make it work right to left, and a new action symbol. You may need to look up documentation on TCLLk to run it.

22.4. Rewrite `WriteOut` to let the visitor pattern itself handle the recursion in a manner shown in Figures 5–12 and 5–13. Put a method `accept(self,visitor)` in the tree nodes that will call `visitor(self)`, and have the node-specific code in `WriteOut` call `node.subtree.accept(self)` in the correct order.

23

Wrap-Up

This book is concerned with the Python programming language and how to write larger programs in it. We devoted the first half of the book to Python itself, and the second half to examples of the kinds of components you might write or use. Throughout, we looked at the kinds of components and techniques that you would use to write larger programs.

23.1 Contents

We looked at Python's facilities for creating *modules* and *packages* in Chapter 3, at *objects* and *classes* in Chapter 4, and at *object-oriented design techniques* in Chapter 5.

While discussing function definition and use in Chapter 6, we looked at Python's built-in functions for use in *functional programming*.

The special methods used in developing *Abstract Data Types* (ADTs), were the subject of Chapters 14 and 15. Chapters 16 and 17 gave examples of abstract container data types: priority queues and sets.

We discussed concurrency in Chapter 18, including the facilities available in Python's threading module, the monitor pattern used to protect data from getting scrambled by concurrent access, and the dangers of deadlock and how to avoid it. Chapter 19 was devoted to an example monitor, SharedDB, that protects a shared database from being mangled by concurrent updates while protecting the transactions that use it from deadlock. Chapter 20 presented another monitor, RunQueue, that allows thread objects to be reused. TransactionQueue is a variant of RunQueue to be used with SharedDB; it automatically reschedules transactions that need to be tried again when they were unable to commit their changes to a database.

Chapter 21 was devoted to Python's `re` module, which provides *regular expressions* that are widely used to process text strings. The chapter included an example, `Scanner`, used by the parser presented in Chapter 22. A TCLLk *parser* is specified by a context-free grammar augmented with "action symbols." Parsers are the next level up from regular expressions, facilitating the processing of text with nested subexpressions. The parser is an example of a *framework*: The parser is in control, and you must write code that plugs into it.

23.2 Software

This book comes with software available through the author's Web site, *toolsofcomputing.com*. Some, but not all, of the software is described in this book.

This book contains code for rational numbers, a doubly-ended queue, priority queues, an implementation of the `union-find` algorithm, and sets. The software at the Web site includes multimaps, directed graphs, undirected graphs, and bit sets. For concurrent programming, this book contains implementations of `Futures`, assign-once variables; `Latches`, single-element buffers; `SharedDB` transaction-oriented monitors to share Python's dictionary-like databases; `RunQueues` to allow reuse of threads; and `TransactionQueues`, a version of `RunQueue` for transactions accessing a `SharedDB` object. Included with the software are translations of classes from the Tools of Computing thread package in Java, described in the book *High-Performance Java Platform Computing* (Thomas W. Christopher and George K. Thiruvathukal, Prentice Hall PTR, 2000, ISBN 0-13-016164-0).

The TCLLk parser generator and parser are available at the Web site. The parser generator takes context-free grammars and generates parsing tables for them, if possible, which are used by the parser to recognize and perform actions on phrases of an input language. The tables can be translated for use in a number of programming languages, including Python, Java, and Icon. All the ports are available, not only the Python. Included with TCLLk is a class, `StringScanner`, that provides an alternative to regular expressions for extracting usable parts of strings.

23.3 Advice to the Reader

Finally, as you go about designing and implementing larger programs in Python, there are several important things to keep in mind:

- *Modularization.* Do not try to write a large program in a single file. Break it down into meaningful parts.
- *Reuse.* Your goal is to minimize the amount of new code you have to write. Use other people's code. Become familiar with Python libraries and frameworks. When you do write new modules, design them so you can use them again yourself.
- *Overdesign.* Design a better and more complete module than you have to for the current use. It will be easier to use again later.
- *Interface.* The interface is the view of a software component from outside: What operations are available and how are they used. The interface should be "clean": functional enough to do what is needed, not too large, and consistent within itself and with conventions in other software components.
- *Encapsulation.* The contents of a software component should be hidden from outside, for a couple of reasons: 1) If you decide to change the implementation, you do not want to break other pieces of software that were dependent on the particulars of the implementation; 2) you do not want to pollute the name space of the users with extraneous names.
- *Abstraction.* Omit extraneous details from the interface. Find its essence.
- *Information hiding.* Do not let the interface commit you to a particular implementation. Hide design decisions that you might reconsider later. Do not allow a change those decisions to break other software using your code.
- *Patterns.* Where possible when designing, use well-known solutions to problems: mathematics, data structures, algorithms, object-oriented design patterns, and concurrent programming patterns. Since other people have used them successfully, there is every reason to believe they will work. Moreover, knowing what patterns they embody will help you remember how to use them.
- *Critiques.* Think about designs. What is useful? What is missing? What is of dubious value? Is its interface consistent with those of other modules? Does it reveal too much about its implementation? Critiquing other peoples' modules as well as your own will help with designs.

Appendix A

The syntax of literals is shown in Figure A–1. The syntax of Python statements is shown in Table A–1. The Python operators and their precedence levels are shown in Table A–2.

The notation used to describe the grammars is the same as the input to the parser generator used in Chapter 22. In the grammars, the identifier in front of the equal sign, '=', is defined by the expression that follows it. The right-hand side ends with a period.

Literal characters are enclosed in either single or double quotes. A sequence of items in the grammar means the strings they describe are concatenated: XY means an X will be immediately followed by a Y. The vertical bar, '|', separates alternatives: X | Y means you will find an X or a Y, but not both. The parentheses, '(' and ')', group alternatives. The braces, '{' and '}', group items that can appear zero or more times. The brackets, '[' and ']', group items that are optional.

identifier = (letter | '_') { letter | digit | '_'}.
number = integer | longinteger | floatnumber | imaginarynumber.
integer = decimalinteger | octalinteger | hexadecimalinteger.
decimalinteger = nonzerodigit { digit }.
nonzerodigit = '1' | '2' | '3' | '4' | '5' | '6' | '7' | '8' | '9'.
digit = '0' | '1' | '2' | '3' | '4' | '5' | '6' | '7' | '8' | '9'.
octalinteger = '0' { octaldigit }.
octaldigit = '0' | '1' | '2' | '3' | '4' | '5' | '6' | '7'.
hexadecimalinteger = ('0x' | '0X') hexdigit {hexdigit}.
hexdigit = '0' | '1' | '2' | '3' | '4' | '5' | '6' | '7' | '8' | '9' | 'a' | 'b' | 'c' | 'd' | 'e' | 'f' | 'A' |
        'B' | 'C' | 'D' | 'E' | 'F'.
longinteger = integer ('l' | 'L').
floatnumber = ('0' fraction |decimalinteger fraction | fraction | '0.' | decimalinteger '.'
) [exponent] |
        decimalinteger exponent.
fraction = '.' digit { digit }.
exponent = ('e' | 'E') ['+' | '-'] digit {digit }.
imaginarynumber = (
        decimalinteger |
        floatnumber | '0') ('j' | 'J').
string = ['u' | 'U'] ['r' | 'R'] ('" " chars '" " | '"' chars '"' | "' ' '" chars "' ' '" |
        '"""' chars '"""').

Figure A–1
Syntax of Python literals.

Table A–1
Python statement types.

Syntax[a]	Examples	Remarks
statement = { targetlist "=" } expressionlist . targetlist = target { "," target } [","] . target = identifier | "(" target_list ")" | "[" target_list "]" | attributeref | subscription | slicing . attributeref = primary "." identifier . subscription = primary "[" expression_list "]" . slicing = primary "[" sliceitem { "," sliceitem } [","] "]" . sliceitem = expression | [expression] ":" [expression] [":" [expression]] | "..." .	A=B a=b=c a,b=b,a x[i],y.f,z(1)[i:j]=p (b,[c])={1,(2,)]	The assignment statement evaluates a right-hand side expression and assigns it to one or more "targets." If the right-hand side is a sequence of expressions containing at least one comma, the values of the expressions are placed in a tuple. (A tuple is a list that cannot be modified.) The targets are separated from the right-hand expression and from each other by equal signs. A simple target is any variable, anything that can be assigned a value: a variable name, an attribute of an object, a subscripted object, or a slice of an object. A tuple can be assigned to a variable. If the value to be assigned is a sequence (list, tuple, or string), then the target may itself be a sequence of targets of the same length, each to be assigned the corresponding element of the right-hand value. Subsequences of targets, within either parentheses or brackets, cause a further decomposition of an element of the right-hand value. The ellipsis slice item, written " ... ", is officially part of Python, but is not currently used.
statement = target opeq expression . opeq = "+=" | "-=" | "*=" | "/=" | "%=" | "**=" | ">>=" | "<<=" | "&=" | "^=" | "|=" .	a+=b	The "augmented assignment" statements combine a binary operation with assignment. The left-hand side of the assignment is used both as the target of the assignment and as the left operand of the operator. Thus, the statement x[i]/=y is equivalent to x[i]=x[i]/y, except that x[i] is evaluated only once.

Table A–1

Python statement types. (Continued)

Syntax[a]	Examples	Remarks

statement = expressionlist .
expressionlist = expression { "," expression } [","] .
	`sub(x,y,z)`
	
	`f(x),g(y)`
		An expression can be used as a statement, as can a list of one or more expressions separated by commas and with an optional trailing comma. The expressions are evaluated left to right.

statement = "pass" .	`pass`	The `pass` statement does nothing. It is used in contexts where a suite is required by the grammar but no operation is needed.
statement = "def" name "(" [paramlist] ")" ":" suite .	`def neg(x):` `    return -x`	The `def` statement creates a function and assigns it to the variable with the name of the function. The suite of statements within the function is executed when the function is called. Functions are discussed fully in Chapter 6, including their parameter lists.

statement = "return" [expressionlist] .	`return`
	
	`return x`
	
	`return x,`
	
	`return f(x),0`
		The `return` statement causes control to return from a function. If no expressions are present, the function returns the value `None`. If one expression is present, its value is returned. If a list of expressions is present, a tuple containing their values is returned.

Table A–1
Python statement types. (Continued)

Syntax[a]	Examples	Remarks

statement = "class" name [inheritance] ":" suite .
 	
 inheritance = "(" expressionlist ")" .
	```class point: pass```
	
	 ```class Q(point):```
	 ``` def where(self):```
	 ``` return \```
	 ``` self.x,self.y```
		The class statement is discussed thoroughly in Chapter 4. The class statement creates a class and assigns it to a variable with the class name. The suite of statements within the class statement are executed when the class statement is. They assign attributes to the class object. Most commonly, they are def statements that create functions that provide the methods of the class. The expressions in the inheritance list following the class name, if present, must yield classes.

statement = "del" targetlist .	```del a,b.f,c[x]```
	
	 ```del d[i:j]```
		The del statement deletes one or more items. A simple variable name deletes the variable. An attribute reference deletes the attribute from the object. A subscript deletes the element of the dictionary or list. A slice removes the elements in the slice from the list.

statement = "print" expression {"," expression} [","]
 statement = "print" ">>" expression [{"," expression} [","]] .
	```print```
	
	 ```print x```
	
	 ```print x,y,```
	
	 ```print >>f, x,y,```
		A print statement prints out the values of expressions on the standard output and ends the line. With no expressions, it prints a blank line. With a trailing comma, it does not terminate the line after writing the expressions. With >> f, it writes to the file f rather than to the standard output.

Table A–1
Python statement types. (Continued)

Syntax[a]	Examples	Remarks

statement = "import"
    module ["as" name] { ","
    module ["as" name] }.
 	
statement = "from" module
    "import" identifier ["as"
    name] { "," identifier ["as"
    name] }.
 	
statement = "from" module
    "import" "*"
    module = {identifier "."}
    identifier.
	`import math`
	
	`import math \`
	`        as mathfns`
	
	`from math import sin`
	
	`from math import \`
	`        sin as sine`
	
	`from math import *`
		The import statement allows you to load and initialize a module (if it hasn't already been loaded).
		
		import m imports module m and assigns the variable m a reference to the module object. You can then get at a variable or other member x in m as m.x.
		
		import m as n imports m but assigns it to variable n.
		
		from m import x imports module m, but doesn't assign the module to a variable. Instead, it assigns the module's attribute x to variable x. With an "as y", it assigns the value of the attribute to variable y.
		
		from m import * imports m and assigns all its attributes to variables with their same names.

statement = "global" identifier { "," identifier}.	`global count`	Within a function definition, global makes the listed identifiers refer to variables in the surrounding module rather than in the function.

statement = "exec"
    expression
    ["in" expression
    ["," expression]].
	`exec "import "+x+ \`
	`        " as modx"`
		The exec statement executes the string value of the first expression as a statement. If "in" is present, the expressions following it yield dictionaries that are used to look up variables. Without the "in," the current environment is used.

statement = "assert"
    expression [","
    expression].
	`assert x>0`	The assert statement evaluates the first expression and raises an AssertionError if it evaluates false. The second expression, if present, is used to provide extra information for debugging.

Table A–1
Python statement types. (Continued)

Syntax[a]	Examples	Remarks
statement = "raise" [expression ["," expression ["," expression]]] .	`raise ValueError`	The `raise` statement "raises an exception," which terminates execution at the current place in the program and takes control back to an `except` clause of a dynamically surrounding `try` statement. See Chapter 11.

statement = "try" ":" suite "except" [expression ["," target]] ":" suite { "except" [expression ["," target]] ":" suite} ["else" ":" suite] .	`try:`
	`    readdata()`
	`except BadDataError:`
	`    print \`
	`        "try again"`
	
	`try:`
	`    search()`
	`except Found, x:`
	`    report(x)`
	`else:`
	`    report(`
	`        "not found")`
		The suite of statements within the `try` clause is executed. If it raises an exception, control will return to the `try` statement. The `except` clauses are examined in order to see if any specifies the type of exception raised. The suite in the first `except` clause that matches is executed. If none match, the exception is propagated back to the next dynamically enclosing `try` statement. If no exception is raised in the `try` clause, the `else` clause is executed.
		    The details are complex. See Chapter 11.

statement = "try" ":" suite "finally" ":" suite .	`lock(x)`
	`try:`
	`    use(x)`
	`finally:`
	`    unlock(x)`
		The `try-finally` statement executes the suite (sequence of statements) contained in the `try` clause. However control leaves those statements, the suite within the `finally` clause is executed. (Returns, breaks, and raising exceptions are all caught.)

Table A–1
Python statement types. (Continued)

Syntax[a]	Examples	Remarks
| statement = "if" expression ":"<br>  suite<br>{"elif" expression ":"<br>  suite}<br>["else" ":" suite] . | ```
if x<0: x = -x

d=cmp(a,b)
if d<0:
    print a,b,
elif d>0:
    print b,a,
else:
    print a
``` | The if and elif clauses are tried one at a time. The suite of statements is executed for the first if or elif clause whose expression evaluates true (non-zero), and then control leaves the if statement. If none of the expressions evaluate true, the else clause, if any, is executed. |
| statement =<br>"while" expression ":"<br>  suite<br>["else" ":" suite] . | ```
while a<n:
    a,b=b, a+b
``` | The suite of statements in the while statement is executed as long as the expression evaluates true. If the expression evaluates false, the suite of the else clause, if any, is executed and control leaves the while statement. If control jumps out of the suite of the while clause (e.g., by a break statement), the else clause isn't executed. |
| statement = "for" target_list "in"<br>expression_list ":"<br>  suite<br>["else" ":" suite] . | ```
for i in \
    range(len(L)):
    if f(L[i]):
        print \
        "found", i
        break
else:
    print \
    "not found"
``` | The variables in the targetlist are assigned the values in the sequence given by the expressionlist. Typically, the expressionlist is a single expression yielding a sequence. For each assignment, the suite following the for header is executed. When the sequence is exhausted, the suite in the else clause is executed and control leaves the for statement. If control leaves before the sequence is exhausted, the else clause is skipped. |
```

Table A–1
Python statement types. (Continued)

Syntax[a]	Examples	Remarks
statement = "continue" .	continue	The continue statement jumps back to the top of a loop (for or while) to start the next iteration.
statement = "break" .	break	The break statement leaves a loop immediately. The loop's else clause, if present, isn't executed.

a. White space is required between adjacent items that would look like a single item if written together, and is optional elsewhere. All items are on the same logical line except suites, which are sequences of statements that normally occupy a sequence of lines and have the same indentation.

Table A–2
Operators and precedence levels.

Precedence	Operators	Comments
1	x or y	This is the logical OR operation. It will return true if either x or y is true, or nonzero. In Python, like C, nonzero is considered to be true and zero false. Like the || operator in C, it is *short-circuited*: It will not evaluate y if x determines the value of the expression. It first evaluates x and returns the value of x if x is true. If x is false, it evaluates and returns the value of y. By "x is true or false" we mean that x would be considered true or false in an if or while statement. Empty lists and strings, for example, also count as false.
2	x and y	This is the logical AND operation. It will return true if both x and y are true, or nonzero. Like the && operator in C, it is *short-circuited*: It will not evaluate y if x determines the value of the expression. It first evaluates x and returns x if x is false. If x is true, it evaluates and returns the value of y.
3	not y	This is the logical NOT operator. It returns 1 (true) if x is false; it returns 0 (false) if x is true.

Table A–2
Operators and precedence levels. (Continued)

Precedence	Operators	Comments

4	`x < y`
	`x <= y`
	`x > y`
	`x >= y`
	`x == y`
	`x != y`
	`x <> y`
	`x is y`
	`x is not y`
	`x in y`
	`x not in y`
		The relational operators are much like they are in other languages. Operators `!=` and `<>` both mean *not equal*.
		The comparison operators `<`, `<=`, `>`, `>=`, `==` and `!=`, can be applied to structured objects, as discussed in Chapter 8. They compare the structured objects' components.
		The comparison operators can be chained, so that `x<y<=z` is equivalent to `x<y` and `y<=z`.
		Operators `x is y` and `x is not y` test whether two names reference the same object, so they will be much faster than `==` and `!=` for structured objects, but they don't compare the contents.
		Operations `x in y` and `x not in y` are discussed with sequence types in Chapter 8.

5	`x	y`	This is the bitwise OR operation, ORing the corresponding bits in two integers or long integers.
6	`x ^ y`	This is the bitwise EXCLUSIVE-OR (XOR) operation, XORing the corresponding bits in two integers or long integers.
7	`x & y`	This is the bitwise AND operation, ANDing the corresponding bits in two integers or long integers.

Table A–2
Operators and precedence levels. (Continued)

Precedence	Operators	Comments
8	x << y x >> y	These are the shift operators. They apply to integers or long integers. The bits in x are shifted left (<<) or right (>>) the number of positions indicated by y. The right shifts are *arithmetic*; the sign bit will be shifted in at the top, preserving the sign of the x operand. Since >> truncates toward minus infinity, it is not a good substitute for division when the left operand is negative.
9	x + y x - y	Addition and subtraction. Operator + also performs concatenation on sequences; see Chapters 8 and 9.
10	x * y x / y x % y	Multiplication, division, and modulus (or remainder). Operator % will also work with floating-point numbers. Operator * also applies to sequence types, and operator % has a special function for strings; see Chapters 8 and 9.
11	- y ~ y + y	Negation, bitwise complement, and unary plus (no operation for numbers).
12	x ** y	Exponentiation, x^y. Associates to the right, so that $x**y**z = x**(y**z) = x^{y^z}$

Table A-2
Operators and precedence levels. (Continued)

Precedence	Operators	Comments
13	f(args) x.attr x[i] x[i:j]	Function call, attribute access, subscription, and slicing.
14	(expressions) [expressions] {expr:expr, expr:expr,..} `expression`	These are used to construct built-in structured objects: tuples, lists, directories, and strings.

Index

536   INDEX

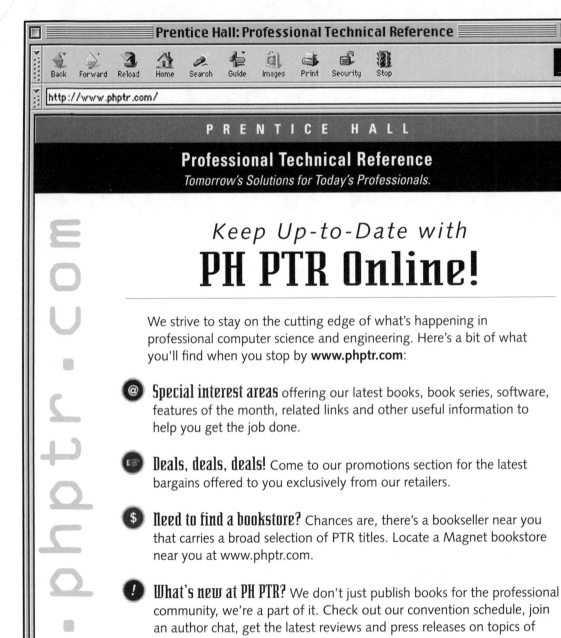